# Deviant and Useful Citizens

# Deviant and Useful Citizens

ع

The Cultural Production
of the Female Body
in Eighteenth-Century Peru

Mariselle Meléndez

Vanderbilt University Press
Nashville

© 2011 by Vanderbilt University Press
Nashville, Tennessee 37235
All rights reserved
First printing 2011
First paperback printing 2021

Publication of this book has been supported by a generous subsidy from the Program for Cultural Cooperation between Spain's Ministry of Culture and United States Universities.

Library of Congress Cataloging-in-Publication Data

Meléndez, Mariselle, 1964–
Deviant and useful citizens : the cultural production of the female body in eighteenth-century Peru / Mariselle Meléndez.
p. cm.
Includes bibliographical references and index.
ISBN 978-0-8265-1768-5 (cloth edition : alk. paper)
1. Women—Peru—Social conditions. 2. Body image in women—Peru—History—18th century. 3. Sex roles—Peru—History—18th century. I. Title.
HQ1572.M45 2011
306.4—dc22
2010040504

COVER IMAGES: E-2: Española con mantilla y bolador; E-21: Yndia de sierra en trage ordinario; E-26: Yndia de lamas con trage ordinario; E-42: Mestiza; E-35: Yndia de Hivito con carga, y su hijito a las espaldas; all courtesy of Biblioteca Real Palacio de Madrid.

# Contents

List of Figures — vii

Acknowledgments — ix

Introduction — 1

1. Micaela Bastidas's Legible Body: Public Spectacle, Violence, and Fear in Túpac Amaru's Insurrection — 11

2. Visualizing and Commodifying Female Bodies in *Truxillo del Perú*: From Colonial Order to Economic Productivity — 41

3. Patriotic Bodies and Corporeal Rhetorics: Sor María Josefa de la Santísima Trinidad's *Historia de la Fundación del Monasterio de Trinitarias Descalzas de Lima* (1783) — 83

4. The Nation and Its Congenital Deformations: The Medicalized Female Body in the *Mercurio Peruano*, 1791–1795 — 127

Epilogue: Prescribing Bodies — 171

Notes — 175

Works Cited — 209

Index — 223

# List of Figures

1. "Estado que demuestra el numero de Abitantes del Obpdo" — 52
2. "E1: Española con solo bolador" — 53
3. "E2: Española con mantilla y bolador" — 53
4. "E28: Yndia de lamas con trage de Iglesia" — 55
5. "E203: Yndia de montaña ynfiel" — 55
6. "E21: Yndia de sierra en trage ordinario" — 57
7. "E26: Yndia de lamas con trage ordinario" — 57
8. "E44: Negra" — 57
9. "E40: Quarterona de mestiza" — 58
10. "E42: Mestiza" — 58
11. "E3: Española con trage a lo antiguo" — 59
12. "E46: Mulata" — 61
13. "E6: Españolas de luto" — 64
14. "E13: Españoles merendando en el campo" — 65
15. "E16: Yndias de Valle a Cavallo" — 66
16. "E35: Yndia de Hivito con carga, y su hijito a las espaldas" — 67
17. "E36: Yndia de Moiobamba cargando platanos" — 67
18. "E83: Yndia pastora pariendo" — 68
19. "E81: Yndio pastor de ovejas" — 68
20. "E99: Yndia de Valles hilando en catre" — 69
21. "E100: Yndia de Valles texiendo" — 69
22. "E98: Yndias escarmenando lana" — 70
23. "E104: Mestizas de Chachapoyas cosiendo rengos" — 70
24. "E105: Mestiza de Moiobamba trabajando en su herrería" — 71
25. "E101: Yndias hilando a torno" — 71
26. "E102: Yndia de Lamas hilando a torno" — 72
27. "E59: Yndias colando chicha y despumandola" — 73

| | | |
|---|---|---|
| 28. | "E197: Yndio con Viruelas" | 74 |
| 29. | "E198: Mestizo picado de Uta" | 74 |
| 30. | "E200: Yndio en agonia" | 75 |
| 31. | "E196: Leprosa bañándose" | 76 |
| 32. | "E202: Yndio de Montaña Infiel" | 77 |
| 33. | "E53: Padron de los Domingos en Huairona" | 79 |
| 34. | Eighteenth-century map showing the Monasterio de Trinitarias Descalzas close to the center of Lima | 85 |
| 35. | "Monstre" | 131 |
| 36. | "Retrato verdadero de una criatura que nació en 12 de marzo del año corriente" | 133 |
| 37. | *Desvios de la naturaleza o Tratado de el origen de los monstros* | 134 |
| 38. | "Jumelles atacheés par les reins" | 135 |
| 39. | A case of a female child born with white stria | 144 |

# Acknowledgments

Completing a book always brings a sense of fulfillment, happiness, and relief. It represents a point in time when one realizes that the conclusion has been possible thanks to the collaboration and influence of people who directly or indirectly impacted our research and daily thinking in multiple ways. This book is the result of many years of continuous dialogue and support with scholars and close friends who have strengthened my approach to a topic that has proven to be a productive tool to read and understand society: the body. I would like to express my gratitude for the generosity of those who have made this book possible.

Maureen Ahern, Santa Arias, Magali M. Carrera, Jennifer L. Eich, Ruth Hill, Yolanda Martínez-San Miguel, Kathryn McKnight, Eyda Merediz, Kathleen Myers, Luis Fernando Restrepo, Stacey Schlau, Karen Stolley, Gustavo Verdesio, Charles F. Walker, and Jerry Williams are among a remarkable group of scholars in the field of colonial studies whose research and conversations have helped sharpen my arguments and prompted me to think harder about many of the subjects discussed in the book. Other scholars in the field whose work is cited in the notes and bibliography have also been very influential in my critical approach. Among all these colleagues, I offer my most special appreciation to Santa Arias (University of Kansas), whose valuable friendship, sense of humor, and intellectual collaboration have been invaluable from the beginning through the final stages of this book. My deepest appreciation to Karen Stolley (Emory University), whose pioneering work in Spanish American eighteenth-century literary studies has had a major impact on the field. Santa and Karen have been instrumental in the conception of this study, and I would like to express my sincere thanks to both of them.

I am indebted to my former professors at the University of Wisconsin, Madison, and in particular Margarita Zamora, for the solid academic training I received as a scholar and for their time spent listening to my ideas and offering suggestions. Margarita's intellectual integrity and discipline have guided my own academic work. My writing and my research have been marked by what I learned with all of them, and for that I am forever grateful.

At the beginning of this project I had the intellectual support of my former colleague Marcia Stephenson (Purdue University), whose understanding of critical theory and studies pertaining to the body played a key role in the formative stages of this book. My colleagues in the Department of Spanish, Italian, and Portuguese at the University of Illinois, in particular Luisa Elena Delgado and Silvina Montrul, have been a source of personal and intellectual support throughout this process, and I am deeply indebted to them for their unconditional encouragement. The University of Illinois Research Board and the Department of Spanish, Italian, and Portuguese offered much-needed financial support to fund several research assistants who helped with different facets of the completion of the book.

My deepest appreciation to Marcos Campillo-Fenoll (West Chester University), whose technical expertise helped this project immensely, especially with regard to the visual material included in the book. As a former graduate student in my department, Marcos was also part of a group of outstanding research assistants who diligently accomplished many important tasks that contributed to the progress of the study, among them Yolopattli Hernández-Torres and Clara Valdano. My most sincere thanks also to Denise Galarza-Sepúlveda (Lafayette College) and Justin S. Davidson (University of Illinois) for their invaluable help and suggestions with many of the translations of primary texts that appear in the book. Their bilingual linguistic expertise proved to be very instrumental in this challenging part of the project. I am also grateful to Carrie Havranek (Lafayette College) for her pointed editorial recommendations.

To the two anonymous readers who provided much-needed constructive criticism and vital suggestions, I offer my deepest thanks. I also thank Eli Bortz, editor at Vanderbilt University Press, for the interest he showed in this study and for his cooperation throughout this process. It has been a great experience working with him. My thanks, too, to Ed Huddleston, managing editor at Vanderbilt, and to the copy editor, Lys Weiss, for her well-reasoned and sensible editing.

Earlier versions of some sections of the book first appeared in other publications. In Chapter 1, some of the material comes from "Public Spectacle and the Fragmentation of the Female Body in Eighteenth-Century Peru: The Case of Micaela Bastidas," in *Mapping Colonial Spanish America: Places and Commonplaces of Identity, Culture and Experience*, ed. Santa Arias and Mariselle Meléndez (Lewisburg, PA: Bucknell University Press, 2002). In Chapter 2, some of the material comes from "An Eighteenth-Century Visual Representation of the Black Population in Trujillo del Peru: Picturing Cultural and Social Difference," *Bulletin of Spanish Studies* 86, nos. 7–8 (2009). In Chapter 3, some of the material comes from "¡Si tal era el dedo, cuál sería el cuerpo! The Archival Project of María Josefa de la Santísima Trinidad (1783)," *Hispanic Review* 74.3 (2006): 251–77, published by the University of Pennsylvania Press. I thank Bucknell University Press, the Bulletin of Spanish Studies, and the University of Pennsylvania Press, respectively, for permission to use this material.

My gratitude also to the personnel of various libraries who granted me permission to reproduce visual materials, including Biblioteca del Real Palacio de Madrid, Spain; the National Library of Medicine (Bethesda, Maryland); and the Rare Book and Manuscript Library at the University of Illinois at Urbana-Champaign. All translations from Spanish to English are mine unless otherwise specified.

Finally, but not least, I would like to thank Chris Jordan for his continuous intellectual and emotional support during the years while this project was developed into a book. His medical expertise was instrumental in my analysis and his recommendations and feedback helped shape my views on some of the topics explored. He, along with our children, Lia and Evan, provided that healthy balance needed when moving back and forth from the construction of the past to the daily challenges of the present. Their curiosity and sense of humor about many of the books they saw lying on my desk enabled me to approach the project with renewed energy and a sense that daily interruptions can certainly work as productive and motivating factors in the writing process. To the three of them I dedicate my book.

# Introduction

In 1783 the Peruvian nun María Josefa de la Santísima Trinidad completed her chronicle, *Historia de la fundación del Monasterio de Trinitarias Descalzas de Lima*, intended to illustrate the religious progress and perfection that characterized her convent as a social institution. In the introduction to the book, Sor María Josefa presents her chronicle as an important contribution to the education of useful citizens. Regarding the relevance of offering domestic examples that the public could follow to become productive citizens, she declares:

> De aquí nace la suma importancia de dar una buena educación a la juventud, ya inspirándole sentimientos nobles y generosos, ya moviéndola con el ejemplo a la práctica de las virtudes morales y cristianas. Y si esto es tan necesario aún en el siglo, para que vayan formando ciudadanos útiles que sean el honor y gloria de las Repúblicas, ¡de cuánto provecho será en los cuerpos religiosos que aspiran a la perfección!

> [And from these examples emerges the importance of granting a good education to young people, inspiring them with noble and generous feelings, and encouraging them to practice Christian and moral virtues. And, if this were very necessary in this century for the formation of useful citizens who could become the honor and glory of the Republics, how beneficial would it be for the religious bodies that aspire to perfection! (25)][1]

In this passage, the Peruvian nun establishes a connection among the formation of useful citizens, religion, and the body. For Sor María Josefa, a religious body is also social and therefore has the potential to become a citizen of use to the Republic. If rightly educated, which in her case meant a religious education based on local examples of model citizens, Peruvian people in general would contribute to the progress of their country. In the context of her work, Sor María Josefa uses the synecdoche "religious bodies" ("cuerpos religiosos") to refer to women who follow a religious life, establishing a coexistence between body and person in which the latter is read, or understood, through what her body does or has the possibility to do. The female religious body, then, represents one of the many bodies that made up the Peruvian nation.[2] Like the rest of those bodies, it exemplifies a crucial component of the country's social and moral progress. The manner in which the body acted or was read within specific historical and cultural contexts determined its usefulness or deviance.

This book examines the cultural production of the female body in eighteenth-century legal documents, illustrated chronicles, religious texts, and newspapers pertaining to the Viceroyalty of Peru.[3] It focuses on the different ways in which male authorities as well as female subjects conceived the female body as a material reality deeply connected to notions of what constituted a useful or deviant citizen in that time and place. Although the body has often been used as a metaphor for society, my use of "material" emphasizes that bodies can also be viewed as historical and physical realities endowed with specific properties. In this sense, it is important to acknowledge "that bodies construct and are constructed by an interior, a physical and a signifying view-point, consciousness or perspective" (Grosz, "Refiguring Bodies," 50). This book demonstrates how these representations and readings of female bodies were used by different sectors of society to illustrate political and cultural preoccupations of the time. I argue that the body, in particular the female body, functioned as a site of knowledge and as a cultural text, and as such became an effective tool to achieve power, to institute order, or to prescribe women's roles within society. I show how utility and productivity became two crucial elements to explain and represent the female body within the context of a highly complex eighteenth-century society.

By exploring the different ways in which masculine authorities (colonial bureaucrats, physicians, and religious men) read, constructed, and codified the female body in visual and written discourse, I show how these representations of women in eighteenth-century Peru responded to the dominant ways in which males themselves imagined women within both public and domestic spaces. At the same time, this book illustrates how women envisioned their bodies as instruments of empowerment. For women such as Micaela Bastidas (see Chapter 1) or Peruvian Creole nuns, their bodies functioned as practical discursive tools to gain visibility and power within society and to resist the codifications of the body imposed on them by male authorities. Finally, how do the tenets of the Enlightenment as well as the Bourbon reforms affect particular readings of female bodies in eighteenth-century Peru? What do those readings of the female body tells us about the social relationships that were coalescing at the time? These questions constitute two of the critical concerns of this book.

Studies about the body are abundant in the literature on Europe, the United States, and contemporary Latin America. Few, however, have addressed eighteenth-century Spanish America or Spain. Still, three significant studies have contributed to the consideration of the body as it pertains to identity construction and as a vehicle for understanding social relationships. Rebecca Haidt's *Embodying Enlightenment* emphasizes that the relevance of the body as an object of study relies on the fact that "the body is the location where beliefs, practices, laws, and institutions of every culture collide" (10).[4] Centering on the case of eighteenth-century New Spain in portraiture and *casta* painting, Magali Carrera analyzes the assessment of social bodies in secular painting where the gaze functions as a vehicle of surveillance. For Carrera, the visual construction of these bodies was "embedded in bureaucratic reaction to demographic changes" that were occurring in eighteenth-century New Spain (107). Carlos Alberto Garcés, in contrast, helps us to understand the mechanisms of punishment in the colonial legal system by emphasizing how the body of the criminal or the accused became a textual exemplum, as well as an instrumental vehicle to impose social and political order.[5] These interdisciplinary approaches to the representation of the body in eighteenth-century Spain and Spanish America underline the importance of looking at the body in relationship to mechanisms of power and social control. They also represent a point of departure from which to examine the processes that become part of such representations and how they are affected by geographic and cultural particularities.

This book is the first to be devoted to a critical examination of the construction of the female body in eighteenth-century Peru as articulated in legal, religious, and scientific discourses—all areas in which hierarchies of power are in place.[6] More important, my study looks at the representation of the female body in periods of political, economic, and religious crises to determine how it was conceived within determinate cultural contexts.[7] As I demonstrate, the body is a site of resistance and social productivity, and it simultaneously functions as an object of speculation and of objectification. I emphasize how the material reality of these bodies was affected by the social, political, economic, and religious reforms that took place in the late colonial period. Eighteenth-century representations of women's bodies read and observed these bodies in terms of their utility or productivity.

The legal documents, illustrated texts, religious chronicles, and newspapers examined in this book offer multiple scenarios for how the body as a social construction was articulated in four different types of discourses that ranged from the legal to the medical. Although these are not traditional "literary" texts in the later sense of the word, they represent fascinating discursive examples of how realities of the time were constructed and the role that the female body played in those constructions. The texts to be discussed were chosen precisely for having been largely overlooked by literary critics and for representing valuable discursive venues to understand the major political, religious, and social preoccupations of colonial authorities, Creole intellectuals, and women at a time of profound reforms and crisis.[8]

## Peru in the Late Eighteenth Century

In Peru, as well in the rest of colonial Spanish America, the eighteenth century was a time when social mobility, profound economic changes, scientific pursuits, and indigenous insurrections became major signs of anxiety and preoccupation for colonial authorities and native citizens. This anxiety was usually directed toward the bodies of those individuals who were perceived as different, including indigenous groups, those of African descent, and women. In Peru, the eighteenth century witnessed major transformations across the entire economic, social, and political spectrum. With the rise of the Bourbon regime of Charles III in 1759 and his successor, Charles IV, in 1788, political, social, and economic reforms transformed the manner in which the Spanish colonies governed, and local authorities envisioned, their citizens. The Bourbon regime's aim to centralize its government in Spain as well as in its colonies, the desire to modernize its state and colonial territories, and the need for more revenues to cover military expenditures prompted Charles III and his successor to impose a series of reforms that affected all aspects of society.[9] National security, the increase of tax revenues, improvement of government efficiency and administration of the colonial territories, and the strengthening of state power through diminishing the power of the Church (and especially religious orders such as the Jesuits) counted as some of the major changes brought by the reforms (Twinam, 311–12). David J. Weber summarizes these reforms as a "revolution in government" that led to what he believes could be considered as a "second conquest" or "reconquest" of America, affecting the very edges of the Spanish colonies, including indigenous communities (6). In contrast, Ann Twinam argues that the Bourbon regime also imposed a series of social reforms, seldom discussed by critics, that facilitated and empowered local elites "to protect the social and racial exclusivity of their family for prosperity" (313). The manner in which these reforms affected all aspects of colonial life is illustrated in the many ways in which different sectors of society, including Creoles, Indians, and people of African and indigenous descent, reacted to new policies on education, hygiene, urbanism, religion, and marriage, to name a few.[10] The impetus for centralization of government by colonial authorities resulted in the appointment of peninsular officials to government and administrative posts, and the decrease of local presence of Creoles in the government, which, in turn, increased discontent in this sector of the population. The expansion of royal authority also contributed to the expulsion of Jesuits from colonial territories in 1767, as the Society of Jesus was perceived as a wealthy institution with powerful influences on local government and economies. Furthermore, the Jesuits' preeminent role in the education of the colonial citizens represented a threat to the administration. Finally, their refusal to recognize monarchical authority above papal authority became a point of contention between the state and the mendicant orders, so much so that the Jesuits even opposed the implementation of royal policies (Burkholder and Johnson, 275). Many of the Jesuits were native born, and the confiscation of their properties (in Peru the value was about 6.5 million pesos) implied significant financial gain for Spanish authorities and a corresponding loss for local families who had benefited from the Society's investment in local goods (Burkholder and Johnson, 276). Following the Jesuit expulsions, the government took control over many social areas that had previously fallen into the realm of the Church. Therefore, the expulsion of the Jesuits caused great discontent in the Creole population.

One of the major results of the Bourbon reforms for Peru's economic situation was the establishment of the Viceroyalty of La Plata in 1776. As Twinam summarizes, the creation of this viceroyalty "deprived Upper Peru of jurisdictions, of captive markets, and of the silver mine of Potosi, with the result that its fortunes sank" (1999, 313). One major consequence for Peru was the loss of Upper Peru to the newly created viceroyalty. The "free trade" treaty known as "Reglamentos de Aranceles Reales para el Comercio Libre de España e Indias" (1778) had an impact on Peru's economic situation at other levels. For example, the once-authorized Port of Callao lost its monopoly in South America and now had to compete with other ports, making the reorganization of the trade route a point of conflict between the urban elite in Lima and colonial authorities (Mazzeo, 133).[11] The port of Buenos Aires, now named by colonial authorities as a new official port, saturated the Peruvian market with material goods that lowered prices to the extent that Peruvian merchants could not make respectable profits. Merchants in Lima seemed to be the major critics of this situation, as they argued that the opening of other Pacific ports, such as Arica, Concepción, Guayaquil, and Valparaíso, decreased Lima's trade through Callao by a third from the pre-1778 level (Fisher, 61).[12] As a result of the free trade, new forms of commercial expansion changed how Peruvians as well as colonial authorities envisioned their role in the management and circulation of natural and material resources. The newspaper *Mercurio peruano* became a fundamental forum in which Creole Peruvians debated many of these changes. Some of these debates are discussed in Chapter 4.

Alongside these complex economic changes, in the second half of the eighteenth century Peru witnessed a period of political instability, reflected in the approximately 140 insurrections that occurred between 1740 and 1780. In the latter year the Túpac Amaru insurrection led by José Gabriel Condorcanqui (known as Túpac Amaru II) and his wife Micaela Bastidas aimed to end the *repartimiento* and *mita* system, to remove the *corregidores* from their administrative positions, and to establish a high court (*audiencia*) in Cuzco (Burkholder and Johnson, 273).[13] The insurrection contributed to an atmosphere of violence and fear that would deepen the Spanish authorities' desire to survey and control the more rural or remote areas of the Viceroyalty in order to impose order.[14] Correspondence between the leaders of the insurrection and their followers, and the legal documentation pertaining to the trials conducted against the leaders, indicate the intense anxiety that characterized colonial authorities' perception of the indigenous population at the end of the eighteenth century. I analyze this situation in Chapter 1, where I focus on how the body of one of the leaders of the insurrection, Micaela Bastidas, a woman of indigenous descent, played a critical role in the discourse of violence and fear that dominated this historical event.

Philosophical and scientific ideas deeply rooted in the literature of the Enlightenment also affected how Peruvians considered and envisioned their territories and the population that inhabited them. Precepts of the Enlightenment were read in Peru (by Peruvians as well as Spaniards) in multiple ways, depending on the specific context of which, from which, and about which they speak. Diana Soto Arango and Jorge Tomás Uribe date this period from approximately 1736 to 1810 (59). In their view, this era witnessed a "Creole adaptation" of the political, philosophical, literary, and scientific ideas emerging from the European Enlightenment that centered on the ideology of utilitarianism. Universities, *tertulias*, *cafés*, newspapers, and homes became popular spaces in which Creole intellectuals discussed and adapted their own historical specificities to the premises circulated by the philosophies of the European Enlightenment. The manner in which Peruvian intellectuals and religious authorities perceived the social and economic colonial lives of Peru, its educational climate, and its religious spirituality and scientific secularization was greatly influenced by the ideas circulated in what is known as "the Age of Reason." As Saldaña argues, the Enlightenment's influence on colonial Spanish America can be seen in its art, history, literature, urbanism, ethnography, philosophy, linguistics, and the sciences (19–20). In this sense, as Saldaña adds, the Enlightenment movement in colonial Spanish America was eclectic and mainly distinguished by a belief in reason and experimentation in the search for usefulness in knowledge (22).

In the case of Peru, this search for useful knowledge was also imbued with a religious perspective or a type of religious modernism ("modernismo religioso," as Víctor Peralta Ruiz calls it), in which a reconciliation between faith and science was understood as a crucial tool to morally rehabilitate individuals and convert them into productive citizens (191). The chronicle compiled and edited by Sor María Josefa de la Santísima Trinidad, a Creole nun, and the *Mercurio peruano*—discussed in Chapters 3 and 4, respectively—offer interesting readings of how the notion of a productive citizen was contemplated and debated from the contemporary Creole perspective within the realms of religion and science. The Spanish bishop Baltasar Martínez Compañón in his *Truxillo del Perú* offers another discursive dimension of the manner in which a productive citizen was envisioned, this time visually, within the precepts of the Enlightenment and from his position as a religious authority representative of the state. His work is discussed in Chapter 2.

This study examines how in eighteenth-century Peru the body became an instrumental tool through which colonial subjects and authorities read and interpreted the political, economic, social, and philosophical preoccupations that marked the Viceroyalty in the last decades of the eighteenth century. My analysis is concerned with the discursive strategies used by the narrators of these texts and their inclination to make of the body a dynamic symbol of social productivity.[15] My book focuses not only on the center of the Viceroyalty of Peru—the capital of Lima—but also on its periphery (specifically Cuzco, the former capital of the

Inca empire, and the Archbishopric of Trujillo) to better illustrate how different localities contribute to distinct forms of interpretation of the body. The ambivalence characterizing these processes of construction is key to understanding the particularities of the bodies that inhabited the distinct territories in the Viceroyalty of Peru. As expected, normative discourses became influential ways to dictate how female bodies should function within the precepts of a modern society.[16] However, for certain female individuals, such as Micaela Bastidas and the Creole nuns who inhabited the Monastery of Discalced Trinitarians, the body took on a more dynamic function. It became a rhetorical tool to express their struggles within the political and religious reforms that were affecting their position in society and their roles as useful citizens of the kingdom of Peru.

## The Idea of the Body and the Construction of Bodies

Early definitions of the word *body* in Hispanic tradition refer to it as everything that can be touched (*Tesoro de la lengua*, 648). They also allude to the physical aspect of the body, such as the trunk; a cadaver; the gracefulness or poise of an individual; a solid substance or matter; and the group of people who constitute a town, a republic, or a community (*Diccionario de Autoridades*, 687). In Western tradition, the body has been also understood as the opposite of spirit; reality as opposed to a representation; a collectivity united by a common tie; a form of government (body politic); the sensual affections or "unrenewed part of man"; a piece of garment used to cover the body; and the matter that can be perceived by the senses (*Webster's Universal Dictionary*, 189).[17] In these early definitions, the emphasis on the physicality and visual nature of the human body is most striking. What we can see or touch is what seems to constitute the reality of that body. The representational nature of the body, as perceived through its physical attributes, was the focus of many of these definitions.

Although my study takes into consideration these definitions, its theoretical framework follows the interpretations of scholars who have looked at the body as a metaphoric vehicle (Barkan, 3) or as a communicative system (Novas and Rose, 237) that is always involved in a process of dynamic construction.[18] Following this line of thought, the body is perceived as a historical, social, and cultural construction and a privileged space of self-expression (Grosz, *Volatile Bodies*, x, 19). The body is a polyvalent reality whose interpretation depends upon its own specific historical context (Rico Bovio, 18). In the eighteenth century it would be important to consider the body as a "visual compendium of knowledge" and as a contentious site of study and experimentation (Stafford, 12). In the context of my discussion the colonial body is also seen as a type of cultural text constantly written by those seeking to consolidate power and control. It is considered part of a scientific and cultural production of meaning deeply rooted in the notion of what constitutes a useful citizen. The processes of bodily construction that emerge from all the texts analyzed in this book stress the importance of the body as a productive tool for making sense of the world. If Michel Foucault emphasizes "the political investment of the body" as tied to "systems of subjection" (*Discipline and Punish*, 25), I call attention to the dynamic nature of representations of the body and the need to view them as part of ambivalent processes of identification.

Susan Bordo reminds us that when talking about the body, we are also referring to the activities involved in its use, such as eating, dressing, and other daily behaviors (90). These rituals are profoundly embedded in the cultural milieu in which individuals live and express themselves. This book also examines how eating habits, fashion choices, cultural practices, and physical expressions of religiosity become part of a discourse that aims to inscribe the body within particular systems of knowledge and forms of consumption that are guided by the notions of what constitutes a useful citizen. The eighteenth century in Peru constitutes a key period in which the body, and in particular the female body, became the center of philosophical, religious, and scientific discussions that significantly influenced the manner in which the body was to be read and codified within the context of particular local realities.[19] As Haidt has aptly put it, in the eighteenth century the body functioned "as one of the most basic tropes by which ethical, political, and social concepts of power may be articulated" (5). My analysis of the body includes a consideration of these particular circumstances in order to demonstrate how the body is read ambivalently as an instrument of disorder, fear, deviance, and danger, but also perceived as an instrument of religious, economic, and social productivity. Within the context of this book, bodies are seen as complex signs of cultural expressions and negotiations that resist unequivocal forms of objectification.[20]

Each chapter of the book explores a different dimension of the body and how it is utilized as a tool to prescribe what a useful or productive citizen should be in the realm of politics, religion, economy, and science. The four different types of body I discuss are the political, the economically productive, the religious, and the scientific or medicalized body. The concept of citizen is key to understanding the multiple readings of the body that take place in the texts analyzed in this book. A citizen is understood in the context of colonial Spanish America as "the social and cultural recognition that one was a permanent member of the community" (Herzog, 55).[21] Reason, progress, and productivity served as three major principles to measure the usefulness of the colonial population.

The first chapter examines the image of the female body as a cultural construct and social reality in the legal texts pertaining to the Túpac Amaru insurrection. I focus on texts that dealt with the wife of the Inca leader, Micaela Bastidas. Through these documents, this chapter demonstrates how the female body became the site of potential insurrection and, as such, the epitome of disorder. For the authorities, Micaela embodied a deviant and dangerous citizen. Chapter 2 centers on the nine-volume chronicle with watercolor illustrations, entitled *Truxillo del Perú*, by Bishop D. Baltasar Jaime Martínez Compañón. The book grew out of the visits he conducted between 1782 and 1785 throughout the Archbishopric of Trujillo, Peru, and was considered by the author himself as a type of "Historical, Physical, Political and Moral Museum." The chapter examines the significance that the female body held in his construction of the visual and material history of these Peruvian territories. I argue that in such a process, visual images of the female body were used to record and encode a particular view of the human geography of Trujillo. In this text, the body functioned as an object of display, desire, utility, commodity, and consumption.

The third chapter focuses on the religious chronicle *Historia de la fundación del Monasterio de Trinitarias Descalzas de Lima*, compiled and edited by the Creole nun Sor María Josefa de la Santísima Trinidad in 1783. It centers on the spiritual and social construction of the female body by focusing on how the economic, religious, and political reforms of the time affected the convent as a national and social institution. I explore how corporeal metaphors and the visualization of the body in terms of control, discipline, and torture became an intrinsic part of a process of identity construction ingrained in Creole national interests and in the notion of a useful citizen. Chapter 4 examines the preoccupation of male intellectuals and contributors to the newspaper *Mercurio peruano* with regard to female bodies, at a time when the female body was the object of intense scrutiny because it was viewed as central to the production of healthy citizens as well as social progress. The news articles and essays published in *Mercurio peruano*, specifically those devoted to issues of monstrosity, defective births, female anatomy, pregnancy, gender transformation, and education, served as discursive venues to highlight the disorders, excesses, and defects that undesirable bodies caused to the Peruvian nation. The Epilogue underlines the implications of constructions of the female body for the cultural and social representation of Peruvian society in the eighteenth century. This book engages in an interdisciplinary reading and critical analysis of texts in which culture in its different manifestations—political, social, religious, and scientific—was read and articulated through the multifaceted images of the female body.

# 1

# Micaela Bastidas's Legible Body

Public Spectacle, Violence, and Fear
in Túpac Amaru's Insurrection

In January 1780, just months before the Inca leader José Gabriel Condorcanqui, known as Túpac Amaru, initiated his famous insurrection, a *pasquín* (subversive poster) was posted in the churches of Arequipa denouncing the abuses of the customs officers and *corregidores* against the indigenous people.[1] The *pasquín* suggested that natives would combat these abuses with violence unless the colonial authorities ceased ordering them to pay new and higher taxes:

> Vuestra cabeza guardad
> y también la de tus compañeros
> los señores Aduaneros
> q' sin tener caridad
> han venido a esta Ciudad
> de lejanas tierras y estrañas
> a sacarnos las entrañas sin moverles a piedad
> a todos vernos clamar.
> ...
> Mas si nuestro empeño
> no se sirven conceder
> tengan por cierto que sangre
> como el agua ha de correr.
> (*CDIP*, 108–9)[2]

[Protect your head along with that of your comrades, the customs officers, because they have come to this city from distant and foreign lands to bleed us dry without any mercy, and they see us crying out for help without showing any compassion.
...
Nevertheless, if you decide not to comply with our request, you can be assured that blood will run in this place as if it were water.]

The author of the *pasquín* clearly indicated that indigenous people would use brutal violence against the foreigners who did not belong to their territories. Peruvian lands would be covered with blood as a reminder of the unnecessary abuses inflicted upon the indigenous population.

This threat would become reality on November 10, 1780, when Túpac Amaru kidnapped the *corregidor* of Tinta, Antonio de Arriaga, and hanged him in front of Spaniards, *mestizos*, and Indians in an act of violence that would serve as a symbol of public defiance, political power, and immediate threat. A witness to the execution portrayed the magnitude of Túpac Amaru's cruelty as he ordered the *corregidor*'s subjects and closest allies to torture their superior and facilitate his death, causing such commotion that the Spaniards "[y]ntimidaronse tanto con este hecho, que nadie osó reclamar, contradecir, ni estorbar lo que se executaba" (became so intimidated with this act, that no one dared to protest, contradict or impede what was taking place) (*CDIP*, 255). According to the witness, this "most horrendous spectacle of perfidy" ("o espectaculo mas orrendo de perfidia") successfully intimidated the foreign population and struck fear into those who dared challenge the indigenous leader's demands (*CDIP*, 254). This act marked the beginning of a series of public punishments and violent deaths carried out by both the Spanish authorities and the leaders of the insurrection, which aimed to instill fear as well as to justify morally and politically the right to inflict pain and punishment.[3]

The great rebellion that Túpac Amaru initiated in 1780 with the help of family members, trusted *mestizos*, *caciques*, and indigenous peasants against the *reparto* system and new taxes imposed on the indigenous people in southern Cuzco culminated in 1781 when the Inca leader, his wife, and commanders were arrested by Spanish authorities and sentenced to death. One of the most important members of the insurrection and a figure crucial to its brief success was Túpac Amaru's wife, Micaela Bastidas. Micaela served as the rebel comptroller, commandant, and adviser of every aspect of the insurrection. Without Micaela's suggestions and decisions throughout the rebellion, Túpac Amaru might not have accomplished many of the victories he achieved against the Spanish troops. Yet historians and literary critics alike seldom discuss Micaela as an important member of the insurrection, and they overlook the influence she held over her husband and its great relevance to the trajectory taken by the rebellious forces against the presence of Spanish authorities in Peru.[4] Some critics, such as Carlos Daniel Valcárcel, however, have noted that if Túpac Amaru had followed Micaela's suggestions about the order in which the rebellion should have been deployed, the Inca leader could have avoided his final defeat in Tinta in 1781 (*La rebelión de Túpac Amaru*, 102–3).[5]

One striking element in the rebellion was the rhetoric of fear that dominated the actions taken by the indigenous leaders and their enemies, the Spanish authorities.[6] Edicts, proclamations, testimonial documents, and letters written during the insurrection demonstrate how fear became one of the discursive strategies employed by all those involved, in an attempt to intimidate and control their enemies. The death proclamation issued by the authorities against Micaela shows how "the cultural elaboration of fear" functioned for the Spanish authorities as a means to control large populations while acquiring power (Taussig, 28). But Micaela, as well as Túpac Amaru, also used fear to achieve important goals. For both sides of the insurrection, it constituted a pragmatic and crucial discursive tool to control the others, one that was imposed as well as read through the human body. The documents circulating during the time of the insurrection point to the image of the body as a legible text marked by the rhetoric of fear and violence. The body as a text requires particular readings, depending on how it is constructed. It is in this sense that we can consider it legible. It is also legible because the body, as Susan Bordo suggests, functions as a "surface on which the central rules, hierarchies, and even metaphysical commitments of a culture are inscribed and thus reinforced through the concrete language of the body" ("The Body and the Reproduction of Femininity," 90).[7]

This chapter examines the image of the female body as a cultural construct and social reality within the legal texts pertaining to the *mestiza* Micaela Bastidas in her involvement in the eighteenth-century Andean insurrection, especially those related to her death sentence. The discussion centers on how the letters and edicts drafted by Micaela or addressed to her by other participants in the insurrection played a crucial role in the manner in which her body was eventually read by colonial authorities.[8] I pay particular attention to how she used the rhetorical tools of fear and violence as a means of persuasion, and how fear itself influenced her behavior in the insurrection. In the context of this discussion, fear is understood as a rational emotion that affects the body and as such is in itself corporeal. As Judith N. Shklar argues, fear "is universal as it is physiological. It is a mental as well as a physical reaction" (29). It is considered a somatic emotion, in the sense that it forces people to be conscious of the imminent danger they might face (Delemeau, 9).[9] I also refer to the corporeal nature of fear. Following Thomas Hobbes, "bodily fear" is understood as fear of "corporeal hurt" delivered by actions that could range from violence to death (343). Fear in its different dimensions (psychological and physical) functions as a powerful rhetorical tool, and it can be used, as Corey Robin suggests, as "an instrument of political rule and advance" (3).

The discussion proceeds with an analysis of the rhetoric of fear and violence that characterized the death sentence imposed on her, particularly the manner in which her body was used by the colonial authorities during her public execution as a type of legible text. Attention is paid to the historical specificity that contributed to the articulation of the body as a visual text or legible narrative to be observed, read, and understood in certain ways.[10] We must consider why colonial authorities viewed the public space as the necessary arena in which punishment, fear, and control were to be executed. Public spectacle in the city center became what Taussig has called "a space of death" (4–5), a space that should be inscribed in the memories of those who witnessed the quartering of Micaela's body. The female body in this context is regarded "as a site of social, political, cultural, and geographical inscriptions, production, or constitution" (Grosz, *Volatile Bodies*, 23). In sum, what do the body and the emotions associated with it tell us about this particular historical and cultural moment in time, and what role does gender play, through a consideration of the body, in the social construction of that moment? These questions are central to my discussion.

## Túpac Amaru's Insurrection: Power and Fear

Túpac Amaru's uprising constituted one of the many upheavals that took place between 1708 and 1783. It is believed that 140 rebellions occurred in the Viceroyalty of Peru during this period, which Steve Stern has called the "Age of the Andean Insurrection" (35), and which has been referred to as the age "of Great Fear" (*Smoldering Ashes*, 55).[11] According to Kenneth J. Andrien, tensions between Spanish authorities and the Indians were caused by the increase in the sales tax (*alcabala*) and the disturbance of regional trade patterns as the result of the separation of Upper Peru from the Viceroyalty of Peru and its annexation as part of the newly established Viceroyalty of La Plata in 1776 (206–7). Through these new policies, Spanish authorities intended to achieve a more effective administrative structure, to stop corruption, and to control the visibility and demands of Creole, indigenous, and *mestizo* populations, as well as groups of African descent. Legal documents as well as historical and literary texts of the time reveal the obsessive desire of the colonial authorities to establish new racial and ethnic distinctions in order to achieve more profound control over their subjects and the lands inhabited by them. As Oscar Cornblit observes, judicial cases that occurred between 1741 and 1781 "show a society in conflict, or, at the very least, one that was quite active and prone to disorder" (37).

Disorder constituted a major preoccupation of colonial authorities, as well as their principal fear, because it hindered their ability to manage and control their territories. Indigenous uprisings became an obstacle that impeded their ability to control the colonized subjects. For the Spanish authorities, the body of the indigenous subject came to represent the vehicle by which power should be restored and imposed, and the basic instrument by which they could gain spatial control. As one of the important tenets of the Enlightenment (Walker, "Civilize or Control?" 80), social control also took effect through the reading and manipulation of the colonial bodies, including those of the protagonists of the insurrection. Power, fear, and violence were inscribed through and upon the body. In the case of the Túpac Amaru insurrection, the colonial authorities instituted corporal punishment to frighten the native population and to make clear that any intention to destabilize the system would result in the most horrific consequences. This politics of punishment was to apply to all members of the indigenous society, both men and women. As edicts pertaining to the insurrection demonstrate, the most violent acts of punishment were chosen for the leaders of the Túpac Amaru insurrection, especially for the indigenous leader and his wife, Micaela Bastidas.

## Micaela Bastidas: A Monstrous Woman

For Spanish authorities, Micaela Bastidas embodied disorder, evil, and a monstrous nature. Many other women were involved in the insurrection, but not to the same extent.[12] Micaela was born in Pampamarca, Perú, around 1742. Although the marriage certificate states that her parents were "españoles" (Spaniards) (*CDIP*, 17), most critics agree that her parents belonged to two different racial groups.[13] Her mother was known to be of indigenous descent, and her father was believed to be mulatto or *zambo* (of Indian and black descent). Some of her enemies during the insurrection referred to her as *Zamba*. However, most critics consider her as a *mestiza* (Andrien, 212) or a *ladina*, the latter term meaning a *mestiza* or Indian who spoke Spanish (Campbell, "Women and the Great Rebellion," 171).[14] She knew both Quechua and Spanish, and her pride in her Indian lineage was reflected after Túpac Amaru's triumph in Sangarará, when the Inca leader commissioned a painting in which he was portrayed as an Inca-King and Micaela as *Coya*-Queen (Campbell, "Ideology and Factionalism," 125).

Micaela's role in the insurrection was paramount; she worked to recruit troops, resolve administrative issues, proclaim and disseminate edicts to spur the propaganda machine, and gather information about the allies' provinces as well as those that were hostile to the cause. Micaela was Túpac Amaru's closest confidant and military assistant during the uprising. He followed her suggestions many times, although in critical instances he failed to welcome her wise advice, which would later prove costly for the outcome of the rebellion.[15] Her gender also made her job more difficult. Many indigenous and *mestizo* rebels found it troublesome to submit to her mandates and accept her policies. They were more willing to follow Túpac Amaru himself, whose messianic fervor led them to believe that he was the one to restore indigenous power and control in the Andean lands (Campbell, "Ideology and Factionalism," 126–27).

Spanish authorities were very much aware of Micaela's influence on the development of the rebellion and considered her at least as dangerous as her husband, if not more so. They offered large amounts of money, rewards, and titles of nobility to those who would help capture Micaela, along with her husband and other leaders of the insurrection. Even when the *visitador* Areche offered pardon to those who in exchange would denounce Túpac Amaru, he made sure to clarify that forgiveness would not apply to "la muger del Rebelde Micaela Bastidas" (the wife of the Rebel, Micaela Bastidas) (*CDIP*, 534). The Spanish government knew that many indigenous people and *mestizos* feared Micaela's threats of death to those who did not cooperate with her cause, which is why the authorities were willing to entice them with the promise of forgiveness. Micaela's power to convince the rebels to proceed with the insurrection and her threats to punish those who contradicted her caused the authorities to perceive her as a woman with no moral or spiritual attributes. According to them, she represented the opposite of what a traditional woman should be: tender, submissive, and weak.

In an account drafted in 1780 by Melchor de Paz referring to the execution that Túpac Amaru ordered against Arriaga, Micaela was described as a monster of cruelty: "Micaela Bastidas (que no es menos monstruo de crueldad que él)" (Micaela Bastidas who is no a less monster of cruelty than him) (*CDIP*, 257).[16] As the definition of monster at that time entailed, Micaela was considered someone who went against the common order of nature; someone who was wicked, excessive, ugly, and cruel (*Diccionario de Autoridades*, 598–99).[17] The use of the epithet "monster" in reference to Micaela emphasized the highest level of fear that her body could impart to others.

Some accounts described her as a woman who behaved with "resolución varonil" ("manly determination") (*CDIP*, 439). Other negative qualities conferred upon her were her rebelliousness, arrogance, and pride. According to Manuel Galleguinos, a witness who testified against her during the trials, "conocía más rebeldía en ella que en su marido; más arrogancia y más soberbia, de modo que se hizo más terrible que su marido" (In Micaela one could see more rebelliousness, arrogance and pride than in her husband; for that reason she became more terrible than he) (*CDIP*, 712). All these accounts emphasize the image of someone who had little in common with the behavior of a traditional woman. Instead, she was detached from her humanity and gender specificity, and was represented as an evil being whose cruelty could only be seen in those opposite to her sex (men) and human nature (monsters). This claim was necessary for the authorities because it would justify her eventual punishment.[18] Micaela's body and behavior required her to be read in a certain manner, which could evoke repudiation, hatred, and aversion.[19] When Micaela was eventually detained and accused of the crime of *lessa magestad* or "rebelión contra la magestad . . . contra el Reino, y especialmente contra la ciudad" (rebellion against the Majesty, the Kingdom and especially, the city) (*CDIP*, 727), the authorities made great efforts to clarify that her crime was "el más execrable y atroz . . . más enorme que pueda cometerse por un vasallo contra su Soberano y Señor natural" (the most execrable, and atrocious, the greatest that a subject could commit against his/her King and natural Lord) (*CDIP*, 727).[20] The greater the crime, the more severe the punishment; this principle, according to the authorities, served to justify her death penalty in their minds.

But what did Micaela say or write in her letters that caused these particular witnesses to form such harsh opinions of her? Edicts and letters drafted by Micaela offer a window into how her behavior might have been interpreted by others. On December 13, 1780, Micaela proclaimed an edict in Tungasuca addressing all Indians as well as Spaniards in the town, asking them to recognize and obey the two leaders whom she had designed colonel and captain of the forces in Tungasuca.

The document was "to be read loudly" ("a voz de pregón") so everyone present could hear and understand. Failure to obey, added Micaela, would result in severe punishment: "bajo de la pena, que los que fueren inobedientes, desleales y andaren con controversias, serán castigados severamente, según el mérito que diesen" (under the penalty that those who were disobedient, disloyal, and created controversies, will be punished severely, according to the nature of their crimes) (*CDIP*, 353). At the end of the edict she reiterated that those who opposed her order were to be publicly executed, with no leeway for forgiveness: "Todo lo que se guardará y cumplirá sin falta en lo menor; y al que contraviniese, se le castigará en público cadalso, sin que valga excusa ni pretexto" (This order should be respected and fully carried out; those who go against it will be punished to death on a platform, without considering any excuse or pretext (*CDIP*, 353). When giving instructions as to where to post the document so that people (including those under her command) would not forget what was stated in it, she stated that the document was to be posted on her door, warning that anyone who dared to remove it would suffer the death penalty ("Y el que lo quitare tambien tiene pena de la vida") (*CDIP*, 353). Micaela consciously employed fear as a rhetorical tool in order to persuade the inhabitants of that region to obey her orders. Fear as a threat allowed Micaela to pursue and to achieve her goals. Fear provoked anxiety and uncertainty about the potential outcomes that awaited them if they failed to obey. Death as the maximum and ultimate expression of fear for a human being (Rosas Moscoso, 28) was what made these types of threats effective.

Letters and mandates (*salvoconductos*) sent by Micaela portray a woman of strong character with a clear vision, extremely committed to the cause of the insurrection. In these documents, the rhetoric of fear goes hand in hand with the threat of violence. In a mandate drafted in Tinta on January 23, 1781, Micaela addressed the *caciques* and mayors of Marcapata, ordering them to report to José Salazar, a lieutenant-priest of those territories, "so pena de ser castigados si se les notare leve omisión" (under the penalty of being punished if caught omitting anything in this order) (*MHDI*, 15). In another mandate addressed to the mayors of Sanca, Micaela demanded that they supply Túpac Amaru with any cattle needed "siempre que se pida, sin que ninguna persona tenga intervención en su destino; pena de que serán castigados, si lo contrario lo hicieren" (every time that is asked, under the penalty of being punished if doing the contrary) (*MHDI*, 17). When giving orders to her army pertaining to the *corregidores*, whom Micaela called "ladrones" (thieves), Micaela was even more emphatic. Writing to the governor Don José Torres, she instructed him "to immediately gather all the town people to enter Cuzco, and to totally ruin the great number of detrimental thieves . . . it is necessary that these thieves leave the town or pay with their own lives" ("para que inmediatamente conduzca usted toda la gente de este pueblo, para hacer la entrada al Cuzco, y arruinar de raíz a tantos ladrones perjudiciales . . . es preciso que salgan los ladrones o paguen con sus vidas") (*MHDI*, 13). For Micaela, violence and ultimately death represented two crucial tools toward the achievement and justification of her ends, as well as a means to emotionally affect the psyche of her enemies or those who dared to disobey her.

In a letter sent to two governors from provinces close to Cuzco, Micaela urged them to help with plans to attack and control the city, as well as to stop the mistreatment and bad government imposed on the indigenous people: "arruinar de raíz todos los vejámenes y mal gobierno" (to completely ruin the source of all the aggravation and bad government) (*CDIP*, 357). Micaela also instructed the governors to put to death those who would disobey: "y al inobediente, con buena guardia y custodia, que tendrá pena de la vida" "(and the disobedient, with good guard and custody, will suffer the death penalty) (*CDIP*, 357). As a sign that this was the least she could expect from the two leaders, Micaela concluded the letter by emphasizing that essentially they had no other choice but to obey her commands. For Micaela, threat of death served as the best antidote to make people follow her commands. The fear she hoped to instill in the psyche of the inhabitants worked as a political tool to mentally subdue others. Robin argues that there is a type of political fear that "preys upon some real threat" (16). The individuals—such as Micaela—for whom fear becomes a political tool are the ones who "identify a threat to the population's well being, who interpret the nature and origins of that threat, and who propose a method for meeting that threat" (Robin, 16). In the case of Micaela, the method to meet that threat relied upon reminding the population that death could become an ultimate reality if they dared not follow her commands. Micaela was well aware of what would evoke fear in the population, and as a result took full advantage of this. For her, violence and death represented two material realities that could keep the bodies of the population in constant threat and fear. This political strategy certainly contributed to the success—albeit short-lived—of the insurrection.

It is important to examine how Micaela's subalterns internalized her threats or reacted to her commands. Letters written to her offer a glimpse of the manner in which she was viewed and treated by those who lived under her commands. The salutations of these letters showed extreme respect and obedience toward Micaela. They addressed her as "Muy Señora mía y toda mi veneración" (My most venerated Lady), "Muy apreciada Señora mía" (My most esteemed Lady), " Muy Señora mía de todo mi respeto y amor" (My most respected and beloved Lady) or "Muy Señora mía de mi singular atención" (Lady of my singular attention), expressing their unequivocal reverence toward her. Obedience was also reflected in the letters with phrases such as "en igual obedecimiento" (in the same obedience) (*CDIP*, 350); "estamos esperando órdenes de Vuestra Merced para practicarlas con la prontitud acostumbrada" (we are waiting for your orders to execute them with the same promptness as usual) (*CDIP*, 351); and "pasamos a Capana y a Cateca y a otras estancias como me ordena" (we proceed to Capana and to Cateca as you order it) (*CDIP*, 353). Clearly, her orders were followed without hesitation.

At the same time, the letters reflect fear of the repercussions of neglecting Micaela's orders. In a letter written on March 4, 1781, Gregorio de Yépez, chaplain of Pomacanche, felt cornered into defending himself against accusations that he had disobeyed Micaela's orders to keep his brother from leaving for Cuzco. Gregorio states that he would have been incapable of dismissing her orders "pero como hallo en mi consciencia de haber dado el menor motivo, ni con la más minima intención" (I know deep in my conscience, that I have not given any reason nor it has been my intention) (*CDIP*, 532). The chaplain accepts that he indeed did let his brother go, but that he did so because he had no other option. His brother feared for his life, as rumors circulated that Gregorio was hiding Spanish authorities in his house. He subsequently feared that Micaela or her husband would have them all killed. Gregorio assured Micaela that his brother had no intention of joining the Spanish authorities in Cuzco, and that he merely left for Cuzco to pursue his priestly vocation. The chaplain concluded his letter by stating that those who spent their lives lying, stealing, damaging the reputations of others, and accusing him were the real criminals. Fearing what Micaela could do to him, Gregorio pleaded for her trust, offering his utmost respect and obedience: "a quien ruego, por quien es, no crea nada, y más en orden a mí; porque no soy dos caras. Y le soy su más agradecido, como lo ha acreditado el tiempo, y en adelante espero en Dios sea lo mismo" (I beg you for who you are, to not believe anything but believe me, because I do not have two faces. Time has shown that I am your most grateful follower. I hope in God that you will from now on believe me) (*CDIP*, 533). Fear echoes throughout Gregorio's correspondence with Micaela; fear of death, specifically, prompted Gregorio to defend his brother and himself, as he knew that for the leaders of the insurrection, treason was an unforgivable act. Unfortunately, we do not have Micaela's response to the chaplain, but we know what Micaela was capable of doing when her orders were not obeyed, thanks to the testimonies of witnesses during her trial.

Francisco Molina, a neighbor of Sicuani and former *escribano* (clerk) of Micaela,[21] testified in April 1781 that he had been imprisoned under the orders of Túpac Amaru, but that it was Micaela who constantly terrorized him: "estuvo el declarante en calidad de preso y sujeto, por temor de la muerte, a las órdenes del Rebelde; porque cada día le amenazaba ella y los indios a influjos suyos, de Micaela Bastidas; que ésta daba órdenes por escrito y de palabra a varias personas, con más rigor que el Rebelde" (the witness felt subject to and a prisoner of the orders of the Rebel for fear of death, as every day he was threatened by Micaela and her Indian followers because she would give written and verbal orders to different people that were more severe than those given by her own husband) (*CDIP*, 709). Francisco portrayed Micaela as crueler than her husband, as she was very cognizant of the fear that she wanted to instill in orders. He recounted how Micaela exacted the death of many Spaniards and Creoles who disobeyed her husband, and how she found joy in every single death (*CDIP*, 709). According to him, she enjoyed forcing the population to attend executions they had organized against Spaniards and Creoles, as she wanted the people to witness the negative consequences that would come to them should they dare to disobey her. She also threatened those who refused to attend the events, with different tactics such as requests and intimidation: "contándolos para atemorizar a los que no querían asistir a su parte, esforzando a los indios a la concurrencia de su inequidad, ya con ruegos, ya con amenazas de que los había de desamparar" (she terrified those who did not want to attend the executions, encouraging the Indians through requests and intimidations to attend her acts of injustice, else they would be abandoned) (*CDIP*, 709). According to the witness, fear, pain, and violence worked well for Micaela as instrumental tools to torture others not only physically, but also mentally.

Two witnesses and former *escribanos* of Micaela, Francisco Cisneros and Manuel Galleguillos, portrayed a similar view of Micaela, emphasizing that she dictated orders, both in writing as well as verbally, "with more severity" than her husband (*CDIP*, 710). According to Cisneros, Micaela "imposed the death penalty on those who did not agree with her" (*CDIP*, 710). Manuel Galleguillos painted an even harsher image of Micaela. He stated that "her orders were even stronger than the ones of her husband and that her only motivation in life was to kill *all the Spaniards through blood and fire*" ("Que las órdenes de esta mujer eran más fuertes que las de su marido; de modo que sus deseos eran pasar *a todos los españoles a sangre y a fuego*") (*CDIP*, 711; emphasis mine). He concluded that people were even more afraid of Micaela than of Túpac Amaru: "Qué conocía más rebeldía en ella que en su marido; más arrogancia y más soberbia, de modo que se hizo más temible que su marido" (That they knew more rebelliousness in her than in her husband, they saw in her more arrogance and conceit, to the extent that she became more frightening than her husband) (*CDIP*, 712). In the words of this witness, rebelliousness, arrogance, and anger made Micaela more terrifying than her husband. The emphasis on the adverb of quantity *más* emphasized that she was the worst of all the leaders of the insurrection. The actions associated with her body, such as verbal orders, instilled fear in the population, who considered her a horrible human being or, even worse, a monster.

Micaela herself was very much cognizant of the uncertainty and anxiety that fear could stir within people. In letters addressed to her husband, she alluded to her own apprehensions, especially her own forebodings of death. Concerned that Túpac Amaru was not attacking Cuzco as early and fast as she wanted, and hoping to persuade him, Micaela wrote:

> Yo ya no tengo paciencia para aguantar todo esto, pues yo misma soy capaz de entregarme *para que me quiten la vida*, porque veo el poco anhelo con que ves este asunto tan grave *que corre con detrimento la vida de todos*, y estamos en medio de los enemigos, que *no tenemos ahora segura la vida*; y por tu causa están a pique de peligrar todos mis hijos, y los demás de nuestra parte.

[I do not have the patience to withstand this any longer, so that I am capable of turning myself in to the authorities *so they can take my life away*, because I witness the little interest with which you treat this serious issue, *putting in danger the lives of all of us*, and we are in the midst of the enemies and *now our lives are not safe*; and because of you the lives of all my children are in danger, as well as the ones on our side.] (*CDIP*, 329–30; emphasis mine)

She concluded the same letter, reiterating that his delay would provoke their death, as their enemies' "only interest was to remove our eyes from our faces" ("solamente van al interés y a sacarnos los ojos de la cara") (*CDIP*, 330). In these passages, Micaela takes advantage of the somatic character of fear to alert Túpac Amaru of what could happen to his own family. From the removal of the eyes as an act of punishment to the final ending of their lives and active bodies, these were reminders of the constant fear in which she lived. Rhetorically, for Micaela, fear worked as an instrument of persuasion aimed to convince her husband to act promptly; otherwise he might lose his wife and children. In a period referred to as "the Great Fear" (Walker, *Smoldering Ashes*, 55), fear in its different dimensions (psychological, moral, and political) also epitomized an act of survival and preservation of life. It acted as an ever-present reminder of what could happen. Violence, pain, disorder, and ultimately death would be the unfortunate results of undermining the power of fear.

It is important to remember that during Micaela's trial, she also mentioned that she participated in the insurrection out of fear of her husband. According to her deposition, Túpac Amaru physically abused her when she refused to follow his orders. She added that he had whipped her, slapped her, kicked her, hanged her from one of the beams of their house, and hit her with a stick (*CDIP*, 733). During his trial, Túpac Amaru acknowledged "that before the insurrection took place, sometimes he whipped her, slapped her, and hit her with a stick, but after the insurrection he no longer did" ("que antes del alzamiento, algunas voces dio azotes, bofetadas y palos a su mujer; pero que después no lo ha hecho") (*CDIP*, 735). It would be difficult to attest the veracity of these confessions, as they were made under duress through the fear of torture (O'Phelan, 250). Micaela could have made a false accusation in order to justify why and how she had been dragged into the insurrection. Consequently, she may have thought that it could save her life. As her trial confession demonstrates, she denied all the charges brought against her, alleging that she had acted out of "the blind obedience" and "blind fear she felt toward him" ("la ciega obediencia" . . . "el ciego temor que le tenía conciliado") (*CDIP*, 734). However, it is possible that Micaela could have been telling the truth and had indeed lived under constant fear of losing her life.[22] Still, it is clear from this confession that Micaela viewed physical abuse as a ubiquitous threat, one that affected the state of her mind and that of others, too.

For Micaela, fear was not considered an uncontrollable passion, but instead a rational one. She was very aware that its usage was dual purpose: as an instrument to achieve control and power, and as a reason to feel perpetually threatened. Fear simultaneously brought security and insecurity. In the case of Micaela, she would rhetorically and consciously use fear to subdue or, just as easily, to persuade others. Regardless of whether she portrayed herself to her husband or to the colonial authorities as a fearful human being, she did so knowing the emotional impact it would have on them. As Robin suggests, those who are fearful "move forward, maximizing whatever means they have at their disposal in order to obtain their future ends, which is the very definition of power" (41).[23] In Micaela's case, fear equaled power.

However, for Spanish authorities, fear acquired a more corporeal nature. When Micaela warned her husband that failing to act promptly could result "in the removal of her eyes" or even potential death, bodily fear was at the forefront of her consciousness. For instance, in one of her letters she pleaded with her husband: "and in this way do not permit that they kill me, because your absence has been the cause of all this" ("y así no permitas que me quiten la vida, pues tu ausencia ha sido causa para todo esto") (*MHDI*, 53).[24] Even at her trial Micaela confessed that her major fear was "eternal death" (*CDIP*, 730). The possibility that her body and that of her children's bodies would be eradicated from the face of the earth was Micaela's ultimate fear. Ironically, she used this same type of fear consistently to intimidate others.

The letters written by Micaela and the letters addressed to her, along with the accounts of the witnesses who testified against her, offer a glimpse into Micaela's personality. Certainly, she was regarded as cruel, fearless, controlling, arrogant, frightening, and rebellious. There were no limits to her desire to make the insurrection a successful one. She would even question the actions of her own husband when she thought they were affecting the outcome of the insurrection.[25] She declared that his lack of practical sense and his ineffectiveness had started to wear on her body: "Yo creí que de día y de noche estuvieses entendiendo en disponer estos asuntos, y no tanto descuido que me quita la vida, que ni aun ya tengo carnes ni estoy en mí" (I thought that you were going to devote your time to these affairs day and night, your carelessness is ruining my life, I have no flesh on my bones and I feel beside myself) (*MHDI*, 50). The phrase "I have no flesh on my bones" lies at the heart of the corporeal image that Micaela used to frame the narrative of the insurrection. Every day that passed, with Túpac Amaru unable to seize Cuzco, contributed to Micaela's fearing for her life or symbolically losing her flesh. The phrase "lacking flesh" ("no tengo carnes") emphasizes the idea of a body on the brink of disappearing.[26] Her own suffering was hyperbolically expressed in bodily terms, or what Fraser and Greco refer to as somatization.[27] She reminded him that she was able to feel the mistakes of his acts upon her very own flesh. For Micaela, the social construction of her own body as one about to dissolve, yet still able to feel pain, emphasized that the fear of death constituted an effective rhetorical tool to mobilize all those involved in the insurrection. It could be used to force others to act promptly, effectively, and without question.

Unfortunately for Micaela, the end was near. Her suspicion that the Spanish authorities and their allies were taking control became a reality when the Spanish army prevented Túpac Amaru from taking Cuzco, and instead captured him and his family in the town of Langui. In May 1781 the Spanish *visitador* José Antonio de Areche proclaimed the death penalty against Micaela Bastidas, underlining that such a sentence should be accompanied "con algunas cualidades y circunstancias que causen terror y espanto al público; para que a vista de espectáculo, se contengan los demás, y sirva de ejemplo y escarmiento" (with qualities and circumstances that will send terror and shock throughout the public; a spectacle of this kind should serve to contain the rest of the native people and serve as an example and a lesson) (*CDIP*, 727). According to Spanish authorities, the grim death that Micaela was to suffer would be staged in order to instill terror in the indigenous people and also to serve as an unforgettable lesson; consequently, it became a spectacle. She was to be dragged by a horse to the place of her death, with her feet and hands tied, while her sentence was read aloud to the public. Upon reaching the site of execution, she would first have her tongue cut out, and would then be garroted (strangled) by means of an iron collar with a screw clasped about her neck.[28] Once garroted, she was to be hanged until dead, leaving her body exposed in public for some time. Later, her body was to be quartered, with her head destined for the Piccho Hill and exposed upon a pillory with a description of her crimes on its façade. Her arms and legs were to be taken to three different sites at which the rebellion had taken place; her arms to Tungasuca and Arequipa, and her legs to Carabaya. The remnants of Micaela's body were to remain on Piccho Hill, where they were burned along with her husband's body. Micaela's death, along with the public punishment and display of her tortured body, thus functioned as a reminder of the fatal consequences in store for those who dared to disobey the system. As Foucault has observed with regard to eighteenth-century Europe, public execution was to be regarded, as in this case, "as a political operation . . . inscribed in a system of punishment" that was intended to reactivate power (*Discipline and Punish*, 53).

What lies behind the logic of public execution and fragmentation? Why was it so important that this horrendous death took place in a public space, in front of every marginalized sector of society? Why was it so necessary for the legal authorities to execute her in the form of a spectacle? Finally, what did Micaela's body represent within the context of the public space, and how did Spanish authorities want her body to be read, understood, and remembered?

## Public Execution and the Female Body as a Legible Text

As a component of the Spanish legal system, public execution lasted until approximately 1826. Since medieval times, people sentenced to death had become part of a "symbolic process" in which decapitation, and in some instances dismemberment or mutilation of the body, seemed the most rightful acts of punishment (De Quirós, 68).[29] The executions were systematized in a manner that assumed order as the norm. Offenders were taken from jail (usually on horseback), accompanied by priests, law officers, lawyers, and executioners. In procession, they were later taken to the *plaza*, where in front of hundreds and sometimes thousands of spectators, their crimes were read aloud. In many instances, the malefactor was asked to accept his or her guilt or to plead forgiveness. The lawbreaker was then hanged, garroted, or decapitated, depending on the person's gender and the nature of the crime.[30] Finally, in those cases where the authorities wished to set a stern example, the offender's body was dismembered and exhibited in the most public and frequented places. Spanish authorities transferred this legal system of punishment to the colonial territories, in which crimes of *lessa majestad* (treason against the crown) were severely punished, as established since the *Siete partidas*. On both sides of the Atlantic, law clearly functioned as "a powerful instrument of social control designed to mold the bodies and the souls of those subject to its rule . . . the legal sphere is a 'theater' or forum in which a pedagogic work takes place in continuous fashion—from here emanate normative messages about illicit behavior, crime and, punishment" (Aguirre and Salvatore, 13). These normative messages, in the case of colonial Spanish America, were sometimes molded to fit the local and particular circumstances that made the American territories different from Spain.[31]

In the case of the Túpac Amaru insurrection, the colonial authorities sentenced three women: Cecilia Túpac Amaru, Tomasa Titu Condemayta (*cacica* of Acos), and Micaela Bastidas. Cecilia, a first cousin of Túpac Amaru, was accused of participating as an accomplice in the insurrection by providing financial assistance and coca to the rebels. She was also found guilty of working with Micaela from Piccho, and of proclaiming openly her hatred against Spaniards.[32] As an accomplice, she was not sentenced to death. Instead, on July 17, 1781, Cecilia was ordered to walk the public streets of Cuzco while receiving two hundred lashes. She also was sentenced to ten years in exile in a convent in Mexico.[33] The public exhibition of her punished and bloody body served as a visual reminder of the consequences of her act.

The sentence imposed on Tomasa Titu Condeymata was harsher, as she was accused of being one of the "main conspirators" ("principal fomentadoras") of the insurrection, as well as of encouraging and forcing Indians to join the rebel troops.[34] Tomasa was sentenced to death by garroting. On May 18, 1781, she was taken to the main plaza by horse with her hands and feet tied, while her crime was read aloud. Once she was garroted, authorities hanged her body from the scaffold and left it open to the public view for six hours. The corpse was later beheaded, and the head was exposed on a pillory in the town of Acos, where Tomasa had once ruled as a *cacica*. As in the case of Cecilia, the authorities used her body as a visual tool to exemplify the consequences of engaging in similar acts and to serve as a deterrent as it became an emblem of fear. Additionally, her body served as a visual reminder of the extreme and violent retribution that would be employed against those who contributed to social chaos and disorder, as it also made clear who held the power to reestablish order. Her body went through a three-part process of immobilization, starting with the tying of hands and feet, then the garroting, and ending in a beheading, which emphasized the final act of domination. If the punishment imposed on Tomasa Titu Condeymata seemed merciless and harsh, the one rendered against Micaela reached greater proportions, in which "the spectacle of punishment" as Mitchell B. Merback calls it, became "the sight of the body-in-pain" (125).

In the sentence handed to Micaela Bastidas, Peruvian authorities were following the Spanish norm of punishment, but with a few noteworthy differences. In the decree issued on May 2, 1781, the prosecutor announced that Micaela was accused of *lessa Majestad* and that the accompanying punishment would follow what was described in "Leyes 2, título 27. Partida; la tercera de la citada Partida, título 1; la 6, título 27 de la 2, Partida; y todo el título 18, Libro 8 de las de Castilla" (Laws 2, Title 27. Order; the third aforementioned Order, Title 1; Order 6, title 27 of Order 2; and everything in Title 18, Book 8 of the Castilian laws) (*CDIP*, 728).[35] Death sentences on the gallows and mutilation of the bodies were the traditional punishments imposed on those accused of treason against the crown (although they were applied most often to men). The public prosecutor in charge of Micaela's case issued a decree stating: "Que en obrando en justicia, se ha de servir Vuestra Señoría mandar se le imponga a la citada Micaela Bastidas la pena ordinaria de muerte, *con algunas calidades y circunstancias que causen terror y espanto al público; para que a vista del espectáculo,* se contengan los demás y sirva de ejemplo y escarmiento" (Executing justice, the King ordered that Micaela Bastidas be sentenced to death, and that her death be *accompanied by conditions and circumstances that cause terror and astonishment in the public; that in the form of a spectacle,* this would prevent others from committing similar actions as well as serve in this way as an example and a lesson to those who witness it) (*CDIP*, 727; emphasis mine).

It was paramount for colonial authorities to carry out the execution in public, and in Cuzco this meant in the most frequented space: the Plaza Mayor, or what had formerly been called the Plaza del Pregón of the Incas.[36] The plaza became a space in which exemplariness, fear, threat, vengeance, pain, and power converged. Its accessibility greatly enhanced the authorities' ability to present their example and display the chosen mode of punishment. The act of execution would become one that looked to reaffirm power and to create fear: "con algunas calidades y circunstancias que causen terror y espanto al público" (with some conditions and circumstances that cause terror and astonishment in the public) (*CDIP*, 727). As Foucault reminds us, it also served "as a political tactic" and as a "complex social function" (*Discipline and Punish*, 23). If we consider a *spectacle* (from the Latin verb *spectare*) an extraordinary act to be viewed and attended by the public, we can then visualize the scene of execution as an exhibition and representation of domination.[37] The execution became a spectacle, whereby Micaela's body functioned metaphorically as a text to be written, read, and interpreted within a spatial context: the Plaza del Pregón of the Incas. This space of punishment would remind the natives of their history of colonization, including their victories and eventual defeat. In this sense, the plaza functioned "both as a school and a theater where the rudiments of *policía* were taught" (Kagan, 34). It also represented a space where memory reinscribed history.

Micaela's execution involved acts of pain that authorities very rarely inflicted on women who were sentenced to death, including the dragging of her body by horse while her hands and feet were bound; the decision to garrot her; the cutting of her tongue prior to death; the quartering of her body; and the burning of some body parts. This was the wording of her death sentence, issued by special investigator and *visitador* Areche on May 16, 1781:

> Fallo, atento al mérito de ellos y por los crímenes que se hallan comprobados, que debo de condenar y condeno a Micaela Bastidas en pena de muerte; y la justicia que le mando a hacer que sea sacada de este cuartel, donde se halla presa, arrastrada con *una soga de esparto al cuello, atados pies y manos*, con voz de pregonero que publique su delito, siendo llevada de esta forma al lugar del suplicio, donde se halla un tabladillo, en que por su sexo y consultando la decencia, se le sentará y ajustará al garrote, *cortándosele allí la lengua, e inmediatamente se le hará morir con el instrumento*; lo que verificado se le colgará en la horca, sin que allí la quite, hasta que se mande, persona alguna. *Y luego será descuartizado su cuerpo*, llevando la cabeza al cerro de Piccho, que será fijada en una picota, con una tarja en que se leerá su delito; un brazo a Tungasuca, otro a Arequipa, y una de las piernas a Carabaya conduciéndose lo restante de su cuerpo al mismo cerro de Piccho, donde será quemado con el de su marido, en el brasero que estará allí, dando razón documentada los respectivos Corregidores de haberse efectuado y publicado esta sentencia por Bando. (*CDIP* 736–37; emphasis mine)

> [Conviction. Based on the nature of the crimes committed, I ought to and I do condemn Micaela Bastidas to death. I sentence her to be taken from this barracks where she has been imprisoned, dragged *by the neck with an esparto rope, with feet and hands bound*. Her crime is to be proclaimed by the town crier, while she is taken in this manner to the place of torture, where a wooden platform is found. Out of respect for her sex and in observance of common decency, she will be seated and the garrote adjusted. There, her *tongue will be cut out, and immediately thereafter the instrument will be applied until she is dead*; once this is verified, she will be hanged on the gallows where no one shall remove her until so ordered. Following this, *her body will be quartered*, her head taken to the Piccho Hill where it will be placed on a pillory next to a wooden tablet where her crime can be read.

One of her arms will be taken to Tungasuca, another to Arequipa, and one of her legs to Carabaya. The rest of her body will be taken to the very top of Piccho Hill, where it will be burned on a brazier along with her husband's body. The respective *corregidores* should give notice that this sentence has been carried out, and they should make it public through an edict.]

For the authorities, these actions (again, more common in sentences given to men) were justified because Micaela, in her attempts to challenge the system, had demonstrated behavior the authorities would normally expect from a man. According to the Spanish authorities, Micaela did not deserve to be treated as a woman because her behavior was perceived as masculine, as the plentiful edicts and testimonies related to her trial indicate.[38] Indeed, the act of her execution was to become a repetitive act of death. The plaza became a space of suffering and terror for the victim and the spectators, as well as a space for the celebration of power for the Spanish authorities as they looked down in satisfaction from their lofty balconies.

In this space of terror, the garrote and the gallows became, as Pieter Spierenburg reminds us, symbols of authority in a dual sense, which "warned potential transgressors of the law that criminal justice would be practiced" and "warned everyone to remember who practiced it" (55). Micaela embodied that which needed to be contained, repressed, and dominated. The use of the aforementioned instruments of pain, violence, and destruction—the garrote, knife, rope, and gallows—represented the means by which such subjection would be guaranteed. Nevertheless, in the case of Micaela, these instruments of power were not the only means available to inflict pain and suffering. According to a witness of the execution, when Micaela was taken to the wooden platform, the garrote did not work properly (meaning quickly enough) because her neck was too slender. As a result, the executioners were only able to kill her by tying a rope around her neck, pulling from opposite sides, and kicking her in her breasts and stomach. This excessive violence against female body parts by the authorities was intended to inflict additional pain and to guarantee death. Furthermore, Micaela's own physical traits (her slender neck) made the punishment more severe, as they violently pulled the rope tight about her neck as she was being kicked. Throughout this process of torture, pain, and death, the body of Micaela became another vehicle of intimidation for the colonial authorities: it guaranteed the execution of power and the implementation of fear.

In the description of the sentence, Micaela's body functioned as a locus of pain and torture. The tying of the neck, feet, and hands; the cutting of the tongue; the hanging of the body; and the partitioning of the body all represent actions that reinforced torture as the instrument par excellence to inflict and display pain. Elaine Scarry argues that torture, aside from constituting "a language, an objectification, is also itself a demonstration and magnification of the felt-experience of pain" (27). Scarry adds, that for the torturers, the process represented a "wholly convincing spectacle of power" (27). In the context of Micaela's execution, her body became a visual, legible text in which torture and pain worked as the grammatical tools to make sense of the textual message.[39] This type of grammar needed no written-language competency except the ability to witness and visually experience the body in pain. For the authorities, the anatomy of meaning in this spectacle of death consisted of the manner in which Micaela's body was able to exhibit the power of torture. In this regard, her body, along with the other bodies executed during the insurrection, fulfilled one of the many functions that made the body a prime target for government officials in the Enlightenment: "inscribing and broadcasting the messages of power" (Bennett, 60).

The message of power could not have been completely conveyed without taking into consideration the topography of punishment that continued after Micaela's death. The logic of fragmentation that ruled her death, expressed in the quartering of her body, became another crucial element within the production of this public spectacle of death. It represented the culmination of the "function" put on by the authorities.[40] The body, which as Jonathan Sawday argues, "had always been available as a rich source of metaphors with which to describe systems of government which were held to be both organic . . . and hierarchical" (29), took on further connotations in Micaela's case.[41] For the spectators, her body represented the subjected and eradicated body. However, for the authorities, it also symbolized terror and disorder, which is why dismemberment of the body was crucial. This aspect of the execution was mainly aimed at the spectators and residents of Peru, and specifically toward those who belonged to the marginalized groups. As Spierenburg rightly observes, "A corpse can no longer feel the pain. Hence its punishment is meant for others" (56).

Therefore, each part of the body dismembered by the executioners carried a determinate meaning, not only for the part of the population that needed an appropriate example, but also for the authorities themselves. In this sense, each body part symbolized a type of grammar that would have made the body, as a text, legible to all. Each part in itself also represented designated tools for communication. The quartering of the body, as Foucault reminds us in a different context, became part of the "quantitative act of pain that is regulated by the act of torture" (*Discipline and Punish*, 33). As he adds, "punishment does not fall upon the body indiscriminately or equally; it is calculated according to detailed rules" (34). The Spanish authorities' decision on this last stage of the punishment was certainly a deliberate one, and one that resided in the power to inscribe upon the body an unforgettable act of violence.

David Hillman and Carla Mazzio argue that individual parts of the body are "increasingly marked and elaborated upon a range of visual and textual spaces," and are "frequently imagined to take on attributes of agency and subjectivity" (xii). Because of the functions that each corporeal part carries, often the individual parts "can become concentrated sites where meaning is invested and often apparently stabilized" (Hillman and Mazzio, xii). If we pay close attention to the order in which Micaela's body was quartered and the public sites that were carefully chosen to exhibit the process, we can easily understand why her corporeal parts represented concentrated sites of meaning and parts of a topography of power centered on the connection between body and space. The body that had once fought for certain political ideas and later had been tortured and put to death had now (so the colonial authorities thought) lost its agency to become part of a political strategy. It also became more manageable and easily controlled in the process.

The partitioning of Micaela's body began, as described in the death sentence, with the cutting out of her tongue. The tongue is characterized by its discursive nature and its power to denounce, convince, challenge, and threaten other people. The tongue also represents the organ through which the self is expressed. As Olivia Vlahos observes, it is part of the "power of speech" and points to "its flexibility and mobility" (112). Because of Micaela's influence within the insurrection and her capacity to dictate orders, impose punishments, convince conspirators in the rebellion, and denounce the colonial powers, her tongue was viewed as an instrument of danger by the legal authorities. The decision to sever her tongue meant that Micaela's ability to attack the system through her organ of speech would be completely thwarted. It is extremely important to consider that the tongue represented the first bodily part detached from her body, while she was still alive. For the authorities, the agony involved in cutting Micaela's tongue seemed to parallel the damage that she inflicted upon the Spanish forces as the logistic leader of the insurrection. Mazzio observes that if the tongue "is imagined as the site where discursive and moral contagion begin and end, it seems logical to detach it in the act of punishing transgression" (64).[42] The removal of the tongue translated to the elimination of the potential for disorder, and evoked a symbolic representation of what would await those who dared to denounce or criticize the colonial system. It also implied a symbolic silence and, further still, the possible end to social disorder.

As documents related to the events that followed her execution attest, the second part of the body quartered was her head. For the authorities, this seemed the logical next step, as the head represented the place where thinking and reasoning took place. Indeed, the head is where the brain as well as the senses is located, and for this reason it was associated with intelligence and reasoning. In Western culture the head was associated with wisdom, power, and understanding (Vlahos, 112).[43] Micaela's head symbolized power, attributed to her ability for acute suggestions on the progress and development of the rebellion, her persuasive capabilities (particularly to mobilize forces), her strategic plans to attack and control territories, and the hatred she infused in the indigenous and *mestizo* population against the Spanish authorities. Her ability to organize a military force and to disrupt the political system was located in her head. If the head was also considered "the command center of the body," which provided its balance (Vlahos, 116), its detachment from the body implied an unbalance of that center of power. Furthermore, as the head was also associated with leadership and direction (Barkan, 102), its detachment implied for the authorities the disruption of the insurrection's organized message so that it lacked guidance, leadership, and control. The site so carefully chosen to exhibit her head was extremely important as well. According to the *escribano real* (royal court clerk), her head was put in Callanca, which was the common entrance to the city and the base of the Piccho Hill (*CDIP*, 738). Micaela's head was to be exposed at the entrance of the city, a place both unavoidable and often frequented because of its geographical location. The population would be welcomed by the remembrance of the horrifying destiny awaiting those who committed crimes against the government, regardless of their gender, social status, or race. The entrance of the city and the hill itself became at once spaces of fear and exemplariness, vivid lessons in the politics of violence and power.

The dismembering of Micaela's body continued with the partitioning of her arms, one of which was sent to Tungasuca and the other to Arequipa. Both represented meaningful places from which Micaela organized the rebellion. Micaela's missing arms were to function as reminders for those who dared to follow her. The arms symbolized action, because of their strength and their ability to demonstrate and express desires and mandates. They were also crucial for the essential tasks performed by the individuals who participated in the insurrection (including Micaela herself), which included cooking, curing the sick, fighting, collecting money, gathering arms, and transmitting letters, safe-conducts, and petitions. For the individuals still alive and to whom the lesson was directed, their arms represented an instrument of work and daily survival. In removing Micaela's arms, the Spanish authorities intended to persuade the marginalized groups that the use of their arms for causes against the government would end in suffering and disability.

The authorities proceeded to publicly expose one of Micaela's legs, while the other was to be burned with the remainder of her body. They were to be exhibited at additional sites from which Micaela had organized and taken part in the insurrection: Carabaya and the Piccho Hill. The legs constituted the part of the body where the weight rests. As a result, the base to sustain the torso disappeared, contributing to the body's lack of support and mobility. The legs were also associated with movement, and mobilization of the public during the insurrection became a major fear for the authorities. The indigenous rebels and their familiarity with the space in which the uprising took place caused the royal forces to constantly look over their shoulders to contain this seemingly uncontrollable force. Micaela was equally mobile during the insurrection. She managed to relocate repeatedly as a means to escape the authorities, and also with the aim of recruiting military forces. As Micaela many times expressed to her husband, mobilization was a key factor to elude death; a mere hint of tardiness could have hastened their enemies' ability to destroy them. With the amputation of her legs, the authorities reminded the inhabitants within southern Andean zones that they should pay heed to stepping in the right place (the subordinate place), because any straying would result in permanent paralysis. Her legs were trophies that the authorities proudly exhibited as symbols of their power to suppress and control any movement or disorder that attempted to disrupt the colonial system and the space of order.

Within the economy of partitioning, Micaela's body can be read as a microcosm of the unruly population threatening the social order of Andean Peru. In this sense, as Fraser and Greco maintain, the body functions "as a locus of transgression and a revolutionary tool, one by which social hierarchies can be destabilized" (69). Dismembering the body parts equaled the deconstruction and, ultimately, the destruction of the message of the insurrection exemplified in Micaela's body. Her body, which had once represented a locus of transgression as well as a revolutionary tool, eventually became a political instrument for the Spanish authorities to achieve social order. The cultural meaning of her body as a legible text pointed to the need to achieve social order through the rhetoric of fear. Her body symbolized an unruly world that needed to be kept under total control.

The final act of burning her torso to ashes, after exposing the different parts of her body in strategic topographical points, aimed to remind the public that an incomplete body was indeed a disabled one. The body ceased to be a body in action and became individual parts that could not function as a whole. Without the head, there is no direction and leadership; without the tongue, there is no discourse; without the legs and arms, there is no sense of action and movement. In sum, for the Spanish authorities, to dismember the body and to partially burn it signified fragmenting the message of the insurrection as propagated by Micaela and her husband, and replacing it with the colonial authorities' own message of power and fear. It also meant erasing the memory of what that body had once achieved, and replacing it with the memory of fear and death.[44]

The exhibition of Micaela's body in the plaza before, during, and after execution highlights one of the persuasive metaphors since early modernity, whereby the body functioned as a book or "a text there to be opened, read, interpreted, and indeed, rewritten" (Sawday, 129). But how did those witnessing the execution read Micaela's body? This is a crucial question to ask in order to understand how successful the execution was for those who organized it.

## Reading the Execution: Legal Punishment in the Andean World

Because diverse racial groups witnessed Micaela's execution, we can assume that its impact on Indians, blacks, *mestizos*, and Spaniards was quite different for each group. An account of an anonymous witness might shed light on how this spectacle of death was received by the intended audience. Unfortunately, we do not have indigenous accounts of the events, even if the authorities thought to target this group as their primary public. It is important to discuss—based on notions of legal punishment and violence held in the Andean world before the arrival of the Spaniards—how the indigenous population could have understood the public spectacle of the execution. I shall examine the corporeal nature of legal punishment in the Andean world as captured by major chroniclers, such as Pedro Cieza de León (ca. 1520–1554), Juan de Santa Cruz Pachacuti (sixteenth/seventeenth century), Inca Garcilaso de la Vega (1539–1616), Guaman Poma de Ayala (c.1550–1616), and Bernabé Cobo (1582–1657), in order to understand how such a spectacle of fear might have been understood by the indigenous audience.

In an anonymous document describing the execution of the leaders of the insurrection, an informant described the plaza in which the executions took place as besieged by an army composed of mulattos and Huamanguinos (Indians from Huamanga), well armed with rifles and bayonets (*CDIP*, 774). The area was tightly secured. According to the same witness, the procession to the gallows included the nine prisoners sentenced to death, followed by priests in charge of their last rites, guards, and two executioners.[45] The witness added that a great number of people attended the ceremony, but none made a sound during the horrendous and gruesome spectacle that took place. The witness was quite surprised that he did not see Indians dressed in their native attires among so many people. He added that if they were there, they were probably disguised with capes and ponchos (*CDIP*, 776). It is noteworthy that the witness could not recognize as many Indians as he thought he would have seen there. He was very puzzled, especially since the *visitador* José Antonio de Areche, in issuing the death sentence against the main leaders of the insurrection in Cuzco, had instructed the *corregidores* of all the regions where the insurrection had taken place to publish the death sentence in their jurisdictions, so that all Indians for years to come would be reminded of the negative consequences of engaging in these types of activities (*CDIP*, 770). Areche had emphasized that the message needed to be clear to "la ilusa nación de los Indios" (the gullible nation of Indians), especially those who might plan to claim Indian nobility as a way to mobilize a rebellion (*CDIP*, 770). The intended audience of his death sentence were Indians who, according to Areche, needed to be detached from any artifact or piece of memory that reminded them of the insurrection or of their Inca cultural past.[46]

If the main intended audience for the execution was indeed Indians, it is hard to believe that the Spanish authorities would not ensure that they were present at the ceremony. The same witness who had found it odd that he could not see many Indians dressed in their native attires, and thought they had decided to hide beneath capes and ponchos, seemed unsure how to distinguish among the great numbers of attendees, who were in fact ("visibly") Indians. What puzzled him even more was how on the day of the execution, nature conspired to help the Indian population arrive at a different interpretation of the events they witnessed or heard about on that day. The eyewitness declared that certain things occurred "that looked like they were planned by the devil to foment in these Indians their abuses, presages, and superstitions" ("Suceden algunas cosas que parece que el Diablo las trama y dispone, para confirmar á estos indios en sus abusos, agüeros y supersticiones") (*CDIP*, 776). According to him, the weather before the executions was very dry and sunny. However, on the day of the executions it turned cloudy, and exactly at noon during the execution of Túpac Amaru, a "strong gusty wind" came up, followed by rain, which forced the public, including the army, to seek cover

(*CDIP*, 776). This change in weather, the witness added, prompted the Indians to believe that nature itself felt the death of the Inca at the hands of the "inhumane and impious Spaniards who were killing with so much cruelty" ("los españoles inhumanos é impíos [que] estaban matando con tanta crueldad") (*CDIP*, 776). One can note the disappointment in the witness's account when he realized that the spectacle that had served as a stern example for Indians to prevent them from committing similar actions in future, was in part hampered by nature. For the witness, the spectacle of death would have been successful only if that human identification between the executed criminals and the public had been uninterrupted. Ironically, the act of prevention and intimidation resulted in a sort of presage that kept feeding the indigenous cultural memory of present and past events.

Given the lack of other eyewitness accounts, we must ponder to what extent the indigenous groups that witnessed the execution of Micaela and her husband, and those who heard of it through the voices of the *corregidores*, understood such a horrific event. Did the punishments imposed on Micaela and the others, and based on Western legal codes, have any connection with Andean views of corporal punishments? What place did the body occupy in the economy of punishment enacted in the execution? Some chronicles that speak about the Inca civilization offer clues about similar punishments imposed in Andean societies before the arrival of the Spaniards and suggest how the body was conceived in Inca society with regard to corporal punishment.

For the Incas, the body was central to understanding social structures. As Constance Classen observes, "the body provided a model for the integrated and dynamic totality of the cosmos," functioning as "a basic organizing principle" (3). The body also served as a "paradigm for interpreting Inca religious practices and beliefs" (Classen, 3). For example, the division of the empire was based on two components, Hanan and Hurin, that referred to the two halves of the body: upper and lower. The four quarters of the empire, or Tahuantisuyu, referred to the four quarters of the body. As Classen adds, "the preeminent metaphor of the body of the empire was the body of the Inca," whose head was conceived as the apex of the empire and his heart as its center (96–97).[47] The health and illness of the empire were also associated with the Inca's body. When in 1533 the Spanish soldiers cut off Atahualpa's head, this act was equated to "the dismemberment of the imperial body" (Classen, 114). As a result of this act, chaos and destruction affected the health of the kingdom, as the Inca society perceived this moment as "the literal and metaphorical devastation of the human body" (Classen, 118). When in 1572 Túpac Amaru I, an Inca ruling from Vilcabamba, was executed by Spanish authorities in the same manner as Atahualpa, the execution served to remind the Andean population of the fracture of their empire, played out through the decapitated body of the ruler.

Túpac Amaru II took advantage of the popular messianic beliefs of the Inkarrí myth associated with Túpac Amaru I, which foretold that Túpac Amaru I's decapitated head and body would unite underground and that when this final union occurred, "the Inca would rise up and return to power, bringing order and social justice to the Andes" (Andrien, 214). Undoubtedly, when the public present at the execution witnessed the garroting of Micaela, and the dismemberment of her body, followed by that of her husband, these acts brought vivid memories of those two crucial moments in the past. The executions served as a reminder that the Andean body as a unit was again broken and dismembered.

This reading of corporal punishment can help us understand how the indigenous population at the time might have interpreted the spectacle of death inflicted on Micaela. Corporal punishment was highly regarded within the Inca legal system. Pedro Cieza de León, in his *Del Señorío de los Incas* or *Crónica del Perú*,[48] described some of the harsh punishments that the Inca leaders reserved for specific crimes. According to Cieza, no soldier, captain, or son of the Incas dared to mistreat, rob, or insult anybody, or rape a woman, under penalty of death. Thieves were whipped multiple times, and if necessary they were sentenced to death. In cases of social disturbances and insurrections, the individuals involved were sent to a type of prison filled with wild animals where the wrongdoers were devoured (Cieza de León, 138). The Inca authorities also chose a special place to conduct death penalties and, when necessary, decapitation. According to Cieza de León, the river that ran through Cuzco was that special place (147). Cieza believed it was due to this strict legal system that "reason and order" existed throughout the Inca empire: "y haciéndolo así, en todo había razón y orden" (138).

With regard to decapitation, in *Relación de antigüedades deste Reyno del Perú* (1613), Juan de Santa Cruz Pachacuti mentioned its importance in the context of military warfare. He described how the Incas would attach the heads of the killed enemies to the tip of their spears, and spread llama blood over the rest of the weapon (150). They made use of the gored heads and bloody spears during their attacks upon other groups. Through inclusion of the head as part of their weapons, the Inca warriors aimed to instill fear and mark their power over others. The head was indeed displayed as a military prize.

The Inca Garcilaso de la Vega, in his *Comentarios reales* (1609), emphasized how Indians under Inca rule "gravely feared the laws" to the extent that they never disobeyed them ("fueron temerosísimos de sus leyes") (143). Corporal punishments and death penalties were reserved for special crimes. For example, those who committed sodomy were taken to the central square and burned (117). Those women chosen as the Virgins of the Sun who then lost their virginity were buried alive, while the involved were hanged.[49] Any person who committed homicide was punished by a "violent death" ("muerte violenta") (276–77). Thieves were hanged and adulterers were sentenced to death (277). In Book 9 of the *Comentarios reales*, Garcilaso described the violent punishments suffered by those who killed Túpac Inca Yupanqui's closest ministers. The Inca successor Huayna Cápac ordered that, as traitors, they were to be sentenced to death by beheading. Those who acted as conspirators were to have their teeth removed (382). In the case of insurrections, such as the one that took place in Caranques, the Inca ordered that all rebels be taken to a lagoon and beheaded. The amount of blood spilled in the lagoon led the Inca to name it Yahuarcocha, which meant "lake or sea of blood" (395). According to Garcilaso, the name was chosen to preserve "the memory of the crime and punishment" ("guardase la memoria del delito y del castigo") (395). For the Incas, this would constitute a stern and memorable punishment (395).[50]

The Andean writer Guaman Poma de Ayala, in *Nueva corónica y buen gobierno*, written between 1600 and 1615, stated that the Aucapacharuna Indians, who were said to be descendants of Noah, punished sorcerers, male or female prostitutes, adulterers, and renegades with great penalties (56). For these crimes they were stoned to death or thrown over a cliff. Under Inca rule, similarly harsh punishments were imposed. Traitors and those who rebelled against the government, especially against the Inca, were killed. Their bodies were then partitioned and from the body parts several artifacts were made. The skin was used to make drums, the bones were made into flutes, the teeth into necklaces, and the head was used as a cup to drink *chicha* (163). Female prostitutes and rapists were hanged by their hair or hands and left to die (163). Removing their eyes and then partitioning their bodies were the punishments imposed on those who dared to marry their own sister, mother, aunt, or niece. Their body parts were left on different hills "for memory and punishment" ("para memoria y castigo") of their acts (164). Adulterers were killed and then left unburied so vultures could eat their bodies (281). Based on Guaman Poma's rendition of punishments, native Andeans were familiar with the notion of corporal punishment, as it lay at the center of Inca rule.

Finally, Bernabé Cobo, in his *Historia del Nuevo Mundo* (1653), devoted chapter 26 of Book 2 to a discussion of the laws and punishments by which the Incas governed their kingdom. In his compilation, he listed a series of corporal punishments imposed on those who violated the laws. Torture and execution were reserved for those who killed someone in order to rob them (237). Those who committed treason were executed publicly; so were those who cast spells on others. Cobo recounts that "this punishment was executed with much publicity, bringing together the people of surrounding towns so that they would be present at the execution, and likewise all of his household and family were killed."[51] Stoning was reserved for those *caciques* who killed their subjects for no reason (238). The death penalty was imposed on those adulterers who committed the crime with married noblewomen and on women who had a subsequent abortion (239). Women who killed their husbands or those who lied were hanged upside down in a public place and left to die (238). Stoning and death were imposed on thieves (240). Those who dared to disobey the Inca orders received long imprisonment and eventual death (241). In extreme cases, the Inca ordered the removal of the hearts of their enemies to instill terror in others (283).

Bernabé Cobo comments that these punishments were not imposed equally, as some noblemen who committed crimes were not punished as severely as nonnobles. He explains that the underlying reason "was to say that a public reprimand was a far greater punishment for the Inca of noble blood than the death penalty for a plebeian" (207). When Túpac Amaru and Micaela Bastidas were executed on May 18, 1781, as part of such an elaborated public spectacle, many Indians and Inca followers must have felt that a great offense must have been committed to carry such a heavy punishment. If corporal punishment, death sentences, and fear worked as instruments to maintain order in the Inca kingdom before the arrival of the Spaniards, two centuries later similar but even harsher punishments had been put into place to instill fear and to uphold order in an unruly world.

This brief survey of crime and punishment in Inca society offers clues as to how Micaela's crime may have been read at the time. A death sentence for a woman, as stated earlier, was not foreign to the Andean population. However, the manner in which Micaela's execution took place was harsher than what any women customarily received at the time. From the cutting of the tongue and beheading, to the ultimate partitioning of her body and the burning of the torso, Micaela suffered what the worst Inca male enemies suffered, and more. Areche was correct when he pronounced with paramount importance that her execution be accompanied with conditions and circumstances that would cause terror and astonishment in the public sphere, serving as an example and a lesson to deter others. The body, which was central in Inca culture in order to understand the world and to maintain order in society, now was being used to convey a slightly different yet not altogether unfamiliar message. Although it was employed as an instrument of fear and control, it also served to eradicate indigenous power.

However, this act of punishment was not free from contradictions. Micaela's brutally punished body, along with her body parts topographically dispersed in key areas of the insurrection, left an indelible memory for current and future indigenous generations of the relevance of what had happened there. At the same time, her body had to be burned to erase all memory of her actions. The act of leaving no trace of a complete body constituted a violent attempt to prevent any future interpretations of the Inkarrí myth. The complete bodies of Micaela Bastidas and Túpac Amaru were never to be reunited, as they became ashes that disappeared in the air and along the stream that surrounded the Picchu Hill. If, as Castro-Klarén argues, the visual spaces of the insurrection and execution "bore the capacity to retain and disseminate the narrative of Inca ancestry well beyond the limits of print media" (175), the brutal execution of the leaders represented an attempt to erase any trace of Inca ancestry in these visual spaces through a superimposed narrative of violence, fear, and death.

The space in which the authorities decided to carry out the execution (the plaza) constituted a relevant visual space for Andean society. The plaza itself bore a narrative of Inca history. If the plaza was a convenient strategic space for the colonial authorities to convey their own message, for the indigenous population it also represented a place endowed with cultural memories of the past. Carolyn Dean reminds us that the Spaniards used the Inca's central plaza in Cuzco (*kaukaypata*) as "their own *plaza mayor*," erecting their buildings over "the foundations of Inka structures" (25). For instance, Pedro Cieza de León described the Inca plaza before the arrival of the Spaniards as the center from which the four main *caminos reales* (royal highways) emerged, directing people to the four areas into which the empire was divided (323).[52] The Inca Garcilaso also described the plaza as an important ceremonial place where sacrifices for the imperial festival, Inti Raimi, or Festival of the Sun, and other spirited dances were performed.[53] For Garcilaso, the plaza was also used to punish those who committed crimes (117). Guaman Poma also mentioned that for the Inca ruler, the plaza was selected as a place in which *caciques principales* gathered to eat (166). It was a center of socialization, as it was the most densely populated area of the Inca empire. As Jay Kinsbruner explains, for Inca society, "administrative, religious, and economic life focused on a central main plaza" (21).[54]

When analyzing Micaela's execution, we must take into consideration this syncretic view of the plaza. The *plaza mayor* and former *plaza del pregón* or *kaukaypata* denoted spaces replete with cultural and political meanings. Through the present (that is, the occupation by the Spaniards), the indigenous population was able to remember its past. From this perspective, the colonial plaza can be considered as a dialogical space and as a "visual representation of colonial dominance, cultural resistance, and spatial control" (Low, 103). In choosing the plaza for the execution of Micaela and the others, the Spanish authorities were not only following the process of execution that was usual in Spain, but were also imposing the punishment in a site where once stood the center of the Inca empire. The indigenous witnesses attending the event were undoubtedly familiar with the importance of this particular plaza as a ceremonial space and center of social interaction. Túpac Amaru's forces also used the Andean plazas to torture and display the bodies of their Spanish enemies and those who supported them, including Spanish women.[55] The plaza as a "contact zone" reminded the natives witnessing the execution that what was taking place there was an event endowed with powerful meanings.[56] The message was clear; the bodies of those executed were to be visually read as texts inscribed with colonial power, domination, and fear. This message, as Carlos Alberto Garcés suggests, was to be easily "read" by an overwhelmingly illiterate population (218).

Another aspect of the executions that warrants discussion is the distribution of body parts over particular topographical points. In the case of Micaela, her head was taken to the Piccho Hill and displayed on a pillory along with a summary of her crimes. Once her body was reduced to ashes, it was thrown into the air and into a nearby creek located at the Piccho Hill. The hill in this context constituted an important symbolic space for Andean culture. Andean natives were certainly prepared to understand the significance of choosing that specific location. Scarlett O'Phelan Godoy notes that hills were considered sacred; on important holidays, such as the Day of the Dead (Día de los Muertos), people removed the remains of their relatives' bodies from cemeteries and reburied them in the hills (170). For Andean society, the hills represented the point of contact between the interior and the exterior world (O'Phelan Godoy, 170). Agricultural rites were performed on specific hills, and people went there to pray and ask the spirits who inhabited these places to help them with the planting season. Lastly, hills were also considered natural observatories in the sense that they represented strategic military points. O'Phelan Godoy believes this is why Túpac Amaru chose the Piccho Hill and the Puquín Hill as strategic sites from which to conduct his military operations (170).

Displaying Micaela's head on a hill, a space endowed with deep religious meanings for the inhabitants of those territories, represented an insulting act. In Andean society, once a person died, he or she was supposed to be buried; the body could not be left exposed. In the case of Micaela's torso, which had been burned to ashes, the possibility of paying respect to the remains had been eliminated. The religious aspect of the space was being overtaken by an act of punishment and horror. As a selective ceremonial space for the Andean population, the hill was being used for a different purpose: a political one. The authorities proposed the hills, especially Piccho, as spaces of violent death. Instead of going there to pray for the spirits to bless them in their season of planting, the Andean population was now being made to go there to visually read and witness the result of the act of death. The space of solemn celebration and prayer had been transformed into one of terror. What had been, during the insurrection, an important military strategic point had become a space of deterrence and threat.

In sum, the punishment imposed on Micaela in the public space of the plaza and the subsequent partitioning of her body must have provoked profound shock throughout the native population who witnessed the spectacle, as such bodily punishment was not usually imposed on a woman within the Inca legal system. For the Spaniards, even the crime surpassed the cruelty of death sentences imposed on women under their legal system, making the case of Micaela an extraordinary one—one that, according to the Spanish authorities, deserved "the most severe and strongest punishments" ("las órdenes más rigurosas y fuertes") (*CDIP*, 736). The use of "violencia selectiva" (selective violence), as O'Phelan Godoy calls it (106), made of the body, and in this case the female body, a crucial discursive tool to display pain and suffering and to instill fear in the memories of those who witnessed the spectacle.[57]

## Inscribing the Rebel Body

In a letter dated April 13, 1781, Juan Manuel, bishop of Cuzco, wrote that with the capture of Túpac Amaru and his wife, the authorities in their capacity "as doctors" of society could finally eradicate all the illnesses (that is, disturbances) that the insurrectionists had caused in the Andean territories. With the death of the leaders, the Spanish authorities were able "to restore to these unfortunate provinces their former tranquility" (*CDIP*, 646). In the words of the bishop, the insurrection as a symbolic disease could finally be contained with the execution of the leaders. Their dead bodies were to act as palliatives to exterminate the evil (diseases) they had spread, as well as to restore order and tranquility. In this sense, bodies such as Micaela's also functioned as prescriptive texts.

When dissecting the spectacle of Micaela's death sentence, we need to consider, as Veronica Kelly and Dorothea Von Mücke suggest in a different context, "the body's discursive character" and its role in the "cultural production of meaning" (4, 9).[58] Micaela's body was perceived by the colonial authorities as what Grosz would call a "vehicle of expression" (*Volatile Bodies*, 9), but a painful expression that was to serve as a lesson to the Andean population. Micaela's dead body became a cultural construct through which the social reality of the time determined how it was to be read and understood by the colonial authorities and marginalized groups. For the authorities, her body personified fear and abjection, and contradicted traditional conceptions about women. Micaela was, in the eyes of the authorities, a monstrous being (hideously evil and greatly malformed), one that had to be eradicated by the power of violence.[59] In death, her body became a site of cultural and social inscriptions, transformed into a visual text that the authorities planned to write and subsequently display to spectators. As witnesses and primary targets, the spectators were to perceive the pain expressed in Micaela's face and the dismembering of her body as an act of warning and prevention, which conveyed the ultimate goal of intimidation. The punitive dismemberment of her body sent a chilling message to the indigenous people, reminding them through the display of each body part that pain, torture, and death awaited those who dared to transgress or disobey the colonial system.

Nevertheless, Micaela's body did not represent an ahistorical body, which could have been depicted in isolation from the social reality of the time. She was a woman in a world dominated and governed by men, but she also belonged to a marginalized group that in the eyes of colonial authorities was not to disrupt the system imposed on them. Micaela had violated the social rules the colonial system had imposed on her that were based on her gender, race, and class. She had transgressed into spaces that, according to Spanish authorities, were forbidden to her: the spaces of war, male domination, and colonial power. The spatial relations that dominated the colonial system at the time required a woman to avoid public spaces and remain in the domestic arena, functioning as a submissive woman, exemplary wife, and devoted mother. According to Spanish laws and authorities, Micaela crossed the boundaries of these spaces, which led to the need for her containment.[60] The public space of the plaza was the most efficient arena in which to set judicial exemplariness and to proclaim their message loud and clear: violence would be suppressed with violence to restore order.

Micaela's public execution, and the subsequent partitioning and exhibition of her body parts, demonstrates how the body, as Alan Hyde suggests, could become a "vehicle for political education" and a "symbol of the political order," even if, before death, Micaela's living body had been seen as a sign of disorder (190–91). Documents related to the events that followed the execution corroborate the position held by the authorities when they stated that with the elimination of Túpac Amaru and Micaela, peace and order would at last be restored: "con la confianza de que en un corto periodo quedará tranquila toda la tierra que nos alborotó [Túpac Amaru y los principales de su alianza]" (with the confidence that in a short period of time, the lands that they stirred up would be calmed again) (*CDIP*, 641).

Final peace and order were to be symbolically achieved by burning the rest of Micaela's body at the stake, along with Túpac Amaru's, and reducing their bodies to ashes. For the authorities, the reduction of Micaela's body to ashes and eventual nothingness represented the most significant proof that order was finally on the way to being restored within their lands, and that spatial relations would finally fall under control of the state through the act of punishment and the power of fear. The final memory of her body was that of a criminal not worthy to be buried, but rather publicly exposed to the rest of the population as a sign of shame. Her body as an instrument of deterrence became at the end a legible text that gained cohesion through the grammar rooted in her body parts. The reading of Micaela, along with the reading of many female bodies to be discussed in the rest of this book, points to the dynamic nature of the body as a social, cultural, and political construct, and also as a material entity always affected by its own particular histories and needs.

# 2

# Visualizing and Commodifying Female Bodies in *Truxillo del Perú*

## From Colonial Order to Economic Productivity

In 1785 the bishop of Trujillo, Baltasar Martínez Compañón, decided to record a complete history of the province, based upon his six-year observations of the inhabitants, cultural practices, customs, architecture, indigenous antiquities, and natural history of the provinces. The result was a nine-volume manuscript composed only of watercolor illustrations, entitled *Truxillo del Perú*. An index that listed the illustrations by title and number accompanied each volume. What is most fascinating about this *historia* is that it did not include any narrative about the images depicted. *Truxillo del Perú* was strictly a visual text, considered by Martínez Compañón himself to be a type of "Historical, Physical, Political and Moral Museum of the Archbishopric of Truxillo, Peru" (Museo Histórico, Ficico, Político y Moral del Obpdo. De Truxillo del Perú) (32). Martínez Compañón decided to send the manuscript, or what he referred to as "obra gráfica" (graphic work), to the king and not necessarily to the Council of Indies or to church authorities.

My discussion considers Martínez Compañón's manuscript exactly as the author envisioned it: as a type of museum used to explore the visual renderings of the female population that he compiled while traveling through these provinces. I examine the significance of the female body in his construction of the visual and material history of these Peruvian territories, and how it was connected to a discourse of national progress that was taking place in Spain as well as in Spanish America. Although the majority of illustrations included in his manuscript were related to men, I focus on the role that women played in his political project.[1] I begin by exploring the metaphorical and literal dimensions of the word *museum* at the time, to better understand the implications of its use in terms of how his visual compilation was to be studied and understood. I then turn to the importance of visual images as powerful rhetorical tools, crucial in the construction of specific female cultural identities. As I will illustrate, for Martínez Compañón, class, race, social economy, and cultural habits became signifying factors to categorize female social groups within the colonial system as well as to visually determine their place in society. As a result, female bodies in Martínez Compañón's compilation were to be read according to his own system of classification, which was deeply rooted in the views of the Enlightenment pertaining to the creation of useful and productive citizens. Thus, visual images of the female body were used to record and encode a particular view of the human geography of Trujillo, where the body functioned as an object of display, desire, utility, commodity, and consumption.

## History as a Museum

In the eighteenth century the word *museum* referred to "the place assigned to the study of sciences, human letters, and liberal arts" (*Diccionario de Autoridades*, 636). It also referred to "the place or repository of diverse curiosities belonging to science: such as mathematical artifacts, extraordinary paintings, antique medals, etc" (*Diccionario de autoridades*, 636). The Latin word *museum* meant "of the muses," those Greek divinities who protected a specific art or activity and provided inspiration. More important, these divinities also controlled their own "sphere over learning and the arts" (Hall, 217).[2] In early modern Europe, the word *museum* referred to "a conceptual system through which collectors interpreted and explored their world" (Findlen, 49). The museum was considered a "space to fill" and a "place for looking" (Findlen, 49). It was also understood as a "space of collecting" and a site "of knowledge" (Findlen, 146).[3] Based on the different connotations of the word *museum* at the time, one can underline its intrinsic association with the acts of collecting, observing, studying, and learning. In this desire for knowledge, as Foucault suggests, "a new way of connecting things both to the eye and to discourse" evolved (*The Order of Things*, 131). The museum constituted a repository of knowledge and of valuable information and objects that were to be kept, displayed, and studied. To a certain extent we can associate this notion of the museum with the one developed by Pierre Bourdieu, who describes the modern museum as "an institution for recording, preserving and analyzing works," which ultimately aims to "conserve the capital of symbolic goods" (110, 121).[4] In the eighteenth century the relevance of visual objects in this process of learning and dissemination of knowledge was crucial to discerning the value of what was collected, displayed, and observed.[5] The isolation and ordering of accumulated material emerged from the desire to observe, to study, and to control that which was exhibited or collected. Collecting functioned as "a paradigm of knowledge," which "stretched the parameters of the known to incorporate an expanding material culture" (Findlen, 4).

When Baltasar Martínez Compañón referred to his work *Truxillo del Perú* as a type of "Historical, Physical, Political and Moral Museum," he stressed the importance of his visual representation of Trujillo in the dissemination of knowledge about these territories. He perceived his work as a depository for information that, when displayed, could generate a desire to learn about the province. The eye was to be the vehicle to capture the natural, human, and moral history of Trujillo. The visual images and representations of these Peruvian provinces were to be viewed as texts and interpreted as historical artifacts. The act of seeing was to supersede the missing word in order to function as the intermediary of knowledge. As with any particular object in a museum, the act of seeing, as Bourdieu reminds us, takes place within a space marked by "silence and methodical inspection according to a fixed arrangement and constraint" (298). Martínez Compañón's visual re-creation of the history of Trujillo was certainly influenced by his own cultural values and the fact that his work was addressed to the king. As Rolena Adorno has suggested, one cannot deny the importance of visual representation as an instrument of ideological expression and rhetorical persuasion (47).[6]

However, one must question the value and role that Martínez Compañón's visual representation of Trujillo had in his re-creation of the natural, physical, moral, and political history of the province, and most important, what significance the female body had as an integral part of this representation. The importance of natural history in the eighteenth century and its emphasis on utility or the useful played a crucial role in Martínez Compañón's portrayal of the colonial population. Daniela Bleichmar suggests that an "exorbitant visual productivity" went hand in hand with the desire for utility and profit, which many scientists and intellectuals in the eighteenth century pursued ("Visible and Useful Empire," 299). For those scientists, vision became "the means to investigate and understand" human and physical nature (Bleichmar, "Training the Naturalist's Eye," 1). Natural history at the time was still considered "as a form of inquiry designed to record the knowledge of the world for the use and betterment of mankind" (Findler, 4). Martínez Compañón's work is influenced by this quest for useful and profitable knowledge.

## Baltasar Martínez Compañón: A Man of the Enlightenment

Baltasar Martínez Compañón was born in Cabedro, Spain, between 1735 and 1738.[7] He studied canon law at the University of Huesca and became an ordained priest in 1761. He worked as a doctoral canon for different cathedrals in Santo Domingo and Santander, Spain, until 1766, and in 1767 Charles III offered him the position of cantor at the Metropolitan Cathedral of Lima. His education and experience helped him to undertake his newly assigned position in Peru. From 1767 to 1777, Martínez Compañón occupied different ecclesiastical positions, including general secretary and moderator of the First Provincial Council of Lima in 1773. In 1778 Charles III named him bishop of Trujillo as a result of the respect Martínez Compañón had gained from his peers in Lima. At the time, Trujillo was one of the largest dioceses in Peru, 1,300 kilometers long and 500 kilometers wide, from the coast to the highlands.[8] As bishop, Martínez Compañón built a successful career by locating priests in parishes who had previously lacked guidance, and by repairing the cathedral, which had been left in a fragile state as a result of damage by earthquakes. He played a pivotal role in improving the working conditions and curriculum of the Seminaries of San Carlos and San Marcelo, where he increased the salary of the professors and offered scholarships to those who were unable to afford the tuition. He also founded twenty towns and fifty-four schools, erected thirty-nine churches, and rebuilt many others. He fostered the agriculture of the new towns and created vocational and art schools for indigenous children. In addition, he made a great effort to visit all parishes, convents, and churches that were under the jurisdiction of Trujillo, despite large distances between them and the difficult topography.[9] These pastoral visits were crucial for the creation of his visual representation of Trujillo.[10]

Martínez Compañón's visits began in 1782 and continued through 1785. Matilde López Serrano has observed that the bishop brought with him topographers to draw detailed plans and maps of the territories, along with other artists and painters who were to capture the people in everyday life and their cultural habits (52). A royal decree drafted by Charles III in 1775 and sent to the Americas also motivated his visits. The decree asked for the collection of curious objects from the realm of natural and human history, which were to be sent to Spain as part of the newly founded Cabinet of Natural Sciences in Madrid.[11] The king delegated the task of collecting these materials to the Regimen de Intendencias in the urban centers of the viceroyalties.[12] The *intendentes* were to visit specific territories to gather the information and send it back; in the case of Peru, from Lima to Madrid. The material requested included maps and censuses, as well as detailed statistical information pertaining to the population, geography, climate, and economic production of the territories (Marchena, 160–61).[13] According to Juan Marchena, Peru had a total of twenty-four *intendentes* in forty years (163). The task was so overwhelming that many times these officials were unable to gather all the information requested by the king. In other instances, the *intendentes* sent thousands of documents, which sometimes were not even consulted by the crown. The *intendentes* had to seek the help of priests to complete the visits. Priests and other religious authorities served as primary providers of information thanks to their familiarity and the trust they had earned with the people who inhabited these territories. It was an extremely expensive enterprise, given the number of people required to conduct the census, take notes, prepare maps, and draw visual representations of what was observed. Sometimes it took years for this information to arrive to Spain.

As Marchena reminds us, in order for the reforms proposed by the Bourbon regime to be successful, it was crucial to collect true, exact, extensive, and exhaustive information about a vast number of aspects of this colonial order (152).[14] Between 1788 and 1790 Martínez Compañón sent some six hundred items of indigenous pottery collected during his visit, along with one hundred ninety-five pieces of clay artifacts and a box including partial objects made of gold and silver.[15] The collection also included medicinal herbs; a "sample of minerals, wood, and soil from the region"; and seeds, roots, and plants (De Vos, "The Rare, the Singular and the Extraordinary," 270).[16] The crown acknowledged the receipt of twenty-four boxes, including items that were labeled as "curiosities of nature and of art" (De Vos, "The Rare, the Singular and the Extraordinary," 270). His passion for natural sciences and history can certainly be found in his monumental work, *Truxillo del Perú*. His work can be considered part of the dynamic production that characterized the intellectual and scientific environment of the eighteenth century, an era deeply influenced by the ideology of the Enlightenment and its utilitarian search for knowledge. Within this tradition, "observation and speculation" became two vital instruments for acquiring knowledge (Soto Arango and Uribe, 67). There is no doubt that in Trujillo the bishop became a naturalist who devoted his time to the processes of "collection, observation, and classification" (Bleichmar, "Training the Naturalist's Eye," 13).[17]

Martínez Compañón's illustrated manuscript comprised nine volumes of watercolors on linen paper, with various types of watermarks and color.[18] A table of contents was placed at the end of each volume, and statistical charts, city maps and plans, and musical compositions accompanied the paintings in some of the volumes. The author divided his work into the following subjects:

> Volume 1: maps of Trujillo del Peru and its provinces; statistical charts; portraits of Charles III and Charles IV, as well as all the bishops who preceded Martínez Compañón; drawings of the uniforms and attire worn by military, religious, and civil authorities; the Spanish coat of arms; and the Gualcayoc Hill.[19]
> Volume 2: another illustration of the Spanish coat of arms; portraits of the king and queen; illustrations of the costumes and racial and ethnic characteristics of Trujillo's population; drawings of job-related tasks as well as cultural practices, including dances, festivals, music, games, and other celebrations. The volume also includes drawings reflecting various diseases suffered by indigenous people.
> Volume 3: flora of Trujillo
> Volume 4: flora of Trujillo
> Volume 5: 138 illustrations of medicinal plants
> Volume 6: 104 illustrations of quadrupeds, reptiles, and insects
> Volume 7: 159 illustrations of birds
> Volume 8: 178 illustrations of marine fauna
> Volume 9: pre-Hispanic antiquities of the Chimu, Moche, and Inca culture

According to Martínez Compañón himself, in a letter sent in 1785 to the Viceroy of Peru after his return from Trujillo, the purpose of the illustrations was related to geography, metallurgy, mineralogy, and botany; however, the last of these "was not in the service of idle curiosity, but rather to see its value in matters related to industry and commerce" ("no por servir de una vana curiosidad, sino en cuanto puedan ser material de industria y comercio") (App. III, 52).[20] Natural resources played a major role in his visual description of Trujillo because they were viewed as economic incentives for the Spanish kingdom. Although six volumes were devoted to natural history, the first two volumes dealt with human nature and cultural practices, which occupy an important place in his depiction of Trujillo. Both volumes include topographical maps and plans of Trujillo provinces and its main churches and cathedral, topographical illustrations, statistical charts, handwritten musical notations, drawings of indigenous objects, and pictures of men and women who inhabited those territories. With regard to the population, Martínez Compañón includes thirty-three illustrations of women alone or in which they are interacting with other women, one hundred fifty-six of men, and forty-five pictures in which women are shown with children and or men and are performing specific tasks to their gender or participating in festivals. In the case of women, he starts with the representation of nuns and ends with the illustration of an infidel Indian woman. The pictures in which women are portrayed alone followed this order: portrait of Luisa de Borbón, Queen of Spain; nuns; Spanish; *criada* (servant); Indian; *quarterona de mestizo*; *mestiza*; black; *samba*; *cholas*; leper woman; and the infidel Indian woman.[21] These images are followed by women performing different tasks, such as making *chicha*, dyeing wool, weaving, spinning, and participating in a wedding as well as in dance festivals and religious ceremonies. Men are portrayed in a similar order, starting with the portraits of Charles III and Charles IV, followed by government figures; religious authorities; members of different racial groups; men participating in tasks such as mining, hunting, agriculture, the production of wool, and sheep herding; and men taking part in rituals and festivals.

The manner in which Martínez Compañón ordered these volumes provided a particular reading and representation of the racial groups that occupied those territories. In the aforementioned letter drafted in 1785, he stated that the collection of his drawings was conceived and organized "as a museum" ("disposición de museo") with the hopes of forming a "Historical, Physical, Political and Moral Museum of the Archbishopric of Truxillo del Perú" (Museo Histórico, Ficico, Politico y Moral del Obpdo. De Truxillo del Perú) (App. III, 52). It is important to note that even though Martínez Compañón hired painters and artists to complete the illustrations, ultimately he decided which images would be incorporated, and in what order they were to be compiled. What was included in those nine volumes was what he wanted the king to see.[22]

As Martínez Compañón himself mentioned in a letter to the king in 1786:

> Lo que unicamente necesita es aumentar y hacer mas util su población, y para conseguirlo reducir á sus habitantes á sociedad, dar crianza a la niñez de ambos sexos, impulso á la agricultura y mineria, movimiento y accion á su comercio interior y exterior, y que se fomenten asi mismo aquellos ramos de industria que siendo útiles á su provincias, no traigan perjuicio á las demas del Reyno, ni á esa Peninsula: cuyos objetos he procurado promover

con todas mis fuerzas en mi Visita, y ántes y después de ella, como Prelado, como Vasallo del mejor Soberano de la tierra, y como miembro de la sociedad, y hermano de los demas hombres.

[The only thing needed is to increase the population and make it more useful, and to achieve this it is essential to subject the inhabitants to civil society, give a proper upbringing to children of both sexes, promote agriculture and mining, movement and activity within the interior and exterior commerce, and also develop those branches of industry that, being useful to its provinces, would not be detrimental to the other provinces of the Kingdom or to the Peninsula: these are the ends that I have strived to promote with all my might both before and after my Inspection, as a Prelate, as a Vassal of the best Sovereign in the world, and as a member of society, and brother to my fellow men.] (6–7)[23]

In this letter, Martínez Compañón summarizes the objective behind his visual compilation of Trujillo. The visual representation of the colonial bodies aimed to illustrate and to prove the potential that the inhabitants of these lands had to become useful and productive citizens. In order to achieve success in these particular territories, the government needed to integrate all inhabitants, including women, into society; to educate all citizens, no matter their gender; and to develop a diverse economy. It was time to rediscover the peripheral zones in order to maximize the economic potential therein. Images became central tools in this process of representation and "constituted a tangible evidence that, throughout the empire, naturalists, artists, and administrators strived to carry out [the king's orders] to produce information that was not only useful but also visible" (Bleichmar, "A Visible and Useful Empire," 307).[24]

In another letter, sent to D. Antonio Polier in 1790, announcing the existence of *Truxillo del Perú*, Martínez Compañón insisted on the authenticity of his illustrations as an eyewitness account, underlining that they were composed before "his own eyes and presence" (App. III, 54).[25] To prove his point, he sent to Spain a box that included indigenous artifacts and pottery that would later be compared with the ninth volume of his manuscript. According to him, the comparison was to prove "the conformity and perfect similarity that existed between them, so through this [comparison] one could conjecture and realize the correspondence between the illustrations and the original as depicted in the other eight volumes" (App. III, 54). Martínez Compañón considered his work to be a significant contribution to the study and knowledge of the Peruvian territories, which, from his perspective, possessed a variety of fauna, flora, minerals, and people, all of which deserved to be beneficiaries of future royal investments. That Trujillo at the time was experiencing profound economic difficulties made the compilation of his work even more imperative.[26]

In the 1790 letter, he urged colonial authorities in Lima to send the work immediately to the king, who he believed would undoubtedly understand its value. His manuscript, according to Martínez Compañón himself, had already undergone all revisions and the necessary permits had been secured from the *intendente* of Trujillo and all its ministers of royal treasure, the ecclesiastic authorities, and the Viceroy of Peru, D. Francisco Gil y Lemus. He added that each volume had been approved with "unique praises" (App. III, 54). He was aware of the singularity of his work, meanwhile conceding that in terms of "length, organization of its parts and method [the book] could be seen as general and ordinary" (App. III, 54–55). He argued that despite its lack of refinement, "it could at least serve as an encouragement" for more eloquent and literate people to write "an accomplished and perfect general history of these vast regions" (App. III, 55). Notwithstanding his desire to send the manuscript to the king posthaste, the nine volumes were not sent to Spain until 1803, six years after his death in Santa Fe de Bogotá in 1797, shortly after occupying the position of archbishop of that city.[27] The nine volumes were sent to Spain, already bound in a typical eighteenth-century Peruvian sheepskin binding protected by a fine layer of wax (López Serrano, 36).

The most remarkable aspect of Martínez Compañón's manuscript is that he never envisioned it accompanied by a written text. In the letters sent by him to Spanish authorities in Spain, and the ones sent to the Viceroy of Peru, he never mentioned that the volumes would include any written explanation.[28] The format he chose presented and still presents challenges to the common reader because words were not part of the process of "reading" and interpreting the visual history.[29] Raúl Porras Barrenechea in 1948 considered this a deficiency in the text: "The fact that the illustrations are accompanied by neither a description nor an explanation of the respective drawing is already a defect" ("Informe," 32).

Critics such as López Serrano have considered these particular drawings of the inhabitants to be lacking in originality, to the extent that the only aspects that are altered are the faces and the representative attire of the people portrayed. Based on the "quality" of the drawings, López Serrano argues that the work was the product of different artists, and she points out that some illustrations, such as the ones depicting architecture, flora, and birds, are technically more sophisticated than the rest (12).[30] Technicalities aside, what I believe to be most fascinating about the nine volumes is the decision to draft a visual history of these regions (and the reasons behind that decision), and what the illustrations themselves tell us about the people, their cultural and work habits, and their popular celebrations.

Visuality was extremely important in Martínez Compañón's work, given that the illustrations were envisioned as part of a museum and specifically addressed to the Spanish king.[31] For the bishop, the bodies of the inhabitants represented the cultural reality of Trujillo and were to be preserved as examples of social and cultural history. Through those bodies, the observer would be able to recognize or have a notion of the history of Trujillo and its provinces. If we consider the museum as "a technology of memory," where the body is conceived as "a storage and retrieval device" and through which the past is to be remembered, Martínez's visual collection has an even greater lasting impression (Bennett, 42–46).[32] By recording the present for contemporary authorities, he was simultaneously preserving history. The material text itself served figuratively as a museum, in which the captured bodies specified social and cultural history. These bodies, by representing cultural realities, consequently came to embody knowledge.

*Truxillo del Perú* can also be considered a visual encyclopedia, when considering the definition of encyclopedia as a "general system of instruction or knowledge" and "a work in which the various branches of knowledge . . . are discussed separately (*Webster's Universal Dictionary*, 557). This coincides with Denis Diderot's vision of the "encyclopédie" as an instrument aimed "to collect all the knowledge scattered over the face of the earth, to present its general outlines and structure to the men with whom we live" (17). For the bishop, it was important to organize and manage knowledge. Martínez Compañón's manuscript also followed the inclination, which became increasingly popular in the seventeenth and eighteenth centuries, to "use visual reproduction as a critical aid to the study of and ordering of nature" (Freedberg, 55). The ordering implied an attempt to clarify ambiguities as well as offer a comprehensible, rather transparent representation of the object in question. Nevertheless, one must focus on the cultural context that guided such a process of reconstruction because, as Beth Fowkes Tobin argues, images do not merely reflect; they also mediate (13).

Martínez Compañón's manuscript can be situated within eighteenth-century historiographical production, which, according to Jorge Cañizares-Esguerra, aimed to write a new history of America on the basis of "new critical techniques for creating and validating knowledge" (1).[33] The Royal Academy of History, founded by the Spanish Bourbons in the eighteenth century, functioned as a cultural institution that produced and promoted these types of texts (Cañizares-Esguerra, 3).[34] New natural and civil histories of the New World were solicited, especially if they defended the record of Spanish colonization of the Americas. The Council of Indies established a series of guidelines that members of the Academy were required to follow when writing these histories.[35] Royal orders issued in 1712, 1767, and 1776 also requested the collection "of all types of curiosities of natural history and antiquity," in order to promote scientific studies and economic development (Deans-Smith, 178).

Although Martínez Compañón did not intend to send his nine volumes to the Royal Academy of History, his effort coincided with the aims of the Council of Indies. His compilation offered visual information that could be deemed useful for the writing of future histories. At the time the work was drafted, it also aimed to persuade the Spanish authorities of the continuing need to "discover" and colonize peripheral territories like Trujillo. Each illustration was to be seen as a visual representation to draw attention to the relevance of these territories and their people, and to evoke thought about the possibilities of colonial expansion. The message, so the bishop thought, needed to be clearly illustrated and free of ambiguous meanings. Visual representations were thought to be the very sort of unequivocal material that would lead to the creation of reliable histories. Scholars in the eighteenth century found many ways to eliminate the potential for ambiguity that a written text could produce. As a result, illustrations were integrated as part of an effort toward "capturing an unambiguous, undistorted reality" (Cañizares-Esguerra, 17).[36] Martínez Compañón positions himself on what Santiago Castro-Gómez has called "la *hybris* del punto cero"—a point from which the observer believed he had the power to represent and construct a legitimate and impartial view of the social and natural world that could serve as a potential source of knowledge for the Spanish crown (25). Such epistemological constructions aimed to facilitate both economic and social control of the world (Castro-Gómez, 25).

This claim of transparency is a dangerous one because, as mentioned earlier, visual images always conceal the potential for interpretation in different manners, depending upon who is producing the image, why it is produced, who is observing it, and where it is located. Yet one must take into account that the person who chooses or creates the image always influences the manner in which an object is represented, simply because of his or her own specific cultural context. As W. J. T. Mitchell argues, images "are not stable, static, or permanent" to the extent that they "involve multisensory apprehension and interpretation" (14). In the case of *Truxillo del Perú*, what we have are specific visual interpretations of peoples, cultures, animals, plants, and other objects, based on Martínez Compañón's eyewitness experiences.

My aim is to focus on this process of interpretation, in order to determine the kind of image that Martínez Compañón attempted to capture of the female population of Trujillo, specifically when it came to his portrayal of cultural differences and social relationships. Can we consider this type of inventory another effort within the culture of the Enlightenment to categorize and order people as well as territories? To what extent did visual images offer the "reader" a more complete view of the female population of Trujillo del Peru? To what extent does this manuscript force the reader to see the female population in a certain manner? More important, what place does the female body occupy in this rendition? A look into the significance of this manuscript in the culture of the Enlightenment in Peru must address these questions to better understand the role of visuality in the cultural construction of social life and female bodies at the time. I propose to examine this visual text as a cultural form central to the articulation of a specific local history at a time of profound social, political, economic, and cultural change.

## Visualizing and Marking Difference

The second volume of Martínez Compañón's manuscript offers a description of a sector of the Peruvian population in which class, race, and cultural habits became signifying factors to categorize social groups. It offers a visual representation of the hierarchically structured ethnic groups, starting with the Spaniards, and followed by Indians, *quarterones*, *mestizos*, blacks, mulattos, *zambos*, and *cholos*. Although there was no written explanation accompanying the illustrations, aside from a descriptive label at the end of the volume, the organization followed by Martínez Compañón preserved the social order imposed by colonial authorities by presenting the images related to the Spaniards first and the blacks and other groups of African descent at the end. When addressing labor tasks and cultural practices, we perceive a clear social and racial division in which Indians, blacks, and other *castas* were found among members of their own groups, rarely interacting with others.[37] Women, of course, were part of this visual system of categorization, as their bodies were used as signs of racial and social distinction. This process of cataloguing "the other" confronted the challenge of how to offer a real image of women who belonged to different social and racial groups. Within this context, the body is endowed with "layers of ideas, images, meanings and associations," which determine the manner in which it is read, interpreted, and defined (Synnott, 1). The arrangement of these female bodies within Martínez Compañón's symbolic museum aimed to send a clear message to colonial authorities that class and racial distinction were still in place in the territories making up this large archbishopric. The appropriate eyes and hands were needed to order as well as to separate any social interaction deemed to be dangerous to the racial and social order.

Martínez Compañón placed women in a clear hierarchical order in which race was a determining factor. Not only did the skin color of these individuals work as the decisive factor of difference, but clothing and other cultural artifacts associated with certain social classes played an important role as well. The bishop's watercolor illustrations became, as in the case of *casta* paintings, portrayals of "the social economy of bodies and spaces that constituted late-colonial culture" (Carrera, xvi). Both types of paintings illustrate the tension between America's natural resources and the productivity of the inhabitants, as well as emphasis on order and orderliness to achieve such productivity (Carrera, xvii). Despite differences, the compilation of illustrations in *Truxillo del Perú*, as well as *casta* painting, can be considered a visual practice "that made the colonial body—both elite and nonelite—knowable and visible" (Carrera, 54).[38]

The author offered a visual representation, hierarchically structured, of the groups, starting with the Spaniards, and followed by Indians, *quarterones*, *mestizos*, blacks, mulattos, *zambos*, and *cholos*. The sense of social order was set clear from the beginning of the volume, where Martínez Compañón inserted a chart listing the number of inhabitants from each province that encompassed Trujillo, which were further divided into *castas*. The title states: "Order that shows the number of inhabitants of the Archbishopric of Trujillo with a distinction of the different *castas*, prepared by the current Bishop" ("Estado que demuestra el numero de Abitantes del Obpdo. De Truxillo del Perù con distincion de castas formado [por] su actual Obpdo"). This statistical chart was extremely important because the charts, along with maps and musical compositions, represented the only illustrations that contained written material.[39]

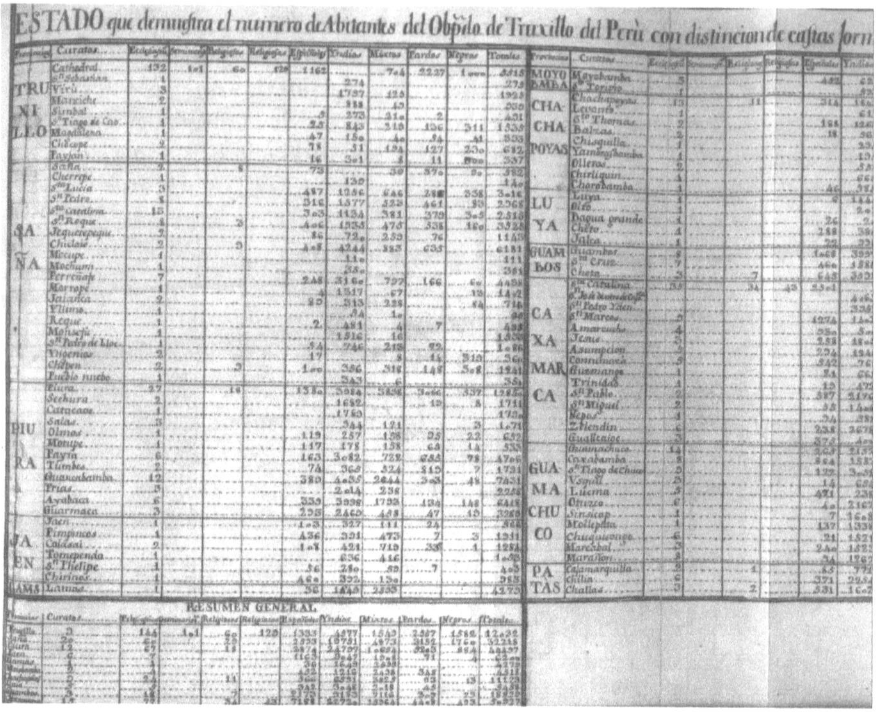
ESTADO que demuestra el numero de Abitantes del Obpdo. de Truxillo del Perù con distincion de castas form

RESUMEN GENERAL

Figure 1. "Estado que demuestra el numero de Abitantes del Obpdo. De Truxillo del Perù con distincion de castas formado [por] su actual Obpdo." (Courtesy of Biblioteca del Real Palacio de Madrid.)

The table therefore served as a point of reference from which to quantify the population he was to depict in his "historical, physical, political and moral museum." The list reduced the different groups to the following order: Spaniards, Indians, Mixed, *Pardos*, and Blacks.[40] According to the bishop, the number of inhabitants in Trujillo was 241,740; of these, 21,980 were Spaniards, 118,324 were Indians, 79,043 were mixed (*mestizos*), 16,630 *pardos*, and 4,846 blacks.[41] The majority of the inhabitants were therefore Indians and *mestizos*, followed by Spaniards, *pardos*, and blacks. For the visual illustrations, the order remained the same, although some groups, including the indigenous population, were subdivided depending upon the region to which they belonged.

Although Spanish women did not constitute the numerical majority in these territories, Martínez Compañón began his visual compilation with a series of pictures depicting Spanish women in various attire and locations pertaining to their social status and *calidad*.[42] Spanish women were portrayed wearing diverse garments with distinct accessories, such as a special handkerchief, a mantilla, and a veil. They were also pictured wearing mourning dresses, riding a horse, and traveling by carriage. All but two of the illustrations of women capture their subject in isolation, with no scenery as a background. The lack of a landscape or other background in these pictures forced the observer to focus solely on their bodies—namely, their clothing. Clothing has always been an important form of identification in the production of portraiture in viceregal America (García Sáiz, 83). For Martínez Compañón, the attire of women became the focal point of these illustrations, as with most of the pictures pertaining to women in *Truxillo del Perú*. Indeed, clothing became a signified and material marker of the specific female bodies he visualizes. Fabrics and accessories indicated the social status and racial category to which the subject belonged. "E1: Española con solo bolador" (Figure 2) and "E2: Española con mantilla y bolador" (Figure 3), for example, emphasize the rich fabrics of the women's blouses and *faldellines*.[43] Silk, lace, and embroidery were characteristics of the dresses worn by Spanish aristocratic women. Embroidered socks, matching shoes, earrings, rings, necklaces, and bracelets complemented their fashion style. In lieu of an atmosphere of luxury represented by a particular

Figure 2. "E1: Española con solo bolador." (Courtesy of Biblioteca del Real Palacio de Madrid.)

Figure 3. "E2: Española con mantilla y bolador." (Courtesy of Biblioteca del Real Palacio de Madrid.)

physical space or surroundings, it is their dresses that are seen as signs of wealth and nobility.[44]

Both illustrations emphasize that what made these women Spanish was not only the color of their skin, but specifically what they wore. It was through their clothed bodies that they were to be recognized and categorized. Their attire also emphasized these women as active consumers, as their selection of the best fabrics highlighted their taste for fashion and illustrated their place in society. As Arnold J. Bauer suggests, in colonial Latin America "cloth represented the major household investment," making it a major element in "the fluid construction of identity" (69, 75).[45]

A particular item of note in these illustrations is the rose that each of the women is holding. In eighteenth-century portraits of aristocratic members of the society in viceregal America, women were sometimes portrayed holding flowers, specifically roses.[46] For example, women who were engaged and prepared for the sacrament of marriage were usually shown with a flower in their hands. In Christian iconography, the red rose signified the "blood of the martyr," while the white rose was viewed as a "symbol of purity" (Hall, 329). Red roses were also symbols of heavenly joy, and were linked to the Virgin Mary, who was called "the rose without thorns" (Hall, 268). The red rose was also a symbol of love and beauty. As the rose is associated with the Virgin Mary, the quintessential female model, one can also conceive that these women holding the flowers were considered by Martínez Compañón to be models of virtue as well. The use of the rose also takes on added relevance when one considers what members of other female social groups were seen carrying in their hands: agricultural tools, weaving paraphernalia, or kitchen utensils. In essence, the rose came to symbolize moral distinction as it is and was connected with purity, divinity, and beauty.

In portrayals of other female sectors of the population, such as native Indians and blacks, clothing again signified social and racial differences. Martínez Compañón introduced pictures of Indian women immediately after representative pictures of the Spanish female population, following the class demarcations popular at the time. The first illustrations of indigenous groups presented in the manuscript emphasized the differences in social class and degree of civilization found among different sectors of the same population. If we compare illustration "E28: Yndia de lamas con trage de Iglesia" (Figure 4) with "E203: Yndia de montaña ynfiel" (Figure 5), we can certainly notice the diversity within the same group. Clothing again played a decisive factor in determining the degree of civilization that distinguished one group from another. In this case, the comparative lack of clothes worn by the infidel Indian woman ("yndia infiel"), along with her bare feet, very native attire, and the leaf used as a blanket to cover her baby placed her remote from civilization.[47] Also, her strong, muscled body seemed to indicate an association between a barbaric state and her moral nature. As I have mentioned

*Visualizing and Commodifying Female Bodies* 55

Figure 4. "E28: Yndia de lamas con trage de Iglesia." (Courtesy of Biblioteca del Real Palacio de Madrid.)

Figure 5. "E203: Yndia de montaña ynfiel." (Courtesy of Biblioteca del Real Palacio de Madrid.)

elsewhere, "naked bodies symbolized within the colonial system lack of civilization and social inferiority" ("Visualizing Difference," 18).[48] The lack of landscape as background also emphasized the subject's nakedness and the absence of civilization that characterized this female sector of the indigenous population. Despite her primitive state, however, it was still important for Martínez Compañón to include her as part of his encyclopedia, as proof of the need to incorporate this sector of the population into a productive society.[49] Religion was still perceived as an instrument to achieve such integration. In contrast, the "Yndia de Lamas" seemed closer to civilization, as shown by her gigantic veil, which covered more than half of her body, and the presence of her *faldellín* and shoes. The body-covering clothing stressed the degree to which she was part of a sector of the population that understood the moral respect that a religious space required. Her solemn facial expression while looking at the entrance of the church emphasized the site she occupied within civilized space and indicated that this indigenous woman was a Christian. Christian bodies were a symbol of social and moral order.

In all, fifteen illustrations pertain to Indian women; they are shown wearing traditional indigenous attire, and for the most part are barefoot. Their costumes were quite simple in comparison to those worn by Spanish women in the preceding illustrations. Their typical hats, pulled-up ponchos and capes, and woven belts, and their lack of accessories are reminders of the social class to which they all belonged. They were all Indians from the mountains and valleys who worked on the land. The landscape that surrounded them emphasized their distance from civilization, as can be noted in the uninhabitable mountains and lack of natural background where Indian women appear standing alone. Their social class was exceedingly visible, as they were depicted mostly in their ordinary daily dress ("trages ordinarios") or with a church dress ("trage de iglesia"). Clothing accessories, such as jewelry and hats, were also used to denote small differences among them, as in "E21: Yndia de sierra en trage ordinario" (Figure 6) and "E26: Yndia de lamas con trage ordinario" (Figure 7). Despite their differences, these indigenous women were categorized by the clothes they wore. Clothing became the determining factor to identify them visually in society. To the Spanish authorities' eyes, social and racial differences between Spanish and Indian women were unequivocally distinguishable and visually obvious. As a result, their bodies were easily legible and indicative of their placement within society.

This phenomenon also occurs with the portrayal of black women, to which Martínez Compañón devoted just one illustration, which characterized the black population in Trujillo by a lack of facial features or expression. In "E44: Negra" (Figure 8), the woman's face is noticeably blurred and she is distinguished only by her profound blackness. The observer can barely locate her eyes, while her lips, nose, eyebrows, and ears seem to disappear into their own blackness. In contrast, her attire and the tools of her labor that she is holding became markers of her racial and social identity. She was recognizable not only by what she wore, but also the type of labor she performed. Her arms as well became prominent features, as they were seen holding the tools that defined her work. She was valued as a useful component of society, as she contributed to the agricultural work force. Her intense blackness emphasized her specific, visible physical features. Her body could not visually be ignored because of her undeniable color. She was easily recognizable and undeniably different. There was no confusion as to who she was, or to which place she occupied in society. Her clothing also emphasized her social status, as the indigo skirt and the white cotton blouse were generally used in these territories within lower sectors of society. That the fabric was locally produced helped make it affordable for these social groups (Bauer, 111). The king, to whom Martínez Compañón addresses his work, should have had no difficulty identifying this female sector of the population.

Although the black population was nearly five times the size of the Spanish population in these provinces (980 Spaniards versus 4,846 blacks), as noted in the statistical chart, in terms of the comparative numbers of illustrations included in the manuscript, they seem to be considered a minority. Their social status and *calidad* determined their placement in this visual museum and in society in general.[50] For women in general, nine images are devoted to Spanish women, while only one

Visualizing and Commodifying Female Bodies 57

Figure 6. "E21: Yndia de sierra en trage ordinario." (Courtesy of Biblioteca del Real Palacio de Madrid.)

Figure 7. "E26: Yndia de lamas con trage ordinario." (Courtesy of Biblioteca del Real Palacio de Madrid.)

Figure 8. "E44: Negra." (Courtesy of Biblioteca del Real Palacio de Madrid.)

Figure 9. "E40: Quarterona de mestiza." (Courtesy of Biblioteca del Real Palacio de Madrid.)

Figure 10. "E42: Mestiza." (Courtesy of Biblioteca del Real Palacio de Madrid.)

portrays a black woman, indicating that this population was easily categorized and cast as unthreatening. For the author, there is little doubt as to the role the black woman performed in society, just as there was no confusion as to who she was: her darkness was unmistakable. This may have been the idea he wanted to convey to his Spanish Majesty. As a collectible object for Martínez Compañón's museum, the black woman became part of the ordering of accumulated material that emerged from the bishop's attempts to classify society. Within this context, one can view the act of reordering things in a museum "as an event that was simultaneously epistemic and governmental" (Bennett, 33). The case of *Truxillo del Perú* is epistemic because it articulates a particular knowledge of the female population. It is governmental because such knowledge is constructed with the aim of directing and controlling a specific representation of them. The author's authority as an eyewitness enables him to direct and control such representations.

However, not all female members of the population were so easily distinguishable; when skin color became an ambivalent determining factor, clothing as well as adornments naturally prevailed as crucial features to categorize mixed racial groups. In illustrations "E40: Quarterona de mestiza" (Figure 9) and "E42: Mes-

Figure 11. "E3: Española con trage a lo antiguo." (Courtesy of Biblioteca del Real Palacio de Madrid.)

tiza" (Figure 10), it is difficult to differentiate based on physical attributes (color of the skin and hair) between the *mestizas* and Spanish women. This is especially evident when we compare both these images to "E3: Española con trage a lo antiguo" (Figure 11), or to Figures 2 and 3. The type of dress, hairstyle, and jewelry the women wore determined their social status. The wealth of the Spanish woman was displayed in the luxury of her clothing's fabric, the detail in the embroidery, and the presence of jewelry and hair accessories. If we also look at the bodices, the style of the Spanish dresses was quite similar to those of the *mestizas* (see, for example, Figure 2). It is in the luxurious skirts where one can see the difference between one female group and the other.[51]

It is interesting to note that even if the *mestizas* were depicted holding flowers, as the Spanish women were, they did not seem to show as much interest in them as the Spanish women did. The Spanish women were portrayed smelling the roses, while the *mestizas* seemed to allow the flowers to fall, as if they were oblivious of their value. It is also worth noting the types of flowers depicted in the portraits: while Spanish women are always holding roses, *mestizas* are holding tulips. Historically, tulips were perceived as a "symbol of the vanity of earthly things" and "the transience of earthly possessions in the face of death" (Impelluso, 82). They were also associated with folly and greed.[52] Wilting tulips, in particular, emphasized "the vanity and frailty of earthly things" (Impelluso, 54). The language and symbolism of these flowers speak to the social and moral differences between these two female sectors of society.[53] As previously mentioned, roses in the Christian tradition and iconography were always considered a symbol of love, of the Virgin Mary, purity, and sanctity (Impelluso, 118). In contrast, tulips were mostly associated with vanity and greed. This floral symbolism therefore pointed to the moral and social inferiority of the *mestiza* when compared to Spanish women. Of course, it is impossible to determine if Martínez Compañón had asked the artists to portray the *mestizas* with the flowers in such a manner.[54] What does seem obvious from the European perspective of the author, based upon the emblematic objects that were associated with both sectors of society, is that the *mestizas* would never be able to achieve the status of the Spanish women, as their attire and material possessions were a constant reminder to everybody of their social and moral status, making it extremely simple to distinguish them from the Spanish women.[55]

The only illustration Martínez Compañón included of a mulatto woman, "E46: Mulata" (Figure 12), highlights the confusing nature of racial categorization. In this picture, her dress shows great likeness to the one depicted for the *mestizas*, except that its fabric seems more greatly elaborated, especially in the bodices, while her socks resemble those worn by the Spanish woman.[56] All women are seen wearing the same type of buckled shoes, which were very popular at the time. It is quite obvious that the *mulata* had mastered the appropriate symbolic fashion icons that made some women of that period socially superior to others. Visually, the use of clothing coupled with the lighter skin tones made social differentiation quite challenging (see Figure 11). However, in Martínez Compañón's museum there is always one visual aspect that can simplify these distinctions, even in instances where easy differentiation is quite challenging. For example, in the case of the mulatto woman, it is her hair that reminds us of her social and racial status; it seems curlier and more closely resembles the texture of the black woman's hair. Symbolic appropriation of Spanish dressing habits would have made class differentiation a very tricky process for Spanish authorities.

Meanwhile, a flower once again becomes a sign of differentiation. The *mulata* is shown holding what seemed to be a wildflower. As opposed to the Spanish and *mestiza*, who were holding what could be considered more sophisticated flowers deeply endowed with Western connotations and material value, the *mulata* is identified by a flower that is uncultivated and to which material value has not been assigned.[57] Within this context, one can argue that the inclusion of this particular flower aimed to emphasize the lower place of the *mulata* within the social strata. The flower as well as her hair served as reminders of her social status, which consequently was determined by her African ancestry.

These illustrations show that Compañón had great difficulties judging women based on visual assessment, especially when women from different racial groups but with similar skin color dressed in comparable fashion. The control of dressing habits, therefore, became very important, because for colonial authorities at the

*Visualizing and Commodifying Female Bodies* 61

Figure 12. "E46: Mulata." (Courtesy of Biblioteca del Real Palacio de Madrid.)

time, skin color was not a dependable factor for distinction. For example, when the skin of a *mestiza* looked lighter, or similar in color to that of a Spanish woman, it became rather difficult for the authorities to deny racially marginalized women (and men) access to spaces reserved for whites.

Sumptuary laws enacted by the crown in the eighteenth century demonstrate the importance of dressing habits in the daily lives of people in the colonies. The royal decrees aimed to legally establish racial and social divisions by controlling and imposing the use of certain clothes throughout all their domains. The *Pragmática*, which was enacted in 1716, clearly stated the type of fabric that lower sectors of the population, such as *mestizos*, mulattos, blacks, and other *casta* groups, were allowed to use. It specified that "herradores, zurradores, esparteros, especieros y de otros cualesquier oficios semejantes a éstos o más bajos, y obreros, labradores y jornaleros no puedan traer, ni traigan vestidos de seda, ni de otra cosa mezclada con ella, y que solo puedan vestir y traer vestidos de paño" (blacksmiths, tanners, esparto and spice workers, and others who perform any tasks similar or lesser to these, and workers, farmers, and day laborers should not display or wear silk clothing, nor other fabrics that contain silk, as they can only wear and own wool clothing) (Konetzke, 130). Visually, items of clothing were to become indicators of the social status of colonial individuals. "Seeing" as a way of "interpreting" was to become intrinsically related to the act of classifying and containing the other (Mirzoeff, 13).

Other royal decrees were intended to limit the racial transformation taking place in the late colonial period. In 1725 the Viceroy of Peru, José de Armendáriz enacted a royal decree that aimed to control "the scandalous excess of the clothing worn by blacks, mulattos, Indians and *mestizos*" ("el escandaloso exceso de los trages que vestían los negros, los mulatos, indios y mestizos de ambos sexos") (Konetzke, 187). It was deemed crucial to prevent these sectors of the population from dressing in such a manner, because of "the frequent robberies committed in order to be able to afford such expensive clothes" ("los frecuentes hurtos que se cometían para mantener tan costosas galas") (Konetzke, 187). Controlling the type of clothing that lower sectors of the society could wear was a vehicle by which colonial authorities could visually clarify the racial and social distinctions needed for a hierarchical society. To this extent, clothing constituted a marker of "status and power" that, when violated, had the potential to cause "disquiet among the forces of order" (Bauer, 113).

There seems to have been an effort on the part of Martínez Compañón to define a clear distinction between the different female sectors of the territories belonging to the Archbishopric of Trujillo. Although female blacks as well as Indians, *mestizas*, and *mulatas* were represented as part of Trujillo's population, they were clearly perceived as occupying specific subordinate positions within the social strata. The illustrations functioned as visual discourses that reflected the ideology of the time. In this sense, the image is part of a "symbolic system of meaning-making" that emphasized the ideology of those in power (Tobin, 13). The images also reinforced the idea of social immobility, keeping the groups constrained to spaces predetermined by specific labor tasks or cultural practices associated solely with their social status within colonial society. More important, although the mulatto and black populations were quite visible in these territories, as the statistical table indicates (see Figure 1), Martínez Compañón offered only one illustration of each group. At a time when *casta* groups of African descent and blacks themselves presented a threatening factor in many areas of the Viceroyalty of Peru in terms of destabilizing the social order, it was significant that in this visual encyclopedia or encyclopedic museum they would appear to represent only a very minor sector of the population. The message the bishop seemed to convey was that their numbers should not be a cause of concern, as these inhabitants were easily manageable and had the potential to be integrated into a productive and well-organized society.

These illustrations also underline the idea that order could be reasonably achieved when these subordinate groups were kept circumscribed and maintained in determinate social spaces. The antidote to a potential "malady" resided in prescribing the appropriate medicine, or in this case, the type of dress, accessories, flowers, and types of fabric every female sector of the population was to wear in order to remain easily recognizable. Their bodies were to be embellished with whatever denoted their particular social and racial group. In sum, each body was isolated from its environment and unequivocally categorized in this museum. However, what visual messages did the bishop try to convey when he portrayed women interacting with other members of society? How were their bodies read, and what intentions underlie such readings? These questions merit some discussion to better understand the symbolic and material meanings that female bodies acquired in Martínez Compañón's description of Trujillo.

## The Productive Body: Active Workers and Efficient Mothers

The compilation of illustrations pertaining to the female population aimed to suggest a certain reading and visualization of the place, as well as space, occupied by the female bodies in society.[58] To that end, the body was central to the process of understanding the material value of these territories. Corporeal location played a major role in the depiction of the female population as productive citizens or members of the colonial system and the community in which they lived.[59] The activities they performed or what they did with their bodies was closely intertwined with the material economy of Trujillo. One must also take into consideration that, at a time when Spain was invested in expanding its own economy, the labor productivity of the colonial subjects became a great focus of interest, along with the natural resources of their territories.[60] For Spain, economic expansion and success depended upon the development and fostering of agriculture, industry, and commerce, especially as they pertained to the American territories (Pérez Samper, 8). Within this context of economic expansion, the bodies of its colonial subjects needed to be reread, redefined, and reorganized, with the goal of productivity in mind. From this location, or "punto cero," following Castro-Gómez's terminology (25), Martínez Compañón positioned himself as an informed observer, someone unquestionably qualified to inform the Spanish kingdom of the potential economic windfall that could be found in the Viceroyalty of Peru.

This productivity was articulated by the images of Spanish women as exemplary mothers. Illustrations "E6: Españolas de luto" (Figure 13) and "E13: Españoles merendando en el campo" (Figure 14) offer depictions of Spanish women as caretakers and wives. In these particular cases, we find no servants surrounding them, as they are portrayed as solely responsible for their children. They also represent key members of the nuclear family (Figure 14). Indigenous women were also depicted as mothers. For example, "E16: Yndias de Valle a Cavallo" (Figure 15) pictures a woman, along with her husband and child, traveling in the hills. She is carrying her child, but is also attentive to the road. Her right hand, which holds the carrier where her child is placed, might project a sign of protection and security. What distinguishes these images are the backgrounds that surround each family. While the Spanish families are set inside their homes or close to them, the Indian family is pictured in transit and within the topographical setting where they belong: the valley.

In *Truxillo del Perú*, indigenous women were portrayed not only as efficient mothers, but as skilled workers as well. They were shown accompanying their chil-

Figure 13. "E6: Españolas de luto." (Courtesy of Biblioteca del Real Palacio de Madrid.)

Figure 14. "E13: Españoles merendando en el campo." (Courtesy of Biblioteca del Real Palacio de Madrid.)

Figure 15. "E16: Yndias de Valle a Cavallo." (Courtesy of Biblioteca del Real Palacio de Madrid.)

dren while simultaneously performing another task. For example, in "E35: Yndia de Hivito con carga, y su hijito a las espaldas" (Figure 16), the woman is carrying her provisions while transporting her child on her back. This is also the case in illustration "E36: Yndia de Moiobamba cargando platanos" (Figure 17), where the Indian woman is nursing her child while carrying plantains that she might be taking to sell in the market. She seems quite comfortable performing both tasks, as one does not seem to interfere with the other. With one hand she holds the child, and with the other she carries the tool needed to grab the plantains from the tree. Both illustrations represent models of useful individuals as the women are able to perform their work tasks without forgetting their roles as caring mothers. They seem to be experts in both capacities. The illustrations also show that "women's economic activities were more publicly visible as one went down the social scale" (Socolow, 115).[61]

One illustration that captures the extraordinary capacity for these women to conduct their jobs while taking control of their role as mother is "E83: Yndia pastora pariendo" (Figure 18). In this representation, the woman seems to take a break from her activities to calmly give birth to her child. The landscape surrounding her

*Visualizing and Commodifying Female Bodies* 67

Figure 16. "E35: Yndia de Hivito con carga, y su hijito a las espaldas." (Courtesy of Biblioteca Real Palacio de Madrid.)

Figure 17. "E36: Yndia de Moiobamba cargando platanos." (Courtesy of Biblioteca del Real Palacio de Madrid.)

also emphasizes the multi-tasking nature of this woman who is able to give birth—a very painful process—while spinning wool. Her sheep as well as the mountains around her function as the only witnesses to such an extraordinary event, as the indigenous woman seems in total control of her body during this process. It is impossible to discern what she would do next, whether it would be continuing with her task, attending to her child, or possibly both. Nevertheless, her capacity to be both a productive worker and a fruitful mother is evident. Both roles represented rewarding and potential gains for the Spanish authorities, if they could be properly used for economic purposes. This is the message Martínez Compañón wanted to convey to the king to whom he was addressing his work. For the bishop, indigenous women were capable of functioning as productive members of the community who did not allow their role as mothers to interfere with their work. We may note the ironic contrast between this image and one of a male Indian performing the same job in illustration "E81: Yndio pastor de ovejas" (Figure 19). While the woman was alert and paying attention to her job, even while giving birth, the man falls asleep watching the sheep, ultimately neglecting his job. The contrast seems to highlight the image of the useful and industrious woman versus the indolent, sleepy man. Indigenous women who are carrying or caring for their children while attentively performing other tasks can be seen in illustrations "E99: Yndia de Valles hilando en catre" (Figure 20) and "E100: Yndia de Valles texiendo" (Figure 21). Their bodies were perceived as potentially useful tools for the economy of those territories. As Bauer observes in a different context, herein lies an intrinsic relationship between "consumption and identity" (xvi), in the sense that the bodies depicted by Martínez Compañón were displayed for the crown, which should have recognized these productive "tools" in order to exploit their potential.

Many of the illustrations highlight the role of the indigenous and *mestizo* women in these territories as specialized and efficient workers. They also represent a markedly diverse work force, involved in different tasks, such as producing textiles (dyeing wool, weaving, spinning), milking cows, or working as blacksmiths. Image "E98: Yndias escarmenando lana" (Figure 22) reflects the sense of complacency with which they performed each task. They are shown in an orderly position, disentangling and cleaning wool without distraction. Even supervision is not needed, as they perform their duties diligently and efficiently. Illustration "E104: Mestizas de Chachapoyas cosiendo rengos" (Figure 23) also shows the skill and care with which this sector of the population conducted its work, as the women sew fabric with point lacework, demonstrating artistry and care.[62] Some of these

Figure 18. "E83: Yndia pastora pariendo." (Courtesy of Biblioteca del Real Palacio de Madrid.)

Figure 19. "E81: Yndio pastor de ovejas." (Courtesy of Biblioteca del Real Palacio de Madrid.)

*Visualizing and Commodifying Female Bodies* 69

Figure 20. "E99: Yndia de Valles hilando en catre." (Courtesy of Biblioteca del Real Palacio de Madrid.)

Figure 21. "E100: Yndia de Valles texiendo." (Courtesy of Biblioteca del Real Palacio de Madrid.)

women seem to have been posing so the painter could capture the total dedication and contentment with which they perform their tasks. The sophistication in the detail and their ease of effort shows how well they had mastered their jobs. At a time when Spain was determined to compete with France and England, with an eye toward taking over the textile market by producing more quality products, these types of images would have certainly appealed to royal authorities. The message conveyed was that the provinces of Trujillo had enormous potential in terms of natural resources and productive individuals.[63] Martínez Compañón apparently hoped to show the king that these territories already possessed the key ingredient for economic expansion: a solid labor force. In these territories, *mestizas* and indigenous women as well as women of African descent constituted a crucial active element of that work force, while elite Spanish women seemed to be in charge of reproducing the future owners of the land. Furthermore, women are shown to be quite involved in both traditional and modern forms of production.

In more demanding jobs, such as that of a blacksmith, *mestizas* displayed their capacity to be productive as well as skillful laborers. In illustration "E105: Mestiza

Figure 22. "E98: Yndias escarmenando lana." (Courtesy of Biblioteca del Real Palacio de Madrid.)

Figure 23. "E104: Mestizas de Chachapoyas cosiendo rengos." (Courtesy of Biblioteca del Real Palacio de Madrid.)

de Moiobamba trabajando en su herrería" (Figure 24), we again witness adept workers conducting their tasks with mastery and ease. That this particular woman seems to own her own smithy, as the title suggests, demonstrates the prominent role women enjoyed as active components of the local economy, and as producers of consumer goods. They had also learned to master European machinery, further demonstrating their ability to learn and be part of the labor force. Illustrations such as "E101: Yndias hilando a torno" (Figure 25) and "E102: Yndia de Lamas hilando a torno" (Figure 26) are prime examples, as Martínez Compañón portrayed these indigenous women in command of a machine that had been introduced to them to facilitate faster spinning In illustration "E99: Yndia de Valles hilando en catre" (Figure 20), the artist depicted an indigenous woman also spinning, but using a more rudimentary tool: the *huso*, which was used before the introduction of the European *torno*.[64] In both scenarios, women are seen as active members of the work force, always completing their tasks effortlessly and independently.

Women as productive members of their own society were also present in the illustrated manuscript compiled by Martínez Compañón. The bishop showed indigenous women working in the production of *chicha*, as captured in illustra-

*Visualizing and Commodifying Female Bodies*    71

Figure 24. "E105: Mestiza de Moiobamba trabajando en su herrería." (Courtesy of Biblioteca del Real Palacio de Madrid.)

Figure 25. "E101: Yndias hilando a torno." (Courtesy of Biblioteca del Real Palacio de Madrid.)

Figure 26. "E102: Yndia de Lamas hilando a torno." (Courtesy of Biblioteca del Real Palacio de Madrid.)

Figure 27. "E59: Yndias colando chicha y despumandola." (Courtesy of Biblioteca del Real Palacio de Madrid.)

tion "E59: Yndias colando chicha y despumandola" (Figure 27). They are portrayed as busy performing their tasks at hand, and attentive to their responsibility of producing this alcoholic drink for local consumption. It is difficult to discern whether Martínez Compañón perceived the production of *chicha* as problematic, especially when one considers the perceptions of the European chroniclers toward the indigenous consumption of alcohol. In this illustration, the emphasis seems to have been placed on production, which highlights the economic thread that runs through all images in this volume: the idea that these subjects have the potential to be productive and useful members of the society if they are well integrated into the work force.[65]

The watercolor illustrations I have discussed portrayed indigenous women as objects of production and as potential incentives for the crown to further its investments in those lands. Martínez Compañón viewed Indians and *mestizos* as peaceful and manageable citizens who were able to execute their tasks with almost no supervision. This is an important message that might have helped to persuade the king, as well as authorities in Spain and Lima, that the territories of Trujillo, along with their inhabitants, were worthy of investment. As Martínez Compañón made clear in his letter to the Viceroy of Peru, Theodoro de Croix, in 1785, all his observations aimed to serve "as matter for industry and commerce" ("en quanto puedan ser material de industria, y de comercio") (App. III, 52).[66] With this goal in mind, the bishop visualized female bodies, in particular, as material instruments to achieve economic prosperity. Their bodies were to be read and exhibited as assets, readily available for productive investment. Their utility made them visible and worthy of inclusion in his own museum of industry.

### The Sick Body: Spatial Constraint and Social Alienation

Not all the illustrations pertaining to the indigenous groups suggest a perfect picture of the ability of women to perform strenuous tasks or to serve as a very productive work force. Images related to disease also functioned as a reminder of the need for colonial authorities to be physically present in these territories. It is noteworthy that all these images were placed at the end of volume 2 along with the images of the infidel Indians, mentioned earlier. It is even more striking that the sick population was not mentioned in the table listing the number of inhabitants of the Archbishopric of Trujillo. Among the illustrations relating to disease we find "E197: Yndio con Viruelas" (Figure 28), "E198: Mestizo picado de Uta" (Figure

Figure 28. "E197: Yndio con Viruelas." (Courtesy of Biblioteca del Real Palacio de Madrid.)

Figure 29. "E198: Mestizo picado de Uta." (Courtesy of Biblioteca del Real Palacio de Madrid.)

29), and "E200: Yndio en agonía" (Figure 30).⁶⁷ These images emphasized the state of isolation, pain, and resignation with which these individuals endured their diseases. One notices in the first illustration, "E197: Yndio con viruelas" (Figure 28), the body trapped by a wrapped white blanket that kept the Indian patient immobile and constrained to a particular space. In the second watercolor illustration, "E198: Mestizo picado de Uta" (Figure 29), we observe a gigantic insect sucking blood from the sores of the patient, who does not even react, so immersed is he in his own misery. The last of these three images, "E200: Yndio en agonía" (Figure 30), sends a clear message when we see the priest offering moral comfort to the Indian in agony. The Indian holding the cross, a symbol of Christianity, against his chest highlights the acceptance with which indigenous people received the word of God.

In the case of the only sick female body pictured in the volume, "E196: Leprosa bañándose" (Figure 31), the patient is portrayed in total isolation, somewhere in the mountains, with what appears to be a divided curtain separating her from her surroundings. This curtain also covers her genitals from the observer. Her upper body is used, however, as an instrument to depict the illness, acting as a symbolic space through which we can observe the physical manifestations caused by the disease. That leprosy was a chronic, contagious disease makes the woman's

Figure 30. "E200: Yndio en agonía." (Courtesy of Biblioteca del Real Palacio de Madrid.)

Figure 31. "E196: Leprosa bañándose." (Courtesy of Biblioteca del Real Palacio de Madrid.)

isolation more understandable, as it justifies in the eyes of the observer, including Martínez Compañón himself, the need for spatial and social isolation. The sick body is perceived as a dangerous one, as it carries communicable diseases that could affect an entire population.

Segregation helped prevent the spread of disease and keep the rest of the population safe. A diseased body epitomized a wasted body, as it was not able to be productive. As Foucault points out in a different context, in the eighteenth century the healthy body versus the sick body was viewed within an "economic management," whereby the bodies needed to be organized in order to guarantee an "increase of their utility" (*Power/Knowledge*, 172).[68] Likewise, the sick body always needed to be cured, corrected, and improved. Martínez Compañón located the illustrations of these sick bodies at the end of his compendium, setting them apart from the rest, in which productive bodies were portrayed. It is important to note that in terms of physical proximity, they were closer to the depictions of the most primitive sectors of the population: the infidel Indians, as illustrated by the portrayal of "E202: Yndio de Montaña Infiel" (Figure 32) and "E203: Yndia de

Figure 32. "E202: Yndio de Montaña Infiel." (Courtesy of Biblioteca del Real Palacio de Madrid.)

Montaña Ynfiel" (Figure 5). All are located at the end of the volume, which suggests their lesser value in relation to the other productive bodies represented in his manuscript. However, as Susan Deans-Smith comments in a different context, the significance of including images of barbaric Indians (and, I would add, sick Indians), emphasizes "the unfinished nature and limits of Spanish imperialism" (173).

Disease and primitiveness represented two elements with which the colonial administration had to contend in order to achieve control and establish order in those lands. Controlling and cleaning those bodies was seen as necessary for the transformation into industrious elements of society. They had the potential to be part of the bigger picture that Martínez Compañón captured through his visual compilation, mainly by becoming active and productive members of society. As Sander L. Gilman argues, "the healthy citizen" is always considered the "good citizen," as the sick body always denotes danger and anxiety (66). If every disease carries the potential to be treated and contained in order to avoid fatal consequences, one could argue that the visual representation of these bodies and the images themselves constituted a way to stop the spread of disease. These images remind the viewer that these problems have the ability to be remedied if the appropriate "medicine" is prescribed. In this sense, these bodies became visual because their skin conveyed the message of urgency to control potential danger and disorder. As Mary Douglas maintains, "the powers and dangers credited to social structure" are reproduced on the human body (142).

Illustration "E53: Padron de los Domingos en Huairona" (Figure 33) demonstrates the extent to which these bodies could be the target of control. In this case, violence became a solution. In the ceremony "Padrón de los domingos," in which indigenous people were physically punished for sins and infractions they had committed, the author shows how the body could serve as a target of violence when order was needed. The woman's body is clearly under colonial control, as she is seen receiving lashes. Her position in the picture underlines her subordination, as religious authorities are located in the upper portion of the picture while the woman remains kneeling and in a lower position with respect to the authorities. Her face cannot be seen, while her bottom becomes the specific part of the body on which the punishment is inflicted. This illustration demonstrates how bodily control was exercised in these territories, with corporal punishment serving as a final resort. The visual images show that for Martínez Compañón, social control was easily achieved in these territories, as bodies can be organized, alienated, used, and managed.

Through the images discussed here, Martínez Compañón reminds the eighteenth-century viewer that colonial religious authorities were necessary in these regions of the Spanish empire at the time. Without a religious presence, the inhabitants of Trujillo would have lived and died in total ignorance and abandonment. Religious authorities served as spiritual healers, conveying a moral message that was to maintain indigenous communities within a productive society that could benefit all.

## A Visual Compendium of Knowledge

Walter Benjamin argues that the act of collecting constitutes a type of "practical memory" and an epistemological system that aims to construct an "encyclopedia of knowledge" (205). Within this process, the objects that make up the collection are devised as a "historical system" as well as material possessions (Benjamin, 205). In eighteenth-century Spain and Spanish America, collecting became "a proof of the value of one's colonial territories" and a way for the crown "to fashion itself as both enlightened and progressive" (De Vos, "The Rare, the Singular, and the Extraordinary," 288). Following Benjamin's and De Vos's remarks, one can argue that *Trujillo del Perú* itself constitutes that type of collection: an encyclopedia of knowledge endowed with utilitarian purposes. In this encyclopedic museum, images of women played an important role, as women were conceived as indispensable members of society. They were identified by the materiality of their bodies,

Figure 33. "E53: Padron de los Domingos en Huairona." (Courtesy of Biblioteca del Real Palacio de Madrid.)

having been endowed with specific spatial and visual attributes. The visualization of the female body became part of an epistemological system in which the body exemplified the potential for social order and economic success. For many intellectual and colonial authorities, the body came to represent an instrument to explain and to categorize society. In the case of *Truxillo del Perú*, female bodies were displayed and read as part of an orderly system embedded in political and economic intentions. As Antonio Barrera argues, for the Spanish kingdom "knowledge became a commodity and a tool to control nature" (50). For Martínez Compañón, the physical body was unequivocally connected to material culture, and to this extent his visualization of those female bodies aimed to send a clear message to the king as to how they were read and understood. Following the philosophical tenets of the Enlightenment, the bishop represented female bodies as "valuable economic resources" filled with the potential of the inhabitants of these lands to become useful citizens (Outram, 40).

Weber argues that "human observation and reason," as understood in the Enlightenment, represented key elements needed in order to "increase trade, industry, agricultural production, and not incidentally, public revenues" (36). In the case of Martínez Compañón, there is little doubt that observation became a primary tool to study and interpret female bodies that occupied these regions of the Viceroyalty of Peru. Integration of this sector of the population into a productive economy also became a goal for the colonial administration and the Bourbon regime.[69] The bishop of Trujillo was keenly aware of the relevance of providing evidence of how to integrate female bodies as part of a productive economy. The manner in which these bodies were fashioned is important to an understanding of Martínez Compañón's political agenda. The images discussed throughout this chapter point out, on one hand, an attempt to facilitate through illustrations the concrete possibility of achieving a social order in which women constituted a crucial component. On the other hand, the images made clear the need for a political apparatus and/or individuals who could set the machine into motion. There was an obvious need to demonstrate to Spanish authorities that these bodies had to be monitored. The organization and numerical placement of the images clearly conveys that Martínez Compañón wanted this type of museum and collected knowledge to be seen and understood in a certain manner. The objects displayed, as Bennett argues with regard to the museum, were expected "to be not just *seen* but *seen through* to establish some communion with the invisible to which they beckon" (35). In this sense, Martínez Compañón's museum becomes "a repository" of the "imagination" of the society he wanted to represent (Findlen, 9).[70]

Anthony Synnott states that the body is always a "social category," whose construction is defined by "the different meanings imposed and developed by every age" (1). In the case of *Truxillo del Perú*, this is certainly the case. However, more significant is how female bodies in this particular case were constructed by selecting specific meanings that appealed to an era and to the figure of the king who went in search of categorizing society for the sake of productive utility. In this sense, as Synnott adds, the "symbolic value" of the body is marked by its "social utility" (7). The commodification of the body as delineated by Martínez Compañón became part of an imperial project that aimed to develop useful citizens who could contribute to the progress of the Spanish nation. The potential of Trujillo's natural resources was reflected in those bodies, which were capable of maximizing the material space in which they lived. Nevertheless, in order to achieve economic success, these bodies needed to be monitored and controlled for the sake of a successful social and political order.

The Bourbon regime thought that economic progress could be achieved through commercial, industrial, and agricultural development (Pérez Samper, 15). The crown's efforts to gain a position in the global market prompted many of the reforms that would motivate works like *Truxillo del Perú*. In Spain, intellectuals were also aware of the importance of economic development for the future progress of their nation. Critics such as Pedro Rodríguez Campomanes in his *Discurso sobre el fomento de la industria popular* (1774), Bernardo Ward in his

*Proyecto económico* (1787), and José Cadalso in *Cartas marruecas* (1793), among others, discussed the need for Spain to become a dominant nation in the world market.[71] It is within this discourse of national progress that we can better understand Martínez Compañón's *Truxillo del Perú*. National progress at this point in time depended upon the correct insertion of men and women into the work force, as well as the articulation of their roles within the private and public spheres.[72] To achieve this goal, it was paramount to understand how their bodies would fit within the new economic and political projects taking place as a result of the Bourbon reforms. Martínez Compañón showed the king, by means of categorization, the orderly and productive manner in which these bodies could function within the colonial system.

In *Truxillo del Perú*, female bodies derived their meaning from the specific places they occupied in society, their occupations, and the clothing they wore. Ultimately, their bodies became what Martínez Compañón and colonial authorities in Spain wished to see within the great scheme of social, economic, and political reform. The visual representation of female bodies aimed to leave no doubt of the potential for this sector of the population to become useful members of the community, not only as efficient mothers, but also as competent workers. Every woman, no matter her social and racial status, could be integrated into society and consequently could contribute to its progress. According to Martínez Compañón, religion was still considered to be a vital tool for the integration of those bodies into a productive society. Their inclusion in this type of encyclopedic museum underlines the governmental manner in which intellectuals strongly influenced by the Enlightenment perceived the human body. For Martínez Compañón and many others, the body was considered a material entity and a source of knowledge. In this visual representation of Trujillo, the female body itself functioned as an object of display, desire, utility, and consumption, and as the most effective tool for contributing to the progress of the Spanish nation.

# 3

# Patriotic Bodies and Corporeal Rhetorics

Sor María Josefa de la Santísima Trinidad's *Historia de la Fundación del Monasterio de Trinitarias Descalzas de Lima* (1783)

In an article entitled "Discurso histórico sobre la fundación del exemplar Monasterio de Trinitarias Descalzas de esta Ciudad de Lima" (Historical discourse on the establishment of the exemplary monastery of Discalced Trinitarians of this city of Lima), published in the *Mercurio peruano* on October 23, 1791, by the Sociedad Académica de Amantes de Lima (Academic Society of the Lovers of Lima), the editors called attention to the relevance of this "illustrious and venerable monument," which made Lima's citizens feel fortunate to consider it as part of their cultural patrimony (*Mercurio peruano* 3.84 [1791], 137) (see Figure 34). The editors took it upon themselves, as guardians of the country, to disseminate to Lima's natives the history of such a memorable institution in order to validate its importance as a national monument and to preserve its history for future generations. According to the editors, because "heroic actions are barely known by those who live at the time in which they take place, it is necessary that a spirit of social responsibility make them public, so their glory can survive into posterity" ("las acciones heroycas apenas son conocidas por los que existen en la epoca fortunada en que se practican: es preciso que el espiritu social las dé á la luz pública, para llevar hasta la posteridad mas retirada su memoria") (137–38). For them, the distinguished monastery of Trinitarias Descalzas of Lima occupied such an important place in Peruvian history that only the act of writing could preserve it for future generations.[1] This was not the first time that a native of Lima had called upon the importance of preserving the memory of such an institution. Eight years before, a member of the monastery itself had already proclaimed the importance of disseminating the history of the institution as a national and religious patrimony. This Peruvian nun was Sor María Josefa de la Santísima Trinidad, who in 1783 decided to write the *Historia de la fundación del Monasterio de Trinitarias Descalzas de Lima* (History of the Foundation of the Monastery of Discalced Trinitarians of Lima). Sor María Josefa and her history constituted a prime example of the intrinsic connections between religiosity and social concerns that were so prevalent in the colonial world.

It is well known that since the arrival of the Spaniards in the New World, religion had become an instrument of political expansion, social control, and identity construction.[2] Literary critics and cultural historians have emphasized the political and social significance of the women's monasteries in colonial Spanish America and their vital role in economic activities and social services. Their social function and political significance were achieved thanks to the work of many religious women who as founders, directors, or practitioners established a close connection between the outside, secular world and the inside, spiritual world of the monastery. As Electa Arenal and Stacey Schlau have indicated, "women's monasteries were educational, economic, political, and social institutions as well as religious ones" (339).

In the monasteries, women worked as administrators, musicians, accountants, playwrights, actresses, entertainers, salespeople, and managers of real state. They also participated in traditional roles performed by secular women, such as cooking, baking, sewing, and cleaning. Their lives inside the monastery space were connected in many instances to the outside world. Their help was greatly needed to tend to the poor and sick and to deal with the effects of natural disasters, as well as to bail out influential colonial citizens who required emergency loans. Having a daughter in the monastery was a sign of prestige for parents, as well as an easy opportunity to obtain loans if or when the need arose.

In Spanish America, monasteries also became "repositories for daughters of the nobility and wealthy urban classes, prisons for the 'dishonored' or 'disobedient,' and sanctuaries for the studious, who had little access to higher education" (Arenal and Schlau, 3). More significantly, these institutions became one of the biggest employers within the viceroyalties, hiring gardeners, surgeons, lawyers, painters, and servants, while also contributing to the economy of the country as active and reliable consumers. Many times nuns also had to depend on the outside world in order to keep their institutions alive. Dowries and contributions became two of the most needed sources of economic stability, especially in small monasteries with lesser means.[3] As Kathryn Burns aptly states, for nuns "spiritual and economic goals" were "inextricably connected" (208).

The discussion in this chapter approaches the Monasterio de Trinitarias Descalzas precisely as a national and social institution deeply connected to the sociopolitical outside world. It focuses on the efforts made by Sor María Josefa de la Santísima Trinidad to write the forgotten history of her own monastery in order to preserve a glorious past and to produce a written account that could serve as a spiritual guide for future generations. The analysis centers on the role that the female body and corporeal metaphors play in the archival project she compiled

Patriotic Bodies and Corporeal Rhetorics   85

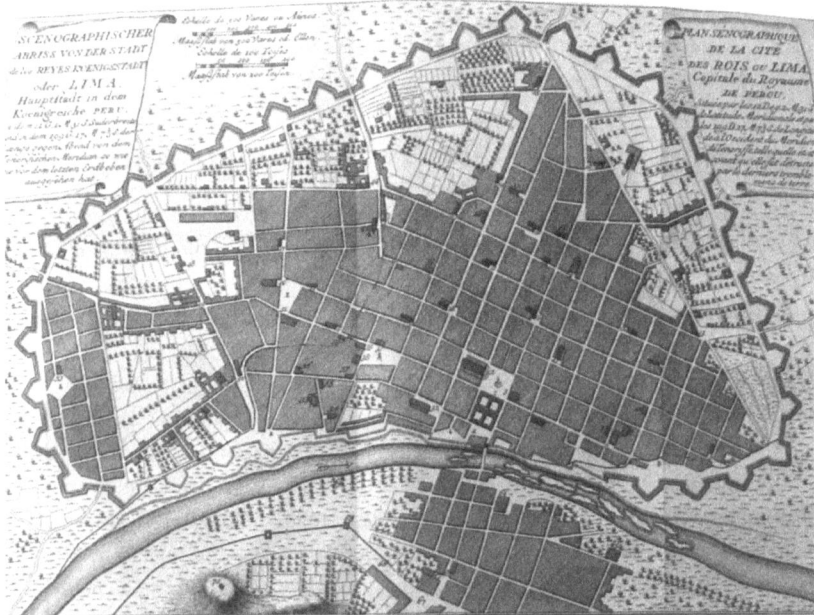

Figure 34. Eighteenth-century map showing the Monasterio de Trinitarias Descalzas close to the center of Lima, as delineated by Jorge Juan and Antonio de Ulloa in *Relación Histórica del Viage a la América Meridional* (1748). In the French translation of the map, the convent is identified as No. 36 (*Voyage Historique de l'Amerique Meridionale*, 1752). (Courtesy of Rare Book and Manuscript Library, University of Illinois.)

and edited in 1783.[4] María Josefa's efforts rely on presenting her chronicle as a cultural patrimony and written evidence of the religious heroic virtues that characterized the lives of many of the nuns who inhabited the Monasterio de Trinitarias Descalzas. At a time when many monasteries were facing a period of crisis and decay, documenting the history of a monastery became a crucial tool to justify the intrinsic and necessary existence of the monastery as a religious and social institution.

María Josefa de la Trinidad's archival endeavor went hand in hand with the articulation of a local sense of national identity that served as an exemplary religious model to be followed by future generations, as well as a testimony of Peru's religious prestige. Her project was anchored in what I call a religious patriotism—a type of discourse that claimed a love of one's country on the basis of religious principles. In such a project the body functions as a crucial rhetorical tool to illustrate the prestigious nature of an institution that sanctity and religiosity together made one of a kind and Lima's "precious jewel." For this nun, the reconstruction of a glorious past was transformed into a process of representation for a religious institution in search of social recognition and cultural visibility, deeply couched in the body as a sign of religious and cultural legitimization.

## Religious Reforms and Their Impact on Peruvian Monasteries

Charles F. Walker states that in the eighteenth century the Bourbons "stressed reforming or 'improving' the Church itself, limiting its numbers, controlling its property, and channeling its efforts to aid in the absolutist project and the improvement of the country" (*Shaky Colonialism*, 110). In the case of the Americas, the deterioration of religious institutions prompted Charles III to call for new *concilios provinciales* in 1769.[5] As a result of this mandate, a *concilio provincial* was held in Lima in 1772. Continuous denunciations made by religious authorities to the king over the lack of discipline observed in many of the nunneries provided much of the impetus for the ordering of the Peruvian councils. Another important reason was the large number of nuns who were entering the monasteries without a religious vocation and who contributed to a supposed lack of discipline. The difficult economic situation of many of these monasteries was exacerbated by the increasing number of nuns as well as secular people who inhabited them, to the extent that many of these institutions became incapable of supporting their overwhelming economic needs (Vargas Ugarte, 230). This constant complaint had been voiced by several archbishops of Lima, dating back to the late seventeenth century. For example, Archbishop D. Fr. Juan Almoguera y Ramírez wrote to the king in 1675 complaining of this precise problem:

> El peso mayor que esta dignidad de Arzobispo de Lima tiene es el gobierno de los monasterios de monjas, porque siendo muchos están todos sujetos a ella y son algunos tan numerosos que pasan de 300 religiosas de velo negro, fuera de legas, donadas y criadas que componen número de más de mil mujeres en cada uno y los demás son a esta proporción. Esta numerosidad tan grande, governada de una mujer con dependencia mía o, por amistad, parentesco o por otro fines, mal puede governarse, que es una de las causas para la relajación a que an venido.

> [The major responsibility of the bishop of Lima is the governing of the female monasteries, because there are so many of them and they are subject to him and some of them are so populated that in them there are more than 300 religious nuns of black veil, not counting secular women, *donadas*, and servants, who count for more than one thousand women in each convent, and this is similar to other convents outside Lima. This large number of women that are ruled by a woman who depends on my authority, be it by friendship, kinship, or other means, can be badly governed, and this is

one of the reasons for the slackening we have witnessed in these convents.] (cited in Vargas Ugarte, 177)

This situation was not as prevalent within monasteries known for more austere rules of religious observance, such as the Capuchins, Carmelites, and other "discalced" orders.[6] In Lima, these monasteries had witnessed another type of problem; namely, a decline in the number of women interested in joining them (Vargas Ugarte, 230). Still, these institutions were forced to decrease the number of servants who worked for them as a way to reduce expenses.

Asunción Lavrin mentions that the three major goals of the royal decree issued by Charles III in 1769 were to examine reported excesses, to improve the behavior of regulars in the missions, and to create seminaries for the instruction of future clergy (184).[7] Ordinances imposed by the *cédulas* affected the monasteries in many ways. As a result, Lavrin adds, bishops and archbishops were ordered to supply the crown with "statements on the observance of their Rules and the vow of enclosure, on abuses which had been introduced in regard to the rule, on the administration of monastery incomes, and on the appointment of confessors" (184–85). Subsequent tighter control and vigilance over the nunneries by the church caused resentment in many religious women, who perceived the new mandates as a threat to their authority and relative freedom within the monastery.

In the Viceroyalty of Peru, many abbesses and nuns legally challenged these new orders in an effort to protect their own religious autonomy.[8] In other instances, they blatantly refused to abide by the new rules levied by the *cédula*. In Lima, royal intervention was needed to compel the nuns to follow the authority of the bishops. The archbishop of Lima was even forced to convince the viceroy to prepare an Auto General de Reforma (General Charter of Reform), which was approved by the king in 1785 (Martín, 236). According to Luis Martín, a "harsher, more specific language, more severe ecclesiastical penalties, and the threat of criminal prosecution by royal authorities" were used to coerce nuns into obeying their male religious authorities (236). Nevertheless, the reform did not hinder the nuns in their fight against the jurisdiction of male religious orders, which the nuns saw as a means by which male authority could and would control their daily lives and religious expressions.

Economic difficulties represented another element that altered their religious lives in the cloister and had an impact on the manner in which some nuns expressed their religiosity. Monasteries confronted new economic responsibilities in the late colonial period.[9] At the beginning of the eighteenth century, the Spanish monarchs imposed additional taxes upon the convents, which worsened the economic situation of many Peruvian monasteries. In March 1700 a royal decree was issued, asking ecclesiastical authorities in the Viceroyalties of New Spain and Peru to contribute a total of one million ducats (*ducados*) to subsidize the wars against Dutch buccaneers attacking Spanish territories (Vargas Ugarte, 4). The Peruvian archbishop and other religious authorities complained about the inability to collect such money from nunneries and churches given the economic burden already weighing on them from previous tax impositions. In 1704 the viceroy of Peru, Conde de la Monclova, also revealed similar concerns to the king. In a letter addressed to the king, Monclova declared: "que es público y notorio que el cabildo padece la escasez que significa con la grande esterilidad que ha más de doce años experimenta todo el distrito de este arzobispado, que considerada por esta real Audiencia y las excesivas pérdidas de los labradores, les ha concedido moratorias por espacio de cuatro años" (that it is public and known that the town council suffers financial scarcity, which attests to the great sterility that the whole district belonging to the archbishopric has experienced for more than twelve years, and considering the excessive losses of the landowners, the royal court has given them moratorium for more than four years) (cited in Vargas Ugarte, 5). Each time a new economic imposition was established by the Spanish crown, ecclesiastical authorities voiced similar complaints. As a result of the Bourbon reforms, nunneries that owned *haciendas* (estates) also were required to pay taxes for each and every indigenous person under their employment. Refusal led to threats that their estates would be confiscated (Paniagua Pérez, 280). This action proved critical, as it was from these estates that nuns produced much of the food they consumed. Consequently, many nunneries had no choice but to comply with the law. Unfortunately, both alternatives—compliance or confiscation—represented a loss of income.[10]

Natural disasters also contributed to economic instability. For example, the powerful earthquake in Lima in 1746 caused great architectural damage to the monasteries.[11] Restoring the buildings to livable condition caused some monasteries, especially the smaller ones with less money, to use nearly all their savings. In the larger monasteries, overpopulation also created economic difficulties, as the number of nuns sometimes rose to double or triple the numbers allowed by the monasteries themselves.[12] Consequently, more money was needed to feed the extra nuns, and additional servants were required as well. Many dowries went unpaid because of the economic problems faced by some families at this time, stemming from the crisis in the mining industry of the Peruvian Viceroyalty; insufficient income made paying for extra expenses extremely difficult (Paniagua y Pérez, 279).

Additionally, in an effort by colonial authorities to improve the cleanliness of the cities and avoid other health problems, viceroys ordered monasteries to pay to pave sidewalks adjacent to their buildings. When the abbesses complained about insufficient funding to cover these expenses, the colonial government responded by threatening to cut water supplies. The cost of these urbanization projects caused deep economic problems for the small monasteries, and often led to ruin.[13]

These financial changes by no means affected all monasteries to the same degree. Smaller monasteries, which usually had survived thanks to the endowments made by their founders, confronted many difficulties as they attempted to maintain themselves once that money was gone. As Lavrin states, the crown "did not provide economic aid," assuming that "the institutions would find mechanisms to sustain themselves," so it therefore became crucial for these institutions to depend on private and community patronage ("Female Religious," 179).[14] As a result, many monasteries saw themselves as having to compete against each other for the financial support of the community. This competition contributed to the realization by many religious men and women that in order to attest to the religious prestige of their own institutions, it was necessary to chronicle their own histories.

The need to convince patrons that their monasteries were deserving of economic protection became a crucial issue in how these institutions presented themselves to the outside world. The willingness of numerous patrons to sustain many of the monasteries arose from a desire to gain "social prestige" or as a result of "civic pride" (Lavrin, "Female Religious," 169). In return for their economic support, they "could demand and obtain special privileges from the nunneries, such as masses for their souls and those of their families, burial in the monastery church, and the right to appoint members of their family or protégés as endowed nuns" (Lavrin, "Female Religious," 169). For their part, patrons saw the presence of a monastery as an enhancement of the city and as a sign of social prestige, as well as a contribution to "individual and urban perceptions of prosperity and of a fitting reflection of the glory of God" (Lavrin, "Female Religious," 169). As Lavrin makes clear, "support of nunneries thus became an index to the wealth of a given city" ("Female Religious," 169).

In the eighteenth century, there were still nunneries in the Viceroyalty of Peru that engaged in social celebrations within their walls, including representations of plays opened to the secular world, commemoration of birthdays and baptisms, and other social gatherings. In the second part of the century "the nunneries were still centers of public entertainment" (Martín, 235). However, what remained constant throughout the period was the attempt by religious and royal authorities to drastically change the institution of the monastery by imposing new and reformulated rules of control and vigilance. As Walker explains, "the discussions, particularly those about the convents, focused on the perceived moral disorder or disarray in Peru and the search for a remedy" (*Shaky Colonialism*, 129).[15]

We can ask how the lives of the nuns who inhabited the monasteries were affected by the reforms imposed on them. How did these changes affect the economic situation of smaller nunneries that participated in more austere rules of religious observance and had less financial means to sustain themselves? Can we perceive any indication in their writings as to how outside politics and economics affected them? What did the monastery as a social institution represent for nuns such as Sor María Josefa de la Santísima Trinidad? In the following pages I address these questions by focusing on how Sor María Josefa's chronicle entered into a dialogue with the cultural and political situation that characterized Peru, and in particular Lima, at the time in which she wrote. Crucial to this discussion is an elucidation of the extent to which her writing was permeated by a sense of urgency: she hoped to create cultural recognition and visibility for the monastery by representing the physical institution, along with its members, as symbolic bodies of religious perfection and national prestige.[16] The body as a tool of identity construction became a material source of patriotic pride.

## Preserving Local History and National Pride

In many texts written by Peruvian nuns, one can notice the authors' zeal to emphasize the exceptional devotion of the nuns, their ability to manage their institutions, and the extraordinary holiness that guided and characterized their lives. The prologues that accompanied some of the biographies, *vidas*, or chronicles in the eighteenth century were marked by a preoccupation that went beyond merely religious concerns to what I call the social.[17] I consider the initial remarks with which many nuns began their works to be important in framing my discussion, particularly since editors and authors alike viewed these histories as part of a developing national treasure that should serve as a model and guide, and would instill pride in future female generations. The content of those histories was intrinsically connected to the outside world, in the sense that writing was not a personal exercise addressed exclusively to the nuns' own communities. Some of these nuns were writing for the world surrounding them and for a public from which they expected recognition as well as emulation. This is exactly the case of the chronicle compiled and edited by Sor María Josefa de la Santísima Trinidad, which aimed to become a public text as well as a treasure of her institution and her homeland.

The chronicle described the first one hundred years of the monastery, including the lives of its twelve principal founders and other exceptional nuns who entered the institution.[18] Sor María Josefa dedicated the chronicle to her mother superior and the fellow nuns with whom she resided. *Historia de la fundación* was written at a pivotal time, when the monastery was celebrating one hundred years of existence.

This chronicle has three important and fascinating aspects. First, it was a product of a collective female authorship. Second, it was edited by a woman and disseminated to a female audience. Third, it was compiled not at the request of a confessor, but on the female writer's own initiative. Furthermore, the voice of the confessor seems to be lost in some of the accounts and is only quoted when his remarks corroborated the extraordinary life of the nun in question. Sor María Josefa's introduction to the *Historia de la fundación* offers a vivid example of how, for some religious women in the eighteenth century, writing became an act of identity construction deeply rooted in national interests.[19] Those patriotic interests pertained to all those who inhabited the same country or territory and were united under the same government.

*Historia de la fundación* can be considered part of the "countless patriotic" sermons, treatises, and histories produced by Creoles in the eighteenth century that, according to Jorge Cañizares-Esguerra, "praised the wealth of their ecclesiastical establishments, as well as their own learning and piety, including that of many New World saints that the Church had canonized, or should have canonized" (205). Traditionally, these types of female religious texts have not been considered within the discursive production of what Castro-Klarén refers to as "homegrown nationalisms" (163). Although the critic is referring to other "modes of encoding discourse and circulating memory," such as iconography, archeology, clothing, or public ceremonies (163), I would add that female religious chronicles in the eighteenth century were also part of a homegrown nationalism deeply rooted in religious sentiments. That the religious patriotism evoked in texts like María Josefa's was framed within the tradition of hagiographical narratives and confessional accounts has contributed to the notion that they were not articulations of a local sense of national identity or deeply rooted in patriotic sentiments. It is important to understand that the language of the Enlightenment was not the exclusive vehicle to instill national pride and identity or to promote the notion of the good citizen in the eighteenth century. Patriotic sentiments were also found in religious narratives. In some cases, both types of languages were present, provoking not tension but rather a productive discourse of cultural and national identity.

Sor María Josefa's *Historia de la fundación* followed some of the typical and formal characteristics of the genre known as monasterial chronicles. This type of chronicle offered an interesting view as to how nuns articulated the history of their own monasteries. These documents were always written by women, although their publication could at times rest upon the decision of male authorities. Josefina Muriel notes that chronicles were primarily initiated by the founder of a monastery, or by their successors, or, in extraordinary cases, written by a group of nuns together (*Cultura femenina novohispana*, 47). In rare cases, the chronicles were published by the director of the monastery. The dual purpose was, first, to present the history of the institution and, second, to relate the story of its exceptional founders and members. In addition, the chronicles also called attention to activities performed by nuns within and outside the monastery walls. Monasterial chronicles aimed to leave written documentation of the exemplarity of their institution (Muriel, *Cultura femenina novohispana*, 47), as is the case with the chronicle compiled by Sor María Josefa de la Santísima Trinidad.

Sor María Josefa's *Historia* was divided into two parts, preceded by a *dedicatoria* (dedication) and a proem addressed to her fellow nuns.[20] The first part dealt with events related to the process of foundation and the principles governing the monastery, and was based on the *relación* of Sor Isabel Francisca de la Presentación, written in 1744. The second part, also written in 1744 by different nuns, constituted an account or *relación* of the lives and virtues of the other twelve founders. In the case of one particular nun, Sor Inés del Rosario, two nuns were involved in the writing of her *vida*.[21] Because original documents dealing with the lives of the other twelve founders had been lost, the authors had to complete their *relaciones* with oral testimonies given by some of the nuns who were still alive. Sor María Josefa, as compiler and editor, relied on all these documents and other oral accounts to produce her *Historia de la Fundación*.[22] Sor María Josefa herself also served as a transcriber and commentator of a *Relación suscinta de los principios y progresos del monasterio*, which she transcribed based on a "cuaderno antiguo" (old notebook) that she had found in the monastery. This notebook listed the names of all the nuns who had entered the monastery between 1675 and 1718, and in some cases also included the reasons why some were asked to leave.[23]

This chronicle has what Arenal and Schlau have called a "patchwork character," because of the "multiplicity of hands" that contributed to "the making of the book" (309). This patchwork character can be easily identified in the "Dedicatoria" with which Sor María Josefa began her book: "Imagen del primer siglo del Monasterio de Religiosas Descalzas de esta ciudad de Lima delineada con las noticias de su origen, fundación y progresos, hermoseada con la vida de sus trece principales fundadoras a las que se agregan las de algunas que entraron después y *reducidas a un solo punto de vista* por Sor María Josefa de la Trinidad quien la dedica a las Reverendas Madres y religiosas de dicho Monasterio a Mayor honra y Gloria de la Santísima Trinidad. Año de 1783" (Portrait of the first century of the Monastery of the Discalced Religious Women of this city of Lima, delineated with the news about its origin, foundation, and progress, beautified with the lives of the first principal founders to which are added the lives of some other nuns who entered the monastery later, and *reduced to a single point of view* by Sor María Josefa de la Trinidad who dedicates the work to the reverend Mothers and the religious nuns of the Monastery to the Major honor and Glory of the Holy Trinity. Year 1783.) (24; emphasis mine). Even before the reader had the opportunity to learn about the history of the monastery, Sor María Josefa emphasized that her *Historia* was a cohesive text because of her ability to research and appropriately gather information about her institution. Her pen acted as the organizing principle of the *Historia* and as a crucial tool to save the memories of a glorious past.

Sor María Josefa underscored her role as compiler in her introduction. This was evident in her "Dedicatoria," where she indicated her sole responsibility for the compilation of all these *relaciones* by reducing them to a single point of view. She later stated that to maintain the vitality of the information which had survived for one hundred years, she decided to preserve it by gathering all items together "in just one body": "Mas, viendo que las pocas noticias que han quedado dan indicios claros de lo que ha sido este Monasterio en los cien años que han corrido desde su erección, me he resuelto a conservarlas reuniéndolas en un solo cuerpo" (And realizing that the scarce news that has survived gives clear indications of the nature of this Monastery in the one hundred years since its foundation, I have decided to preserve the news in one single body) (27). A major concern for her was that some of the written documentation that could testify to the exceptional nature of the monastery had been lost.[24] She saw an urgent need to save the memories that did remain, in order to better preserve and make available for future generations the history of the origin, foundation, and first one hundred years of existence of her institution. Her articulation of the past is not an innocent act of recording. As Castro-Klarén argues with regard to texts emerging from colonial situations in which history and memory play a major role: "A reiterated memory of the past" is always "a task of deliberate construction" (169). The result of this construction would constitute a "body" to be made accessible to a broader audience targeted to learn about the glories of those who had inhabited the monastery. The importance of her task relied on integrating "parts into wholes" and making "the body as a whole" a "concentrated" site where "meaning is invested" (Hillman and Mazzio, xi–xii). Sor María Josefa's chronicle would be read as a textual body whose parts would help in understanding the significance of the whole.

Sor María Josefa mentioned additional reasons for deciding to write her *Historia*. She began with the firm assertion that "the monastery, in its one hundred years of existence, had nothing to envy in other institutions in terms of the number, multitude and accomplishment of heroic deeds" ("Pero ¡ay! Que aunque en un siglo que cuenta de antigüedad, no tiene que envidiar a ningún sagrado cuerpo en el número, multitud y asombro de proezas de santidad") (26). For this reason, she proposed that a written testimony should be left, chronicling each of the many exceptional women who had lived there and who in their totality constituted a "sacred body" (26). According to her, this would follow in the tradition of many religious institutions that had deemed it important to collect and disseminate the history and lives of their most holy people: "Tal ha sido el origen de la loable costumbre de todos los cuerpos religiosos; de recoger las venerables memorias de cuantos los han ilustrado con sus heroicidades" (This has been the origin of the laudable customs of all religious bodies; of compiling the venerable memories of those who have decorated the institution with their heroic deeds) (26). A written testimony of the history of the monastery, its founder, and its most heroic nuns would make a contribution to future generations. New religious women would then have their very own, native holy heroines to admire and follow. Her institution as a religious body was to be represented physically in the corporeality embodied in the text itself to subsequently be read as a part of sacred history.

Sor María Josefa also indicated in her introduction that the *Historia* aimed to contribute to the good education of young generations with the purpose of instilling noble and generous feelings: "De aquí nace la importancia de dar una buena educación a la juventud, ya inspirándole sentimientos nobles y generosos, ya moviéndola con el ejemplo de la práctica de las virtudes morales y cristianas" (Here resides the importance of offering a good education to the young generation, either inspiring them with noble and generous feelings, or moving them with the practical examples of moral and Christian virtues) (25). The *Historia* as a teaching tool and example of Christian and moral virtue for future generations—mostly women—became one of the major justifications for the need "to make" this book. It represented a contribution to their homeland in terms of helping to produce good citizens. With the Enlightenment came an increased significance of education as a vital instrument in the creation of useful citizens, and to that end, Sor María Josefa stated: "Y si esto es tan necesario en el siglo, *para que se vayan formando útiles ciudadanos que sean el honor y la gloria de las Repúblicas*, ¡de cuánto provecho será en los cuerpos religiosos que aspiran a la perfección" (And if this is so necessary in the century in which we live, *so that useful citizens can be developed to become the honor and glory of the Republics*, how much benefit this would be for the religious bodies who aspire to perfection) (25; emphasis mine). Honor and fame were seen as two obvious legacies that the book would leave for her country, by bringing to light the lives and virtues of many heroic women who had lived in such an exceptional monastery. From a religious perspective, the book enabled religious women to achieve a path of perfection so that these "religious bodies" could, in a practical manner, identify with and emulate the paths of the bodies gathered in her chronicle. This dual legacy of national pride and religious perfection lay at the heart of Sor María Josefa's desire to compile the history of her institution precisely at a time when the economic importance of the monasteries in Peru had declined.

Nothing was more important for Sor María Josefa than to offer the young population of Peru "domestic examples" that could move them to imitate and practice moral and Christian virtues: "Nada tiene más eficacia en cualquier género que los ejemplos domésticos, para mover a la imitación. Lo que ven practicar los hijos a los padres, los niños a sus maestros, hermanos e iguales, tiene tanta fuerza, que queda impreso por toda la vida" (There is nothing more efficient when encouraging imitation than the illustration of any kind of domestic example. That which daughters and sons see their parents practicing, and what children see in their teachers, brothers, and other children has so much power that it remains imprinted in their minds for the rest of their lives" (25). This statement is extremely important because of its placement at the opening of the introduction. From the very beginning, Sor María Josefa made clear the powerful sense of identification that a local hero or heroine could instill in fellow countrywomen and countrymen. Peruvians needed only to look to their own religious people to find models of guidance and imitation. Although according to Sor María Josefa many books had been published pertaining to the amazing lives of holy people from other countries, she insisted that nothing was more powerful than learning and identifying with their own, local spiritual heroes (26). She added that any citizen of Lima would be more affected by the sanctity of her fellow *paisana* (countrywoman) Saint Rosa de Lima than by a saint from a remote region. The ability to recognize places where the native saint lived, the miracles she performed, and the clothes she wore helped women with the identification process in a way that saints from other places could not match (26). The case of Saint Rosa de Lima, the first American saint, was used by Sor María Josefa as a justification for the importance of making all the lives and virtues of their own, local heroes accessible to all.[25]

Preserving the memories of fellow countrywomen famous for their religious heroism was paramount to the successful education of young Peruvian women, as well as instilling pride in all citizens who viewed local heroes as worthy of social prestige. Sor María Josefa was engaged in the national promotion of local holy people, which was a trend in Spanish America during the seventeenth and eighteenth centuries. During this time, as Kathleen Ann Myers states, "Local holy people were depicted in Spanish American hagiographies for a dual purpose: they served as models to emulate and as symbols for the building of a local history and identity" (5). Sor María Josefa seems to justify her chronicle, as an archival project that ultimately would bring national pride and prestige to her country, by referring to her *paisana*, Saint Rosa de Lima, and the spiritual connections that Peruvians felt for her. If we consider the nation the way Ernest Renan describes it, as a "soul and spiritual principle" based on "the possession in common of a rich legacy of memories" and "the will to perpetuate the value of the heritage" (19), Sor María Josefa's chronicle is indeed a work characterized by a firm desire to promote local religious patriotism and national pride.[26]

National interests and concerns for the future of Peru emerged from Sor María Josefa's remarks. She believed that Christian and moral virtues were necessary for the creation of good citizens. She portrayed religious women as occupying a vital role in the education and production of solid, moral Christian citizens; this type of education was to produce citizens who would bring religious fame to the country. The word "República" used by Sor María Josefa emphasized her social preoccupation with the future of her homeland. In the eighteenth century, the word was used in reference to *pueblos* (towns or a group of people), and also connoted "a common public cause that was beneficial to all" (*Diccionario de autoridades*, 386). However, the task of preserving national pride and history through researching and collecting oral and written testimonies was not an easy one, as Sor María Josefa clearly explained in her proem.

Sor María Josefa compared her task to that of a painter named Finantes, who was asked to paint a giant within the confines of a small canvas. Owing to his talent and inventiveness, he was able to achieve this task by painting only the giant's finger in all its size and irregularity so that others reflected upon it and said: "¡Si tal era el dedo, cuál sería el cuerpo!" (If that was the finger, imagine how the body must be!) (27). The purpose of Sor María Josefa's comparison was threefold. First, she clarified from the very beginning that her chronicle could capture only a small part of the exemplary history of her extraordinary institution, analogous to the giant's finger. Second, she stressed her ability to perform the arduous task of editing and compiling the history of one hundred years of the institution. Finally, she emphasized the difficulties involved in such a chore, especially when the material was insufficient: "Veis aquí lo que yo también he discurrido: no teniendo espacio donde extenderme por lo reducido de las memorias resolví ofrecer las que han quedado a nuestra religiosa posteridad" (Here you see what I have pondered: as a result of not being able to expand on news about the monastery because of the reduced number of written memories that exist, I decided to offer the ones that have survived into posterity) (27). Not having enough written documentation ("memorias") made her job challenging, though crucial. However, like Finantes, she would rely on her ingenuity to accomplish this challenging task.

If a painter's job at the time was to capture, through color and line, a visual image in an attempt to imitate the object itself, Sor María Josefa undertook the challenge to metaphorically paint, through the act of writing, a history of her illustrious institution in order to more accurately reproduce its one hundred years of existence as well as its significance.[27] As a "painter," her goal was also to preserve the history of the monastery to make it available for future generations.[28] She envisioned that history as a body, of which she would be able to reproduce only a part ("un dedo," or a finger), leaving to the imagination of the reader the rest of that giant body. Her chronicle metaphorically functioned as a body in which the parts needed to be assimilated by the act of writing, as well as the imagination of the reader in visualizing the rest of that body. In Sor María Josefa's case, the act of representation became, as Scarry reminds us in another context, "an act of embodiment," in which the history of the members of the institution would be represented in the text itself and fully rescued through the act of description (216).[29] Sor María Josefa's task was to overcome the obstacles in such a rescue, including the delay and subsequent loss of important documentation pertaining to the history of the monastery and its founders.[30]

For Sor María Josefa, this task was not an easy one, especially because of the lack of written information. As a result, she had to rely heavily upon two sources: the oral testimonies of fellow nuns who had known some of the founders of the monastery and the very brief accounts written by other nuns. Sor María Josefa commented that she had no choice but to work with the histories previously written by other female chroniclers. According to her, although these histories were not rhetorically sophisticated, they were able to simply and sincerely capture the history of their institution and founders: "El naufragio que sumergió tanto tesoro en el olvido, reservó algunos preciosos restos que dan a conocer lo que se había perdido. Son unos apuntamientos, unas bien historias hechas por nuestras mismas hermanas. Lo más apreciable de ellos, es la *sinceridad, llaneza, y simplicidad conque estaban escritas*" (The shipwreck that submerged so much treasure into oblivion preserved some beautiful remains that give us an idea of what was lost. They consist of notes, very well-written histories by our own sisters. What is most precious about the documents is the *sincerity, frankness, and simplicity with which they were written*) (28; emphasis mine). Sor María Josefa credited this female collective authorship to legitimize their importance as reliable and truthful sources for her compilation of the *Historia*. She praised their plain writing style for its ability to communicate effectively and for its high degree of sincerity.

What stands out in these comments is Sor María Josefa's need to justify the validity of her sources, even if her fellow nuns had not received ecclesiastical approval to do so. Sor María Josefa emphatically declared the veracious nature of their accounts: "Así, pues, me persuado a que reluce la veracidad de nuestras cronistas, en la llaneza del estilo, en las explicaciones y frases mujeriles de que usan, y en el mismo desorden, que a veces se nota en los períodos" (Therefore, I do attest to the veracity of our chroniclers, as it is seen in the simplicity of their style, in the womanly explanations and phrases they use, and in the disorder itself that may often be observed in the sentences) (28). The truthfulness of the accounts would overcome the lack of rhetorical sophistication usually found in historical and hagiographical narratives written by women. Sor María Josefa also had to justify the validity of narratives that had been written by women but not officially approved for publication by a male authority figure, the confessor. He had the power to decide whose lives merited a written account and publication. As Myers states, "the confessor's interpretation and judgment of the account" ultimately granted validity to these texts (11). In lieu of that, Sor María Josefa provided coherence to the narratives, based on the fact that these nuns had at one point reported to their confessors what they had witnessed and heard (28). The documents that had been ignored by male ecclesiastical figures now acquired a special value, because they constituted the only written testimonies of a historical period crucial to the knowledge of the exemplary nature of the monastery.

Sor María Josefa was very aware of the political and religious consequences that would come from making the *Historia de la fundación* a text worthy of publication, even if a male religious figure had not requested it.[31] To address this issue, she made the following clarification: "No por eso pretendo que se les dé una fe superior meramente a la humana, ni prevenir el juicio de la Iglesia. Sólo se intenta darles aquel crédito a que nos sujetan los Vicarios de Jesucristo, siempre que se trata de virtudes y milagros, mientras no lo ha aprobado la silla Apostólica, en la que está reservado su examen y declaración" (I do not intend that this work received a faith superior to the human faith, neither do I intend to prevent the judgment of the church. My intention is to give credit to that to which we are subject by the Vicars of Christ when it comes to matters of virtues and miracles, meanwhile understanding that it has not been approved by the Holy Office, which is in charge of the final examination and decision) (28). Here, Sor María was referring to the highly controlled process that had been established by the church after the Council of Trent, and that had determined which heroic lives were deemed worthy of beatification, who could be considered a holy person, and what kind of writings complied with the church's new exigencies. As Myers explains, in the Americas, literary practices were closely monitored by the Holy Office, to the extent that at the turn of the eighteenth century it drafted a set of fourteen rules, called "Reglas, mandatos y advertencias generales del novissimus libros et expurgandorum," that determined "a book's fate when examined by the Inquisition" (64).[32] Sor María Josefa was very aware of the danger involved in her efforts to produce a book that could be perceived as a challenge to the precepts imposed by the Holy Office.[33]

However, her fear was overcome by an urgent need to recover and preserve the history of an institution where, according to her, since its foundation, many religious women "with special reputation of sanctity have flourished" (174). Religious and local pride lay at the heart of her commendable task.

Sor María Josefa de la Santísima Trinidad concluded her introduction by indicating what she believed could be considered her greatest contribution to her religious institution, fellow nuns, and future generations. She declared: "He dado a vuestras reverencias razón de mi trabajo de poca consideración aunque algo laborioso. Lo único que tiene de aprecio es la buena voluntad con que he deseado ser útil a mi religión, promoviendo sus glorias en cuanto ha estado de mi parte." (I have given to your reverences the reason behind my lowly esteemed, albeit challenging piece of work. All that is deemed of value is the good will and the desire I have of being useful to my religion, by promoting its glories.) (30). As this passage suggests, Sor María Josefa viewed herself as someone who rescued the memories of her model institution, thus contributing to the preservation of knowledge of the lives of the heroic religious women who had inhabited the holy walls of the Monasterio de Religiosas Trinitarias Descalzas de Lima. Through the process of "accumulation and presentation of knowledge," Sor María Josefa constructed the monastery's subjectivity in order to legitimize and validate its existence, a project that, as Antony Higgins reminded us, was quite prevalent within the *criollo* intellectual culture of the eighteenth century (8–9).

Sor María Josefa's nationalist sentiment was echoed by the Sociedad Académica de Amantes de Lima, in the aforementioned news article published in the newspaper *Mercurio peruano* in October 1791. In the article, the Academic Society also proclaimed the patriotic need to publish the history of this illustrious monastery, which had come to represent a national symbol: "Nosotros añadimos que este insigne Monasterio no hace solamente la edificación y el exemplo, sino que tambien es el escudo y presidio de la Patria" (We add that this distinguished Monastery not only represents a useful spiritual benefit and an example, but rather also the shield and fortress of the Homeland) (161).[34] The availability of the history of the monastery to the public was perceived as a way to make fellow Peruvians aware of the monastery's current prestigious status, as well as to preserve in writing its memorable historical past. According to the members of the Academic Society, gaining familiarity with the history of the Monasterio de Trinitarias Descalzas would help Peruvians realize how special their land was: "Esta es una tierra privilegiada, tierra santa en cuya posesion puesto habra de entrar un Pueblo singularmente escogido del Señor" (This is a privileged land, a holy land, which God's chosen people will enter and possess) (161). Members of the Academic Society seemed to agree with Sor María Josefa that this particular religious institution was and should be considered as a symbol of religious prestige and national pride.

There is, however, a preoccupation that I believe was a catalyst for the Academic Society to write such an article in 1791, and was also an underlying factor behind Sor María Josefa's impulse to write her *Historia*. When referring to the actual condition of the nunnery, both parties emphasized the economic difficulties prevalent at the institution at the time. The editors suggested that the monastery did not have adequate funds to meet basic needs (156). They stated that the institution did not have enough money to cover its expenses and that even if the public or readers of the newspaper were not obligated to make donations to alleviate the situation, they at least needed to share a sense of responsibility to economically aid the preservation of the monastery (156). To a certain extent, this call to the people of Lima to recognize and feel proud of the importance of this "illustrious and respectable monument" also constituted a reminder of their responsibility as citizens to preserve the image of their city, and to economically support institutions such as this, which were seen at the time as representatives of the economic wealth of the city (3.86 [1791)], 137).[35] Lack of funds could eventually contribute to the ruin and disappearance of these illustrious institutions that contributed greatly to preserve social and religious order and prestige.[36]

It became paramount to prevent this happening to the Monasterio de Trinitarias Descalzas. The monastery was undoubtedly endowed with religious virtue and divine blessings. Based on this, and on the religious perfection that characterized the lives of the nuns who inhabited the monastery, the authors of the *Mercurio* article emphatically concluded that the Monasterio de Trinitarias Descalzas indeed ought to be considered the shield and fortress of their homeland. There was an implicit call to all citizens who loved their country to protect and defend this national patrimony.

Eight years before, Sor María Josefa had issued a similar call for the recognition of the exemplarity of this monastery as a space of religious perfection, sanctity, and national prestige. Her attempt to write the hundred-year history of her institution was fueled by a desire that it be recognized as an important treasure of the city of Lima. Taking into consideration that from an economic standpoint, the monastery could not have been in a stronger position then than it was in 1791, when the editors of the *Mercurio peruano* pleaded for financial support from their subscribers and citizens of Lima, Sor María Josefa could very well have been writing with the same intention. For her, writing represented simultaneous acts of persuasion and legitimization. The account of the lives of the nuns who inhabited the monastery represented the best proof of the extraordinary nature of her institution. The life of each nun symbolized a crucial member of the body that exemplified the text itself. At the same time, it would be through their bodies that such exemplarity would be demonstrated. Their bodies were to function as "symbolic spaces," vital to the illustration of the exemplary history of the institution; through their bodies history was being written.[37] Physicality would become an integral part of the accounts related by Sor María Josefa's *Historia de la fundación*, to the extent that religious devotion, perfection, and exceptionality were all going to be expressed through bodily acts, including the act of writing itself.

## Religious Bodies within the Architectural Body

The first part of Sor María Josefa de la Santísima Trinidad's *Historia* focuses on the history of the foundation of the monastery and the principles that governed it. As mentioned earlier, she based this part on the *relación* written in 1744 by another nun, Sor Isabel Francisca de la Presentación. The protagonists of the second part of the history were a collective group of nuns known as the twelve founders, one of whom was Ana de Robles, who professed with the name Ana María de la Santísima Trinidad and was considered the principal founder of the institution. The *Historia* concluded with a third part, entitled "Relación de los sucesos del monasterio" (Accounts of the events of the monastery), written by Sor María Josefa, in which she also offered brief accounts of other nuns who inhabited the monastery. All three parts aimed to offer a cohesive history that would bring about a better understanding of the monastery's exceptional nature.

The first part conveyed the idea of the monastery as an architectural body, or a body in parts, whereby the principal power relied on the "heads" of those first twelve founders who supported the institution in its incipiency. They were described as "the twelve bright stars that crown the head and foundation of this monastery, or the heads of the monastery that function as its crown" ("las doce rutilantes estrellas que coronan la cabeza y principio de este monasterio, o las cabezas de este monasterio en su principio para que él siempre sea su corona") (50). This metaphor highlights the idea of interdependency that existed between the institution and those religious women who lived there. The institution as a body relied upon those heads that supported it and were the locus where reasoning and thinking took place. The remaining nuns came to represent the other corporeal parts of the metaphor constituting the body as a cohesive unit. The metaphor functioned to illustrate the idea of an institution that stands unified and physically strong.

Further, there is a correlation between space and body to the extent that, as Henri Lefebvre contends in a different context, "each living body is a space and has its space; it produces itself in space and it also produces that space" (170). Within this framework, physicality became the perfect venue to emphasize the extraordinary character of those who inhabited the monastery, as well as the monastery itself. Indeed, it was in those bodies where the presence of God was to be recorded (Scarry, 204).

The narrator of this *relación*, Sor Isabel Francisca de la Presentación, emphasized the crucial role that the main founder, Ana de Robles, played in the existence of the institution. She made clear the limitations she had confronted while recounting this part of the history: "El *corazón* bien quiere, pero la *lengua* no puede, ni la pluma que, como de mujer, y tan rústica é ignorante impropria para referir cabalmente un caso, que por singular y portentoso, es digno tanto de reflexión como de admiración" (the *heart* does want, but the *tongue* cannot, neither the pen that, belonging to a woman, is so rustic, ignorant, and improper to recall a case exactly, even though the case is worthy of reflection and admiration) (34; emphasis mine). For this narrator, writing became a bodily act confronted with the challenge to capture "with tongue and hands" the extraordinary nature of the founding of her institution. For women like her, speaking and writing were concomitantly dangerous acts, given the women's lack of authority to take control of the written word or to attempt to master the religious official discourse.[38] Nevertheless, these difficulties did not deter the narrator from conveying the exceptionality of the main founder.

Ana de Robles was born in Spain, and was the daughter of a widow whose husband had died on their way to the Americas, leaving her with little money and two children. After much economic hardship, the mother became a successful bakery owner in Lima, while her son became a priest. As for her daughter, Ana de Robles, marriage was thought to be the best path. Ana did marry a wealthy man and had a child, but soon afterward her husband and son both died. She then married another wealthy man, Diego de Bedía, with whom she had a daughter. Twice again death struck, when she became a widow for the second time and later when her daughter died at the age of eleven. These episodes, according to the narrative, along with the subsequent death of her mother, prompted her to follow a path of religion.

In 1671 Father Alonso Riero encouraged a group of women for whom he was a confessor to buy a house in which they could devote their lives to God without the strict rules of confinement. After two years spent searching for economic assistance to buy this house, Ana de Robles decided to buy one on her own and convert it into a *beaterio*.[39] Her goal was to eventually request royal permission to transform the *beaterio* into a monastery. Ana became a *prelada*, adopted the name of Sor Ana de la Santísima Trinidad, and enjoyed the trust of her fellow sisters. The archbishop of Lima, Melchor de Limán, then named her *ministra perpetua*, a position she held until her death. She had power to decide who could or could not enter her *beaterio*. Along with the other eleven so-called founders, she took a vow of complete silence and devotion to God. They were successful in getting official approval to turn the *beaterio* into a monastery in 1682.[40] Ana de Robles donated all her money to the *beaterio* and subsequently the monastery, facilitating the entrance of nuns who previously had not been able to pay the dowry.[41] The first eleven nuns or founders of the monastery did not pay any dowry.[42] According to Sor Isabel Francisca de la Presentación, while Ana de Robles was alive, the institution avoided financial difficulties, and the *rentas* provided by the founder were enough to cover the expenses of the thirty-six religious women who lived there (53). Sor Isabel Francisca pointed out that many people viewed the monastery as a wealthy institution, to the extent that still in 1744, while she was writing and despite many financial difficulties, the monastery was still erroneously viewed in this manner.

We learn more about the founder in the second part of the *Relación*, also written by Sor Isabel Francisca de la Presentación in 1744. In it, we find a recounting of Ana de Robles's life, along with the lives of the other eleven founders who contributed to the establishment of the monastery as an institution.[43] The narrator begins her account by referring to Sor Ana as the "principal founder" and as the "column and foundation" of the spiritual building ("porque habiéndola el Señor destinado para columna y fundamento de este religioso edificio") (75). In the first part of the *Relación*, Sor Isabel Francisca offered us a portrait of the founder related more to her business acumen—as a financial provider and diplomat in the process of establishing first the *beaterio* and then the monastery. In the second part she focused more upon the founder's merits as a spiritual leader and an exemplary nun. Physicality becomes a pervasive aspect of this narration through a focus on Sor Ana's body as a sign of symbolic power and perfect devotion.[44] The narrator made clear that her pen was sufficient to portray only the external qualities of the founder, but not the ones of her soul: "Ahora quisiera, que mi pluma tuviese ojos con que registrar los interiores retretes de su alma, y escondidos secretos de su vida interior en que atesoraría preciosidades su ambiciosa virtud, pero como esta no se puede pintar en si misma, por que no hay otros colores que la retraten, sino las señales sensibles con que se manifiesta" (I would like now for my pen to have eyes with which to register the interior rooms of her soul and the hidden secrets of her interior life, as well as the ambitious and beautiful virtues that she treasured, but the interior cannot be painted since there are no colors that can possibly picture it, and one can only see the sensible signs in which it manifests itself) (76). Attention was to be focused on what was witnessed and captured by the eyes of her contemporaries, as well as upon the persistence of her corporeality.

Corporeal parts were used by the narrator to exemplify the crucial role of Ana de Robles in the history of the monastery. She referred to the founder as a "column" and as the "main head" of the institution: "la más querida por ser la más cabeza de todas" (83). The head of Ana functioned within this context as a sign of thinking, deliberation, and power. The head is the location of the brain, the organs responsible for seeing and hearing, and parts of the organs of speech. It is the location of "the center of mental and emotional activity" (Hillman and Mazzio, xxiii). As a head, Sor Ana—owing to her mental faculties—was able to oversee the direction of her institution and to make decisions relevant to its success. She was also the principal leader of the monastery. Furthering the narrator's metaphor, as the vertebral column, which attaches muscles, ligaments, and passages to blood vessels, and as the "center of reflex action containing the conducting pacts to and from the brain,"[45] Sor Ana also served to keep the monastery alive. As an architectural column, Sor Ana represented that "solid body . . . standing upright, and generally serving as a support to something resting on its top" (*Webster's Universal Dictionary*, 330). Sor Ana also epitomized the religious connotations of a column, which was considered "a symbol of spiritual strength and steadfastness" and an "attribute of the allegorical figures of Fortitude and Constancy (Hall, 247). She embodied all the functions associated with these body parts, as she was viewed as the center, support, joining, strength, dependability, and spiritual as well as economic power of the institution.

Spiritual perfection was also exemplified through Sor Ana's body. Eating habits and illness constituted two valuable venues to express her religious devotion and exemplarity. The narrator commented how little the principal founder would eat, to the extent that her fellow nuns were not sure if she ate at all. She ate what was given to her, but never asked for anything. Her meals usually amounted to a small piece of bread. Furthermore, many times she would take food to her room, where the nuns were not sure if she ate at all (79). Her only two vices, according to the narrator, were her taste for hot cocoa and her inclination to smoke tobacco. With regard to her love of hot cocoa, the narrator was careful to point out that Sor Ana would only partake if it was given to her and had not been bought. She was, however, able to contain her inclination for this American drink by refusing to drink it during the time of Advent or Lent. When she indeed drank it, she made sure to use a small cup made of clay and not porcelain. The narrator wanted to focus not so much on the drink itself as on how she was able to control her desire for it when it was most necessary. After all, cocoa was considered a food needed to regain energy; it was indeed a "refección."[46]

Her second inclination was more difficult to justify, because at the time it was considered a vice by some.[47] According to comments made by the narrator, she was not the only one in the monastery who consumed tobacco; others also shared this inclination. The narrator stated that the reason Sor Ana did not break this habit was because she did not want her fellow nuns to feel shame for sharing it (79). It is important that the narrator used the word *imperfección* to refer to this inclination because at the time, *imperfección* referred, from a moral standpoint, to "a light fault that that does not become guilt, nor even venial guilt; however, those who aspire to perfection should stay away from it" (*Diccionario de autoridades*, 223).[48] Although *imperfección* was seen to be a *defecto* (fault), it was not considered a major moral fault. Here again, the potential fault is minimized by Sor Ana's willpower to control her tobacco consumption and the fact that the tobacco was given to her by fellow nuns without her having to purchase it. Indeed, she refused to accept it if she knew it had been bought specifically for her (79). The passage emphasizes not her inclination for a vice, but rather her ability to overpower that inclination by accepting it only under circumstances in which she did not appear as a consumer of material goods. The narrator's decision to highlight Sor Ana's other sign of perfection is the focal point of the narration. However, as the Europeans in the Americas had known since the sixteenth century, tobacco could function as a hunger suppressant (Goodman, 42). Depending on how it was consumed, it could have been used to control pain as well as hunger and thirst or "to counteract weariness and induce relaxation" (Goodman, 45).[49] Within certain sectors of the church it was believed that tobacco helped people resist lust because of its perceived ability to repress sensual urges (Goodman, 79).[50] Although the narrator did not specify how Sor Ana used the tobacco, the product had an obvious impact on her body. It aided her as a vehicle to control bodily temptation in the enjoyment of food, or by alleviating her precarious physical state.

Illness constituted a conspicuous element of this process of identity construction that the narrator delineated in the *Relación*. According to her, Sor Ana suffered numerous illnesses in her life, but always confronted them with resilience. The illnesses and subsequent anxiety did not pose obstacles to her desire to work tirelessly helping others. According to the narrator, the illnesses were able to "wound her without hurting her" ("la herían y no la lastimaban") (85). Despite the physical pain, she never stopped helping others who were also ailing. Medically, it could be surmised that the cocoa or tobacco helped her to endure the pain. She continued to take care of her fellow sick nuns, forgetting her own pain through the healing of others. This "saintly wish" ("santo deseo") and "perfect charity" ("caridad perfecta") made her an exemplary nun, one who ignored her own pain for the sake of the well-being of others. Illness functioned within this context as an instrument to achieve martyrdom and recognition, also constituting part of the process of *imitatio Christi* as an "effort to plumb the depths of Christ's humanity" (Bynum, 131).[51] It was that innate humanity that the narrator wished to emphasize in her account of Sor Ana's illnesses.

Even the blindness she suffered in the later years of her life did not deter her from feeling the pain of others or devoting her life to help those in need. She accepted her blindness with resignation, and contrary to Saint Tobias, who endured his blindness with sadness and affliction, she always accepted it with almost a sense of enjoyment (86). This attitude gained her the respect and reverence of those who surrounded her, making her an exceptional human being. If God had denied her physical vision, He had nevertheless endowed her with a "spiritual and intellectual vision" to understand and feel the pain of others (88). What was considered extraordinary in the case of Sor Ana was her ability to see her surroundings despite being blind. According to the narrator, she was able to feel and witness "the body's ailments" of other nuns. Whenever the nuns would decorate her cell, she was amazingly able to recognize the attempt, and would ask the nuns to remove everything from her room. She was also able to cure fellow nuns, despite not being able to physically see their illnesses. Again, God had given her the power to see in spite of her blindness, as well as the ability to see and understand the pain of others.

The ability to confront physical limitations with spiritual optimism was considered by the narrator to be an element in the lives of those who followed a religious path of perfection. As the narrator stated, "para conseguir la corona del cielo, no son bastante mérito todos los trabajos, que se padecen en la tierra" (to obtain the crown of Heaven, it is not of sufficient merit to go through the hardships we suffer in life) (86). Suffering, endurance, sacrifice, resignation, and love for others constituted signs of the exemplarity and sanctity of this principal founder. Indeed, the suffering of illnesses at that time was perceived as a sign of sanctity in religious women (Bynum, 188).[52] The narrator was well aware of all the requisites that would have made an exceptional nun—one who had the potential to be considered for canonization, or at the very least revered as a holy woman. She made sure that in the brief account of Sor Ana's life, all these elements were conspicuously present, thereby underlining the importance of corporeality when narrating the lives of saintly women.

The final illness endured by the principal founder would represent a climactic demonstration of her exemplarity. At the end of her life she was diagnosed with a tumor in her throat ("parótida") that led to her death. This particular illness became the major testament to her endurance of pain and suffering. According to the narrator:

> Los dolores que le ocasionó el accidente, con ser tantos y tan crecidos, se dejaron rendir a la constancia de su sufrimiento, que heroico lo supo vencer apostando la dolencia a atormentarla, y su mortificación a sufrirla con tanta paz y mansedumbre, que causaba ternura a quien consideraba lo mucho que padecería naturalmente, en tan penoso achaque, pero nuestra Madre no daba muestras de lo que padecía, por ser más lo que deseaba padecer, no solicitando alivio alguno.
>
> [The pains that the accident caused her were so many and attacked her so often that, giving in to the perseverance of her suffering, she was able to heroically overcome the ailment that was tormenting her, and she suffered her mortification with so much peace and gentleness that she provoked tenderness in those who knew how much she was naturally suffering from the heavy ailment, whereas our Mother did not show any signs of suffering and never solicited any comfort.] (91)

Sor Isabel Francisca de la Presentación witnessed the indelible pain and the exceptional manner in which Sor Ana endured it as symbols of her exemplarity and sanctity. Sor Ana viewed her suffering as an opportunity to be closer to God. After all, it is in the body, as Scarry suggests in another context, "that God's presence is recorded" (204). In her case, illness would provide proof of her sanctity. Illness as "a fact and as a metaphor" united the nun's pain to the pain Christ suffered during the crucifixion (Bynum, 48). It elevated the principal founder to the level of God's humanity and pain, and also allowed her to identify with Christ's suffering and achieve the ultimate consecration of her sacrifice. Pain and suffering of the body were viewed as requisites of exemplarity, and the body was seen as a symbol of endurance, sacrifice, and sanctity. The nuns themselves envisioned her body in that manner, as it was difficult for them to watch her body erode. The narrator commented that they were so concerned that they refused to leave her side for fear of losing her and her body forever: "creyéndolo y temiéndolo, así las religiosas, ninguna tenía valor para apartarse de su vista, ni aún de noche *a darle al cuerpo el preciso descanso de dormir*, teniéndolas desveladas el justo sentimiento que las tenía tan afligidas, y *les amenazaba la pérdida de su amada Madre, a quien quisieran eternizar*" (and the religious women, believing and afraid that they were going to lose her, did not have the courage to take their eyes away from her, *nor even at night did they want to give the body the rest it needed*; the feeling that afflicted them kept them awake all night, *and the loss of their beloved Mother, whom they wanted to live forever, kept threatening them*) (90; emphasis mine). Sor Ana's body at that point had become a symbol of sanctity and eternity, as well as an architectural column that sustained her institution as a privileged spiritual space.

The ugliness of the tumor would later constitute another crucial element offered by the narrator in the process of identity construction for the principal founder. "Parótida" was considered at the time to be a tumor located behind the ears. It was also viewed as a monstrous disease because of the size of the growth. Parotidoscirrhus, as it is known today, creates swelling in the area around the ear, as well as a lot of pain when the person attempts to chew or swallow. It is a hard tumor because of the overgrowth of fibrous tissue.[53] Visibility was an important issue in this case, because the fellow nuns were identifying the size of the tumor with the level of pain Sor Ana was enduring. However, the ugliness of the tumor itself, and the odor produced by the secretions expelled from the parotid gland into the oral cavity, were more than offset by a wonderful scent that seemed to emanate from her cell. Sor Ana's illness, as it was sent by God, was thought to be a divine affliction that proved her exceptionality. We must not forget the intrinsic association between odor and sanctity. Instead of the uncomfortable odor that should have come from her room as a result of the tumor, the nuns sensed "a very soft fragrance" ("suavísima fragancia") that overpowered the smell emanating from the tumor (91). Although the tumor was consuming her throat, beauty could still exist in the ugliness of her disease, as a pleasant smell would emanate from her room. Only a divine power could exercise such a miracle, eliminating the putrid odor and replacing it with a soft, sweet yet powerful fragrance: "suavísima fragancia." The sweet-smelling fragrance turned ugliness into beauty and pain into a pleasing act—in other words, a truly miraculous act.[54]

After her death, Sor Ana's body became an even more powerful and visible sign of her sanctity. Sor Ana died in 1707 at the age of eighty-nine. Her renown was evidenced by the famous individuals who attended her burial, including representatives of the town council (*cabildos*) and royal advisory and judicial bodies (*audiencia*), all the important ecclesiastical authorities, and many *fieles* of Lima. Her death also caused great commotion because of the great number of people wishing to show their devotion and touch her body as a relic. The narrator, Sor Isabel Francisca de la Presentación, described the scene as a spectacle:

No cabía en la iglesia la gente y unos en la reja del Coro por donde llegaban a verla dando r[o]sarios para que los tocasen en el cuerpo de la sierva de Dios, sortijas para que las pusiesen en sus dedos, siendo las señoras más principales en esta pretensión. Y esto fue tan continuo que se cansaban las religiosas, como ellas lo dicen, porque las señoras pedían las flores que tenía el cuerpo, y daban otras que le volviesen a poner, quitándole unas y poniéndole otras, para tener más que repartir ambiciosas de su contacto.

[All the people could not fit in the church, and some of them arrived and threw rosaries through the bars of the choir so that the rosaries could touch the body of the servant of God, whereas the women of better means threw rings so the nuns could put them on the body's finger. And this happened so often that the religious women themselves said that they grew tired because the ladies were asking them for the flowers that covered the body, while simultaneously giving them more flowers to cover the body again. The religious women kept taking and putting back flowers, so they could please the ladies who ambitiously wanted to give others flowers that had been in contact with the dead body.] (93)

Sor Ana's body had already become a relic: a sacred symbol as well as a religious treasure. Furthermore, everything she had worn or touched also became a relic. The principal founder's body had become a powerful symbol of devotion and a sign of the divine nature of the monastery. Her body brought the monastery public recognition and prestige. It endowed the monastery with significant distinction, as it was recognized as a chosen space where God's divinity had made a mark.

Her remains also became a site of power struggle when the monastery nuns and local priests engaged in an argument over who had the right to carry her body to its final resting place. The discussion turned violent when the priests forcibly seized the dead body from the arms of the nuns who were carrying it: "Las religiosas llegaron como debían a cargar el cuerpo cuando fue hora de que lo sepultasen, y los señores sacerdotes se lo quitaron diciendo que a ellos les tocaba" (The religious women arrived to carry the body as they were supposed to at the time of burial, but the priests took it away from them, claiming that it was their responsibility to bury it) (93). The dispute over Sor Ana's body was therefore between two groups who conceived it as a symbol of worship and religious prestige. For the first time, Sor Ana no longer held control of her body, as it was instead locked in a power struggle over who had the power to own it during the last minutes of the solemn act of burial. The nuns believed it to be their right because they had shared their lives with her in happiness and pain. The priests envisioned themselves as the chosen ones based on the highly patriarchal role that male authorities played in the hierarchy of the church.

Ultimately, her fellow nuns were triumphant, as a decision was reached that

Sor Ana's body was to be buried in their monastery, where only they would have access to and ownership of it. The nuns enjoyed watching the remaining faithful followers, as well as noted government authorities, desperately attempt to see Sor Ana's face one final time. The followers were to remain separated from the solemn burial act by the bars that divided Sor Ana's body as well as the nuns themselves from the rest of the world. Sor Isabel Francisca de la Presentación commented: "sintiendo todos los que estaban allí presentes, no poder introducirse por la reja, pero las religiosas se alegraron de que tuviesen este estorbo, sirviéndoles de libertad la misma prisión de su clausura, pues sin el muro de la reja, hubiera sido muy difícil poder concluir con el entierro" (the people who were present were upset because they were unable to get past the bars, but the religious women were glad to have this obstacle, as what was supposed to represent their enclosed prison was working now as a sign of freedom: without the bar that served as a wall, it would have been very difficult to finalize the burial) (94). It was the nuns' opinion that these people were guided only by their material desire to obtain a relic, or what the narrator called a "devota codicia de lograr alguna reliquia" (a devout greed to obtain a relic) (94). Ultimately, they thought, the body as a relic should have belonged only to those who had lived with her and witnessed her prodigious life. Their coexistence with her in that religious space endowed them with the right to maintain possession of her dead body; they were always the true believers. Nevertheless, after the burial they were ordered to surrender Sor Ana's only three material possessions to the three highest official authorities. The archbishop of Lima at the time, Don Melchor de Linán, upon learning of the acts of love toward God that Sor Ana had committed throughout her lifetime, wished to preserve one of her rosaries as a relic (94). Another of her rosaries was taken by Don Melchor de la Nava, and the third, which she had worn around her neck, was taken by Dr. Mesía.[55] The material loss of these three relic items was not envisioned by the nuns as a loss in itself; rather, they viewed the transfer of possession of these items to superior religious authorities as a sign of victory. That these three high ecclesiastical and political authorities in Lima recognized Sor Ana as a potential saint, or at least viewed the possibility for her to become one, made the nuns feel the loss of the rosaries as a triumphal act.

The last miraculous act performed by Sor Ana's dead body reiterated her status as a chosen one. At the end of the *Relación*, Sor Isabel Francisca de la Presentación recounted a "remarkable event" that occurred during Sor Ana's burial. According to witnesses at the ceremony, as her dead body was being lowered into the *coro*, they could hear "celestial music" (94). Don Juan de Illescas, a lawyer, was one of those who heard the music. He called other nuns who, along with various servants from the monastery, corroborated the sound of the music. At that precise moment, one of the servants who had kept a handkerchief as a relic passed it along Sor Ana's face, and immediately the pain that the servant had been suffering instantly withdrew. This also was believed to be a miraculous act. The *Relación* concludes with this passage, leaving a profound image of how Sor Ana indeed complied with all that was expected of someone deserving beatification. Everything that her body touched, before and after her death, became a symbol of her sanctity and exemplarity, as illustrated in this last miraculous act. Her body was perceived by her fellow nuns, as well as by other natives of Lima, as a patrimony to her monastery and as a sign of their religious prestige.

Ibsen argues that in colonial times, "the moral superiority of the colonies over Spain [was] expressed with the greatest natural resource: the female body" ("The Hiding Places of My Power," 254). This is certainly the case of Sor Isabel Francisca's *Relación*, which endowed the monastery with religious excellence and superiority by emphasizing not only the exemplary life of the founder but also that the space of the monastery was blessed from that point on because its principal founder was such an exceptional nun. Sor Ana's body epitomized religious prestige and recognition for the importance of this institution. However, as Sor Isabel Francisca de la Presentación mentioned at the beginning of her *Relación*, Sor Ana represented just one of the pillars that made the monastery such an exceptional place. There were eleven other founders, who also contributed to the relevance of the monastery as a place endowed with divine favors. If Sor Ana was perceived as "the most head" of the monastery, the other eleven founders, metaphorically speaking, represented those other parts of the body that epitomized the monastery as a complete religious body. They kept the monastery alive—in movement, so to speak—and played a crucial role for the increased visibility of the monastery as a proud Peruvian patrimony. They were all symbolic images of the architectural body that represented the monastery itself—an institution that, according to Sor María Josefa de la Santísima Trinidad, the editor of the *Historia de la fundación*, deserved the recognition of future generations as it represented a privileged place in the history of Peru. These other eleven so-called founders and natives of Peru also had a central role in the recognition of the monastery as a sacred place. In their biographies, the body would continue to be a key element toward the construction of the history of the Monasterio de Trinitarias Descalzas and its legacy as one of Lima's most prestigious institutions.

## Corporeality and National Icons: The Peruvian Native Bodies

Sor María Josefa de la Santísima Trinidad organized the *vidas* of the other eleven founders, starting with the account of four nuns native to Lima. Their *relaciones* are very brief because, as she made clear in her introduction, most of the documents related to the lives of the twelve founders were lost when Dr. Clerque took them with him to the highlands.[56] With the exception of the life of Sor Inés de la Madre de Dios del Rosario, a native of Ica, the *relaciones* varied in length from one paragraph to six pages.[57] Another reason for the shortness of the accounts was that in many cases, the founders' lives were reconstructed mainly through the oral accounts of some of their fellow nuns, relating what they were able to remember. Remembering became a very selective act by which the nuns chose to narrate and share those episodes that had made an indelible mark on their lives. More important, they remembered what they wanted readers to bear in mind when learning of the exceptionality of their saintly lives. Because all memory "is necessarily archival" (Radstone and Hodgkin, 52), the nuns who narrated the *vidas* found themselves with the power to select the images that were deemed worthy of remembering and sharing with future generations.

The narrators who recounted the lives of the eleven additional founders recognized that history could be found in the bodies of those eleven nuns. In their accounts, the body came to constitute an essential part of history and a type of mnemonic device. In this context, as Susannah Radstone and Katherine Hodgkin remind us, the body could be conceived as "a storage and retrieval device in which the past was remembered" (46). But what did the narrators remember that made the bodies of the founders a prominent element in their accounts? They undoubtedly remembered the symbolic power of the body to epitomize religious perfection and exceptionality, essential requirements that would have endowed the founders as well as the monastery itself with the necessary prestige to occupy a special place in the history of their country. The idea of the body as a sacred space became a significant part of the recollection of their lives as seen by their fellow nuns.

A noticeable element in the description of the lives of the first four nuns, all natives of Lima, is that the narration focused almost entirely on their lives after entry into the monastery, with barely any recollection of relevant events from their childhood. The episodes remembered dealt with three relevant aspects: suffering of illness, self-starvation, and examples of stigmata.[58] These had constituted three important manifestations of sanctity for religious women since medieval times (Bynum, 188).

One case in point is the life of Sor Francisca de San José, who was described as one of the "first columns" of the monastery. Since joining the *beaterio* at the age of fifty, she had suffered bleeding from her mouth, as well as high fevers, described as "burning fire," which she attempted to contain by soaking her clothes in cold water (96). However, the fevers became so intense that she would consistently need to be in the *coro*, where she ultimately would faint after suffering "profound ecstasy" (96). But the changes that overcame the body after she lost consciousness awed the nuns even more. According to the narrator, once Sor Francisca de San José lost consciousness, her face turned beautiful, almost as if it were "flashing lights" (96). Despite her continuous ailments, her fellow nuns considered her to be favored by God, who they believed was helping her to stay alive. However, her illness became acute to the point that the nuns noticed Sor Francisca appearing lost, taciturn, and detached. As the narrator commented: "Ya no vivía como en el mundo" (It was as if she were not living in the world) (96). Although the disease itself was never named, based upon the symptoms and considering the sanitary conditions at the time, one can infer that Sor Francisca may have been suffering from either tuberculosis or typhoid fever. Typhoid fever is known today as an acute infectious disease characterized by symptoms of high and sustained fever, headaches, "general weakness, indefinite pain, and nosebleed" (Thomas, 1928). As occurred with Sor Francisca, the fevers worsened at night. In addition, other symptoms of the illness involved the tongue becoming tremulous, and in some cases "stupor, muttering, delirium, twitching of the muscles, and coma vigil may be present" (Thomas, 1928). What the narrator and other nuns described as "bursting in a profound ecstasy" and "applying to herself cloths of cold water in order to mitigate the fire" could easily have been Sor Francisca suffering from typhoid fever (96). That she was vomiting blood could have meant that she was suffering from tuberculosis, stomach cancer, acute gastric ulcer, or pneumonia. Gastric ulcers also can be affected by other diseases, such as anorexia, which is caused by loss of appetite.[59] It is not uncommon for pneumonia to occur in connection with a systemic disease, such as typhoid (Thomas, 1428). Lack of sleep made these diseases even more dangerous, as weakness of the body will worsen the immune system. As we know, many nuns did limit their hours of sleep to the extreme minimum, which indeed compromised their immune systems. Within this religious realm, real illnesses and diseases became transformed into religious sufferings, conferring sanctity on their lives. In the case of Sor Francisca and her fellow nuns, they perceived pain and suffered symptoms in religious terms. In many cases, illnesses were perceived as divine or chosen by God. They were used discursively to establish a parallelism between human agonies and the ones suffered by Jesus Christ. As Carolyn Bynum argues, illness was conceived as "an *imitatio Christi*," which made the chosen nun closer to God (131).

The final disease Sor Francisca suffered reiterated her sanctity as a woman who endured her pain with patience and resignation, and served as an example for her fellow nuns of how to accept pain and adversity. She was diagnosed with "hidropesía," which at the time was considered to be an anomalous accumulation or discharge of serous liquids within the body.[60] A common manifestation of the disease was an abundance of blisters or the destruction of tissues. Hydropsy or edema, as it is commonly known today, may result from, among other things, "increased permeability of the capillary walls . . . due to venous obstruction of heart failure," or "disturbances in renal functioning; reduction of plasma proteins; inflammatory conditions; fluid and electrolyte disturbances" caused by sodium retention, malnutrition, starvation, and certain chemical substances (Thomas, 560). Because of the extreme fasting practiced by nuns at the time, malnutrition and starvation became two main causes of hydropsy. The lack of a balanced diet made their bodies more prone to acute diseases. It is again important to emphasize that they were suffering from actual diseases. Their internal pains were tangible, and what was seen as "éxtasis" (ecstasies) or "arrobamientos" (flights of spirit) was caused in many instances by genuine illnesses that affected their bodies, their posture, and their overall state of being. Fellow nuns viewed these illnesses as true signs of God's divine will. The physical transformations, the convulsions, the anemic state in which many nuns lived, the vomiting of blood, the ulcers, inflammations, and nosebleeds were material aspects of their suffering, and not merely constructions of a symbolic ideal. These illnesses were not necessarily a simple metaphor or act of manipulation controlled by the nuns to underline their signs of sanctity, but legitimate medical maladies that caused the women to lose control of those very bodies they so adamantly sought to control. The pain, even when the nuns themselves did not induce it, was the result of a physical suffering that went beyond anything they could have envisioned. In the case of Sor Francisca, the *hidropesía* ultimately led to her death.

The case of Sor María de la Encarnación represented another prime example of how some of the nuns abused their bodies in order to live a life full of sacrifice while attempting to emulate Christ's suffering. This particular nun's sacrifice made her a model nun and an emblem of the monastery's religious perfection. For Sor María de la Encarnación, abstinence from food became her major obsession. In the brief account of her life, the narrator emphasizes Sor María's propensity to eat very little or nothing. As Patricia Curran explains, one of the means to achieve spiritual perfection was to deny everything that the body enjoys, including "food, sleep, comfortable clothing, and lodging" (55). For Sor María, food represented an obstacle to the achievement of religious perfection. The narrator, Sor Rosa Catalina de San José, emphasized Sor María's aversion to food, pointing out how she was "abstinentísima" (99). She ate only what was given to her, and only then if it was something that did not look appealing. Her body became so weak that her confessor and mother superior had to request that she moderate her abstinence: "le mandó su confesor y prelada que comiese carne. La moderaron el rigor de las penitencias, la comía en tan corta cantidad, que admiraba, como se mantenía con fuerzas para el trabajo, que este nunca decaeció de él" (the confessor and prelate asked her to eat meat. They regulated the rigor of her penance, but she ate meat in such a small quantity that it was admirable how she was able to keep her strength at work: she never stopped working) (100).

The lack of protein and other appropriate nutrients made her lose bone marrow, to the point that while performing manual work, Sor María broke both wrists. "Unresponsiveness to pain," as Rudolph Bell reminds us, constituted one of the "expected outcomes of extreme self-starvation" (116). From that point on, she worked in constant pain. Another incident that underlined her exceptional sacrifice occurred toward the end of her life, when she was not even strong enough to chew a small piece of meat she had been asked to eat. Her confessor had also asked her to eat either eggs or "mazamorras," a type of pastry made from corn flour, milk, and sugar—a request that to her represented "a mortification" (100). The nuns in charge of distributing food denied the cook access to the ingredients needed to make the "mazamorras," demanding that Sor María eat what the rest of them were to eat. Ultimately, Sor María de la Encarnación was unable to follow the diet recommended by her confessor. In her final days, she became very sick, suffering high fevers while refusing to drink any liquid, despite feeling an "extreme thirst" (102). She therefore died thirsty, similar to Jesus Christ at the crucifixion. Despite what the nuns could have rightfully expected from a weak, malnourished body—a pale, bony face—Sor María's body, according to the narrator, was more beautiful than ever: "Quedó su cuerpo muy flexible y más hermoso que cuando estaba vivo" (Her body remained very flexible and more beautiful than when it was alive) (102). The beauty of her body underlined Sor María's exceptionality, providing a sign that she was chosen by God as a model of perfection and sanctity. The lack of food made her body more beautiful and even stronger in the eyes of those who revered her. The case of Sor María is a perfect example of what Carolyn Bynum calls "miraculous anorexia" (194), or what Rudolph M. Bell describes as "holy anorexia" (118).[61]

Sor María de la Encarnación's saintly nature was corroborated a year after her death, when she appeared to another founder, Mother Ana de la Santísima Trinidad, and invited Mother Ana to join her in the glory she now possessed. The founding mother was in awe, asking Sor María if what she was witnessing was true. A day later Mother Ana did indeed pass away, which demonstrated to everybody Sor María's ability to prophesy the future. While still alive, she was famous for her ability to foretell the future; according to the narrator herself, Sor María prophesied that the narrator's two nieces, despite suffering from smallpox, would not die if she would pray to Saint Felix. Furthermore, she told Sor Rosa Catalina that her nieces would eventually become nuns in the monastery. The narrator did as Sor María had asked, and her nieces did indeed survive the disease and join the monastery as nuns. The life of this founder was depicted as yet another member of the architectural body of the monastery who contributed to creating an exceptional place. Religious perfection, the ability to maintain strength while experiencing physical weakness, and the capacity to prophesy life and death were just a few of her many characteristics that were those expected of a saint. Again, the exceptionality and religious prestige of the monastery were epitomized in the religious bodies of those who inhabited it.[62]

Another founder whose ability to stay strong despite her constant aversion to eating was Sor Petronila de la Santísima Trinidad, who at the end of her life avoided sustenance completely. Prior to that and throughout her life she had followed strict abstinence, with the exceptional instances of Fridays and Saturdays, when she would eat "potaje," a type of stew made from vegetables and legumes that was popular during periods of abstinence. The narrator of her life, Sor Madre Teresa de la Santísima Trinidad, pointed out that even when eating the stew, Sor Petronila consumed only the broth and not the solid food. Rarely, she would eat breadcrumbs dipped in water, and occasionally a small piece of cheese. Meanwhile, she spent every minute of her life giving her own remaining food to others and refusing to rest. She spent most of her time standing or walking and always helping others, especially the poor. Her body emanated kindness toward all those whom she helped. In an extreme case, she came to the aid of a black male servant in the monastery who had slit his own throat to the extent that his head remained barely attached to the rest of his body, by only a few nerves. She held his bloody head in her own hands and implored God not to let him die until he had received the blessing of the confessor. Father P. M. Gabriel de Barrenechea, a member of the Jesuit Order, did arrive and was able to give absolution and unction to the man. After this, he died in peace, and Sor Petronila felt relief that he had received the last blessings and the forgiveness of God. This miraculous act gained her the respect and reverence of all those who saw in her an example of religious perfection and sacrifice.

The physical transformation of her body in the last years of her life reflected the sacrifices she had imposed on herself. Despite suffering from trembling hands, a visibly humped body, high fever, and difficulty walking, she refused to lie down or sit down. On days of extreme cold she would walk barefoot and never wear extra layers of clothes. She endured her pain on her own two feet until she was forced by her superiors to rest in bed, when finally she refused to be fed. After nine days of intense fever, she died at the age of seventy-five on April 5, 1733, which coincidentally was Easter. The significance of the day she died emphasized Sor Petronila's blessings as an exceptional religious woman who sacrificed her own body to be closer to God. She was known among her fellow nuns as one who made her own pain visible while herself feeling the pain of others. As the narrator mentioned in her account, "Descuidada de sí con su ardiente caridad cuidaba de las necesidades espirituales y corporales de los prójimos" (Not caring about herself, she took care of the spiritual and corporal needs of others with passionate charity) (163). Sor Petronila's body exemplified religious perfection, ultimate sacrifice, and spiritual strength, which ultimately gained the absolute devotion of those who had witnessed her great life. As Bynum argues in a different context, for some religious women, as for Sor Petronila, "the rejection" of their own "physicality" was concomitant with an elevation of that physical being, which allowed them "access to the divine" while reiterating their own religious perfection (182).

The desire to emphasize the saintly character of the nuns was a prominent element in the accounts of the lives of the twelve founders. It was undoubtedly their bodies as well as the actions performed by those bodies that made them worthy to consider as holy women. For example, when narrating the life of the first vicar, Mother Josefa de San Pedro, the aspect that the narrator underlined—from the little information that she was able to gather—was that despite the many illnesses the vicar suffered, she refused to receive any treatment or to take any medicine that would help her. Her stomach and liver diseases were the narrator's focal point. These illnesses were so painful that the fellow nuns were in awe of how Mother Josefa was able to endure them without any attempt at remedy: "Era modestísima, nunca permitió ni por enfermedad, que le hiciesen remedio con que le llegasen a su cuerpo" (She was very modest, never allowing, even when she was sick, that homemade remedies touched her body) (105). Mother Josefa certainly envisioned her body as a sanctuary of sacrifice and religious perfection, which she strove to keep under complete control. Her real diseases were doubtless a result of her refusal to eat and sometimes to drink, and for her fellow nuns who witnessed her pain, they constituted material examples of the sacrifice and resignation with which she accepted them. She likely was suffering from extreme ulcers because her only food intake was breadcrumbs left by others and the water she would drink six of the seven days of the week. Her disease, described by the narrator as "enfermedad de escrúpulos" (scruple disease), made her a real martyr.[63] Her exceptional will to endure suffering also made her worthy of consideration as a saint, as the narrator commented in the last sentence of her account. Sor María Antonia de San José, in concluding her account, wrote to the confessor that she had done what she could to gather information about the vicar's life, discovering only that which she had recounted to him. However, she emphasized that despite the little information that could be gathered, "the unanimous belief of those nun who met her was that she was a Saint" ("Que la voz común de todas las Religiosas, que la conocieron, es, era, una Santa") (106).[64] The narrator was able to offer what she believed was enough evidence to prove Mother Josefa de San Pedro's sanctity. The testimony of her sanctity again rested upon the symbolic power of the nun's body, as well as her physical ability to endure pain in the pursuit of religious perfection.

A major sign of sanctity and proof of the religious perfection of the monastery could be found on the body of Mother Juana de Jesús María y José after her death. She represented another perfect nun renowned for her obedience, humility, penance, mortification, poverty, and discipline.[65] The narrator, Madre Sor María Teresa de la Santísima Trinidad, quoting from Mother Juana's second confessor, commented that Mother Juana was a saint (109).[66] Her ability to prophesy deaths and fortuitous events also contributed to her image as an exceptional religious woman, and earned her the faith of many. Fellow nuns, government officials, and merchants approached her, asking what future was awaiting them, and soliciting assurance for the decisions they were about to make. Everything she told them came true. Even the archbishop of Lima, Don Melchor de Linan y Cisneros, deferred to her when wishing to know about future events, such as the earthquakes that would strike Lima. He also learned from her of the burning of a ship in Paita before the event even happened. According to the confessor himself, the archbishop "communicated with her frequently, helping her with what she needed" (114).

The major proof of her sanctity occurred four months after her death, as the nuns prepared to transfer her remains to the *coro*. To the amazement of those who attended her funeral rites, they witnessed the incorruptibility of her dead body: "Salió su cuerpo incorrupto y entero, estando a la vista de todos, cuanto duraron las exequias" (Her body emerged incorrupt and visible to all, for the duration of the funeral rites) (115). Since the early modern period the "incorruptibility of the cadaver in death" had been considered "a virtual requirement for female sanctity" (Bynum, 187). This Peruvian nun exhibited one of the elements that had made other famous European religious women worthy of being revered or considered as saints. The incorruptibility of Mother Juana de Jesús's body represented material evidence of how the Monasterio de Trinitarias Descalzas had been blessed by the glory of God. It was indeed a holy place inhabited by holy women who had nothing to envy of the rest of the world. Peru had its own holy women who deserved to be recognized as such. It was not by chance that the extraordinary transformations suffered by the bodies of the religious founders were always witnessed by a group of people as evidence of the truthfulness of the accounts.

Incorruptibility of the body was also the case for another founder of the monastery, Sor Nicolasa de San José, whose body several years after her death was found uncorrupted. This event was the culmination of an outstanding body that had survived self-starvation and self-inflicted pain. Sor Nicolasa avoided the consumption of food, by alleging to have suckled milk from the Virgin's breast and to have satisfied her hunger by "smelling a flower" that the Virgin herself had offered her. According to the narrator, Mother Sor Cipriana María de las Llagas, Sor Nicolasa had sustained herself from this smell for an entire Lenten season (116). This apparition represented a very convenient way to avoid real food, and emphasized her body's superiority and miraculous nature by being able to survive with no food at all. Her eating habits were always extreme. She never ate meat, only ate bread, and drank water during Lent and every Friday of the year, except when she sustained herself from the smell of the celestial flower. She also never tasted fruit, sweets, or any food that appeared tempting. At the end of her life, she suffered terrible rib pain on one side, probably due to acute osteoporosis as a result of a lack of calcium and phosphate in her daily diet.[67] Of course, she endured the pain in heroic fashion, never complaining as her spiritual strength overcame her physical weakness and pain. Nevertheless, her ultimate proof of sanctity, as was also the case with Sor Juana de Jesús, was that her body was found uncorrupted years after her death. Only her clothes were found to have disintegrated. They proceeded to clothe her again, as well as spread a white dust over her taken from a white stone—a custom popular at the time when handling uncorrupted bodies. As Mother Sor Cipriana wrote, everything with Sor Nicolasa was "admirable" (118).

Bynum emphasizes that "illness was the major element of sanctity" for women who were canonized or revered as saints between 1000 and 1700 A.D. (188). A prominent element that was present in most of the biographies of the twelve so-called founders focused upon each nun's final illness as a sign of her religious sanctity. For example, in the very short account of the life of Sor Micaela de Jesús, native of Ica, we find that the last illness she suffered left her motionless, lying on a wooden plank that served as her bed for the last three days of her life.[68] Although the name of the disease was not mentioned, the narrator did point out that Sor Micaela died with "her body immobilized and positioned in the shape of a cross"

(119). Her dead body—immobilized—became a legible space in which those who witnessed the death were able to read the undeniable sanctity that characterized this woman; in her death, she assumed the position of Christ's painful crucifixion, making her an exceptional divine being.

The extreme transformations suffered by these nuns' bodies highlight the awareness that they all possessed with regard to the potential symbolic power of their bodies. They were cognizant of the legibility of their own corporeality and how fellow nuns and other religious authorities would read them. In the end, it was acknowledged that sanctity was not an individual act of recognition, but rather a collective acknowledgment by other members of the religious community.[69] Witnesses were paramount to this process of recognition.

The case of Mother Juana de Santa María, another so-called founder, is a prime example of how the corporeal transformations were read by fellow members of the monastery. Mother Juana had entered the *beaterio* when she was eight years old, in 1683, a year after the license to turn the *beaterio* into a monastery had arrived. She was considered to be a founder since she had been one of the eleven nuns to first inhabit the monastery. She always lived a life of total humility, charity, patience and suffering. She was known as a very knowledgeable and religious woman to whom her fellow nuns could turn to find answers to their questions. Later, she became a teacher of novices, and in this task she excelled. However, one day before meeting with her novices, she retreated to a secluded location within the convent to flagellate herself. Subsequently, to the perplexity of the novices, Mother Juana did not arrive in class on time but was later carried in by two servants, unable to walk on her own. What they were witnessing left them in a state of shock. Her face was broken and quite pale, almost to the point of being yellow. She appeared almost dead. Her mouth was full of blood, and she had two broken teeth. The novices immediately asked her what had happened, but Mother Juana refused to share any information. One of the nuns decided to contact Mother Juana's confessor to see if he could be pressed for details, but his response was quite puzzling: "respondió, que había sido mucho lo que había visto, que no lo podía decir hasta su tiempo, el cual hasta ahora no ha llegado" (he responded that he had seen a lot, and that he could not say it until the proper time, which had not arrived yet) (168). It is difficult to determine whether his response was an act of concealment, or if he had to some extent witnessed this or any other violent acts involving Mother Juana's self-inflicted corporal punishments. The mystery was never cleared up. What seems likely is that he indeed had witnessed extraordinary circumstances that emphasized her incredible ability to endure torture. As he mentioned to the nuns, the time would arrive when he would finally share his thoughts with the rest of the world. There was an unmistakable sense that he viewed Mother Juana de Santa María as a sign of religious perfection that set her apart from the rest.

It was not a coincidence that this sign would become manifest in the last illness suffered by Mother Juana. According to the brief account, she suffered a serious case of *tabardillo*, or what is known today as typhoid fever, accompanied with an acute side pain in the area between her chest and back.[70] The narrator did not offer details of all the physical ailments she was suffering, except to emphasize that she endured her illness with "patience and resignation" (168). The miracle following her death and the circumstances of the last days of her life amazed all who witnessed them. When she was about to die, all her caregivers were said to hear horrendous screams, accompanied by loud noises and jumps that seemed to emanate from above her cell. The noises were so loud that a neighbor of the monastery even came to discover the source of the uproar. Meanwhile, the confessor had asked one of the nuns to seek out who was making these terrible noises, because they were disturbing the silence within the convent. The nun checked several times, but did not see anyone screaming or jumping. To the dismay of the confessor and the nuns who were present in the cell that day, they suddenly realized that an image of the Virgin Mary's face that was next to Mother Juana had begun to change color, becoming pale and yellow. At the moment of Mother Juana's death, the image returned to its original color and appeared more beautiful than ever, compelling the confessor to bless Mother Juana by telling her: "**Dichosa tú mil veces dichosa tú, que ya saliste en paz de esta mortal vida**" (Lucky you, one thousand times lucky you, that you left this mortal life in peace) (170).[71] The original words in the text were printed in bold, which serves to emphasize the symbolic importance of Mother Juana's death. To a certain extent she had received the approval of the Virgin Mary, since the image reacted to Mother Juana's death beautifully and peacefully. Owing to her divine nature, Mother Juana had received the ultimate absolution; the Virgin had been identified with her during her moments of pain (the last minutes of her disease, when the Virgin's image had turned yellow) as well as right at her death, when peace and joy returned beauty to the Virgin Mary's face. Unfortunately, there is no additional information concerning what followed, except that the powerful image of the Virgin's corporeal transformation was received as a sign of Mother Juana's exceptional religious virtue. Mother Juana died quite young, at the age of thirty-five. At her death her body was clearly ravaged by the horrendous conditions that characterized such a disease: high fever, headache, abdominal pain, general weakness, constant pain, nosebleeds, tremulous tongue, extreme bowel movements, anemia, and desquamation (shedding of the skin)—in sum, "general mental and physical debilitation" (Thomas, 1927–28). To a certain extent, the terrible state of her body was overshadowed by the beautiful physical transformation of the Virgin Mary that occurred beside her. The Virgin seemed almost to take it upon herself to put an end to the extreme physical suffering endured by Mother Juana. The Virgin's body restored peace to a body that previously had been deeply disturbed by the powerful disease.

Another example of the endurance of an extraordinarily painful illness in the moments leading up to death was the case of Sor Luisa de la Madre de Dios de Belén, whose life occupied the tenth *relación* in the *Historia de la fundación*. As the narrator commented, Sor Luisa never complained about the many diseases that tormented her. Nevertheless, one in particular demonstrated the exemplary character of this Peruvian nun. At the end of her life, she suffered a tumor ("apostema") that began to abscess. According to the narrator, the lesion had to be bluntly excised at one point, as it had become cancerous, but she never complained (167).[72] The abscess itself was certainly a major source of pain. As we now know medically, as inflammation increases, pain takes on a throbbing, more prolific nature, with impaired or lost function of the afflicted site (Thomas, 8). The situation was exacerbated by the openness of the wound, coupled with the potions being poured into it, which were attracting insects that seemed very bothersome, according to witnesses. Nevertheless, Sor Luisa never complained. She subsequently died from what was diagnosed by physicians as "enfermedad de hidropesía" (dropsy disease) (166). In this case, it is possible that the cause of death could have been the inflammatory conditions present in her illness, which acted as a precursor to heart failure.[73]

However, what the narrator considered more extraordinary was the eerie transformation that came over Sor Luisa's dead body. The reader is told that the swelling of her body increased to the point that the nuns begged the mother superior for its immediate burial. The nuns regarded this corporeal transformation with fear, as if the body could become another entity entirely, transforming into the image of a monster. One must remember that in the eighteenth century, the word *corrupto* (corrupt) had obvious negative connotations, and was associated with something "malignant, evil, perverse and detrimental" ("maligno, dañado, perverso y prejudicial") (*Diccionario de autoridades*, 623). These connotations created the notion of the dead body as a dangerous object. Nevertheless, even more remarkable were the events surrounding Sor Luisa's remains shortly after the nuns had requested that she be buried immediately, and that all ceremonies that usually followed the death of nuns be canceled. The mother superior decided to speak to the body itself as a method to communicate with Sor Luisa, and she begged, "**Pues fuiste tan obediente en vida, te mando no te hinches más**" (Because you were so obedient in life, I order you to not swell more) (166). These powerful words, highlighted in bold in the original text, emphasized the miraculous nature of what was about to occur. After the mother superior's request, and to the astonishment of all those who were present, the body's inflammation immediately dissipated, replaced by "an attractive and radiant appearance" ("un semblante halagueño y resplandeciente") (166). To increase the credibility of this miracle, the narrator mentioned that at that precise moment, two surgeons who were visiting the monastery had entered, and in awe reiterated that what they had witnessed was truly supernatural (166). What had begun as a solemn act consequently had become a tremendous spectacle that testified to Sor Luisa's extraordinary sanctity.

Her burial held miraculous connotations as well. The narrator mentioned how at the time, the mother superior had commented that she had only five pesos to pay the funeral expenses (which included the ceremonial rites), and that they were unable to spend more than that. However, after celebrating the burial and the novena, she found that she still had money left. Furthermore, given the seemingly impossible event that had happened, many devotees began to worship Sor Luisa, and to ask for help and favors that were repeatedly and miraculously granted. Addressing this aspect, the narrator concluded her account by stating: "Y espero nos alcance de la Divina Trinidad, el que la alabemos por toda la eternidad" (And I hope that the Divine Trinity helps us to praise her through eternity) (167). Locally, Sor Luisa had become a saint who listened to and helped those who sought her aid. She, along with the other so-called founders, embodied the exceptionality of the monastery, as their bodies were endowed with religious talents that created in the institution a source of national pride.

Herein lay the importance of publishing the *Historia de la fundación*: the book would become the archival source of an institution where religious perfection was an integral part of its character and a solid example of patriotic pride. Peru, and in particular Lima, had nothing to envy in other nations when discussing the devotion of religious figures, as within their own territories existed one of the best examples of religious perfection and sanctity. It is important to note that during a time in which cases of beatification had decreased drastically within colonial Spanish America, an emphasis on publicizing the religious lives of women such as Sor Luisa was an attempt to demonstrate the continuing need to seriously consider such lives as unquestionable examples of divine perfection. To this extent, the life of another founder, Sor Inés de la Madre del Rosario, became the epitome of national and local pride, as well as religious perfection.[74]

The case of Sor Inés de la Madre de Dios, a native of Ica, represented a perfect example of the heroic life of a holy woman who had, from an early age, become a local example of religious virtue. It is important to note that this is the lengthiest account we find in the *Historia*. The *relación* is thirty-five pages long, and is divided into five chapters. The first two chapters were written by her natural sister, Sor Micaela de Jesús, and the last three chapters were written by Mother Josefa de San Pedro, who functioned as vicar and second minister in charge of the monastery in 1745. Inés was born a blessed child. According to three of her sisters, when she was born they could see the image of the infant Jesus reflected upon her beautiful face. Her childhood was atypical, in the sense that she never engaged in childish activities, instead preferring to spend her time alone or in confession. When leaving the house, she always covered half of her body, including her face, with a mantle. Sor Inés survived a devastating earthquake that caused her house to collapse, killing two of her sisters, whose bodies were partially buried by the debris. Meanwhile, Sor Inés miraculously survived, suffering minor injuries when one of her arms was also buried. According to one of her biographers, from an early age Sor Inés won the admiration of her town, whose residents regarded her as a saint. According to the account, Inés already seemed sanctified, as evidenced by the manner in which she practiced her fasting, discipline, retreat from society, continuous prayer, and disdain for mundane things. Her life was an example and object of admiration for all the citizens of Ica who already considered her to be a saint: "Inés ya parecía profesaba el serlo, en ayunos, disciplinas, retiro de criaturas, continua oración, menosprecio de las cosas del mundo, siendo su vida ejemplo y admiración de todos los ciudadanos de Ica quienes ya la miraban con la estimación de Santa" (Inés already seemed to be a saint, in her fasting, disciplines, retreat from people, continuous praying, and disdain for earthly things; her life was an example and the admiration of all the citizens of Ica who already looked at her with esteem as a saint) (127). Indeed, according to Sor Micaela, she was physically often confused with Saint Rosa de Lima. When the first portraits of Saint Rosa de Lima arrived (at Ica), some people uttered: "Inecha de Buendía." This episode clearly signaled how closely Inés resembled Saint Rosa. Her town had already raised her status to that of a local holy figure; they identified her with the revered Peruvian saint.

The town of Ica, however, zealously wanted to keep its local holy spiritual daughter close to home, despite Sor Inés's interest in joining a monastery in the city of Lima. Her brothers attempted to prevent her from leaving town by offering her a very unfavorable view of the capital city. On one occasion, when she was ready to depart with her sister, the muleteer who was to take them to Lima refused, fearing the threats he had received from the priests of the church of San Francisco of Ica. The priests had told him that they would do him harm, and that many other ominous things would occur if he were to bring the sisters to Lima. This episode did not discourage Inés and her sister from fleeing their town and arriving in Lima. Her successful escape was evidence of God's wishes for Sor Inés to be a blessed woman.

Once in the monastery, Sor Inés led the life of an exceptional religious woman. Her biographer commented that despite Sor Inés's continuous extraordinary illnesses, physical sufferings, constant *arrobamientos* (flights of spirit), and ecstasies, and the insults she received from those who envied her, she always fulfilled her tasks to perfection (138).[75] Sor Inés also performed miracles by curing other nuns' ailments without the need to touch their bodies. Her popularity as a model holy woman gained the admiration of her fellow nuns. She was deemed "ejemplarísima" (very exemplary), "perfectísima" (very perfect), and as a woman of "grande calidad en el ingenio" (great ingeniousness). The nature of her death and the nuns' reaction to it strongly illustrated Sor Inés's indisputable holy fame.

Sor Inés died at the age of forty-nine, on September 30, 1697, as a result of a tumor in the glands located under her ear. Even after her death, her body, and especially her face, remained beautiful and striking: "Quedó su rostro hermoso y apacible y el cuerpo notable" (Her face was beautiful and calm and her body remained noteworthy) (159). Her religious sisters frantically asked the mother superior for any objects that had belonged to Sor Inés, in order to keep them as proof of her holiness: "sin tener el horror que suelen tener a los cuerpos muertos: pedían por reliquia (como queda dicho) sus cosas y fue menester mucho, para satisfacer la devoción de todas, por ser más las que pedían que las alhajas que se habrían de dar" (without feeling the horror that sometimes people do from dead bodies, they asked, as it is stated, for relics associated with her. It was very difficult to please everybody's devotion, as the number of religious women asking for treasures was higher than the number of objects available to be given to them) (160). Sor Inés had already become an object of devotion among her religious sisters. They believed in her sanctity and wanted to be the first to keep the items that they thought would eventually be considered relics by religious authorities. Because of the material austerity in which she lived all her life, there were not many objects that could be shared with anyone. The only material items she had owned included a picture of a cross, the instrument that she had used to flagellate herself, scissors, and other tools she had used in her occupation as a seamstress. Evidence of her sanctity continued to increase when Sor Inés's dead body performed miracles. According to one of the biographers, a nun who was suffering an extremely painful headache after spending so much time crying in the wake of Sor Inés's death had approached the nun's body, touched it, and was immediately cured.

On another occasion, the painter commissioned to paint a portrait of Sor Inés, in order to depict her holiness so it could be preserved for future generations, complained that he was unable to clearly see her face because everything around it appeared dark. The nuns opened windows; however, her face remained impossible to see clearly. He finally asked the abbess to allow him close proximity to the body by passing the bars that separated him from Sor Inés. When he passed, he noticed that Sor Inés's face showed signs of anger and that it was changing color: "empezó a mudar el semblante el cuerpo difunto, y mostrar un ceño, y obscurecerse el rostro, que si estuviera viva, no podía hacer mayores demostraciones" (the face of the dead body began to change, and it began to frown and become dark; if she were alive, she would not be able to show any greater expression) (161). The transformation prompted the abbess to ask Sor Inés's dead body to allow that it be painted by the man. In a final act of obedience, her body seemed immediately to cooperate, and the painter was finally able to portray her. The nuns explained to him that this miraculous act reaffirmed Sor Inés's sense of morality, as she had never allowed herself to be looked upon by a man when she was alive.

In Sor María Josefa's chronicle, the case of Sor Inés presented one of many concrete pieces of evidence depicting the various exemplary lives of the nuns that inhabited the Monasterio de Trinitarias Descalzas in Lima. Although differences existed in terms of the nature of holiness expressed by each founder, every nun's life in the chronicle offered a clear instance of the outstanding holy vocation of these Peruvian women. Like Saint Rosa de Lima, these women, according to Sor María Josefa, represented perfect models for future generations to follow. Her *Historia de la fundación* not only would preserve the history of her institution, but would also facilitate the promotion of Peru's own local holy people. In a time when many monasteries in Peru were experiencing a financial crisis and the church was unable to subsidize many of their expenses, many monasteries perceived an even greater need to justify the spiritual exemplarity of their institution and their social need for existence.[76] The Monasterio de Trinitarias Descalzas was perceived by Sor María Josefa de la Santísima Trinidad as a privileged space that could enable the production of useful citizens, by instilling religious and moral perfection into the population. For Sor María Josefa, religion ought to be considered an important "spiritual principle" that could positively contribute to the character of her homeland (Renan, 19).

## Religious Prestige and Local Patriotism

Sor María Josefa's decision to compile this volume aimed to save the past in order to preserve an identity. She clearly envisioned herself as the protector and rescuer of a historical patrimony that ran the risk of becoming forgotten: "viendo yo que andaban exparcidos varios fragmentos sueltos, expuestos a experimentar la misma desgracia que las noticias más abundantes que se nos han perdido, creí los salvaría del naufragio" (seeing that some of the loose fragments were already scattered, and in danger of experiencing the same misfortune of the other documents that we had already lost, I thought I could save them from another shipwreck) (28). Her major contribution for future generations in her country, especially women, was to offer them a written account that testified to the holiness of her institution. The stories included in her *Historia de la fundación* were indeed part of a national treasure that aimed to inspire religious patriotism within those who read it. If, as Homi Bhabha suggests, we stop reading the nation restrictively "as the ideological apparatus of state power" or as "the incipient or emergent expression of the 'national-popular' sentiment," we can then consider a text such as Sor María Josefa's to be an example of the diverse ways in which the idea of a particular nation was articulated or constructed in the eighteenth century (3).

Sor María Josefa's written compilation was also an attempt to cultivate admiration and respect for the monastery's own *paisanas*, who, according to her, deserved recognition. Their spirituality, extraordinary behavior, and great virtues could be viewed as inspiration for the education of the useful citizens of their land. It was within this context that her text strove to justify the existence of the monasteries as special places from which holy local people emerged. As Myers reminds us, many of the hagiographies written and published in colonial Spanish America aimed to demonstrate "the importance and efficacy of local holy people bringing special divine favor to their community" (49).[77] The life stories that Sor María Josefa compiled, with the exception of Ana de Robles, who was born in Spain, were simply the lives of many exemplary Peruvian Creole religious women from the regions of Lima, Ica, Potosi, Pellico, Quisquipanchis, Huambacho, and Callao. They all represented models of virtue and obedience, and demonstrated evidence of their desire to devote their lives to God from an early age while enduring a life of suffering, sacrifice, and difficulties in order to become exemplary nuns.

The body as an instrument to achieve and demonstrate religious perfection therefore played a fundamental role in Sor María Josefa's patriotic project, as an instrument of legitimization as well as religious prestige. In these women's bodies, the glory of God was lived and witnessed. Their bodies also epitomized the institution itself, as the founders were viewed as corporeal components of the monastery. They represented the columns and spiritual support of the institution. For some of them, who were visualized as saintly, everything that came in contact with their bodies (rosaries, clothes, crucifixes) became relics. These relics constituted corporeal reminders of the sanctity of these women for future generations (Corbin, 79). Their bodies also served as pieces of history that enabled the compiler of the *Historia de la fundación* to construct a religious discourse that underscored the need for recognition of the exemplariness of their institution. Each body constituted a narration of their own holiness. Within this context, the material and symbolic nature of the body pointed to the importance of recognizing the spiritual and social value of the monastery as a cultural and religious institution. To this extent, the individual bodies, as Jaime Borja argued, served as an excuse to appeal to a "social body" that created in their own locality a place of prestige and recognition.[78]

Sor María Josefa's chronicle was also the result of a corporeal act itself, as her writing became a process of remembrance and part of an urgent need "to evoke the past" in order to reconstruct it and preserve it for future generations (Hutton, xxi). In the end, what would always be remembered from the past would be the manner in which it was represented, and the sources from which it emanated. In this sense, her chronicle functioned as an archive of knowledge and as a repository of collective memory, deeply centered on the religious perfection of the monastery. Sor María Josefa and the other nuns who contributed to the writing of the *Historia* imposed a series of ideas, images, and meanings over these bodies, aimed to demonstrate their religious perfection. To this extent, the body, as Anthony Synnott reminds us, "is not a 'given,' but a social category" to which specific meanings have been assigned (1). In the case of *Historia de la fundación* these meanings are social, religious, and political, as they intended to persuade possible donors and other colonial authorities of the moral responsibility of preserving their monastery as a social patrimony playing a vital role in the production of model citizens. As the editors of the *Mercurio peruano* argued in the aforementioned article about this monastery, it was the responsibility of truly patriotic Peruvians to acknowledge the relevance of what they considered an "illustrious and respectable monument" that brought religious prestige to the city of Lima (3.84 [1791], 160). An institution that they also considered to be "the shield and fortress of the Homeland" deserved a collective recognition that only the act of writing could preserve for present and future generations.[79] Ultimately, what Sor María Josefa was able to offer, as she warned in her introduction, was just a glimpse of the exemplarity of her institution, similar to that finger painted by Finantes in his efforts to capture the figure of the giant upon a small canvas. The onus was upon the reader to imagine the remaining illustrious history, so impossible to capture in its totality given the lack of written documentation. For this, readers were to engage their imagination and serious deliberation after reading her *Historia de la fundación*. Readers, as Sor María Josefa suggested, needed to evoke the enticing quote by Finantes, when he expected the observer to come to the following reflection: "¡Si tal era el dedo, cuál sería cuerpo!"

# 4

# The Nation and Its Congenital Deformations

The Medicalized Female Body in the *Mercurio Peruano*, 1791–1795

In January 1795, the *Mercurio peruano* (1791–1795) published a brief news article entitled "Operacion Cesarea" (Cesarean Operation), describing a cesarean surgical procedure performed in Tucumán that resulted in the death of a woman in an advanced state of pregnancy.[1] The author did not mention the name of the woman, only referring to her as a *Zamba*, which at the time meant the offspring of black and Indian parents. According to the article, a lightning strike led to her death. The lightning entered through the middle of her brain, leaving through her right side after "superficially running" through her whole body.[2] The day after the incident, the mayor of the town requested a cesarean operation to save the child, despite "the refusal and repugnance" of members of the family. Nevertheless, the surgeon proceeded with the operation without the presence of the relatives, and was instead surrounded by various government and religious authorities, as well as other gentlemen who "enthusiastically attended the operation" ("concurrieron gustosos a la operacion") (12.595 [1795], 111).[3]

The article proceeded to point out that the timely surgery was a success as they found the fetus alive, although it survived for only half an hour. The child was a boy, and the author commented that his death was unfortunate, particularly since he might have survived had the woman's family, whose members witnessed without understanding how the woman's abdomen continued to move after her death, acted more promptly. He blamed the death on the "pernicious silence" ("silencio pernicioso") of the parents, who waited until it was too late. According to the author, this case provided proof of the importance of cesarean surgeries in cases like this and moreover demonstrated "the need for vigilance toward people who neglected the significance of the health of the soul as well as the body" ("que la vigilancia con que todos debemos vivir contra las gentes que se descuidan en un punto tan importante a la salud del alma, y del cuerpo" (12.595 [1795], 111–12).

This case highlights some of the recurrent themes explored and discussed by the editors of the Peruvian newspaper in the larger context of Peru's social progress. The notion of the female body as an object to be studied, and its significance with regard to the health of the country, was a topic often discussed in detail by these male contributors, from a scientific, philosophical, and moral standpoint. The central figure of this event, the woman of African descent, represented another trait of many of the news articles and dissertations, the focus upon female sexuality and social deviance. As this news article illustrates, the anatomy of the body became the epistemological object par excellence to discuss some of the social preoccupations that the white Creole elite thought were fundamental for the good social order and progress of society. In this particular case, the cesarean surgery functioned as a spectacle as well as a male enterprise where the female body served as an exercise of speculation, knowledge, curiosity, and entertainment. That the woman was not referred to by her real name but only by her social categorization, a Zamba, emphasizes that her body had more relevance than her own personal situation. The editor concluded by urging vigilance on the part of his readers with regard to ignorant people such as the Zamba's relatives who were obviously unaware of how to care for their own bodies. Lack of medical knowledge had kept these people in the dark, and as a result, intellectuals such as those conducting the surgery or the editors of the newspaper themselves (mostly Creoles, whites, and members of the upper classes) had an obligation to monitor these bodies. A primary goal of this Peruvian newspaper was to awaken fellow citizens to reason, so they could become more aware of the intellectual, historical, religious, economic, and cultural qualities of their own country.

In the following pages I examine the preoccupation with female bodies shown by male intellectuals and contributors to the *Mercurio peruano*, at a time when the female body was the object of intense scrutiny and viewed as central to the production of healthy citizens and to social progress. It is important to recognize how eighteenth-century scientific and medical approaches to the human body became critical instruments to define women's role within society. The urge to examine the medical defects as well as the limitations of the female body, especially those bodies of African descent, worked as an incentive to determine the proper rules to be prescribed for those bodies in order for them to contribute to the progress of the nation. The news articles, as well as dissertations published in the *Mercurio peruano*—specifically those devoted to issues of monstrosity, defective births, female anatomy, pregnancy, gender transformation, and education—served as discursive venues to highlight the disorders, excesses, and defects that would affect the image of Peru as a distinctive and intellectually developed nation. Central to this discussion is the question of why these deviant bodies were primarily those of women of African descent or belonging to the lower sectors of the social spectrum. Patriotism was used as an excuse to denounce the causes that contributed to that deviance, with the aim of cleansing the kingdom of Peru of unhealthy as well as undesirable citizens. The bodies of these women functioned symbolically as "the sites of unreason," which, according to Chris Philo, constituted "the despised and darkened places" integral to the philosophies of the Enlightenment (374–75). The following sections illustrate the ambivalences implied within the discursive efforts made by the male contributors to the *Mercurio peruano*, as they described female bodies by their anatomical functions. This was done in an effort to demonstrate to the local population, as well as to the outside world, how Peru from a social and cultural standpoint was to be considered not on the fringes of modernity and progress but instead as synonymous with intellectual progress itself.

## Patriotic Enlightenments in the *Mercurio Peruano*

The *Mercurio peruano* was founded by the Sociedad Académica de Amantes del País, a group of young Creoles mainly from Lima, whose fields of expertise included medicine, commerce, science, geography, religion, literature, and law.[4] The choice of name for both the society and the newspaper is revealing of the founders' aims and the role of this particular newspaper within Peru. To distinguish themselves from the similarly named Sociedad Económica de Amigos del País (Economic Society of Friends of the Country) that functioned in Spain at the time, the Peruvians decided to identify themselves as the Academic Society of Lovers of the Country. With this name, they emphasized their ambitious aim to educate their country and their will to demonstrate their passion for it.

The founders perceived themselves as spokesmen for their native country, the chosen few in charge of educating not only their homeland, but also the rest of the world. According to them, foreigners had erroneous ideas about Peru and its inhabitants. Eloquence and reason, two distinctive principles of the Enlightenment, would characterize their discursive approach with regard to Peru's past, present, and future. A crucial goal for the founders of the newspaper was to depart from reporting news events from other parts of the world and instead focus primarily upon news of their own homeland: "que mas nos interesa el saber lo que pasa en nuestra Nacion, que lo que ocupa al Canadense, al Lapon, ò al musulmano" (we are more interested in knowing about what happens in our nation than what worries the Canadian, Laplanders, or Muslims in their nations) (1.1 [1791]). Special attention would be given to that which was deemed useful for the country in terms of the production and dissemination of knowledge. As "lovers of public enlightenment" ("amantes de la ilustracion publica"), the contributors to the *Mercurio* supposedly addressed all Peruvians, including female residents of Lima (*limeñas*), for whom learning and education had always been important aspects of their lives. The first issue expressed the sentiment: "el amor Nacional, la pureza, la Fidelidad, y la constancia [que son] las guias de mis pasos, y caracteristicas del *MERCURIO PERUANO*" (national love, purity, faithfulness, and perseverance are the objects of my writings, as well as characteristics of the *MERCURIO PERUANO* (1.1 [1791]).

There was clear evidence of an idealistic sense of marriage or union in this exhortation of "national love."⁵ However, despite the sense of inclusiveness, the founders targeted a particular sector of the population: those members of the upper class and colonial administration who were able to afford the subscription cost of the newspaper. Addressed to those who had the economic power to transform the political, economic, and social future of their nation, the newspaper was therefore a didactic instrument with the aim of providing the necessary tools to enable those changes. Within this context of cultural and social reform centered upon Enlightenment views on medicine, and as part of science and education, every aspect of Peruvian society was to be discussed. As many articles in the newspaper demonstrate, women were to be the focal point and main vehicle to discuss the production of useful citizens. Their bodies, as the article on the cesarean section demonstrated, became sites for medical speculation. In this manner, the way in which those bodies were to be viewed, read, and understood could be controlled from the male perspective.

## From Monstrous Bodies to Monstrous Births

In March 1792 a member of the Sociedad Académica de Amantes del País published an article in the *Mercurio peruano* entitled "Descripción de un ternero bicípite seguida de algunas reflexiones sobre los Monstruos" (Description of a bicephalous calf followed by some reflections about monsters).⁶ According to the author, the point of the article was to satisfy the curiosity of all who looked with admiration upon this kind of phenomenon, and to invoke keen reflection on the Peruvian medical intelligentsia. The article begins with the description of a calf that was born with two different but perfect heads, and an otherwise perfect male body.⁷ The heads looked in opposite directions at a seventy-degree angle, and the calf was able to alternately suckle milk with each mouth, which helped it survive fifteen days. More amazing to the author than the calf's two heads were the results of the autopsy performed after its death. Several vital organs were found to have been duplicated, including heart, lungs, and other organs, except the intestine. The author concluded that the duplication of the calf's organs and its anatomical constitution were sufficient to consider the calf a "monster."

The word *monster* was defined in the ancient world as "something outside the existing order of nature" (Friedman, 3). To the Greeks, this referred to "unusual births of a highly individual nature" of mainly "unusual races of men." In Latin it included "a disruption of the natural order" and a "warning" (Friedman, 3). The word derives in part from the Greek word *teras*, which means "both horrible and wonderful, object of aberration and adoration" (Braidotti, 61–62). It encompasses ideas of disorder, ambiguity, deviance, and anomaly (Friedman, 109). As Dennis Todd observes, this singleness with superimposed doubleness threw "all conventional categories created by law, theology, and metaphysics into confusion," baf-

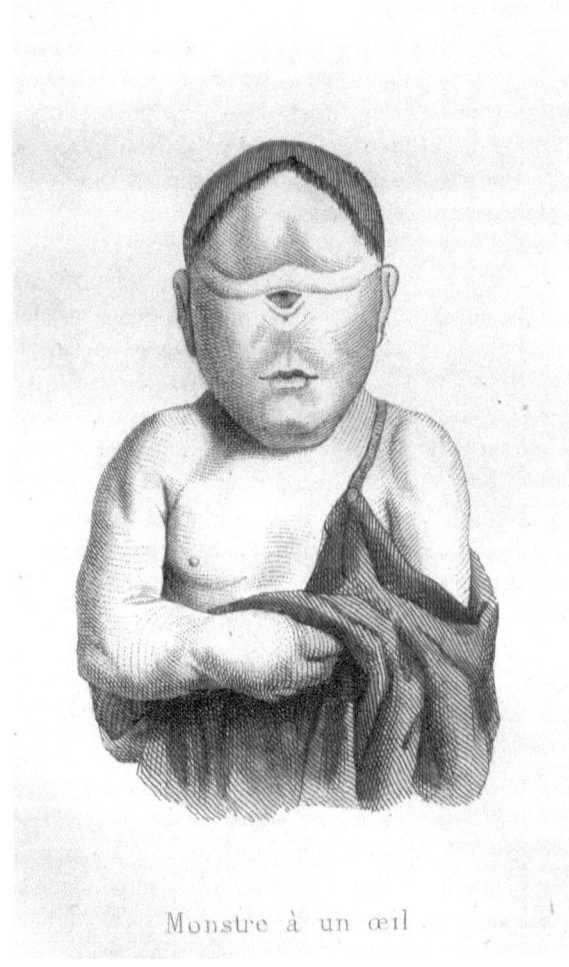

Figure 35. "Monstre." Georges Louis Leclerc, Comte de Buffon, *Histoire naturelle, générale et particulière*, 1785–1790. (Courtesy of Rare Book and Manuscript Library, University of Illinois.)

fling any attempt "at definition" (133). In the seventeenth century Sebastián de Covarrubias had already identified a monster as "cualquier parto contra la regla y orden natural," or "any birth out of the ordinary course and order of nature" (1294) (see Figure 35).[8] Definitions found in eighteenth-century Spanish dictionaries corroborated the associations of monsters with disorders. For example, in the *Diccionario de autoridades*, a monster was defined as "a birth or production against the order of nature," "what is extremely ugly," "serious disorder in terms of the proportion that things should have according to what is consider natural or regular," and "physical and moral disproportion" (598–99).[9] In the context of such definitions, order was represented by the categories of beauty and the perfect male body. Difference was seen as an aberration.

The attempt to decipher the mysterious origins of monsters never stopped, and the late seventeenth and eighteenth centuries saw numerous publications and discussions with regard to the origins of monstrous births. In the late eighteenth century the experimental science of teratology emerged, and the monster came to be studied within the institutions of the anatomy clinic.[10] Teratology had as its objective "to study malformations of the embryo so as to understand in the light of evolutionary theory the genesis of monstrous beings" (Braidotti, 72). In an age when the human body, as Barbara Stafford suggests, "represented the ultimate visual compendium, the comprehensive method of methods, the organizing structure of structures" (12), the image of the monster served as a paradigm for surgeons, physicians, and anatomists to debate the social conditions of human nature and the deficiencies and errors found in them. It is not surprising that at the center of these discussions was the image of the female body as an important factor in the engendering of such monsters. According to medical authorities of the day, two familiar elements of monstrosity were "the deformed child and the aberrant mother" (Huet, 24). It is no coincidence that when the author of the article on the bicephalous calf concluded with the description of the animal, he proceeded to a summary and discussion of the many theories that offered explanation as to the origin of the monster. As this chapter will illustrate, the female body and anatomical constitution lay at the core of many of the explanations.

According to the author, there were four types of monsters: "monstruos por transposicion" (monsters due to transposition); (2) "monstruos por defecto" (monsters due to defects); (3) "monstruos por exceso" (monsters due to excess); and (4) "monstruos por conjuncion" (monsters due to conjunction). "Monsters of transposition" referred to creatures whose internal organs did not occupy their natural positions. "Monsters of defect" were those born with fewer organs or body parts than normally expected (see Figure 36). "Monsters of excess (or surplus)" were those born with superfluous body parts or internal organs, such as a child born with two heads (see Figure 37).[11] Finally, "monsters of conjunction" were those with two distinct and separate bodies, each with its autonomous organs and attached in one particular place (a set of twins born bound together at the chest) (see Figure 38). The author went on to summarize the three main theories—all plausible—that had attempted to explain such phenomena.

The first theory held that monsters had existed since the creation of the world, and that they were the result of primitive developmental processes in which the germs in one egg did not evolve properly.[12] The second theory asserted that monsters were the result of violent accidents that had occurred in the womb, causing a confusion of germs in one egg, which gave rise to the creation of monsters by excess or defect. The third theory was argued by Nicolas Malebranche (1638–1715), who believed that the majority of monstrous births stemmed from strong imaginations of mothers.[13] According to this theory, "the child bore witness to the violent desires that moved the mother at the time of conception or during pregnancy"

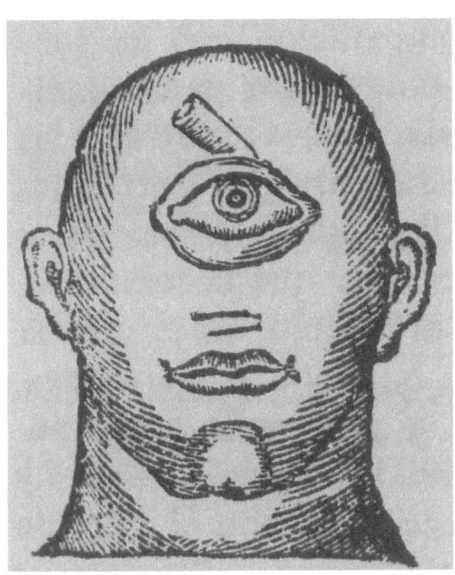

Figure 36. "Retrato verdadero de una criatura que nació en 12 de marzo del año corriente." *Gazeta de Mexico*, 1784. (Courtesy of Rare Book and Manuscript Library, University of Illinois.)

(Huet, 1). As an example, the author of the newspaper article explained the impact that horrible feelings have upon our brain when we witness a monstrous image or horrendous event. He stated: "Si una muger preñada experimenta esta propia sensacion, sucede en ella lo referido, y por imitacion en su feto; mas como las carnes de este se hallan aun muy delicadas ceden facilmente a la impulsion de los espiritus, quienes varian su figura imprimiendo como en cera la imagen del objeto percibido por la madre. En consequencia él nace con esta deformidad" (If a pregnant woman experiences this feeling, what she has seen has an impact on both her and her fetus; but because the flesh of the fetus is very delicate, it easily gives way to the impulse of the spirits, who vary according to their figure and imprint what the mother has witnessed on her fetus as if were waxed. As a consequence the child is born with deformities) (4.126 [1792], 191).

The contributor concluded by stating that all three theories were acceptable. However, none of them could be established autonomously as a general rule for every case. Each theory needed to be applied dependent upon the case in question. For example, he clarified that the genesis of monsters by transposition could only be explained by the power of God's creation. Nevertheless, he argued that Nicolas Lemery's (1645–1715) theory better explained the birth of monsters by defect, by excess, and by conjunction. According to him, the bizarre accidents that affected the fetus in the mother's womb contributed to anomalous births by dislocating or breaking the child's organs or the membranes that protected the development of eggs. Finally, he reached the conclusion that "the imaginationist thesis of Malebranche" offered a clear explanation as to why there were some children born with

134  Deviant and Useful Citizens

Figure 37. *Desvios de la naturaleza o Tratado de el origen de los monstros. A que va anadido un compendio de Curaciones Chyrurgicas en Monstruosos accidentes,* José de Rivilla Bonet y Pueyo, 1695. (Courtesy of the National Library of Medicine.)

animalistic or plantlike features. It was the mother who, through her imagination, because of "fevered and passionate consideration of images," shaped her progeny with monstrous features (Huet, 5).

In this context, it is interesting to note that monstrous creatures always de-

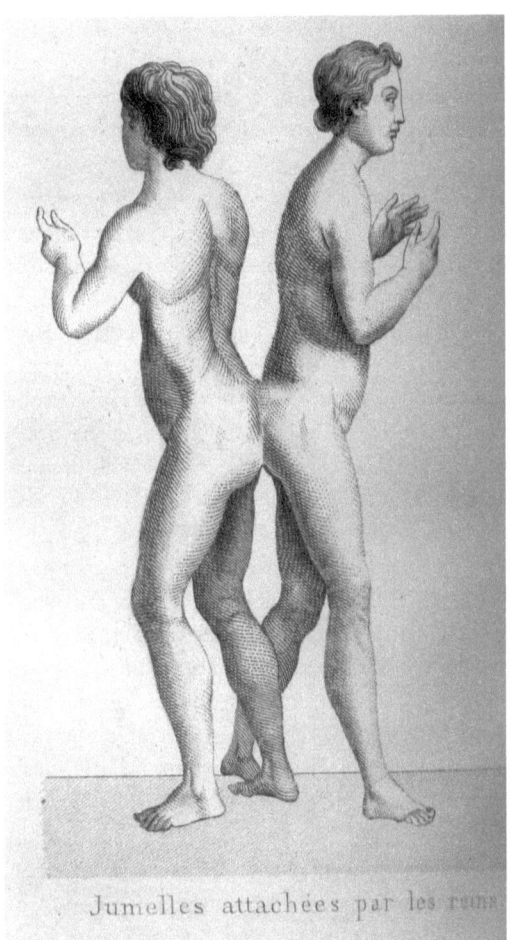

Figure 38. "Jumelles attacheés par les reins," Georges Louis Leclerc, Comte de Buffon, *Histoire naturelle, générale et particulière*, 1785–1790. (Courtesy of Rare Book and Manuscript Library, University of Illinois.)

noted disorder, ugliness, or excessiveness—attributes that in some fashion were always associated with the female body. These disturbances occurred in the mother's disordered imagination, while her body was responsible for the creation of such horrendous beings. Not surprisingly, the author's position was the same as those of the main anatomists, philosophers, physiologists, and surgeons of his time, in which "ugliness, evil, and discord [were] associated with bestiality, femininity, and duplicity" (Hanafi, 104). They (women and monsters) represented nature's deficiency, deviation, and mistakes. This association dated back to Aristotle's *Generation of Animals*, in which, as Huet observes, there was "a decisive association between the monstrous and the female as two departures from the norm," always implying "dissimilarity" (3). It was difference that constituted confusion, disorder, and fear.¹⁴ Every birth defect and deformity was seen as an evident sign of monstrosity. The monster's body was a disabled body in need of regulation because of its physical difference. However, because disability, as James Porter states, "defies correction and tends to operate according to its own rules" (3), it represented a constant challenge to medical writers and scholars.

There was another relevant yet underlying aspect in the literature concerning monstrous births, particularly in the eighteenth century. The great concern exhibited by male authorities with regard to anything that represented a mosaic or hybrid existence spurred many authors of the time to begin scientific inquiries in search of explanations for such phenomena. The female body in particular became an object of intense scrutiny and observation. The eighteenth-century preoccupation with the production of useful citizens constituted an important factor in the discussion of monstrous births. As Zakiya Hanafi suggests, elements of the "real," such as "deformed fetuses, anomalous births such as twins, animals with humanoid parts, humans with animal-like features, [and] peoples that have different skin or unusual customs," provided the basis for all writings about monsters (7).

Medical authorities began to examine the issue of monstrosity from a non-metaphysical perspective. As a result, they began to question the role of the imagination in the act of conception. This is reflected in the articles published in the *Mercurio peruano*. As Hanafi states in a different context, "The ability to discern and identify latent animal tendencies . . . [was] seen as essential for the development of good citizens, not only to be able to positively encourage children in their future pursuits, but also to eliminate those that [were] tainted from birth" (101). The objective was to categorize and explain everything that was outside the norm in order to avoid future errors that could hinder the progress of the nation. Contributors to the *Mercurio peruano* were very concerned with this problem, and their many articles on the subject proposed ways to save Peru from the horrendous consequences of monstrous citizens. A monstrous child was considered a detriment to the progress of the nation, as it could not contribute to the work force.¹⁵

This fear of the unknown had been evident in Peru years before, when in 1694 the viceroy of Lima ordered a distinguished physician of the time, Joseph de Rivilla y Bonet y Pueyo, to perform an anatomical examination on a supposed monster born in Lima, and to draft a document explaining the nature of such a birth.¹⁶ As a result of this task, one year later there appeared, under the name of Rivilla Bonet y Pueyo, professor, member of the Royal Protomedicato, and surgeon of the cabinet of the viceroy, a book entitled *Desvios de la naturaleza o Tratado de el origen de los Monstruos. A que va anadido un compendio de Curaciones Chyrurgicas en Monstruosos accidentes* (Deviations of Nature or a Treaty about the Origins of Monsters to Which Is Added a Compendium of Surgical Treatments of Monsters).¹⁷ The book was based on the monstrous birth of a set of twins, or "bicorporeo infante," born in 1694 with two heads and two sets of arms attached to one body and only two legs (see Figure 37). The author mentioned that the "monstrous twins" ("monstruosos mellizos") were born from a nineteen-year-old married woman, whose internal organs were torn ("dilaceraron") and later rotted because of such an extraordinary birth.[18]

The treatise, which he called a "literary birth," aimed to be a helpful tool to the kingdom through offering a better understanding of possible causes of such births. As one of the dedications of the book stated, this kind of explanation would bring "unity in thought, in the Republics peace, and in the governments fortunate tranquility" ("cabeças union, en las Republicas paz, y en los goviernos dichosa tranquilidad"). The author made clear that when he spoke of monsters, he meant their corporeal and not spiritual manifestation.[19] Rivilla's book helped calm the authorities' preoccupation with and fear of the different monstrous births in Lima during the time.[20] Among them, the author mentions one case of a mulatto woman who had given birth to a set of twins, one black and one white; another case of different women who had given birth every two months; and the case of a stillborn child who at birth appeared to be already between five and six months old.[21] After reviewing the literature on the nature of monstrous births, Rivilla concluded that the possible reason behind the birth of the "bicorporeo infante" was "the tortuousness and inequality of the uterus" ("la tortuosidad pues, y desigualdad de el utero").[22] The female body was seen to be always at the center of social disorder, as mothers were responsible for all birth defects. Articles published in the *Mercurio peruano* certainly followed the notion that to understand the corporeal monstrosities of society, one had to examine the constitution of the female body itself.

It is within this context that the preoccupation with monstrous births in the *Mercurio peruano* emerged. Discussions of the nature of monstrous births were intrinsically related to social concerns. Articles were crafted to serve the country, as the authors strove to act as "prophets of their land" ("ser Profetas en nuestra Patria") through education of their fellow countrymen and -women. Their objective was to focus on issues vital for the future and progress of their country. The construction of the nation as an enlightened and prosperous country was the underlying motivation for their newspaper articles. For them, the monster signified a destabilization of order, an abject being that needed to be eradicated in order to facilitate the strong foundation of Peru.

In an article entitled "Idea general del Peru" (A general idea about Peru), the editors of the *Mercurio peruano* emphasized that the goal of their publication was "to make their kingdom known," in order to avoid erroneous assessments that had been popularized by foreign writers (1.1 [1791], 1). According to their brief description, Peru was "a kingdom" in which intellectual achievements and natural resources created a special environment endowed with the necessary means to achieve economic, cultural, and political progress.[23] The aim of the newspaper was to disseminate that information and bring to the forefront every piece of news that could contribute to the progress of the country. Interestingly, a piece of news published in the second issue of the *Mercurio peruano* dealt with the issue of monstrosity. The article, "Descripción anatómica de un *Monstruo*" (An Anatomical Description of a Monster) described the case of a slave and *negra bozal* named Mariana who gave birth to a monster in Lima.[24] The editors were perplexed, claiming that this phenomenon should have gained the attention of the medical experts. The child was born with no brain, missing the forehead (frontal bone) and the sides of the skull (parietal bones), as well as the medulla. The space that should have been occupied by the bones was covered instead with a membrane to which the eyes and eyebrows seemed to be loosely attached, making them appear "extremely frightening" ("extremadamente espantoso") (1.2 [1791], 9). To add to the oddness, the child's ears were rounded, and in lieu of cartilage there seemed to emerge something that looked like a small female breast. Finally, the editors mentioned that the child was born with two sets of genitalia, male and female, almost merging into one. They marveled most that the child was born alive and was able to live without several vital organs.

The article concluded with questions directed to the medical authorities, asking how it was possible for a fetus to develop in such a manner and asking about the nature of the black slave's body, since a year before she had given birth to a similarly monstrous creature, born with long ears and many deformed protuberances: "Y expliquenos los fisiológicos ¿de que arte se valio la Naturaleza para dar el incremento regular á un Niño, faltando organos tan precisos aun para sostener la vitalidad" (Physicians please explain to us how did Nature allow this child to live when lacking organs vital to survival?) (1.2 [1791], 8). Even more puzzling for the editors was how the woman was able to give birth to normal children after giving birth to monsters.

In this brief article, the body of the black woman and her pregnancies became objects of scrutiny, serving to underline the inferiority and natural difference of her reproductive capacity. Her questionable physical condition and lifestyle appeared to explain the birth of the creature. It is important to note that the woman was identified as a *negra bozal*, which according to stereotypes prevalent throughout the colonial period, was an epitome of barbarity or a person without reason.[25] The author seems to suggest this as a cause for her propensity to engender monsters. This became his major concern, something he declared in need of intensive study by male authorities (physicians, anatomists, and philosophers) because of the perceived negative repercussions that could arise within a developing Peruvian population.

The realization that a "monster" was able to survive and physically develop into an actual member of society presented an appalling and vexing dilemma. For the author, the monster represented that which was outside the realm of normality because of its physical malformation. After all, it was in the eighteenth century that factors such as race and social class came to play a major role when defining what was to be considered a useful citizen. The cause of a monster's congenital malformations had historically been believed to arise from the woman's anatomical nature and her behavior throughout the development of the fetus. Such claims placed women's bodies under constant scrutiny and judgment by medical authorities.

In this case, the body of the black female slave was perceived as diseased and malfunctioned, in need of proper observation, diagnosis, and correction to avoid the birth of future monsters. The context of the article epitomized the black female body as abnormal, an abject element that needed to be contained. Also illustrated in the newspaper article was the manner in which the female reproductive capacity constituted "a key aspect of women's otherness" and how any changes or variations in her body or reproductive capacity were construed "as disease states" (Jackson et al., 363–64). In the *Mercurio peruano*, the body of every pregnant woman commanded the scrutiny of the male gaze. However, the body of the African woman prompted even greater evaluation and surveillance as a result of its ability to spawn such despicable bodies, of no use to the progress of the nation. In this article the image of the monster functioned, as Hanafi suggests, as "the other face of humanity, some bestial or demonic alter ego that must be repudiated and effaced in order for the authentically human being to assert its civilized selfhood" (4). Disability constituted a sign of disorder and futility, as well as an excuse to scrutinize the female body in order to better determine its functions and roles within a productive society.

However, even when black women were able to give birth to healthy children, their bodies were still conceived as anomalous or monstrous. In another newspaper article published in May 1792, Joseph Torpas de Ganarrila brought to publication a letter written by a surgeon entitled "Disertacion de Cirugia sobre un fetus de nueve meses que sacó a una muger por el conducto de la orina el año de 1779 el Autor de ella" (Treatise on the surgery of a nine-month-old fetus born through the urinary canal in the year 1779). His letter was a discussion of abnormal childbirth cases and the possible causes of such extraordinary events. His aim was to validate the importance of surgeons as medical authorities, on the basis of their knowledge of the female body.[26] Their anatomical expertise granted them the power to explain and perform surgical procedures on the bodies of pregnant women in order to ensure successful childbirths.

As part of his dissertation, Ganarrila mentions the case of another *negra bozal* named Francisca, who in 1759 allegedly gave birth via her anus.[27] According to him, the case was perceived as a "rare phenomenon" ("raro fenomeno") by the two surgeons who were consulted by the midwife in charge of the delivery (5.147 [1792], 66). In this instance, the anatomical configuration of the *negra bozal* and its abnormal constitution were blamed for such an unprecedented event: "[Los cirujanos] pasaron al reconocimiento de la parturiente, y observaron con bastante admiracion, que el conducto de la orina llamado *uretra*, se hallaba situado en el mismo lugar que debe ocupar naturalmente la rima menor ú orificio del útero, y que por el ano era por donde se anunciaba el próximo parto" (The surgeons examined the woman in labor, and they observed in awe that the urinary conduct named the urethra was located in the place where the orifice of the uterus should be located, and that it was through the anus where the birth was taking place) (5.147 [1792], 67). The black female body again became a sign of difference—a body substantially marked by monstrosity in the Greek sense of the word, seen as horrible and aberrant yet simultaneously able to stir admiration.

The scene described by the surgeon conjured the image of the male surgeons standing about the woman, wholly perplexed by such an "outrageous event." They felt as through they were the only spectators for this "marvelous and mysterious work of Nature" (5.147 [1792], 68). The surgeons awaited the fetus's arrival, if only to discover whether delivery would occur in the same mysterious manner in which they thought the child had been conceived (that is, anally) (5.147 [1792], 68). Francisca's case became part of a legal battle between theologians and *canonistas* (experts in canon law) with regard to whether a woman who had become impregnated through "unnatural" means should be allowed to marry.[28] In actuality, their concern posed a dilemma with moral repercussions, as they were forced to ponder the possibility of acceptance of anal intercourse within the walls of marriage: "si sería válido el matrimonio, en quien no tenia vaso natural para el coito, ó si este se hacia por un criminal nefando" (if marriage was valid in the case of a person who did not have a natural orifice for intercourse, or if the intercourse took place through an abominable criminal act) (5.147 [1792], 68). To resolve the dispute, the two surgeons who had witnessed the case were called in, both of whom claimed that the lone determinant for the event was the anatomical constitution of the black woman. Francisca's anatomy revealed that her pubic bones and urinary canal were improperly located, the latter found in the actual site of the uterine orifice. As a result, the opening of the uterus was forced to remain enclosed in the superior part of the anus. The theologians and *canonistas* accepted the surgeons' explanation and allowed Francisca to remain married.

However, we must bear in mind the anatomical impossibility of Francisca having conceived a child anally or given birth in like manner. The unusual anatomical orientation of Francisca's female reproductive organs and anus might have confused the surgeons, probably because of their close proximity to one another. The medical authorities likely found it difficult to distinguish among the three orifices. Nonetheless, the relevant pervading thought in their diagnosis of the situation, as well as the author's assessment, is that an apparent abnormality in the female body once again served as an excuse to generate a discussion of the sexual and moral behavior of the black woman, also considered by the author to be monstrous.

This case highlights how conceptions of the female body were intrinsically related to social and moral concerns. That Francisca allegedly was able to conceive a healthy child in a manner considered abnormal by male authorities prompted concern on the part of religious and legal authorities. In colonial times, anal intercourse was perceived as an "abominable sin" ("pecado nefando"), to be avoided at all costs.[29] Women were to abide by sexual rules imposed on them, and they were required to use their bodies in appropriate manners. What was considered abnormal instantly became an object of examination, discussion, and surveillance. As Haidt observes, it is within this frame of reference that in the eighteenth century the body functioned "as one of the most basic tropes by which ethical, political, and social concepts of power" were articulated (5). Francisca's body therefore represented a dangerous and monstrous one that could be contained only through intense scrutiny. The monster as a symbol of difference reappeared in this newspaper article. The idea of a monstrous act caused concern and anxiety, and for that reason needed to be eradicated. In this context it served as a sign of "transgression, of breakdown in hierarchy; it [was] a symbol of crisis and undifferentiation" (Hanafi, 55).

The surgeons used Francisca's case to elucidate how the science of anatomy could help decipher abnormal cases of conception and childbirth, such as the one described by the author. His aim was to disparage superstitions that such cases were the product of horrible things that women witnessed or ate during their pregnancy. He argued that the anatomical constitution of the female body offered explanations for its biological processes. Accurate knowledge of each anatomical landmark, with its respective location and function, was fundamental to understanding the process of conception and reproduction. Nevertheless, his ostensible objectivity and more scientific approach to explaining the anatomy of the female body did not eliminate the prevalent tendency that had dominated male perceptions of the female body since antiquity. Women's bodies were viewed within society as key to the process of reproduction. Anatomical knowledge in the age of the Enlightenment merely offered a new vocabulary to use to categorize body parts, in hopes of maximizing their function and thus avoiding any obstacles that would interfere with reproduction.[30] In the cases mentioned by the author, there was a tendency to indict female anatomy, especially that of the black woman, for all anomalous childbirths based on anatomical difference. The case of Francisca also demonstrates the limitations still confronted at the time with regard to knowledge of female anatomy and the means to interpret what was considered to be outside the norm. It is clear, however, that the author viewed the body and its functions as "the site of scientific diagnosis" and as a "space of scientific knowledge" (Livingstone, 72).

He continued by offering another interesting example: the case in 1779 of a young woman, aged fifteen to sixteen, named Feliciana. Through reference to her job as a washerwoman, as well as the disparaging manner in which he referred to her nickname (Pichita), the author offers another example in which race or social class (in this case, class) is associated with the issue of monstrous births. Feliciana's dilemma, which required the intervention of three surgeons, was the pain and difficulty she endured for two days in labor, allegedly as a result of hitting her abdomen against a door. He claimed this to have been the result of "an emotional problem" ("pasion de ánimo") she had experienced two days before. The scene of the childbirth became a spectacle when the three male surgeons, including the author himself, examined Feliciana's body. The abnormality of her case was rooted in the duration of her labor as well as the entity to which she was giving birth. The first day produced the emergence of a single foot, followed the second day (with the surgeons' assistance) by the extraction of part of a leg that bore virtually no flesh. After five days, the author extracted three bones (cubitus, humerus, and radius), which completely lacked flesh. Finally, after eight days, Feliciana gave birth through the urinary canal to four phalanges encased in an infected and thick membrane. For eleven months, the author witnessed numerous bone fragments discharged from her urethra. After this, she remained practically healthy, with the exception of part of a cranium that, after almost four years, began to emerge between the opening of the urethra and the vulva. The services of another surgeon had to be enlisted to remove this last part. This circumstance provoked the author to pose two questions: first, he pondered how such things could have descended from the bladder instead of the interior orifice of the uterus; second, he wondered how it was possible that Feliciana had survived.

The author never clearly answered the first question. His lone conclusion was that the natural constitution or physical nature of a person could be very powerful. Quoting Aristotle, he stated that "Natura daemonia est" (77), which means that nature is demonic or filled with divine spirits. He added that further study was needed before such a complex phenomenon could be resolved. However, his discussion did suggest that by hitting her abdomen violently against a door, Feliciana might indeed have affected the development of the fetus. She appears not to have cooperated fully with the surgeons, as the author himself noted that she never divulged to them how long she had been pregnant. According to the information given, Feliciana's interest lay more in the relief of her pain than the well-being of her baby. She also was a single mother, and because of her youth, she was not able to completely understand the damage being inflicted upon her own body. Nevertheless, the author was able to answer his second question: Feliciana was able to survive because the body parts of the fetus had not been fully developed. Therefore, because of their diminutive size, they were too tender to cause any damage to her bladder. What seems to stand out in his dissertation is that during the four years the author treated and examined Feliciana, her body parts and anatomical constitution seemed more important than her proclaimed physical pain. A clear separation was made between her body and her persona, with the former also enduring objectification. Her body was viewed like a puzzle in which pieces needed specific rearrangements to make sense. Her abnormal body represented a sign of aberration and also fascination, a feeling overtly expressed when he stated: "Este es el maravilloso y raro fenómeno que observamos ahora doce años" (This is the marvelous and rare phenomenon that we have observed for twelve years) (5.147 [1792], 71). Similarly, he considered Feliciana's case to be an example of "the marvelous and mysterious works of Nature" ("las admirables y misteriosas obras de la Naturaleza") (5.149 [1792], 84). The final image of her body was that of a broken machine in need of proper examination. This was necessary for a diagnosis of the etiology of the problem as well as subsequent attempts at possible solutions in order to avoid any future monstrous births.

For modern readers, Feliciana's case raises question about the facts of her situation. Was it conceivable that her labor process lasted approximately four years? Was it possible to give birth solely to body parts and not an entire body? Was it feasible to give birth through the urinary canal? Was Feliciana's silence a product of a carefully executed hoax? Did Feliciana receive financial compensation for allowing the surgeons to use her body as an object of medical inquiries? It is difficult to answer these questions, given the lack of information the author provided, but previous and contemporary cases in Europe had shown that carefully planned frauds involving monstrous births were very common in the eighteenth century. Monetary motivations guided some of these hoaxes, as the indigent often collaborated with surgeons who were in search of money, fame, and notoriety. Animal parts and other objects were hidden in the vagina or other internal organs in order to simulate the direct birth of monstrous beings.[31] Extreme pain, blood hemorrhages, and infections were widespread consequences of such acts. Cases of children born boneless or with broken bones were also documented in Europe in the eighteenth century. We cannot be sure if Feliciana really gave birth to body parts; however, we can entertain the idea that her case might have been fabricated by herself or the surgeons. Nonetheless, her case served as an excuse for the surgeons to objectify and give meaning to the amazing power of her monstrous birth. It offered them the opportunity to illustrate the consequences confronted when female nature deviated from the norm. It also served as an excuse to examine the female body in order to question women's behavior and to suggest how they were responsible for the production of such abnormalities.

However, if up to the eighteenth century deformation of the fetus was blamed mainly on women's active imaginations, Francisco de Rebollar (another contributor to *Mercurio peruano*) offered his own version of the phenomenon. He firmly believed that women's sexual habits were the direct antecedent to the births of many deformed children. To prove this, in December 1793 Rebollar presented the case of a girl from Cotabamba named Maria Josepha Batallanos.[32] Because of her rural origins, as well as the author's reference to her mother as a rustic woman, one can assume that this is another case of a woman from the lower classes. The girl was born with horrendous red marks over her entire body. The blemishes on her feet almost appeared like ankle boots and the spots on her hands were like red gloves highlighted with white stria (lines) (see Figure 39). Only her chin, eyebrows, and a line similar to a ribbon from her nose partway up her head and from her neck to her navel was white and unmarked.

Rebollar immediately suggested that such an abnormality certainly developed in the fetal stage. Unable to obtain any information from the mother, who refused to disclose any facts related to her activities during pregnancy, or to state whether she was married, the author angrily proclaimed her ignorant. According to him,

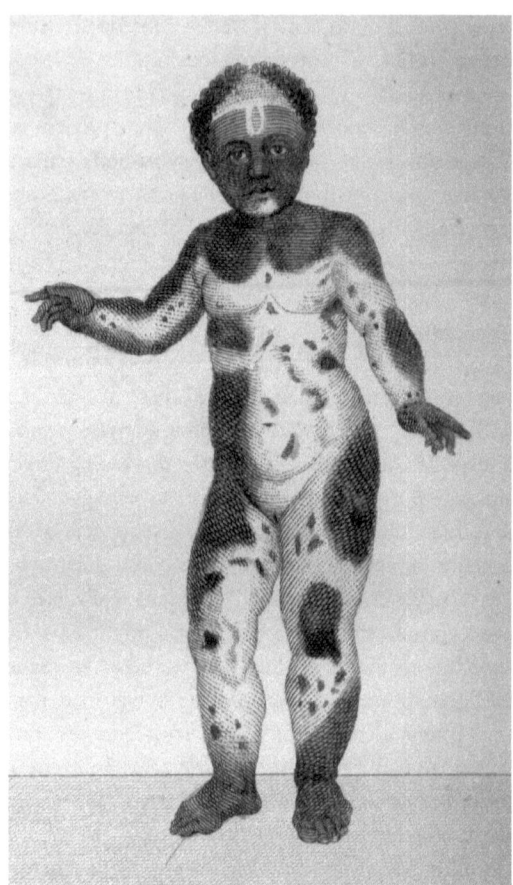

Figure 39. "Négre-pie." An illustration of a case of a female child born with white stria, similar to the one described in the *Mercurio peruano*. Georges Louis Leclerc, Comte de Buffon, *Histoire naturelle, générale et particulière*, 1785–1790. (Courtesy of Rare Book and Manuscript Library, University of Illinois.)

"in the end it is the tenacity, caprice, blush and fear" that cause women not to tell the truth (9.311 [1793], 268). The mother's refusal to disclose what he wanted to hear prompted his own conclusions. For Rebollar, this case would not be explained by ridiculous arguments made by poor and ignorant people, who claimed that such childbirths were the result of witnessing the devil bearing the face of a dog, or any other "illusory visions" ("visiones ilusorias") (9.311 [1793], 268). He went on to suggest two possibilities that could explain monstrous deformations in general: (1) venereal diseases suffered by the mother which affected the fetus; (2) the many concoctions ingested by women who did not want to have their babies.[33] Rebollar concluded that the cause of the child's red blemishes had been such concoctions.

The refusal to carry a baby to term was perceived by Rebollar as an awful moral act: "la composicion de brebages, ó pócimas que se hace, y se da á tomar á las mugeres que estando en cinta, pretenden librarse de tal incomodidad y sus resultas, *por un modo tan contrario á la naturaleza como pecaminoso*" (these women take an arrangement of drinks or concoctions while they are pregnant, trying to free themselves from the discomfort of pregnancy and its consequences, *through a manner so sinful and contrary to nature* (9.311 [1793], 281; emphasis mine). This passage offers an excellent example of how women's control over their own bodies was seen as dangerous and immoral. In the mind of Rebollar, the acts of women to contest nature and to transgress the norm were viewed as inexcusable, barbaric acts punishable by condemnation.[34]

Indeed, the author followed up by suggesting that the sexual practices of the mother were also to blame for the birth of such a monster. According to his scientific knowledge, a fetus would receive lymph from the mother, which if contaminated by venereal diseases could badly affect the child's development. Rebollar emphasized that venereal diseases could be transmitted to the fetus, thus affecting the development of bones. "The licentious life of the parents" was therefore blamed for the development of this disease, which questioned the type of sexual behavior the mother had engaged in when the child had been conceived (9.311 [1793], 279). That she was a single mother who did not share with the surgeons any information about her sexual partners made her an easy target of Rebollar's denunciations and scientific objectification.

It is interesting to note that Rebollar opposed the idea, very popular at the time, that the mother's imagination was to blame in cases involving skin coloration. Following Buffon's position on this issue, he maintained that the mother was still at fault because of the wrongful behavior of controlling her body.[35] Achromatism was perceived with horror by the author, as the girl's skin coloration came to represent a sign of deficiency. Improper pigmentation was considered abnormal because, according to eighteenth-century beliefs, "proper pigmentation," furnished by the male, was thought of as a symbol of "potency and life" (Stafford, 318). Cases that deviated from this norm were strictly the responsibility of the mother, as Rebollar has illustrated. The blemishes on the girl's skin were viewed as visual reminders of imperfection.

Rebollar's article emphasizes how the physical nature of female bodies dictated that they abide by rules that would facilitate the healthy and numerous reproduction of society. Transgressions were criticized through punitive discourses aimed to portray women as ignorant and substantially immoral. The author also adopted the position that "in the everyday indicative world, women and their bodies, in certain public framing, in certain public spaces, are always already transgressive—dangerous and in danger" (Russo, 323). In this case Rebollar inscribed his own beliefs and knowledge upon the mother's body, and made her an example of the negative consequences a child would suffer when a mother committed any wrongdoings. According to him, this type of behavior could in turn generate disorder within the social body. Recall that he began his article by stating that the news he was going to relate constituted "a good service to his homeland" ("en bien y servicio de la Patria") (9.311 [1793], 267). For Rebollar, these types of social monsters constituted a detriment to the progress of the kingdom. The phenomena of anatomical deformation and monstrous births served as an excuse to examine, judge, and define the female body. Deviance served to justify the pursuit of knowledge and intellectual capacity, as well as to empower men to categorize women's bodies.

Another article, published in the *Mercurio peruano* by the editors, concerned a disfigured girl. The authors stated that cases of human deformations (especially female) served as a source "de asombro al Pueblo, de exercicio á la piedad, y de materia á las reflexiones del Filósofo" (of astonishment to the People, as an exercise of piety, as a matter of reflection to the philosopher) (2.55 [1791], 197). Ironically, it was the abnormal female body that functioned as a male instrument of analysis for the extrapolation of what was to be considered normal. The news articles discussed here constitute examples of what Braidotti has called "normative discourse" that "requires difference as perjoration in order to erect the positivity of the norm" (64). At a time when upper-class women were becoming more visible in the public space, while lower-class women were crossing and transgressing numerous social boundaries in order to survive economically, medical texts became a type of antidote for the prevention of social disorder. In this context the female body projected an image of danger because of its perceived irregularity and difference.

Helen King reminds us that "medicine is never neutral" because it always "carries cultural values, including beliefs about the human body and about the roles and relative importance of different age/gender groups. It constructs its object in a dialogue with culture; before treating sickness, it is necessary to decide who is sick and who is not, what behavior is abnormal and what is normal" (114). The articles included in the *Mercurio peruano* clearly exemplify how normal behavior had to be defined in terms of the abnormal. Monsters and deformed children all became symbols of social malformation. Their bodies were constructed in these articles as "factories" in need of constant examination and repair. They symbolized what was aberrant in nature as well as dangerous for the social order. As was prevalent during the Enlightenment, the body became "a space of scientific endeavor," as well as a "site of medical experiment" (Livingstone, 73). In the case of women of African descent, the body was always in need of diagnosis, treatment, and cure.

Michael Palencia-Roth observes that "monstrosity need not to be overtly physiological; it may be moral, behavioral, or social" (35).[36] In the case of colonial Spanish America, monstrosity was an important issue in the histories written about the conquest of the so-called New World. The predominant view from the first encounter to the seventeenth century emphasized the moral and behavioral nature of monstrosity. At the time, chroniclers and historians such as Cristóbal Colón, Hernán Cortés, Pedro Cieza León, González de Oviedo, and Antonio de la Calancha, among others, mentioned the possibility that monstrous beings existed in the Americas. Some of these authors alluded to particular cases that came to their knowledge. In the eighteenth century discourses of monstrosity were integrated into political, philosophical, and scientific discussions about the need for useful citizens within a productive economy.

In the age of the Enlightenment, monstrosity began to be viewed from a scientific perspective. As the articles in the *Mercurio peruano* have illustrated, monstrous births became part of philosophical and scientific debates related to the specialized fields of anatomy and embryology. The monster was transferred "to the newly established institution of the anatomy clinic, where it could be analyzed in the context of the newly evolved practice of comparative anatomy and experimental biomedicine" (Braidotti, 71–72). The eighteenth-century search for an orderly conception of nature made the "monster" an enticing topic of research in cases of congenital malformations. The monster was studied not so much because of its marvelous or prodigious nature, as because of the need to explain how the anatomical constitution of the female body could have contributed to the monstrous birth. As we have noticed, the "new" epistemological search for a clear explanation of such phenomena did not break completely with the old tradition based on Aristotelian and Galenic presuppositions. However, for eighteenth-century scholars, birth defects and deformities were a reality that needed to be explained so problems could be corrected or prevented. In that sense, the female body, especially the internal organs, became the site of great speculation. From this speculation arose the science of teratology as we know it today.[37]

Susan Bordo observes that despite the many ways the body has been defined throughout history, "what remains the constant element throughout historical variation is the *construction* of the body as something apart from the true self (whether conceived as soul, mind, spirit, will, creativity, freedom . . .) and as undermining the best efforts of that self" (5). There is no doubt that the authors of the articles about monstrosity in the *Mercurio peruano* subscribed to this construction, which detached women from their bodies and left them to be seen merely in terms of their materiality and the function of their organs. Women were judged and defined by their anatomical constitution, which determined their character and behavior. In the end, the future and prosperity of society and the Peruvian nation wholly depended upon the economy of the female body and the avoidance of congenital malformations. This utilitarian vision of the body constituted for the authors of the newspaper articles, or, as they called themselves, "the real lovers of the homeland" ("verdaderos amantes de la Patria"), a key to understand the obstacles that could affect the kingdom of Peru in their search for progress.

## Anatomical Wonders: How Can Women Become Men?

The search for understanding the emergence of deviant citizens came along with a strong desire to standardize the female body. Medical discourse again worked as the tool par excellence to understand, explain, and "cure" those bodies. The bodies in their materiality always became the object of knowledge endowed, as Judith Butler reminds us, with cultural and historical meanings (521). As Butler adds, in this sense the body has been "an intentionally organized materiality . . . always an embodying of possibilities both conditioned and circumscribed by historical convention" (521). The philosophy of the Enlightenment, with its emphasis on progress, citizenship, reform, reason, and education, informed the historical context in which the contributors of the *Mercurio peruano* envisioned female bodies as signs of deviance.

In August 1792 Joseph Torpas de Ganarrila, surgeon and professor of medicine, published a dissertation entitled "En que se trata si una muger se puede convertir en un hombre" (In which the possibility of a woman becoming a man is discussed). This dissertation was prompted by a letter written by the archbishop of Granada, Doctor Don Juan Manuel de Moscoso y Peralta, and circulated in February 1792 throughout Lima as well as in a *papeleta* in Madrid.[38] The focus of the dissertation was a nun of New Granada who, after eighteen years in the convent, confessed to the bishop that she had become a man. The bishop consulted physicians who examined her body, agreeing that indeed, the nun had certainly become a man. According to Torpas de Ganarrila, cases such as this had been related since classical times; he cited Virgil, Jovian, Ovid, and Hippocrates, as well as contemporary scholars such as the Spanish physician Fragoso.[39] The author did not discuss in depth the validity of the arguments used by these authors, but rather summarized some of the most famous cases mentioned in their works.

Torpas de Ganarrila stated in a note that it was difficult for him to find a detailed account of the type of examination performed on this nun and the findings that had led physicians to believe that she had indeed been transformed into a man. He pointed out that the letter did not mention exactly when the episode had happened, which was a crucial piece of information because, as he had mentioned, the knowledge of human sexual nature in the eighteenth century had changed profoundly from the previous centuries.[40] Already in the seventeenth century "the body was no longer regarded as a microcosm of some larger order in which each bit of nature is positioned within layer upon layer of signification" (Laqueur, 10), but rather was understood as an epistemic object of study to help explain the sexual differences that separated a man from a woman. Women's bodies increasingly began to be seen and explained in terms of their reproductive organs (Laqueur, 149). That no one could tell Torpas de Ganarrila exactly when the event had happened prompted him to conclude that the archbishop, along with the physicians, were not conversant with the latest medical and scientific knowledge with regard to human anatomy.

To explain the possibility of this phenomenon, Torpas de Ganarrila listed three main anatomical features that distinguish a man from a woman: (1) the difference in the perineum; (2) the distinction in the urethra; and (3) the presence of the scrotum.[41] He emphasized that these three differences were key in analyzing such cases (5.167 [1792], 234). He added that the examination of the clitoris should also be required when studying these extraordinary cases of women who allegedly became men and vice versa. By carefully examining the human body, male authorities were able to clarify any confusion arising from gender deviations. According to him, most of these cases were the result of misinterpretations.

To prove his point, he documented cases in which women had been born with what anatomists believed was an abnormal clitoris—namely, cases in which the clitoris was too long. Citing examples that had been referred to him by his former professor, he mentioned the case of a black woman in Lima named Mariana, who was expelled from a monastery where she had worked as a servant because they had found her clitoris to be of extraordinary length. As was common practice at that time, surgeons as well as anatomists believed that the only cure to restore the normality of this organ was to cut the length of the clitoris, a painful surgery that was performed in this case, as well as in those of many other women who suffered the same problem. The female organs had to be transformed into what was believed to be the norm in terms of the anatomical features of the female body. Torpas de Ganarrila also mentioned two cases that he himself had witnessed: one of a six-year-old girl and another of a fifty-year-old woman who had been born with a clitoris that was three fingers long. Torpas de Ganarrila warned medical and religious authorities, as well as common people, that they should be extremely careful not to confuse these cases as evidence that a woman had been transformed into a man. It was imperative for them to understand that the length of the clitoris could not be confused with a penis, as the former lacked a urethra. According to him, the time had come to stop believing Galen's understanding of the anatomic body.[42] In Torpas de Ganarrila's own words:

> Por las pocas luces que ofrece el capitulo de la Papeleta citada me dispensan los lectores el que explaye algunas mas reflexiones en una material tan importante; pues aunque se asienta de plano que la Monja fué reconocida y examinada de facultativos por orden del Obispo, no se dice si esto sucedio en el mes de Diciembre del año pasado, ó en Enero de este, ni aun como se manifesto este fenomeno; o si en este siglo de las luces, por equivocacion de los Profesores se ha vuelto á renovar el engaño que padecieron en el siglo proximo pasado con la Monja de Ubeda y en el anterior con la de Madrid.

> [Because of the few reasons that the cited *papeleta* offers, I would ask the readers to excuse me for offering my thoughts on such an important subject; because it was stated that the nun was recognized and examined by the bishop, they do not explain if this happened in the month of December of last year or January of this year, nor do they explain how this phenomenon was manifested. It is also not explained if, in the age of Enlightenment, the same misunderstanding that happened last year with the nun of Ubeda and

two years ago with the nun from Madrid, because of an error of professors, has been repeated.] (5.168 [1792], 242)

Torpas de Ganarrila had known from the beginning that the case of the female nun transforming into a man was impossible. However, he did take the opportunity to correct the public as to what made the female anatomy defective. He obviously visualized the human body as endowed with specific organs that distinguished the sex and gender of each individual. Furthermore, he also believed it incumbent upon each body to display certain characteristics that would mark it as normal. If a female body did not display the proper anatomy conferred upon it, it was considered, as the author mentioned in his dissertation, "a bad composition" or "a regular deviation of nature" ("un regular desvio de la naturaleza") (5, nos. 167–68 [1792], 236, 240). In a search for a proper social order, female bodies were scrutinized to determine what was to be their assigned nature. The author subscribed to the position held by many medical theorists influenced by the philosophies of the Enlightenment, for whom "the body provided a solid foundation, a causal locus of the meaning of male or female" (Laqueur, 163). To this end, certain parts of the body were found to determine special differences. In the case of women's organs, such as the clitoris, this became a determining factor for their anatomical normality. As Torpas de Ganarrila explained, "El clitoris, que debe examinarse ante todas cosas para la mas cumplida y perfecta decision, segun todos los Anatomistas, es un cuerpo, cuya composicion es toda semejante á la del Pene, y no se diferencia de él mas que en que no tiene uretra" (The clitoris has to be examined with the most complete and perfect judgment; it is, according to all anatomists, a body whose composition is similar to the penis, and the only difference between them is that the penis does not have a urethra) (5.167 [1792], 235). Within this context, the female body became the receptacle of moral, social, scientific, and historical ideas that predisposed the difference of its nature.[43] The science of anatomy came to represent the field that would help to decipher this nature. It became, as Stafford suggests, "the basic science for surgeons" to explain the human body (49).[44] Nonetheless, this emphasis on the study of the human body was geared toward the understanding and expression of the body's utility. As Charles III made clear in his *Real Provisión* of 1777, medical students needed to study the "fabrica y mecanismo del cuerpo . . . la situación y naturaleza de todas sus partes, que es el asunto propio del catedrático de Anatomía, sin la cual no puede saberse ni practicarse la Medicina con el logro de su utilisimo fin" (makings and mechanism of the body . . . the condition and nature of all its parts is the proper subject of the professors of anatomy, and without the science of anatomy, one cannot practice medicine nor fulfill the object of its utility) (cited in Granjel, 16).

It is noteworthy that Torpas de Ganarrila also considered any attempt to transgress the laws of nature to be aberrant and monstrous. As an example, he referenced the case of a very young Roman emperor named Heliogabalus who, according to him, clandestinely engaged in sexual activities with other men while also inviting a group of physicians and surgeons to his palace to ask them if they could perform a type of surgery that would transform him into a woman: "*si podrian abrirle las carnes con los instrumentos de Cirugia para convertirse en muger*" (if they could open his flesh with surgical instruments so that he could become a woman) (5.168 [1792], 239; original emphasis). Fortunately, according to Torpas de Ganarrila, God punished his behavior when his vassals murdered him in a latrine at the age of twenty. That the author referred to the young emperor as a "monster of incontinence" ("monstruo de la incontinencia") underlined the disgust he felt for any human being who attempted to transgress their sexual nature and appetite (5.168 [1792], 239).[45] For a man, the desire to be female represented an aberration of nature. Torpas de Ganarrila made clear in his dissertation that the fixity of the body was crucial for good social order. His interest in the possibility of whether a woman could become a man, as he discussed in "En que se trata si una muger se puede convertir en un hombre," had to do with his intentions of prescribing the natural order of the female body, as well as the social body in general, based specifically on the notion of a normative anatomy. In this sense, the female body becomes a "text to be read—as inferior, sick or even monstrous" (Conboy et al., 8), especially when it did not conform to what was believed to be the norm.

Torpas de Ganarrila's particular reading of the female body centered on contemporary theories of anatomy that emphasized, as Laqueur observed, two structures of the body, one male and one female, underlining their sexual differences (157).[46] In a world economy in which a citizen came to be recognized for the productivity of his or her body, this emphasis on sexual difference and the normative body became a key factor in discussions related to good social order and progress. A body that did not subscribe to a determinate anatomy or structure came to be perceived as abnormal or monstrous; the body served as an excuse to explain the limitations as well as the possibilities of individuals within a determinate society. Science and medicine helped to explain the reasons for these phenomena, in which women seemed to embody the causes of corporeal disorder or monstrosity.

Haidt reminds us that if in the eighteenth century "reason" conditioned "the human capacity to know the world, the body [was] the instrument and origin of that light [of reason]" (185). This became the center of discussion when debating political, social, and cultural issues pertaining to the progress of the nation. The attempts to rationalize the body through "objective" observations during the Enlightenment rendered certain bodies targets of debates with regard to how a body should function within society. This was the case for women as well as for individuals of African or indigenous descent. Male intellectuals such as Torpas de Ganarrila, as well as other contributors to the *Mercurio peruano*, envisioned themselves as the authorities who were best qualified to explain to the rest of their *compatriotas* what constituted good social order. It is important to note that the news articles and dissertations published in this newspaper were aimed mainly toward a very specific public population: the upper-class white Creoles and Spaniards who constituted the powerful sector of the society. Within this sector, women represented a key group to whom they addressed many of the public debates published in the newspaper, in particular, those related to sexual reproduction and child rearing. The deviant bodies of the black population or women of lesser means were used as examples of what needed to be avoided, fixed, cured, and eliminated. As the selection of articles discussed here demonstrates, signs of difference and deviance were always a main concern for the contributors of the Peruvian newspaper, as deviance became a vehicle to illustrate the norm. This obsession with prescribing social rules that could enable upper-class women to understand the limitations of their own bodies became a central issue in articles addressed to pregnant women.

## The Female Body as a Machine

The desire to prescribe the behavior of female bodies is evidenced in another dissertation published in the *Mercurio peruano*, entitled "Disertacion primera en la que se proponen las reglas que deben observar las Mugeres en el tiempo de la preñez" (Treatise first proposing the rules that women should observe during pregnancy). The author, Joseph Erasistrato Suadel, published the first part of the article on June 5 and 9, 1791, while the second part was published in the format of a letter on December 25, 1791. These articles represent salient examples of the relationship that many intellectuals in the eighteenth century established between women's bodies and good social order. Bear in mind that this exposition was included in the news pertaining to "hygiene," which at the time referred to a branch of medicine whose objective was to preserve the health of individuals through the prevention of disease.[47] The author gave several reasons why it was critical to publish this type of information. In a letter accompanying the "Disertacion primera," he submitted that one of the ways in which the Academic Society of Lovers of the Country could contribute to the usefulness of its fellow citizens, as well as foster the real patriotism that guided the group as an academic society, was to publish articles in its newspaper specifically devoted to the problems confronting pregnant women: "Entre los cuidados con que una Sociedad de Amantes del Pais, puede contribuir a la utilidad de sus Conciudadanos, y acreditar el verdadero Patriotismo que la anima, merecen sin duda el primer lugar las reflexiones destinadas á impedir los daños que frequentemente acaecen a las Preñadas" (Within the news with which the Society of Lovers of the Country can contribute to the usefulness of the Fellow Citizens, and as a credit to the real Patriotism that encourages them, the news on how to avoid the harms that Pregnant Women suffer deserves special attention) (2.45 [1791], 87). That he capitalizes several key words in this passage underlines the intrinsic connections that many eighteenth-century intellectuals perceived between the progress of their homeland and the role of women within it.

As he pointed out, this type of news should occupy "first place" when it came time to determine what sorts of issues merited publication in its newspaper.

In his letter, Erasistrato Suadel regretted the number of women who had died in childbirth or were otherwise unable to fulfill the role God had bestowed on them. Their ignorance about their own bodies and the proper behavior during pregnancy, in his mind, contributed to failed pregnancies. As the author mentioned: ";Quantas personas del bello-sexo, capaces de fecundizar unas proles, *honor y lustre de su nacion*, han miserablemente pagado el feudo a la Parca; *o por un vicio irremediable se hallan ineptas para desempeñar el principal fin, á que el Supremo Autor las destino segun el orden natural*" (How many women, who are able to engender offspring who can become the *honor and luster of their nation*, have miserably paid their tribute to the Fates with their own lives; *or because of an irremediable vice have become inept to fulfill their main responsibility that the Supreme Author has given them in accordance with the order of Nature*) (2.45 [1791], 87; emphasis mine). For the author, procreation contributed to "the honor and splendor of the nation" and was to be considered women's primary natural responsibility. As Erasistrato Suadel highlights, women were assigned the greatest responsibility of all: the propagation of humanity and the foundation of the nation. Their main goal in society was to give birth to healthy babies who could eventually become useful citizens. Their contribution to the Peruvian nation or their patriotism depended upon the correct use of their bodies, which ultimately meant the successful birth of healthy children.

To fulfill their role within society, it was crucial for women to learn the appropriate ways to take care of their bodies. Because of their ignorance or lack of reason, it was essential for others to teach them and guide them in such tasks. Of course, male authorities in the field of medicine were thought to have the power and knowledge to prescribe women's behavior. Erasistrato Suadel made this clear when he commented: "No es menos propio de la prudencia y de la razon del hombre, corregir los males presentes, que precaver los futuros" (It is not less proper for man's prudence and reason to correct the present problems, and to prevent future ones) (2.45 [1791], 88). As had been the norm since classical times and still in the eighteenth century, philosophical and scientific investigations of women viewed them as "incapable of understanding general principles," as beings who acted "on the basis of desires and tastes" and who followed "the guide of the senses rather than that of reason" (Tuana, 82). Following this tradition, many of the authors of the news articles published in the *Mercurio peruano* aimed to teach the female population about how to behave during pregnancy. Those women who did not follow instructions would suffer the consequences of giving birth to horrendous creatures that would not and could not serve the nation's progress, as was the case for the Zamba who paid for her ignorance with her life. Prescribing women's conduct with regard to their bodies was viewed as a patriotic duty and sacrifice. As Erasistrato Suadel claimed: "Mi empleo, mi amor á la Patria, à las Ciencias, y à la

*Sociedad*, me ponen la pluma en la mano para presentar unas reglas de conducta à las Preñadas, por las que puedan evitar las desgracias enunciadas, si ellas fuesen bien admitidas" (My occupation, my love for the Homeland, for the Sciences, and for the *Society*, force me to take up the pen and with my hand present to Pregnant Women some rules of conduct, so that they may avoid misfortunes if they are well received) (2.45 [1791], 88). Homeland (Patria), Science (Ciencias), and Society (Sociedad), words common in the theories of the Enlightenment and key to the diverse processes of modernization around the world, became three key elements for the author to justify the reform of female citizens and the regulation of their own bodies. It is within the discursive frame of the homeland and science that the female bodies in the Peruvian newspaper would materialize. As Judovitz explains in a different context, these processes of the materialization of bodies were determined by the "conceptual and cultural frameworks" that made their construction and representation possible (3).[48]

The author began his treatise by placing all responsibility for disastrous pregnancies squarely on the mother. Yet he argued that women were not aware of the responsibilities they had to fulfill based on their sexual nature, and that through their own ignorance, they put the development of the fetus in grave danger. Women's "depraved appetites" had rendered them unable to control their own bodies, causing great harm to the fetus (2.45 [1791], 89). Erasistrato Suadel's public writing aimed to propose a set of rules for a female population unable to comprehend the repercussions of their own behavior. Writing became a fundamental regulatory activity that reconfirmed male power over women's bodies. According to him, the rules he aimed to propose would help to prevent any problem during pregnancy, consequently helping the nation to have "permanent heirs" ("sucesiones permanentes") as well as "fertile mothers" (Madres fecundas") (2.45 [1791], 89). With regard to successful population growth and the role of the mother in the production of healthy citizens, the author perceived the crucial need to propose "rules of conduct" and a "regimen" that would prevent abortive births.

Erasistrato Suadel identified two groups of pregnant women whose bodies reacted in two different ways, depending upon their conduct and their health. The first group he referred to as "hystericas debiles" ("weak hysterics"), who because of their sedentary lives suffered numerous tragic consequences in their pregnancies.[49] Their lack of appetite, symptoms of nausea, the irregular circulation of blood, and vomiting affected "all the internal organs of the body machine" ("todos los órganos de la maquina"), in many instances causing the death of the fetus (2.45 [1791], 90). The second group of women he referred to as "fuertes y robustas" ("strong and heavy"), who thanks to moderate exercise had maintained their internal organs and fluids in equilibrium. Their healthy "machine" (that is, body) helped the fetus to develop properly and successfully. Erasistrato Suadel viewed the female body as a machine that worked better when properly fixed and maintained. The materialization of the female body into an object enabled him to propose the proper measures to keep that machine working efficiently. Following the Cartesian notion of the body as a machine, the author saw it as having the potential to maximize its function. This Cartesian impulse to conceive of the body "as an anatomical, technological, and philosophical entity" witnessed the "anatomical redefinition of the body in terms of the circulation of blood, its technological resynthesis as a machine, and its philosophical reduction to a material thing" (Judovitz, 67). In the case of Erasistrato Suadel, it provided him with the opportunity to prescribe the female body according to particular cultural and historical circumstances that highlighted what he perceived to be Peruvian women's lack of knowledge regarding their own bodies.

The author considered the mother's diet a key factor in the government of women's bodies. He emphatically stated that "the responsibility of all women was to preserve the fetus, avoid miscarriage, and facilitate a natural delivery" ("Todo el objeto de la Madre debe dirigirse, como se ha dicho, á conservar su feto, precaver el aborto, y facilitar un parto natural") (2.45 [1791], 90–91). It was her obligation to contribute to society by fulfilling her role as a healthy mother. The author considered the mother's eating habits to be a crucial factor in avoiding miscarriages. He believed that special attention should be paid to the so-called *antojos* (cravings) that pregnant women often used to get what they wanted. Although he knew that some authorities had criticized the tendency to let women satisfy their "antojos," he found that it was better to avoid risking the pregnancy by denying them certain foods. He asked: "¿Pero aun quando asi fuera, la privacion de lo apetecido no puede causar tal *desorden en su maquina*, que facilite el aborto?" (But even if that is the case, can't the denial of appetites cause such *disorder in the bodily machine* that it ultimately leads to abortion?) (2.45 [1791], 91; emphasis mine). According to Erasistrato Suadel, "the field of physiology had already called attention to how easy it was to alter *the economy of the human body* because of the impression caused by a sensitive appetite" ("la Physiologia, explicando lo facil de alterarse, *la economia del cuerpo humano* por la impression del apetito sensitivo") (2.45 [1791], 91; emphasis mine). He also appealed to the work of Sir Richard Manningham (1690–1759), a physician and fellow of the Royal Society in London. In his manual *Artis obstetricariae compendium* (1739), devoted to the science of obstetrics and the anatomy of the female body, Manningham argued that it was better to allow women to eat foods they enjoyed rather than forcing them to consume healthy foods they despised, as this could affect their appetite and consequently the development of the fetus.[50] Coincidentally, Manningham also in his manual referred constantly to the female body as a machine and called for knowledge of the female anatomy in order to guarantee a successful pregnancy. Erasistrato Suadel followed Manningham's call to understand the female body as a machine in order to govern it better. This is exactly what Suadel meant when he referred to "the economy of the human body," with the allusion of the word *economy* to mean the notion of "disposition or arrangement" and the "system of rules and regulations" that controlled the body.[51]

Another key factor to facilitate the government of the female body during its pregnancy state was to understand what could be harmful with regard to women's dietary habits, the environment, and sleeping habits. The author defined "diet" ("dieta") as the proper use of elements that necessarily contributed to preserve health but were not considered natural. If wrongly organized, they could alter and destroy the human body (2.45 [1791], 91). Among those elements, he mentioned air, food and drink, sleep and wakefulness, movement and stillness, the passions of the soul and the excretions that passed and those that did not ("excreciones detenidas ó evacuadas"). He proceeded to briefly discuss the necessary precautions to be taken with each.

First, he cautioned pregnant woman to avoid close proximity to strong odors, as well as exposure to extreme heat or cold. He also claimed that being exposed to burned charcoal or breathing the smoke of a snuffed candle could contribute to abortion. It was important to always breathe pure air. With regard to food consumption, it was important for women to eat in moderation, as this allowed skinny women to retain what they ate and enabled heavier women to avoid premature labor. Certain foods were considered detrimental, such as those high in fat, those that produced flatulence, raw fruits and vegetables, meals containing lard, and especially any kind of chili peppers, which, according to him, were heavily consumed by women in Lima. He added a lengthy note explaining the health problems caused by consumption of peppers, such as intestinal ulcers, dysentery, strong headaches, and colics.[52]

Drinks were also to be consumed cautiously, with women avoiding those that were hot as well as the new popular drinks made with liquor and snow water ("agua de nieve"). According to Erasistrato Suadel, some of these beverages could cause issues with the uterus or cases of "hydropesia," or swelling caused by the retention of water. The author's recommendation was to simply drink clean and pure water to avoid affecting "the mechanics of the body" ("la mecanica del cuerpo") (2.45 [1791], 93). Not only did the consumption of water constitute a detriment to the pregnant body, but also bathing in rivers where the water was too cold, which could contribute to abortions, as extreme temperatures could cause convulsions or affect the circulation of blood. In sum, if women still insisted on bathing in the river, they were to avoid doing so at night, when it was extremely cold. In addition, they were to refrain from jumping abruptly into the water, were to stay in the water for only brief periods of time, and were to avoid swimming aimlessly.

Excess constituted a great preoccupation for the author, as he also stated that pregnant women should avoid oversleeping as well as not sleeping enough. Quoting Hippocrates, Erasistrato Suadel mentioned that excessive sleep affected blood circulation and produced "plethora" (excess of blood and humors in the body), while lack of sleep contributed to melancholy.[53] A similar problem occurred with excessive movement or lack of exercise, the latter more prominent in upper-class women, while the former affected women of lower social class. The "movimiento desordenado" (disorderly movement) constituted the main reason for abortion in lower sectors of the population, while "la quietud" (stillness) was said to affect the position of the uterus in upper-class women. He failed to offer any recommendations for the first group of women; however, he made certain to recommend moderate exercise for women of the upper class. His rules sought to impose orderly behavior and to regulate women's bodies so that they would accomplish their assigned goal in society: to procreate effectively. Women of the upper class seemed to be his targeted group; for him, that sector of the population represented a social status that would garner more pride for Peru. Conversely, women of lower strata, and especially those who had any African and indigenous ancestry, seemed to be more like experimental bodies, as they were used to justify biologically and medically the excesses and social disorders of congenital malformations. However, what remained clear was that women in general needed to be told how to control their own bodies for the well-being of the nation.

Erasistrato Suadel also pointed out that women in general were to avoid "the passions of the soul," such as anger and terror—the first because it would thin the liquids of the body, which would lead to abortion, and the second because it altered the nervous system as well as the soul, producing epileptic seizures that would contribute to the death of the fetus. For the author, the bad behavior of women could have a negative impact on the healthy function of their bodies. For example, he criticized women's dressing habits, in particular the use of corsets ("cotillas") because their extreme tightness in the upper body pressed the abdomen so severely that the expansion of the uterus was affected, causing frequent abortions or, at the very least, births of very weak babies. He called this fashion style "a depraved practice" ("depravada practica"), which deserved "the sternest punishments" ("los mayores castigos") (2.45 [1791], 94). The author's comments emphasized the crucial task of taming women's bodies and their concomitant corporeal behavior not only with the censorship of the pen but also with the suggestion of physical control. Such control, insisted the author, could be achieved by practical as well as legal means. Writing and legal impositions—two typically male activities at the time—would help to reconfirm male power over women's bodies.

Erasistrato Suadel's article demonstrates that the field of medicine was very much a male enterprise. What did not change from Hippocrates to Victorian times was that "women [were] sick, and men [wrote] their bodies" (King, 246). For Erasistrato Suadel, the female body epitomized a machine in need of maintenance, repair, and proper order. The economy of that body pointed to the need for constant organization and order. The guide he proposed for pregnant women aimed to keep that machine in order to ensure the development of healthy citizens. Within this context shaped by the philosophies of the Enlightenment, the female body functioned as an object to be scrutinized and prescribed specific actions, movements, and behavior for the sake of a good social order. As Margarita Eva Rodríguez García reminds us, a main goal of Enlightenment intellectuals in Spain as well in Spanish America was to invoke the importance of civilization and progress for the transformation of modern societies and public happiness (278–79). That goal was to be achieved via the manipulation of those bodies, central to the reproduction and preservation of its citizens.

Suadel published a second letter closely related to his first dissertation, covering the rules that women were to follow during pregnancy. This letter, which he called his "Carta segunda de Erasistrato Suadel relativa a las precauciones que debe observarse en los *Partos* en continuacion de las publicadas en el *Merc.* Num. 45" ("Second Letter of Erasistrato Suadel pertaining to the precautions that should be observed during Childbirth, a continuation of the news published in *Merc.* No. 45"), addressed the issue of midwives and the cautionary measures to be taken during delivery. He began this letter by stipulating that his goal was to preserve a "healthy body" and to examine those elements that could affect women's health (4.102 [1791], 291). For him, it was necessary to instruct those responsible for the successful birth of children. The midwife, or as he called her in Spanish the "partera," was this person. He acknowledged that "el arte de Partear" (the art of delivering a baby) was critical in many societies, as these women had the responsibility to facilitate the birth of healthy children. Citing the Bible, Hippocrates, and Galen, among others, he argued that dating back to classical times, midwives had been in charge of this task. According to him, not until 1663 in France did a trend develop to hire a "partero" (a man-midwife) to aid in deliveries. Other European countries followed the trend, although the great majority of deliveries continued to be handled by midwives except in difficult cases, when surgeons were asked to be present. However, he mentioned that the field of obstetrics was gaining in professional status in Europe at the time, and government authorities were controlling the participation of midwives, privileging male surgeons as the only people with the scientific knowledge to conduct this job. He immediately pointed out that Lima was lacking an adequate number of professional surgeons who could handle this need, causing many inexperienced women to be thrust into challenging cases of birth deliveries. As he stated, "Las parteras en Lima se apropian de este titulo, sin mas principios y reglas que una asistencia ciega, y sin mas conocimientos que los que ofrecen la experiencia propia, é inspeccion de otras" (The midwives in Lima appropriate that title for themselves, without any principles and rules other than a blind assistance, and without more knowledge than what the experience offers them and the manner in which they are observed by other midwives like them) (4.102 [1791], 294).

To understand the imperative nature of addressing midwives at this juncture, one must remember that in the eighteenth century the Spanish government, through the royal protomedicato, initiated a campaign to reform the medical field. As part of the Bourbon reforms and its "process of modernization," as Claudia Rosas Lauro calls it, the Spanish government aimed to regulate the medical field in the belief that physicians and surgeons needed to play a pivotal role in the correct functioning of society ("Madre solo hay una," 104, 120). In the context of this attempt to professionalize medicine, the Spanish government proceeded to examine the role of midwives and their heavy involvement in the process of childbirth. As the rate of child mortality was so high in Europe, as well as in the Americas, the Spanish government considered it crucial to address the role of those involved in the birthing process. As had been the case in Europe since the late seventeenth century, the attack on midwifery was also prompted by an interest of male intellectuals "to take over control of the potentially lucrative field of obstetrics" (King, 175).[54]

The author lamented the sad situation in Lima, where there was not a single well-prepared woman with the proper knowledge of female anatomy to better deliver a baby. He argued that it would be very beneficial for the crown to name an expert (that is, a surgeon) who could monitor and teach those interested in becoming midwives, while prohibiting the practice of those who refused to learn the art of obstetrics. He considered it crucial to avoid the frequent damages caused by "the ignorance of these midwives" (4.102 [1791], 294). To resolve this problem, he recommended the presence of male surgeons during delivery while limiting the role of midwives in the process, especially in cases in which the health of mother and child were in danger. Understanding that at the moment it was impossible to ban midwives from working, he opted to offer them a list of measures to be followed during the delivery of babies.

Erasistrato Suadel had three goals in mind when addressing midwives. First, he wished to denounce the ignorance so prevalent in this female sector of the society, stemming from their lack of knowledge about how the female body machine works. His second goal was to save mothers' lives by preparing midwives to safely deliver babies. His third and final objective was to "preserve children's lives" ("conservar los hijos") (4.102 [1791], 294). The female body again became the center of observation and experimentation; the better it was understood, the more successfully it could be treated and controlled. Childbirth had been a female enterprise, dating back to antiquity, as women had always given birth with the help of female relatives or midwives. In the eighteenth century, as Erasistrato Suadel's article demonstrates, the emphasis was on institutionalizing the process of childbirth by determining who would participate in it and how it would take place. The division between the supposed "normal" childbirth and complicated labors became the focus of intensive debates over who should be in charge of this task. The attack against midwives and the desire to reform their profession became the focus of many debates, always centering on the nature of the female body. With regard to complications fatal to the mother or child, such as breech presentation, twins, and prematurity, the presence of an expert was necessary since "a woman laboring alone [could not] manipulate her own body and the body of the child to facilitate a difficult birth" (Rich, 131). In these cases, a male authority figure, such as the surgeon, was needed. For Erasistrato Suadel, it was extremely important to instruct women who aimed to practice midwifery about the precautions to be taken when delivering babies. He felt it necessary that they be prevented from assisting in complicated childbirths, as these were to be reserved for male surgeons, considered far greater experts on female anatomy. Within this context, the figure of the physician or surgeon came to be perceived as the one who possessed science and experience—"an inseparable binomial" that united theory and practice to form a scientific knowledge useful to society (Rosas Lauro, "Madre solo hay una," 121).

In sum, Erasistrato Suadel's articles emphasize the notion of the female body as a machine. He perceived women anatomically and in terms of their corporeal functionality. Their bodies had to work perfectly, and as a result, the midwives were to be sure not to interfere with the natural process of that machine. Understanding the female body anatomically, as well as in terms of the function of its reproductive organs, constituted a critical step toward increasing the number of successful childbirths. Healthy children represented the ultimate goal of his deliberation and recommendations. To better achieve this, it was necessary to prescribe the proper procedures to follow for those involved in the process of childbirth. The process had to be controlled by medical authorities within the field of science, widely thought to have the superior intellectual knowledge to oversee female bodies. For Suadel, the bodies of pregnant women represented sites for medical reasoning. They were construed, as David Livingstone suggests in a different context, as "biologically fecund and ecologically risky" (2003). To avoid the risk of wasted fecundity, it was deemed crucial to establish a set of rules that would enable the healthy reproduction of future citizens. These rules had to be respected not only by pregnant women themselves, but also by those who had traditionally been in charge of the childbirth process: the midwives. Questions then arose, such as, what happened once that child was born? What needed to take place in order for that child to become a productive citizen? What obstacles would impede this process? Again, contributors to the *Mercurio peruano* found an excuse to use women's bodies as a means to address these preoccupations.

### *Amas de Leche* and Their Unruly Bodies

In January 1791 a man writing under the pseudonym Eustachio Phylomathes submitted two letters to the editors of the *Mercurio peruano* expressing his concerns about the dangerous behavior of the *amas de leche* (wet nurses) in the households of the colonial elite. Like the articles about women's responsibility for congenital malformations, these news articles expressed deep concerns held by a sector of the male Peruvian population toward the lower sectors, specifically women of African descent. However, in this case it was the body of the *amas de leche* that was used as the instrument to delve into issues of the education of healthy and productive citizens. Black wet nurses were perceived as disruptive and unruly bodies in need of containment and denunciation. Nevertheless, they were also regarded as individuals who played a major role in the education of Peru's future generations as well as the maintenance of class distinction and social recognition. Two letters published in the newspaper in 1791 that dealt with the wet nurses' social role in the private world of the colonial elites served as a podium to inform the public of the dangers of uncontrolled wet nurses in the domestic sphere.

The essential role wet nurses played in the cultural and economic world of Spanish American colonial society has not yet been fully studied, perhaps because documentation about the role of wet nurses in public and private spheres is not readily available. Nevertheless, wet nurses were very common in the Spanish American colonies, as their services were persistently needed to ensure the survival of the elite colonial offspring. Indeed, some newspapers in eighteenth-century Spanish America published occupational classified advertisements in which *amas de leche* were touted as profitable objects of commodity. For example, the *Diario de Lima* (1791) printed the following ads:

> Quien quiera comprar una Mulatilla de todos haceres, natural de Buenos Ayres, con un hijo de siete à ocho años, en cantidad de 450 pesos libres de Escritura y Alcavala, ocurra à la calle Plateros, donde Gregorio Palacios.
>
> [Whoever wants to buy a mulatto woman who has everything, who is a native of Buenos Aires with an eight-year-old son, for 450 pesos and free of contract and sales tax, go to Plateros Street, and contact Gregorio Palacios.] (May 18, 1791)
>
> *Ama de leche.* Quien quisiere una ama de leche entera, que es una Negrita de 18 annos, ocurra à la calle del pozo, N. 1055 en la casita del doctor Manzano.
>
> [Whoever wants a capable midwife, who is an eighteen-year-old black woman, go to Pozo Street, N. 1055, to the small house of Doctor Manzano.] (May 31, 1791)[55]

These advertisements illustrate the demand that existed in the colonies for this type of labor. It represented a profitable business for those involved in the process of selling, as well as a much-needed income for those who belonged to marginal sectors of the society. Historically, wet nursing has been perceived by lower sectors of the population as a well-paid occupation, especially when compared with the income earned by women in other jobs, such as washers, cleaners, cooks, or farmhands. At the time these ads were published, wet nursing had become a profitable market and an opportunity for social mobility.[56] Because in many countries, such as Spain, nursing until the age of three was required by law, the job served as a steady source of income for some women, while it fulfilled a need for others.[57] Unfortunately, the wet nurse's opportunity to earn a better income came at the expense of her body being controlled by those who held the power to dictate her services.

The constant preoccupation of the Spanish authorities with determining that a wet nurse was clean, honest, and free of any social deviance was illustrated in legislation and in printed manuals that specified the characteristics a good wet nurse ought to have. For example, Alfonso X (1221–1284), in the *Siete partidas*, strongly urged the public to find healthy and well-reputed wet nurses who would not compromise the upbringing of their children:

> E esto es en dar les amas sanas, e bien acostumbradas, e de buen linaje ca bien assi como el ninno se govierna, e se cria en el cuerpo de la madre sassta que nasce, otrosi se govierna y se cria del ama, desde que le da la teta, shasta que gela tuelle: e por que el tiempo dessta criança, es mas luengo, que el dela madre: non puede ser que non reciba mucho del contenente e de las cosstumbres del ama.
>
> [And it is important to hire healthy wet nurses with good manners and of good lineage because in the same manner that the child is sustained and reared in the body of the mother until he is born, he is sustained and reared from the breast of the wet nurse until he is weaned, and because the breastfeeding period is longer than the time the child spends in the mother's womb: it would be impossible for this child to not receive the disposition and customs of the wet nurse.] (Partida 2, tit. 7, law III)

In the eighteenth century, the negative consequences that could result from a bad wet nurse's upbringing of a child became a major issue of debate. As a result, the practice of wet nursing came to be questioned by scientists, medical practitioners, and philosophers. Their discussions revolved around the critical influence a wet nurse had upon the early development of a child. More specifically, male authorities were concerned that many children grew closer to those who fed them and nurtured them than to their own mothers. Because wet nurses generally belonged to lower sectors of society, many of these men saw danger in how children were inclined to learn wet nurses' cultural habits, language, and manners. Strongly influenced by Rousseau's *Emile* (1762), male intellectuals in Europe, as well as in the Americas, began to emphasize that the mother was the person best equipped to successfully nurse the child by setting a good example for her children.[58] As Valerie Fildes suggests, it was at this time that the notion of the family "as the ideal and natural environment in which to raise children" and of the mother as the ideal person in charge of raising her own offspring began to be idealized (111). Consequently, the paid wet nurse began to be seen as a disruption to the natural and social order. Jaime Bonells, a physician of the Duke of Alba, wrote the most popular Spanish book on this subject, published in 1786 and covering both the negative consequences that professional wet nurses could have on society and the refusal of mothers to breast-feed their own children. Bonells stated:

> Las calamidades que había de traer al Género Humano y al estado este notable trastorno del orden natural y civil, no pudieron ocultarse a la perspicacia de los sabios, los quales para atajar con tiempo sus progresos no han cesado desde el principio de declamar contra las madres que quebrantan tan expreso precepto de la naturaleza.[59]

> [The calamities that this remarkable disruption of the natural and civil order would bring to society and to the state were impossible to ignore by those learned men who, in order to stop the progress [of hiring wet nurses], have worked nonstop since the very beginning to denounce the mothers who break this very clear rule of nature.] (cited in Sarasúa, 179)

In the Spanish colonies an attempt was made in the eighteenth century to redefine the role of maternity within society. Subsequently, many male intellectuals were prompted to question the role of wet nurses in the domestic space (Rosas Lauro, "la visión ilustrada," 329). Such debates aimed to instruct noblewomen how to fulfill their obligations as responsible mothers. At the expense of the bodies of the wet nurses, the lives of noblewomen, as well as their social space, were being redefined. Spanish families that moved to the Americas continued the practice of hiring women from lower sectors of the population to work as wet nurses. As a result, in colonial Spanish America most wet nurses belonged to indigenous groups, as well as to black and other *casta* groups of African descent. In urban areas, most were of African descent, especially after the sixteenth century, when the black population increased throughout the colonies. This was the case in Lima, where by the end of the seventeenth century half the population was black or of African descent (Klarén, 100).[60]

Giving this racial sectoring, it was not a surprise when in January 1791 Eustachio Phylomathes offered the Peruvian public an example of the problems that the presence of an unruly wet nurse within a noble household could stir up. The letter, entitled "Carta escrita a la Sociedad sobre el abuso de que los hijos tuteen a sus padres" ("Letter written to the Society about the abuse of how children address their parents informally"),[61] was addressed to the members of the Academic Society of the Lovers of the Country. Phylomathes justified the publication of his letter within the *Mercurio peruano* by stating that the case he would expose should be the focus of serious consideration by his fellow countrymen. The editors published the letter to emphasize the implications of the situation presented by Phylomathes upon the social order and well-being of the Peruvian nation. The letter was going to unveil the danger in the intimate contact, so persistent in Lima, between elite children and *amas de leche*. Phylomathes joined the thinking of many intellectuals in the eighteenth century as they began to question the role of wet nurses during the formative years of children and in society in general.[62] His letters certainly fit well within the debates that had become so prevalent in Europe and in colonial Spanish America with regard to regulating the practice of wet nursing. These letters should be read in dialogue with the articles published by the Franciscan Juan Antonio Olavarrieta in his Peruvian newspaper *Semanario crítico*. In 1791 Olavarrieta delivered a scathing diatribe against the practice of wet nursing in Lima in an article that garnered many enemies and, as Premo mentions, earned him the nickname of "Fray de las Amas de Criar" (Friar of the Midwives) (*Children of the Father King*, 170).[63]

The first letter sent by Olavarrieta was a brief description of the many problems he encountered within his household after being absent for seven months while conducting business in Cuzco. Despite praising his wife for being a "beautiful and nice" woman, he added that she suffered from the same weaknesses that the rest of the female population inherently possessed. He did not elaborate on what those "prejuicios" (prejudices) entailed; however, after reading both letters one can extrapolate that he was referring to a lack of judgment that was characteristic of women, according to male philosophers since antiquity.[64]

Phylomathes mentioned that after hugging his children upon his return from Cuzco, he began to notice a change in their patterns of speech; they now referred to him with the pronoun *tú* instead of the more formal and socially required *usted*. He immediately questioned his wife about this unexpected and socially unacceptable practice. She responded by blaming the new habit on the children's contact with their grandmother, who had stayed with them while he was away. Yet she seemed unconcerned, since according to her, this form of parental address had become customary within many families in Lima. Phylomathes was unable to contain his indignation and proceeded to scold his children in the presence of his mother-in-law, whom he referred to sarcastically as Democracia. The mother-in-law retaliated with insults and undermined his authority by suggesting that his complaints were inconsequential. Phylomathes concluded his letter with a series of questions addressed to the editors of the newspaper: "¿Que idea tienen del respeto filial, y de la superioridad paterna? ¿Por que hemos de acostumbrar a los hijos à que hablen à su madre en el mismo tono que à su esclava, y à que no distingan à su padre de su calesero?" (What kind of idea do they have about filial respect, and about paternal superiority? Why should we accustom the children to addressing their mothers in the same manner as they address the slave, and to not distinguish their father from the driver of a calash? (1.5 [1791], 37–38). Finally, he wrote that he hoped his letter would prove beneficial to the public.

The answers to these questions were found in the second letter he sent to the editors, entitled "Amas de Leche. Segunda carta de Filomates sobre la educación" (Midwives. Second Letter about education from Phylomathes).[65] The letter, which was addressed to all members of the Academic Society of Lovers of the Country, delved into what he believed to be the real problem underlying his children's behavior. Indeed, the problem revolved around "who" was in charge of raising and educating the children, and the potential problems arising from such a relationship.

Phylomathes opened this second letter by expressing his newfound concerns about a current situation he was confronting at home with one of his children and the wet nurse. According to him, the letter was to serve as a benefit to his homeland, but it also allowed him to channel his frustration. Phylomathes related the case of the wet nurse, a "negra criolla" (Creole black woman) named María whom they had hired to nurse their daughter.[66] He stated that María had displayed exemplary behavior at the outset of her employment in the house, always obeying his wife and following the family's rules. However, upon his return from an absence of several months for one of his trips to Cuzco, he noticed a great change in the relationship that had developed between Clarisa (his daughter) and the *ama de leche*. He noted how the wet nurse "tuteaba" (addressed as "tú") Clarisa, while Clarisa called the wet nurse "mi mama" (my mama). What he found further disconcerting was how they slept, ate, and played together, to the extent that Clarisa ignored her siblings and even her own mother. The wet nurse had become such a powerful influence on his daughter that she was perceived to be a close member of the family. For the author and father, this perilous friendship was disrupting the sense of family that he had striven vigorously to promote and maintain.

Additional impetus for him to submit the letter came from what he had learned about the ubiquity of this type of behavior by *amas de leche* in Lima: "Yo bien se que lo mismo sucede con todas las amas de leche" (I know very well that this is the case with all the wet nurses in Lima) (1.8 [1791], 60). As a result, such behavior was affecting the character and education of children everywhere. According to him, such relationships were bestowing power upon the wet nurses, who in many cases perceived themselves as the most indispensable members of the household, even daring to give orders and demand respect. As a perfect example, Phylomathes offered his own experience with the wet nurse: "En efecto *Maria* es la que manda en casa: todos los criados la obedecen y la acatan mas que à mi mugger, y à mi mismo: hace lo que le da la gana" (In fact, María is the boss of the house: all the servants obey her and listen to her more than to my wife and myself: María does what she feels like doing) (1.8 [1791], 60). The situation was compounded when he tried to scold the wet nurse, and his wife and mother-in-law intervened in defense of María.

This passage demonstrates how María transgressed every rule that dictated the role of a wet nurse at the time. According to popular belief, a wet nurse was to be quiet, controlled, submissive, and obedient, but this stereotype did not align with María's behavior.[67] As described by Phylomathes, other servants and members of the household perceived her as a figure of authority. It was also obvious that she had gained the respect of his wife and mother-in-law, who had both defended her against his accusations. Rather than being subservient to others, María now had others answering to her. In Phylomathes's view, the typical perception of the wet nurse had taken a contradictory shape and temporarily turned the domestic world upside-down.

The most difficult task for Phylomathes was to convince his wife that María was endangering the social order of the family by stepping outside the domestic and social boundaries imposed on her. He could not understand why his daughter still remained under the care of a wet nurse, especially since she had "reached an age" ("grandecita") when the services of a wet nurse typically were no longer required. Instead, María was still the person taking the girl to public and private places, a problem exacerbated by the fact that many of these sites were deemed inappropriate for her social class. Such "dangerous" places included the kitchen, the washroom ("la[v]adero"), the streets, and the grocer's shop ("pulpería"), among others. The situation escalated as the wet nurse took the girl "wherever she wanted" ("adonde quiere") (1.8 [1791], 60). Phylomathes warned his wife and readers: "esta libertad de las amas de leche suele ser fatal à la inocencia de los niños que al compartir con la gente de esta ralea se familiarizan con sus modales groseros, y que aprenden y adoptan todas las llanezas que entre sí platican los esclavos" (this freedom of the wet nurses is detrimental to the children's innocence: when they share with these vulgar people, they become familiar with their rude manners, and they learn and adopt all the foolishness that the slaves talk about) (1.8 [1791], 60). He seemed to agree with critics such as Bonells, who a few years before had associated wet nursing with a social evil or, in his own words, "a disruption to the natural order" (cited in Sarasúa, 188).

The body and actions of the wet nurse invoked in this passage were viewed by the husband/father as signs of deviance and contagion. Clarisa's reputation and class upbringing seemed to be at stake because of the inability to control María's actions or "fatal freedom." The black servant embodied a sign of "evolutionary belatedness" that, in the words of Anne McClintock, was evidenced by the sustained colonial perception of the black woman's "lack of history, reason and proper domestic arrangements" (44). The dangerous sexuality that emanated from the wet nurse's body was also viewed by Phylomathes as a potential sign of corruption of the domestic order that he wanted so desperately to maintain. He warned his wife that a "good mother" should never allow her children to learn "the vulgar dances" taught by the black servants (1.8 [1791], 60). She, as a mother, was jeopardizing the future of her own children through her total disregard for the wet nurse's actions and behavior. His remarks served as a two-front attack, in which both women (the *ama* and his wife) were perceived as active contributors to social disorder. His letter aimed to provide, as an example to the rest of the Peruvian elite, news of the dangerous consequences that could arise from hiring wet nurses, both in the domestic world as well as subsequently for society.[68]

Phylomathes was also attempting to prevent his daughter from adopting the same attitude that had already taken hold of his wife: the acceptance of the notion that cultural contact with the black servant was the norm, rather than a sign of moral and social contamination, as he believed. He could barely fathom his wife's reaction to his exposition regarding the dangerous influence of María in their family household: "Asi se estila" (1.8 [1791], 60), which meant "that is the custom." His wife Teopiste viewed her *ama de leche* as a productive source of labor, enabling her to avoid some of the responsibilities expected of her as a mother. Teopiste also trusted María to the extent that she was allowed to become a valuable member of the household. This trust empowered María to make certain decisions that were considered inappropriate by the head of the household. In this case, it was the body of the "negra criolla" that ultimately and literally enabled the freedom of the white Creole woman. However, it was the opinion of the husband that with wet nurses, race as a social factor that implied color, as well as its relationship with the notions of local hierarchies such as *"casta, limpieza,* and *estado,"* was perceived as a polluted element in society (Hill, *Hierarchy, Commerce, and Fraud,* 198).[69] For him, wet nurses had to be eradicated because of their potential to bring social disorder and create unproductive citizens.

Premo suggests that the letters printed in the *Mercurio peruano* on the practice of wet nursing during the eighteenth century resulted from "a coalescing image of creoles as racially degraded and politically stunted" (*Children of the Father King,* 169).[70] That many white Creole children were being nursed by women of African descent contributed to the idea that sucking milk from these women affected the intellect of children. Coupled with a lack of proper education at home, the effect created a deteriorating social order, as these children were not becoming useful citizens. At the same time, the figure of the father was being questioned, as he was losing control of his household. Rosas Lauro echoes these ideas when she argues that the discourse on wet nursing addresses the issue of maternity and the role of women in society as it was being envisioned by intellectuals and male authorities at the time. As she observes, this debate delineated and established the boundaries between public and private space within the tenets of the Enlightenment, for which private space was considered the space for women ("La visión ilustrada" 313). Both positions, Premo's and Rosas Lauro's, are important in understanding the reasons for the publication of the letters. However, it is equally relevant to focus on how the wet nurse as a social body was being constructed to denounce social disorder. It is also noteworthy that owing to the wet nurse, the white Creole woman was able to move freely outside the domestic space. Ironically, the space that should have socially separated these women in the end brought them together. Elizabeth Grosz observes that the body is always "inscribed, marked, engraved by social pressures external to [it]" (*Volatile Bodies,* x). In the case of Phylomathes, the body of the wet nurse is socially constituted by her skin color, her social status, and cultural stereotypes popular at the time.[71]

It is revealing to examine the two notes written by the editors of the *Mercurio peruano* justifying the publication of Phylomathes's letter. The first note emphasized that this type of reflection would benefit not only Lima, but also "all Peru and the rest of America" (1.8 [1791], 62). In the second note, the editors warned the readers that everything published in the *Mercurio peruano* was for the well-being of "their homeland" (1.8 [1791], 64). One must remember that Phylomathes was not denying the importance of employing *amas de leche* for the subsistence of children at an early stage. Rather, he maintained that husbands, as heads of household, had to guarantee the preservation of social order by maintaining those who were subject to their power in subaltern positions. He argued that the role of wet nurses was to be a temporary one. This would also help guarantee that wives and mothers would take on more responsibilities after the wet nurse had fulfilled her services. Legislation passed in 1794 by the Spanish king also emphasized the negative consequences that would occur if children were kept under the care of wet nurses until the age of six and seven, and how it would impede the successful formative education of the child. According to the king, keeping the children for so long with wet nurses represented a loss to the state (Premo, "'Misunderstood Love,'" 240).[72] Indeed, for Phylomathes, early education needed to be in the hands of the parents and not delegated to those who, because of class and racial attributes, had the potential to contaminate the much sought-after purity of the social order. As Ann Laura Stoler has suggested, "strict surveillance of domestic servants" has always been "one way to protect children" from moral contamination (154–55). María's body, along with the bodies of many other wet nurses who populated Lima, represented a type of infection that was affecting healthy domestic spaces. Because private space and public space had always been connected (Lefebvre, 166), Phylomathes perceived this issue as one that ought to be a national concern, because of the social repercussions it could have throughout the rest of society.[73] The healthy preservation of order within the elites' domestic spaces was at stake, with the hope of achieving this by controlling those deviant bodies.

Within this context the body of the black woman was perceived as an ambivalent object, always oscillating between demand and repulsion, the wanted and the unwanted.[74] Because ambiguity had always been a danger sign in colonial discourse, it was crucial to contain and control what seemed to represent a potential sign of disorder. For Phylomathes, the successful control of this social body would have helped guarantee domestic order, reputation, and the incorruptibility of the country. Within this context, the wet nurse herself, as well as his wife's reaction to the situation, came to represent "that dangerous zone[s] against which culture must struggle to retain itself" (Kaplan, 43).[75] Ultimately, it was the husband who needed to take control of the situation by restoring order to the domestic space. Social, gender, and racial order had to be maintained at all times within and outside the confines of the domestic world. Phylomathes seemed to suggest that the time had come to reconsider the role that *amas de leche* were playing in the lives and social spaces of the Peruvian elite, as it was intrinsically related to the education of future generations. In Phylomathes's own words, what was needed was "the entire reform of his family" ("la entera reforma de mi familia") (1.8 [1791], 62). For this reform to happen, the bodies of the wet nurses as well as the wives had to be monitored and controlled. Phylomathes's letters contributed to the apologetic discourse on domestic maternity that had already begun in Europe since the mid-eighteenth century.[76] From this point on, the image of the nurturing mother as a guardian of the home became a vital part of discourses on nation formation, while the image of the salaried wet nurse as a deviant body became solidified in the minds of those in charge of controlling them.

## Female Bodies of the Enlightenment

This chapter has demonstrated how questions of the body in the *Mercurio peruano* were framed within the philosophical precepts of the Enlightenment, specifically the use of science as a vital tool to understanding the functioning of society and the production of healthy citizens. On one hand, female bodies worked as experimental objects of knowledge, to be consumed for social, scientific, and political purposes. On the other hand, female bodies also constituted a cultural medium through which to achieve domestic and social order. Scientific reasoning reduced these bodies to sites of observation and speculation, and prescribed behaviors that helped explain what was considered to be deviant or outside the norm. The monstrosity of the female black body, children born with congenital malformations and deemed as monsters, the abnormality of the female body that could at times cause gender confusion, the pregnant body, and the body of the wet nurses all constituted expressions of social anxiety as well as scientific pretexts to explain perceived obstacles to ideal social order. Thus, the discursive appropriation of the female bodies functioned as an exercise of correction. Furthermore, systematic and disciplined observation, a principle of the Enlightenment (Edney, 191), constituted the means by which those bodies were to make sense within the parameters of good social order and human progress. Within this context female bodies served as an excuse for critical reasoning.

Chris Philo argues that when understanding the Enlightenment as a cultural and geographical process, we should not mistakenly conceive it only as an "age of reason." Rather, we should also devote particular attention to the many "sites of unreason" that made the Enlightenment such a complicated process (373). For Philo, the sites of reason coexisted with those of unreason, the first pointing to those "well-lit places of the Enlightenment from and through which its intellectual, artistic, and architectural brilliance was put together," while the second always entailed "the despised and darkened places which in effect marked an underside of the Enlightenment" (373). Following Philo's remarks, I argue that in the *Mercurio peruano*, the bodies of black women or women of African descent could be considered constituents of those sites of unreason that male intellectuals chose as pertinent to demonstrate what impeded progress and social order.[77] This explained why their bodies were perceived as monstrous or prone to the conception of monsters, becoming subsequently sites of experimentation.

The Academy of the Society of Lovers of the Country and its discursive organ, the *Mercurio peruano*, epitomized those privileged sites of reason that thought to posses the critical tools to contain those other spaces, which carried within them uncertainty, anxiety, and fear. For the authors of these newspaper articles, the body was conceived in its material form and viewed as culturally inscribed within gender and racial parameters. In the context of the *Mercurio peruano*, to view the body as a monstrous incarnation, an anatomical wonder, or a machine thus implied viewing the body as a utilitarian tool to legitimize social order and to foster reform. Within this context of cultural and social reform centered on Enlightenment views of medicine, female bodies became cultural pretexts to dictate a male point of view on the manner in which those bodies were to be read and understood.

# Epilogue

# Prescribing Bodies

In an article entitled "Discurso sobre el destino que debe darse a la gente vaga que tiene Lima" ("Discourse on the use that ought to be given to the indolent people in Lima"), Joseph Ignacio Lequanda, minister and accountant of the Royal Treasury of Lima, denounced the rampant idleness of many sectors of the population of the capital city as a "political disease" needing to be cured (*Mercurio peruano* 10.326 [1794], 122). According to the author, those visible bodies in the streets of Lima contributed to economic ruin, social disorder, and backwardness. Lequanda referred to them as "a pernicious body of indolent people" ("cuerpo pernicioso de araganes") that, like a moth's larvae ("polilla"), callously destroy everything with which they come in contact (10.326 [1794], 112).[1] For the author, it was crucial to target these bodies in an effort to stop them from "eating away the healthy part" of society ("para que no carcoma la parte sana") (10.326 [1794], 112). Lequanda argued that "this disease" could only be cured through the intervention of "a skillful doctor who not only is able to apply the antidote but knows how to apply it slowly and with reason" ("un doctor diestro que no solo applique el antidoto, sino que sepa aplicarlo lentamente y con cordura") (10.326 [1794], 123). Of course, Lequanda presented himself as that skillful doctor who would offer the appropriate remedy to cure this "political disease."

The author suggested that judges, ecclesiastical authorities, and politicians should be involved in the process of eliminating "this disease," as it represented an ailment that affected all sectors of the population, including both men and women. Lequanda also noted that this disease affected not only Lima, but other provinces of the Viceroyalty of Peru as well. He even argued that indigenous revolts that took place in Peru in the 1780s (including that of Túpac Amaru) gained their strength in part thanks to the many indolent Indians who "wanting to occupy the ancient seat of honor of their Inca emperors," joined the insurrections ("queriendo ocupar el antiguo sitial de sus antiguos Emperadores Incas"). As a matter of political and social stability in the capital as well as in the provinces, indolent bodies needed to be reformed and integrated into a productive economy. Lequanda's suggestion was to assign them jobs based on their gender and physical ability, but jobs that would benefit the economy of the Peruvian capital. The development of mechanical and liberal arts, as well as agriculture, the mining industry, and commerce, would depend upon the inclusion of those indolent bodies in the work force. In the case of women, Lequanda argued that because of their innate weakness ("sexo debil"), they should be closely monitored by delegating tasks appropriate to their gender. With the exception of those who suffered physical disabilities—who should instead be locked away in hospices ("hospicios")—every "body" should be transformed into a useful one as they would then contribute to the "good order" of society ("buen orden").

Lequanda's article touched on the importance of the body as a vehicle to understand and explain society. The works discussed in this book demonstrate that useful and deviant bodies became synonymous with useful and deviant citizens.[2] If all bodies required examination, it was always the female body that deserved more surveillance and guidance. The four different types of body analyzed here—the political body, the economically productive body, the religious body, and the scientific body—all offer examples of how bodies are read and constructed within particular political agendas. The documents examined emphasize the notion that women as citizens or "permanent member[s] of the community" constituted an integral part of the ordering of society (Herzog, 55). In this process of redefining women's role, the body became "an object of reflection" and "intervention," making all bodies, including disabled bodies, subject to rationalization (Grosz, *Space, Time, and Perversion*, 2).

In the case of Micaela Bastidas, her body was constructed as an instrument of fear by the Spanish authorities, who felt the need to contain her through the economy of violence and punishment. But for Micaela, her body became in itself a powerful tool to challenge the colonial system, although that challenge fell short once the colonial authorities captured the leaders of the insurrection. The rhetoric of fear and violence that characterized the death sentence imposed on her, principally the manner in which the colonial authorities used her body as a type of legible text during her public execution, demonstrated the importance of the body as a political tool, and the manner in which deviant bodies were considered symbols of disorder.

In *Truxillo del Perú*, Martínez Compañón underscored the importance of visual images as powerful rhetorical tools, necessary to the construction of specific female cultural identities. For Martínez Compañón, factors of class, race, social economy, and cultural habits became elements used to categorize female social groups within the colonial system as well as to visually determine their place in society. As a result, female bodies in Martínez Compañón's work were read according to his own process of classification, which was informed by the Enlightenment's views pertaining to the creation of productive citizens. The gaze functioned in his text as a "central vantage point from which surveillance or looking occurs" (Carrera, 19). Martínez Compañón viewed women as integral to economic development and to the social order of the Viceroyalty.

The archival endeavor of María Josefa de la Santísima Trinidad went hand in hand with the articulation of a local sense of national identity that promoted her monastery as an exemplary religious model worthy of being followed by future generations. In Sor María Josefa's project, the body functioned as a crucial rhetorical tool to illustrate the prestigious nature of an institution whose religiosity made it one of a kind. For this nun, the reconstruction of a glorious religious past was deeply couched in the construction of the body as a sign of religious and cultural legitimacy. The materiality of these bodies is evident in the symptomatic nature of the diseases these women suffered and the repercussion of the manner in which they understood their own bodies in relationship to their fervent religiosity. Sor María Josefa considered the institution of the monastery to be a model of virtue that had the potential to instill good values in Peruvian citizens, a view that coincided with what the contributors of the *Mercurio peruano* had to say about the monastery.

Scientific news articles published in the Peruvian newspaper by its Creole contributors underscore the need to examine the defects as well as the limitations of the female body, especially those bodies of African descent, in order to determine the proper rules to be prescribed for them to become useful constituents of the nation's progress. Disabled and dangerous bodies, incarnated in the figure of the monster and the wet nurse, respectively, embodied deviance, anxiety, and disorder. That these bodies belonged to women of African descent emphasizes the importance that racial hierarchies held in the construction of social order. The "growing realization of the relationship between knowledge and incipient patriotism," so prevalent in the eighteenth century (Stolley, 367), played a key role in stipulating the corporeal behavior of women. The rules prescribed to upper-class pregnant women were a result of the desire to make sure that they gave birth to healthy children who would later become productive leaders. The utilitarian construction of the body and its emphasis on useful and healthy citizens anticipated nineteenth-century formulations of the mother figure within the public and private sphere. Those bodies subsequently came to be considered responsible for the well-being of the citizens of the homeland. Healthy bodies equated order and progress.

Dalia Judovitz describes the body "as an always provisional construction, grounded in changing worldviews that entail different understandings of representation, subjectivity, and identity" (3). The works discussed in this book emphasize how the construction of the female body was affected by the local positionality of colonial administrative authorities, insurrectionist and religious women, and Creole intellectuals who were actively engaged in the political, economic, religious, and scientific changes taking place in the Viceroyalty of Peru in the late eighteenth century. Representations of the female body in these texts attest to the attitudes of individuals who, from different localities, thought they had a solution to these problems.

Government authorities, such as the ones prosecuting Micaela Bastidas, saw the necessity to exterminate disorderly bodies such as hers in order to restore peace, tranquility, and order to the peripheral zones of the Viceroyalty. Meanwhile, colonial administrators, such as Martínez Compañón, visualized the presence of useful and orderly bodies ready to contribute to the state's economy in other peripheral territories. Sor María Josefa de la Santísima Trinidad's construction of the exemplary religious body responded to the economic crisis that religious institutions such as hers witnessed in the late eighteenth century, when the Bourbon government was trying to diminish the power of the Catholic Church in their dominions. The representation of female religious bodies obeyed a patriotic desire to illustrate the prestigious nature of an institution in which sanctity and religiosity functioned as positive examples for Peruvian citizens, especially women. Patriotism also guided the contributors of the *Mercurio peruano*, who envisioned themselves as in charge of proposing to cure the diseases that threatened the progress of their homeland. As doctors and patriots, they sought in those female bodies the explanations for Peru's maladies. By transforming those bodies into objects of reason, this group of learned Creole men set out to propose the rules that would reform women's bodies so they could contribute to the healthy progress of the nation.

In sum, the body as a "site of governance" is a recurrent theme in all the works analyzed here (Fraser and Greco, 28). The possibility that a body could be objectified, diagnosed, and reformed for the well-being of society emphasized the idea that the body could regulate society once the deviant bodies were controlled or eliminated. The textual and visual representations of female colonial bodies allow us to think how, in eighteenth-century Peru, cultural classifications were formed and political and religious views were constructed for the sake of social order and maintenance of the status quo. Prescribing and assigning the behavior of those bodies proved to be crucial not only for colonial authorities, but also for those whose love for the *patria* made them the real connoisseurs of their own social problems and undeniable cultural prestige. The compatibility between the empirical attitude toward knowledge, Spanish Catholicism, Bourbon centralism, and patriotic fervor present in eighteenth-century cultural production in Peru made of the female social body an instrument of knowledge and a vital part of the formation of healthy and productive citizens. This task proved to be an ever-present concern for future national projects in post-Independence Peru.

# Notes

INTRODUCTION

1. All translations from Spanish into English are my own unless otherwise specified.
2. The concept of the nation used here refers to the place of origin or an ethnic entity. It also implies the population of a particular province, country, or kingdom. Nevertheless, in the eighteenth century the word *nation* also entailed a racial, cultural, and linguistic unity "that connected a group of people" (Mazzotti, 144). In this sense, as Tamar Herzog suggests, "the nation" implied a sense of community rooted in linguistic and ethnic commonalities (1–2).
3. By "Peru," I refer to the Viceroyalty of Peru, which until 1776 comprised what is today Peru, Bolivia, Chile, Argentina, Uruguay, and Paraguay. When it was established in the early 1540s, the Viceroyalty of Peru included Panama and the entire South American continent except a small part of Venezuela. In 1776, with the creation of the Viceroyalty of La Plata, what today is Argentina, Bolivia, Paraguay, and Uruguay ceased to be under the jurisdiction of the Viceroyalty of Peru.
4. The complete title of the book is *Embodying Enlightenment: Knowing the Body in Eighteenth-Century Spanish Literature and Culture* (1998). Haidt examines how ideas about the male body informed the literature and culture of Spain at the time.
5. Garcés relies heavily on *Discipline and Punish* by Michel Foucault, and specifically examines the legal trials that took place in Tucumán and Jujuy, dealing mostly with male suspects. According to him, cases of delinquent women were very scarce and generally amounted to accusations of witchcraft (102).
6. By "hierarchies of power," I refer to the dominion that particular legal, religious, and scientific authorities had in their respective fields, a dominion established by a belief in rank or order. I also follow Ruth Hill's definition of hierarchy as a "norm of inequality" that could be written—in the case of constitutions, edicts, or rules—or could be "unwritten" and related to a "hierarchy of values," such as customs, assumptions, and stereotypes (*Hierarchy, Commerce, and Fraud*, 197).
7. Other studies, such as Mario Cesareo's *Cruzados, mártires y beatos: Emplazamientos del cuerpo colonial* (1995), examine the representation of the male body in the early colonial period to argue that for religious authors, the body represented a symbolic and instrumental space from which to impose their religious practices and ideologies on the colonial population (21). In a more recent book, *El discurso colonial en textos novohispanos: Espacio, cuerpo y poder* (2008), Sergio Rivera-Ayala discusses how in early narratives of conquest, the European image of the male body functioned for Europeans and their hegemonic enterprise as a way to define and dominate Amerindian bodies and the spaces they occupied (5). These books represent important contributions to thinking about the body as an entity subject to social control

and surveillance. However, most of them have focused on the male body rather than the female. Two important contributions focus on the significance of the body in cultures that do not conform exclusively to Western ideologies of the body, such as indigenous cultures before the arrival of Spaniards in the Americas. The first, *Inca Cosmology and the Human Body* by Constance Classen (1993), offers an in-depth study of the interrelation between cosmology and the human body in Inca culture. According to Classen, the body functioned for Inca society as a vital instrument to understand and order its world. In the case of Mexico, Alfredo López Austin has studied the interpretation of the human body in Nahua culture before the arrival of the Spaniards. His book, *Cuerpo humano e ideología: Las concepciones de los antiguos nahuas*, demonstrates the correspondence between cosmogony, political organization, and corporal division in a society in which, for example, eating part of the body had specific social functions.

8. Some of the most important historians who have contributed to the understanding of this time period as it pertains to Peru are David Brading, Kathryn Burns, Jorge Cañizares-Esguerra, John R. Fisher, Bernard Lavallé, Scarlett O'Phelan Godoy, Bianca Premo, Margarita Eva Rodríguez-García, Claudia Rosas-Lauro, Steve Stern, Ann Twinam, Rubén Vargas Ugarte, Charles F. Walker, and David J. Weber. See Works Cited.
9. The Seven Years' War (1754–1763) between Spain and Great Britain resulted in the Treaty of Paris in 1763, whereby Spain relinquished Florida to Britain while obtaining New Orleans and French Louisiana. Spain also regained Havana.
10. For an outstanding collection that touches on multiple aspects of the Bourbon reforms in Peru, see *El Perú en el siglo XVIII. La era borbónica*, edited by Scarlett O'Phelan Godoy (1999).
11. The treaty imposed the need for Spanish American colonies to import more products from Spain while also increasing the export of raw materials (Mazzeo, 128).
12. Callao, as John R. Fisher argues, still represented an important commercial point especially when it came to silver export; however, it now had to compete with other ports such as Buenos Aires and Montevideo that could supply cheaper European goods to the southern provinces of Peru (62).
13. The *repartimiento* refers to "the allocation of an Indian chieftain and his people to a Spaniard to provide labor" (Burkholder and Johnson, 360). *Mita* was a word used in Peru for forced labor draft, and *corregidor* referred to "a magistrate and chief executive office for a provincial jurisdiction" (Burkholder and Johnson, 358).
14. After the insurrection ended, the Spanish authorities promoted a good number of indigenous *kurakas* of Indian nobility to Spanish military positions. These royalist *caciques*, as O'Phelan Godoy refers to them, viewed these promotions as a mechanism of social advancement and potential political control over nonelite Indians (277).
15. In this study, symbol refers to representation. This type of representation can be arbitrary depending on the context from which it emerged.
16. Within the context of my discussion, modernity refers to "institutions and modes of behavior" connected to the development of an industrialized world and to the notion that "the key to human progress and social order is objective knowledge of the world through scientific exploration and rational thinking" (Lupton, 6). It assumes, as Deborah Lupton suggests, "that the social and natural worlds follow laws that may be measured, calculated and therefore predicted" (6). Modernity is then understood as characteristic of Enlightenment thinking and the subsequent globalization that emerged from the multiple debates and exchanges of the late seventeenth and eighteenth centuries. For Aníbal Quijano, modernity refers to "the ideas of newness, the

advanced, the rational-scientific, the secular" and as a phenomenon is "possible in all cultures and historical epochs" (543).
17. Michel Foucault has referred to the biological assessments of the body as the manner in which the body has been seen historically as "the seat of needs and appetites, as the locus of physiological processes and metabolism, [and] as a target for the attacks of germs and viruses" (*Discipline and Punish*, 25).
18. One of the most prevalent metaphoric uses of the body up to the eighteenth century was the organic conception of the state as a body (Barkan, 62). In this metaphor, the sovereign functions as the head; the Senate constitutes the heart, eyes, and ears; the governors or judges of the provinces are the tongue; the financial officers are embodied in the stomach and intestines; and the rest of the population make up the feet of that organic body (Barkan, 73). Other metaphoric interpretations of the body are the Platonic notion of the body as tomb of the soul, the body as the temple of the Holy Spirit as elaborated by Saint Paul, and the body as the enemy of the soul as developed by Saint Teresa de Avila (Synnott, 4).
19. As Kristine Ibsen points out, Spain and Spanish America shared the association, well documented in Western society, of the woman with "the body, carnality, and sinfulness." As "inherently transgressive," the woman's body was viewed by male authorities as in need of constant surveillance (1).
20. By "sign" I refer to the arbitrary association between an image and the meaning of the image. I emphasize the multiple ideas with which the body is associated by those in charge of its discursive constructions. For a detailed explanation of the concept of sign, see *Columbia Dictionary of Modern Literary and Cultural Criticism*, edited by Joseph Childress and Gary Hentzi (1995).
21. According to Tamar Herzog, already by the mid-seventeenth century there was no distinction in colonial Spanish America "between the rights of citizens and noncitizens" (55). Herzog explains that there was not any formal legal process or declaration that individuals followed to become citizens or act as citizens (5). He also reminds us not to confuse the concept of citizen with *vecindad*. In the eighteenth century *vecindad* referred to "a wide range of fiscal, economic, political, social, and symbolic benefits in return for the fulfillment of certain duties" (Herzog 6). *Vecindad* also implied a social and cultural distinction.

CHAPTER I

1. *Corregidores* were magistrates and chief administrative officers of particular provincial jurisdictions (Burkholder and Johnson, 358).
2. Most of the documents quoted in this chapter with regard to Túpac Amaru's uprising and Micaela's role therein come from *La rebelión de Túpac Amaru* in *Colección Documental de la Independencia del Perú*, ed. Carlos Daniel Valcárcel, vol. 2, hereafter cited as *CDIP* with page number. Valcárcel has compiled all documents pertaining to the insurrection into four volumes as part of the document collection honoring Peru's independence.
3. After the first battle won by Túpac Amaru in Sangarará, the indigenous rebels left the naked bodies of the Spanish enemies exposed in the field. According to Jan Szeminski, their decision was also dictated by Andean criminal law, which established that "criminals guilty of evil" did not deserve burial (170).
4. Some critics who have mentioned the importance of Micaela Bastidas as a crucial figure in the Túpac Amaru insurrection are Barrionuevo (1976); Bolo Hidalgo (1976);

Campbell, "Women and the Great Rebellion in Peru, 1780–83" (1985); Cornejo Bouroncle (1949); and Loayza (1945). However, their studies mainly point out the importance of her role as an active participant in the insurrection. They do not conduct a close reading of the legal documents addressed to or authored by Micaela.

5. The greatest tactical disagreement between Micaela and her husband stemmed from her insistence that Túpac Amaru needed to attack Cuzco first and then continue with his attack in southern Peru. He opposed the suggestion, and when he finally decided to attack Cuzco, it was too late. His brother's help failed to arrive in time, and the city did not respond as he thought it would. This failed attempt contributed to his final defeat in Tinta (Glave, 15). According to Charles W. Walker, Túpac Amaru's delay in attacking Cuzco was because "his intent was to extend territorial control and prevent a counterattack from the south before he confronted the bulk of the Spanish forces in the key city of Cuzco" (*Smoldering Ashes*, 45). For more information on the Túpac Amaru insurrection see the work of Steve Stern (1987), Charles F. Walker (1999, 2001), Kenneth J. Andrien (2001), David Garret (2005), Daniel Valcárcel (1973), Oscar Cornblit (1995), and Scarlett O'Phelan (1988).

6. For a specific discussion of this topic, see Meléndez, "La dimensión discursiva."

7. Bordo follows Mary Douglas's argument that the body is a powerful symbolic form. For Douglas, the function of the different body parts "and their relation afford a source of symbols for other complex structures" (142).

8. The number of letters she wrote between November 1780 and March 1781 was nineteen (Guardia, 70).

9. According to Jean Delemeau, the clinic definition of fear appeals to "a shocking emotion" that is often preceded by surprise caused by the individual's acknowledgment that he or she is in imminent danger (9).

10. As Alan Hyde argues, one must not forget the "materiality" of the bodies and the fact that bodies exist in a real world (7). In the case of Micaela Bastidas, the body has a human face, one that is marked by suffering, violence, and pain.

11. Stern refers more specifically to the years between 1742 and 1782 (35).

12. Two other women actively involved in the insurrection were the *cacica* Tomasa Titu Condemayta and Cecilia Túpac Amaru, who were also sentenced by the Spanish authorities. Tomasa was sentenced to death by garroting, while Cecilia was ordered to receive two hundred lashes while walking in the public streets of Cuzco. The participation of women in the peasant rebellions was due in part to the effect that the Bourbons reforms had on the indigenous household unit. According to Leon G. Campbell, these reforms forced many males to conduct labor services in the silver mines (*mita*), leaving women to participate in the peasant rebellions as soldiers, or even as military commanders ("Women and the Great Rebellion in Peru, 1780–83," 167).

13. As mentioned in note 2, most of the primary documents of the insurrection trials come from *CDIP*. However, other mandates of *salvoconductos* come from Francisco A. Loayza's edition, *Mártires y heroinas. Documentos inéditos del año de 1780 a 1782*, hereafter cited as *MHDI*.

14. Micaela's birth certificate has never been found, and most of her biographical information is based on legal documents related to the insurrection trials. For more general information on Micaela's biography, see the work of Alfonsina Barrionuevo (1976), José Antonio Busto Duthurburu (1981), Salomón Bolo Hidalgo (1976); Cornejo Bouroncle (1949); and especially Juan José Vega (1969) and Luis Miguel Glave (1982). For purposes of my discussion, I will refer to Micaela as *mestiza*.

15. I will discuss specific examples in the following sections.

16. The account is entitled, "Relación del más horrendo atentado que cometió José Gabriel Túpac Amaru, Cacique de Pampamarca en la persona del Corregidor de Tinta, jurisdicción del obispado del Cuzco: y otros graves delitos que executó" (Account of the most horrendous attempt that José Gabriel Túpac Amaru, Cacique of Pampamarca, committed against the person of the *Corregidor* of Tinta, jurisdiction of the Archbishopric of Cuzco: and other grave crimes that he committed) (*CDIP*, 252). I will elaborate on the concept of monster in Chapter 4.
17. The exact definition is "birth or generation contrary to the normal order of nature" and "[b]y extension that which is extremely large or extraordinary" and "that which is exceedingly ugly or deformed" (598–99).
18. It is important to bear in mind that many of the confessions of those who once collaborated with the insurrection were the result of torture, humiliation, threats, and offers by the Spanish authorities. For more on this, see Barrionuevo, *Habla Micaela*.
19. As Silvia Arze, Magdalena Cajías, and Ximena Medinaceli observe, the legal documents written against women involved in the eighteenth-century Andean insurrections were drafted by official and masculine voices, men who held an elitist and gender bias against women in society (13–14).
20. *Lessa majestad* refers to crimes and offenses against the king or the state. Carlos Aguirre and Ricardo D. Salvatore observe that Spanish law codes, such as *Siete partidas* (1251–1265) and the *Recopilación de las Leyes de Indias* (1680), "outlived the period of colonial administration" and were still in place into the second half of the nineteenth century (3). Carlos Alberto Garcés has also studied the role of the *Siete partidas* in the practices of corporal punishment in eighteenth-century colonial Spanish America. Garcés explains that the type of public spectacles organized for corporal punishments followed the structure of the *Siete partidas* in terms of public participation in the ceremony (22).
21. It is important to understand that some of the former *escribanos* became witnesses for the royal authorities, as the officials offered them immunity if they testified against Micaela and Túpac Amaru. Some of the eventual witnesses were also physically threatened by the colonial authorities if they failed to testify against the rebels (Barrionuevo, 119).
22. According to the authorities' reaction to Micaela's confession, they did not believe anything she said. They stated that she had had many opportunities to leave the insurrection and escape her husband, especially when he was "in remote regions" away from her (*CDIP*, 730). They also contended that her followers were so afraid of her and so obedient that she had all the freedom to escape without obstacles. However, despite these chances, she had opted to be heavily involved in the insurrection.
23. Robin is referring to the definition of fear given by Hobbes in his works, *The Elements of Law: Natural and Politic* (1640), *De Cive* (1642), and *Leviathan* (1651).
24. Micaela sent this letter on December 10, 1780, from Tungasuca.
25. In the same letter sent to Túpac Amaru on December 6, 1780, one can note Micaela's lack of patience with his manner of proceeding with the insurrection. She reproached him, stating that he had not paid attention to her recommendations and that if the insurrection failed, he was solely to blame. She warned him: "Todo esto te lo prevengo, como que me duele; pero si tú quieres nuestra ruina, puedes echarte a dormir, como tuviste el desahogo de pasearte solo por las calles del pueblo de Yauri . . . Tú me ofreciste cumplir tu palabra, pero desde ahora no he de dar crédito a tus ofrecimientos, pues me has faltado a tu palabra . . . Bastante advertencias te di para que inmediatamente fueses al Cuzco pero has dado todas a la barata, dándole tiempo para que se prevengan" (I warn you about all of this, though it hurts me; yet if you want

our ruin, you can go ahead and sleep, since you already had the audacity to stroll through the streets of the town of Yauri . . . You promised me you would keep your word, but from now on I will not give credence to your assurances, since you have broken your word . . . I gave you plenty of counsel so that you would go immediately to Cuzco, but you have made short shrift of it all, giving them [the enemy] enough time to prepare themselves") (*MHDI*, 50–51).

26. *Carne* was understood at the time as the corporeal matter of every animal as well as human being, including the nerves, bones, and the rest of the components that made up the body (*Diccionario de autoridades*, 184). It was viewed in contraposition to the soul.
27. Fraser and Greco define *somatization* as the expression of suffering in bodily terms (22). The critics refer in particular to the work of Bryan Turner, for whom society expresses itself in somatic terms. For him, a "somatic society" is "a society where our major, political and moral problems are expressed through the conduit of the human body" (quoted in Fraser and Greco, 2).
28. *Webster's Universal Dictionary* described the garrote as "a mode of punishment in Spain, by strangulation, the victim being placed on a stool with a post behind, to which is affixed an iron collar with a screw; this collar is made to clasp the neck of the criminal, and is drawn tighter by means of the screw, until life becomes extinct" (706). The violent punishment was also used in Rome during ancient times and since the Middle Ages in Portugal.
29. According to Pieter Spierenburg, from medieval times "executions were dramatized in order to serve a sort of morality play" (43).
30. Women were usually hanged and men were garroted or decapitated.
31. We cannot forget, as Walker explains, that in the case of colonial Spanish America "the legal system buttressed social and racial distinctions while also providing the means for groups to soften or question these hierarchies. It constituted a contact zone or 'contested terrain' in which the rules of colonialism were imposed yet at the same time contested" ("Crime in the Time of the Great Fear," 36).
32. In Cecilia's trial, she denied the charges and confessed that she was accused only because she had at times visited Túpac Amaru's house (*CDIP*, 758). She also stated that the only reason she was on the Piccho Hill on the day of the insurrection was for fear of Micaela, who she claimed had forced her to be there, despite proofs to the contrary. She even denied that she was a real cousin of Túpac Amaru, alleging that her real name was Cecilia Escalera.
33. It is not clear whether Cecilia was truly exiled to Mexico. Her death certificate, signed by the rector priest of the Cathedral of Cuzco, stated that Cecilia died on April 19, 1783, of natural causes while imprisoned in what had once been the quarters of the Jesuits in Cuzco and since 1767 had functioned as a jail (*CDIP*, 1765).
34. Like the other female participant in the insurrection, Tomasa also denied the charges, confessing that she had helped Micaela and Túpac Amaru because of the pressure she was under from the Indians of her jurisdiction, who had begged her to financially support the insurrection (*CDIP*, 742). She even accused Túpac Amaru of burning some of her property when she refused to help (*CDIP*, 742). She finally confessed that she indeed had participated in the insurrection, out of fear of what Túpac Amaru could have done to her (*CDIP*, 743).
35. By *Leyes de Castilla*, the prosecutor referred to the legal corpus compiled by Alfonso X (1221–1284) in his three legal works: *Fuero Real* (1254), *Espéculo* (1255–1260), and *Siete Partidas*.

36. The significance of the plaza as an exemplary place in which the readings of the bodies and the punishment took place will be discussed later in the chapter.
37. Mitchell B. Merback contends that "the very idea of punishments enacted as a form of spectacle is predicated on the belief in their educative potential" and the ability to emit "cautionary tales" and "brutalizing threats of violent retribution" (135).
38. Micaela's lawyer asked for a lesser punishment for her. He argued that because of Micaela's gender, she should be exiled to Africa rather than executed. The Spanish authorities rejected the request.
39. Mitchell B. Merback suggests that through the spectacle of punishment, the body becomes fully legible to the eyes of those who witness it (102). He refers to the case of medieval and Renaissance Europe.
40. An anonymous witness to the execution referred to it as a "function" ("función"; see *CDIP*, 775), perceiving it as part of a formal ceremony or social occasion.
41. One of the most common metaphors depicted the king as head of the state.
42. Mazzio adds that in early modern anatomical texts, philosophical treatises, and conducts, "the mouth is positioned as a war zone, with tongue and teeth locked in perennial combat" (67).
43. For a lengthy discussion of the relevance of body parts and the human body as an image of the world in Western culture from Plato to the Renaissance, see Leonard Barkan, *Nature's Work of Art: The Human Body as an Image of the World* (New Haven, CT: Yale University Press, 1975). Later in the chapter, I will discuss how the execution, the partitioning of the body, and the body parts themselves might have been interpreted by the indigenous population who witnessed the spectacle of death.
44. To erase the memory of everything related to Micaela was one of the authorities' major objectives. As the prosecutor in charge of the case stated in one of the trial documents, the government ordered: "Que igualmente sea demolida la casa que tiene en Tungasuca y todas las demás posesiones que tuviere; y que en adelante no haya de erigirse ni edificarse casa de habitación de ninguna persona, para perpetua memoria e infamia suya; y que así mismo sea extinguida toda su descendencia hasta el cuarto grado" (That her house in Tungasuca also be demolished along with all the possessions she might have; and that no other house be built there with the intention to perpetuate her memory and infamy; and that also all her descendants to the fourth generation be eradicated) (*CDIP*, 727). Ironically, these events did not erase the memory of the insurrection. As Sara Castro-Klarén states, although the execution of Túpac Amaru and his wife ended with "the physical disappearance of the bodies," it did not erase the "link with the past of the nation as a set of indivisible biological and cultural relations in space and time" (177).
45. The nine prisoners were José Verdejo (one of the main commanders of the insurrection), Andrés Castelo (one of the colonels of the insurrection), Antonio Oblitas (a *zambo* who executed the *corregidor* Arriaga), Antonio Bastidas (brother of Micaela), Francisco Túpac Amaru (uncle of Túpac Amaru), Tomasa Condeymata (*cacica* of Acos), Hipólito Túpac Amaru (oldest son of Túpac Amaru and Micaela), Micaela Bastidas, and José Gabriel Condorcanqui (alias Túpac Amaru). The first four were simply hanged. For Francisco and Hipólito, the executioners cut out their tongues before hanging them. As mentioned earlier, Tomasa was garroted on a special platform in which the iron wheel was placed. Hipólito was hanged before his parents, followed by his mother and finally his father, Túpac Amaru. The witness described the death of Túpac Amaru as a "spectacle that had never been seen in this city" ("espectáculo que jamás se había visto en esta ciudad") (*CDIP*, 775). Túpac Amaru,

after witnessing the death of his family members, was released from his shackles and handcuffs. His legs and arms were bound to the girths of four different horses. Four *mestizos* were in charge of pulling from each horse trying to dismember his body. When they proved unable to do so, and after the *visitador* Areche experienced "compassion," he ordered this torment to stop and had the executioner instead cut Túpac Amaru's head off. The rest of the body was transferred to the gallows, where it was dismembered along with that of his wife.

46. The document reads: "Lo cual se publicará por bando en cada provincia, para que deshagan ó entreguen á sus corregidores cuantas vestiduras hubiese en ellas de esta clase, como igualmente todas las pinturas ó retratos de sus Incas en que abundan con extremo en las casas de los indios que se tienen por nobles, para sostener ó jactarse de su descendencia. Las cuales se borrarán indefectiblemente" (This shall be made known by proclamation in every province, so they can surrender or give to their *corregidores* all the indigenous clothing of this type, and, in like manner, all the paintings and portraits of their Incas which are so prevalent in the houses of the indigenous who deem themselves members of the nobility in order to claim and boast about their [Incan] ancestors. All these artifacts will be inexorably eradicated) (*CDIP*, 771). In the same document, Areche proposed to establish more schools that would force the Indians to learn the Spanish language, Spanish law, and how to dress as Spaniards. According to him, this would help the Indians to "get rid of the hatred they have conceived against the Spaniards" ("para que estos indios se despeguen del odio que han concebido contra los españoles") (*CDIP*, 772).
47. For a detailed analysis of the metaphorical use of the body in Inca culture, especially the role of Cuzco as the navel of the empire, as elaborated by the Inca Garcilaso, see Classen, 98–112.
48. *Del Señorío de los Incas* was the second part of Cieza's *Crónica del Peru* and was published posthumously in 1880. The first part of the *Crónica* was published in 1553. *Tercero libro de las guerras civiles del Perú* was considered the third part of the *Crónica* but was not published until 1877.
49. Garcilaso describes these women as having been chosen by the Inca. He adds that they lived in a place similar to a convent. The Inca chose them for their pure Inca lineage or for their beauty, and they were thereby to remain virgins. They served as wives of the Sun. For a more detailed description of these women, see *Comentarios reales*, Book 4, chapters 1 and 2, pp. 139–41.
50. Garcilaso claimed that the harsh punishments imposed by the Inca rulers were necessary in order "to extirpate the evils from the Republic" ("extirpar los males de la república") (69). Garcilaso added that by imposing severe punishments such as death, they would teach people to abhor death and to love life (69). For Garcilaso, fear of death kept society in order; a similar argument was proposed by Hobbes years later in his work *Leviathan*.
51. The English translation of Cobo comes from *History of the Inca Empire,* trans. Roland Hamilton, 202.
52. Kinsbruner observes that as vertical cities, the central plazas represented one of the most important sites of the Inca cities (21). For as a spatial description of Cuzco in its vertical nature, see Inca Garcilaso Book 7, chapter 8, 289–93.
53. The festival was organized to celebrate the period of harvesting and to honor the Sun, the *huacas,* and shrines of Cuzco (McCormack, 75). It was also a special event to give thanks for the past harvest and to pray for future ones (McCormack, 75). For a description of the festival, according to the Inca Garcilaso, see *Comentarios reales*, Book VI, chapter 20, 248–49.

54. In the case of the main plaza of Cuzco, it was divided into two parts, one devoted to ceremonial events and the other to secular activities (Kinsbruner, 21).
55. According to the *corregidor* of Puno, Joaquín de Orellana, the Indians of Chucuyto committed the most horrendous crimes against Spanish women, such as beheading them and exhibiting their heads as prizes (*CDIP*, 627). He adds that "el que ha visto *el espectáculo de la Plaza,* el camino y las orillas de la Laguna cubiertas de cuerpos muertos, no puede explicar sin dolor suceso tan lamentable" (he who has seen *the spectacle of the Plaza,* the path to the Lagoon and its shores covered with dead bodies, is unable to describe without grief such a deplorable scene) (*CDIP*, 627).
56. My use of the term *contact zone* invokes the now well-known concept developed by Mary Louise Pratt, which refers to "the space in which peoples geographically and historically separated come into contact with each other and establish ongoing relations, usually involving conditions of coercion, radical inequality, and intractable conflict" (6).
57. For an outstanding discussion of how different types of violence were used against all those involved in the insurrection, including Indians, *mestizos,* Creoles, Spaniards, and priests, see O'Phelan Godoy, *La gran rebelión en los Andes,* 105–37.
58. Kelly and Von Mücke argue that knowledge of the eighteenth century is crucial to an understanding of the cultural activities that are informed by how the body is represented and consequently how corporeality "can be thought of in the critique of culture" (1–2).
59. "Hideously evil" and "greatly malformed" are two elements of the traditional definitions of *monster.*
60. For the Andean society, Micaela's role in the insurrection could have constituted part of the "gender complementarity" that dominated their world (Silverblatt, xxvii). According to Irene Silverblatt, the contributions of women to society were manifold (cooking, harvesting, child rearing, preparing fields for cultivation), which is why "in the eyes of Andean men and women, their complementary activities were essential to the reproduction of the Andean society" (10). One can take a closer look into the familial way that Túpac Amaru organized the rebellion, calling himself the father and Micaela the mother. The remaining commanders (who were mostly relatives) were regarded as sons and daughters of Túpac Amaru and Micaela. After the Incas solidified their power over other societies, the ideal of Andean manhood began to emerge as the dominant ideology.

CHAPTER 2

1. Later in the chapter I will discuss the distribution of these illustrations on the basis of gender.
2. For detailed information on muses and their specific attributes, see Hall, 217.
3. Paula Findlen focuses her study of the museum on the formation of a scientific culture in early modern Italy, where the museum came to be considered as the "repository of the collective imagination of their society" (9).
4. By "symbolic goods" Bourdieu refers to "any set of symbolic objects," including clothing, literary works, plants, statues, decorations, and paints (32). These symbolic objects tend to possess a commercial or material value given to them by those who own or control them. He includes the museums as institutions that tried to preserve the accumulation of symbolic objects.
5. Within this context, one can view the act of reordering things in a museum, as Tony

Bennett suggests, "as an event that was simultaneously epistemic and governmental" (*Birth of the Museum*, 33).

6. Rolena Adorno refers specifically to the work of the indigenous writer Felipe Guaman Poma de Ayala, *Nueva corónica y buen gobierno* (1615).
7. Most of this synopsis of the biography of Martínez Compañón derives from the works of Matilde López Serrano, Daniel Restrepo Manrique, and Manuel Gabrois Ballesteros, and from documents found in the Biblioteca Nacional de Colombia.
8. The Archbishopric of Trujillo was founded in 1616. Miguel Feijoo in 1763 comments on the "fertility of the fields and valleys" in Trujillo (12). According to him, "it is impossible to translate into writing the report based on the eyes. I will never be able to offer an exact account of the fertility of these Valleys" ("que es imposible trasladar a la pluma el informe de los ojos, nunca podre dar punctual razon de la fertilidad de estos Valles') (12). In 1766, Cosme Bueno also described the territories as endowed with fertile and abundant valleys where many agricultural goods could be produced (50). However, he also pointed out that the then-current economic decline in the territory was due to two strong earthquakes, one in 1725 and another in 1759, that had left the entire infrastructure in ruins. In 1793 Joseph Ignacio Lequanda also emphasized the great attributes of these lands. According to him, the lands were "tan fecundas y dóciles que sin mas beneficio que el romperlas con el arado siembran los granos, y colocan los plantios, logrando asi los frutos a que aspiran" (the lands are so fertile and docile that by merely breaking them with the plow the grains are planted, and the fields are readied, achieving instantly the fruits they desire) (91).
9. The Archbishopric of Trujillo was composed of twelve provinces: Cajamarca, Chachapoyas, Chillaos, Huamachuco, Lamas, Luya, Moyobamba, Piura, Saña, Trujillo, and the territories of Cholones and Hivitos. The city of Trujillo is located in northwestern Peru.
10. Historian Susan Ramírez of Texas Tech University is in the process of publishing a compilation of records written by Martínez Compañón pertaining to his pastoral visits, including notes, letters, and detailed records. The collection will be published by Pontificia Universidad Católica del Peru Press (personal communication). Daniel Restrepo Manrique, *La Iglesia de Trujillo (Peru)*, has already published some of the correspondence between Martínez Compañón and colonial authorities of Lima and Trujillo, while the priest held the position of bishop between 1778–1790.
11. However, it is important to remember that Spain's interest in collecting material information about its territories had certainly been present since the sixteenth century. As Antonio Barrera observes, already in 1527 the crown issued a decree expanding its "information-gathering activities to cover natural history" (44). However, this process came to a halt when Spain devoted all its attention to religious matters occurring in Europe between the Protestants and Rome (Barrera, 45). In contrast, Paula S. de Vos argues that the "institutional base for imperial science" had its origins in the late seventeenth century with the establishment of the Royal Chemical Laboratory and the Royal Pharmacy in 1695 (60).
12. For a detailed discussion of the search for and collecting of curiosities in the Spanish empire, see De Vos, "The Rare, the Singular, and the Extraordinary."
13. De Vos mentions three different institutions that were established by the Bourbon regime for the collection of "natural and artificial curiosities": The Royal and Public Library (1715), the House of Geography and Natural History (1752), and the Natural History Cabinet (1771).
14. As Marchena adds, many dispositions were sent to the viceroys, governors, *intendentes*, and presidents of the High Court, requesting them to gather systematic infor-

mation about every aspect of human and natural history (155). This information was to be sent to Madrid and other political centers to be studied and accessed. For example, in 1784, after the indigenous insurrections that took place in the Andes, the king decreed another royal order demanding specific information about the indigenous population in these territories. Among the items of information requested were names of the different tribes, the languages they spoke, the communities in which they lived, how many churches were erected in their towns, how many priests worked in those territories, what kind of land property they shared, and if they had any kind of *cofradías* (brotherhoods) (Marchena, 157).

15. According to Ballesteros Gaibrois, those items are found today in the Archeological Museum of Madrid ("Un manuscrito colonial del siglo XVIII," 173). López Serrano states that some of the items are also found in the Museum of America in Madrid (55).
16. For a complete list of items included in the boxes see De Vos, "The Rare, the Singular and the Extraordinary," 271–72. De Vos indicates that between 1745 and 1819 more than 335 shipments of thousands of natural history specimens were sent to Spain from the Americas (272).
17. Martínez Compañón engages in the processes of observation, collection, and classification that were an essential part of a naturalist's job (Bleichmar, "Training the Naturalist's Eye," 13). However, there is no evidence that Martínez Compañón was trained professionally as a naturalist. According to Bleichmar, naturalists were trained "not only to observe but also to draw" and "to identify objects accurately" ("Training the Naturalist's Eye," 11).
18. The use of watercolor technique made Martínez Compañón's task more feasible, as it was considered at the time to be a portable and convenient method when traveling in difficult territories (Finch, 8–10). It was also considered very practical, as the artists themselves were able to produce the colors on the spot. The method was preferred by topographers and botanists to produce maps and illustrations related to natural and human history. In the case of the Andean territories, minerals such as azurite, malachite, vermilion, and red ochre existed in abundance. As Gabriela Sirucasano observes, these pigments were already an influential part of many of the rituals and religious ceremonies practiced by the native Andeans before European arrival (29–33). Martínez Compañón included in his manuscript illustrations related to the production of blue pigments and the process of dyeing fabrics in that color, as well as illustrations of plants such as "brasil" (Brazilian dyewood) and "sangre de drago" (dragon tree resin), which were very popular for the creation of red tones.
19. All volumes except volume 9 begin with an illustration of the Spanish coat of arms.
20. This letter and the one sent to D. Antonio Polier in 1790 were reproduced in the "Apéndice III" of the 1994 facsimile reproduction of *Trujillo del Perú*, edited by Ballesteros Gaibrois (hereafter cited as App. III with page number).
21. In the Peruvian context, *cholas* or *cholos* referred to the descendant of an Indian and a Spaniard, or an Indian who dressed as a Spaniard.
22. Pablo Macera argues that several artists were involved in creating the illustrations (51). He adds that in 1788 Martínez Compañón himself mentioned in a letter to the king that due to the death of one of his artists, a replacement would be needed in order to continue with the job (Macera, 51).
23. For a discussion of selected reforms proposed by Martínez Compañón, see Restrepo Manrique, vol. 1.
24. Bleichmar notes that "images were central to the gift exchange economy that regulated almost any type of transaction at the time" between administrators, naturalists,

and the king. Images became persuasive tools when "soliciting additional funds" for expeditions, when honoring a scientific or administrative patron or when needed "to ask a favor" ("A Visible and Useful Empire," 308).
25. This letter was sent from Cartagena de Indias, where he held the post of archbishop of Santa Fe.
26. In 1784 the viceroy of Lima, Don Teodoro de Croix, had already received requests from members of the Real Audiencia (High Court) of Trujillo, who functioned as his advisers, to help them recover economically. Two major reasons were given as the causes of the problem: the earthquakes that had affected those territories and the lack of African slaves (Croix, 134). They described the city of Trujillo in particular as found in an "unhappy state" ("infeliz estado"), and as "backward" ("ciudad atrasada"), especially after losing the sugar business to the new formed Viceroyalty of La Plata and not being able to find affordable African slaves to work on their lands. The viceroy at that point considered it an obligation for the crown to assist Trujillo in any way possible due to "la antiguedad de su establecimiento, por la constante fidelidad, y por el honor de las familias que la pueblan" (the antiquity of its settlement, its steady fidelity, and the honor of the families who populate it) (Croix, 136).
27. Martínez Compañón was named archbishop of Santa Fe in 1788; however, he did not arrive there until 1791. He was buried in the cathedral of that city in 1797. In Santa Fe de Bogota, Martínez Compañón established a strong friendship with the famous naturalist and scientist José Celestino Mutis. In the "Oración fúnebre" read by Mutis at Compañón's funeral, he refers to the archbishop as a "wise man" whose "name will live eternally" due to his "work and merits" ("Oración fúnebre," December 19, 1797).
28. Ballesteros Gaibrois dismissed the supposition that the illustrations were to complement a written history about Trujillo (*Trujillo del Perú*, Apéndice, 73). However, in 1948 Raúl Porras Barrenechea had argued that the illustrations were to be part of a written history of the archbishopric of Trujillo, which Martínez Compañón had no time to complete (19–21). He suggested that the *Descripciones geográficas de los partidos de Trujillo, Piura, Saña, Lamayeque y Cajamarca*, published by Martínez Compañón's nephew Joseph Ignacio Lequanda, was based on notes compiled by the bishop during his visits to the provinces of Trujillo. Indeed, the organization of Lequanda's account follows the order of the volumes compiled by Martínez Compañón. However, in a dedicatory note written in 1786 to the king of Spain, which accompanied a detailed map he drew of Trujillo and published in the *Mercurio peruano* in 1794, Martínez Compañón mentioned that while traveling to the territories to delineate the map, he also took notes that could serve as a source to write a general history of Trujillo "I have prepared some notes in order to fashion a general history of this bishopric, or at least some memoirs that could serve that purpose" (4). Although there is mention of his notes and memoirs, the letter never mentions that the illustrations gathered were going to be part of that general history. The author also added that he had neither the good health nor the time to write such an encyclopedic work.
29. This was the case as well for geographical atlases, which often were published with no accompanying written material or explanations.
30. Critics agree that further research needs to be done with regard to the number of local artists who were involved in the process of illustrating, painting, and creating maps. Richard Kagan suggests that "there is little doubt that patrons who were themselves Creoles sought artists of similar backgrounds" (132). In Peru, according to Kagan, the main artists were Europeans. However, in the seventeenth century there were also Creoles and native indigenous artists, such as Diego Quispe Tito (16).

31. Gillian Rose, based on a definition by H. Foster, summarizes "visuality" as the "way in which vision is constructed in various ways," specifically what we see or are allowed or able to see in a particular object (6). For Daniela Bleichmar, "visuality" implies "the practices and results of both observation and representation" that can make nature "identifiable, translatable, transferable, and appropriable" ("A Visible and Useful Empire," 310).
32. In his study of the cultural function of the museum and its historical development, Tony Bennett does trace the history of the public museum to the eighteenth century when, according to him, "royal collections were translated into more public domains" (37).
33. Cañizares-Esguerra examines how this new historiographical production began to question "the authority and reliability of the sources that the historians and chroniclers had traditionally used" (1–3). For Spanish writers, it was part of an effort to defend Spain from the attacks of Northern Europeans, who negatively portrayed Spaniards as abusive, cruel, and ignorant. For the American writers, these writings represented a way to defend their cultural past.
34. The establishment of the Archivo de Indias in 1780 served as another example of an institution devoted to categorizing and assembling knowledge. Cañizares-Esguerra views the establishment of this institution as a way to centralize knowledge (379).
35. Cañizares-Esguerra specifies that the council "also asked the Academy to assemble a compendium of facts that would allow anyone to put together different narratives by an almost mechanical permutation of information" (165).
36. Susan Deans-Smith suggests that the incorporation of images also aimed to show Spain's "active engagement and progress in both visual and written media," in order to combat the negative stereotypes of the time, which promoted the idea of Spain's backwardness (176).
37. The word *castas* refers to "group or kind" (Hill, *Hierarchy, Commerce, and Fraud*, 208). As Hill explains, *casta* did not mean someone of mixed blood or a group of mixed-bloods (*Hierarchy, Commerce, and Fraud*, 207). For example, Spaniards could be considered a *casta*.
38. Magali Carrera defines *casta* painting as a pictorial genre developed mainly in New Spain, which portrays "men, women, and their offspring classified in hierarchical order according to their proportion of Spanish blood" (27). Contrary to the conventions of *casta* painting, Martínez Compañón does not show men, women, and their offspring in one single illustration. Another important difference is the absence in Martínez Compañón's work of inscriptions as part of the portrait, as is very common in *casta* painting. He does follow a hierarchical order, but illustrates the different racial groups in isolation. Finally, while *casta* paintings are oil paintings on canvas or copper plate, the pictures in *Truxillo del Perú* consist of watercolor illustrations. For an analysis of the visual strategies of *casta* painting, see Carrera, *Imagining Identity in New Spain*, 44–105. For a discussion of the historiography of *casta* painting, its format, and the influence of race in these representations, see Katzew, *Casta Painting*. Katzew points out that the only known Peruvian set of *casta* paintings was the one ordered by Viceroy of Peru Manuel Amat y Juniet (1761–1776) in 1770. According to her, Amat was familiar with the Mexican *casta* works that preceded his series (150–51). Amat's collection consisted of twenty paintings. Katzew comments that this set of *casta* paintings also "underlines the role of classification as a way of rendering visible and stable an increasingly fluid society" (150). It is not known if Martínez Compañón was familiar with this particular set of paintings. Unfortunately, according to Katzew, these paintings have not been located.

39. The quantitative nature of the chart seems to follow the format of the official questionnaires to which the *relaciones geográficas* responded. De Vos argues that the eighteenth-century bureaucratic collections requested by the Bourbons were part of this tradition ("The Rare, the Singular, and the Extraordinary," 272). The *relaciones* answered to a set of surveys drafted by the Spanish crown in 1577, through which they requested information about Spanish-held territories in the Americas, specifically about natural resources and local customs (De Vos, "The Rare, the Singular, and the Extraordinary," 272). This type of census was still existent in the eighteenth century. For more information on the *relaciones geográficas* see Mundi, 29–59.
40. The statistical chart also made a distinction in order of "Eclesiásticos," "Seminaristas," "Religiosos," and "Religiosas."
41. He also listed within this population 482 clergymen, 101 seminarists, 162 clerics in monasteries, and 172 nuns.
42. As Ilona Katzew summarizes, *calidad* refers to a "combination of economic, social, cultural, and racial factors that defined an individual" (45).
43. The letter *E* plus the number is the format that Martínez Compañón utilized to organize the illustrations and to accompany the titles. "E" might stand for the Spanish word "estampa" (picture). I shall follow the same format when citing the illustrations.
44. Clothing represented a similar role in eighteenth-century *casta* painting. As Ilona Katzew states, clothing was used in these paintings "as an indicator of socioeconomic class" and illustrated "the pervasive concern" in colonial Spanish America and Spain regarding "the loss of social boundaries" (109).
45. Bauer adds that "the quality of cloth and the design of shoes were all finely tuned instruments of social and political standing" (84). For more discussion of the rhetoric of clothing in colonial Spanish America, see Meléndez, "Visualizing Difference."
46. For some examples of these portraits, see the illustrations included in the essays by María Concepción Sáiz, Kirsten Hammer, and Teodoro Vidal in *Retratos: 2,000 Years of Latin American Portraits*, 74–146. For more details on the significance of the rose in both traditions, see Ferguson, 37–38; and Hall, 268.
47. According to David J. Weber, the word *ynfiel* or *infidel* when referring to an Indian meant "heathen Indians" (15). Other denominations for Indians were "indios bravos" (wild Indians), "indios bozales" (wild and ignorant Indians), and "indios salvajes" or "indios bárbaros" (savage Indians) (Weber, 15).
48. For a detailed discussion of the importance of clothing as a social marker and a rhetorical strategy in the processes of identity construction in colonial Spanish American from the fifteenth to the eighteenth century, see Meléndez, "Visualizing Difference."
49. It is important to remember, as David J. Weber explains, that in the eighteenth century the Spanish regime and officials debated the status of "the crown's impoverished Indian vassals" by discussing the manner in which this group could be integrated into Spanish society in order to turn them into productive subjects useful for economic progress (3). Weber adds that Bourbon officials sent trained scientists and travelers to go "beyond the edges of the empire" to better promote "civilian settlements, foster economic development, and forge alliances with native leaders who wielded local power" (5). After all, "for Spaniards, making Indians rational meant putting them into order" (Weber, 93).
50. A total of five illustrations are devoted to blacks. For an in-depth analysis of these images, see Meléndez, "An Eighteenth-Century Visual Representation of *Truxillo del Peru*."
51. Arnold J. Bauer suggests that the *mestizo* population made a great effort whenever economically possible to imitate Spanish and Creole dress habits, as they were quite

aware that the use of gold and lace symbolized a privileged social status (111). Bauer adds that it was almost impossible for the *mestiza* to compete with Spanish women when it came to "the richness of the material" used for the dresses (111). It was indeed through "dress and adornment" that European- and American-born Spaniards expressed their "political and social rivalries" (Bauer, 114).
52. Tulips originated in Persia, where they grew as wildflowers. They were brought to Europe in the sixteenth century and after widespread crossbreeding, became a very popular flower and part of a strong market, especially in Holland. The boom lasted until 1637, when prices suddenly declined. Some scholars argued that the *tulipa silvestris* already was known in Italy, where it grew in fields and meadows. For more information on the symbolism of tulips, see Impelluso and Hall. I would like to thank Mónica Domínguez Torres, professor of art history at the University of Delaware, for her insights on the representation of flowers in visual art.
53. The depiction of the flowers also speaks to the particular training of the artist hired by Martínez Compañón.
54. To date, I have not found any other Peruvian painting in which women are shown holding tulips.
55. In 1793, when talking about the bishopric of Trujillo, Joseph Ignacio Lequanda pointed out the difficulty of distinguishing between *mestizos* and Spaniards. He states: "El [mestizo] quarteron o el quinteron puede pasar por español o español Americano" (The *mestizo quarteron* or *quinteron* could pass for a Spaniard or a Spanish American) (50).
56. Lequanda refers to the mulatto population of Trujillo as "los Gitanos de nuestras Americas" (the Gypsies of our Americas) (51). He adds that the lighter ones want to be and act as Spaniards: "Los que van blanqueando quieren ser iguales a los españoles . . . es gente que tienen la capacidad para disimular y ocultar sus defectos a cambio de conseguir doble aprecio entre nosotros" (The ones who are trying to be white want to be like the Spaniards . . . they are people who have the capacity to conceal and hide their faults in order to feel doubly accepted among us) (51). Lequanda obviously highlights the difficulties the Spanish population and the authorities had when trying to distinguish the inhabitants solely on the basis of the color of their skin or fashion style.
57. As mentioned earlier, the tulip originally was considered a wildflower, but once transferred to Europe, it acquired a material value and was part of a profitable market up to the seventeenth century.
58. By *space* I refer to the physical location where "human bodies interact and where things are contained" (Arias and Meléndez, 16). *Place,* on the other hand refers to "a particular point or location which is occupied by a person or an object" (16). For more on the distinction between space and place, see Arias and Meléndez.
59. It is important to remember that in eighteenth-century colonial Spanish America, a citizen was understood as someone who was recognized as "a permanent member of the community" (Herzog, 55). For Martínez Compañón, these women were productive members of the community.
60. As Daniela Bleichmar observes, "rather than purchasing natural commodities such as coffee, tea, cinnamon, pepper, nutmeg, or *materia medica* (natural specimens with medical uses) from European competitors, Spain hoped to locate profitable substances in its colonial territories" ("Painting as Exploration," 84).
61. Socolow offers evidence of women's participation in the cloth trades, silk spinning, cotton weaving, and the production of food, *chicha,* and brandy (115). Women were very present in the marketplaces where they sold "fruits and vegetables, flowers, and

meat as well as cloth, woven goods, yarn, and cotton" (Socolow, 115). For a discussion of the participation of Indians and *mestizos* in supplying goods for colonial markets in the late colonial period, see Tandeter et al. The authors emphasize the lack of documentation found concerning indigenous participation in the markets, but from the material available, it is clear that these sectors of the population were active in the cultivation of barley, potatoes, maize, and wheat and the production of *chicha*, woolen clothing, and coal, among other things.

62. *Rengos* were pieces of a gauze-like material, similar to starched lace, that were sewn with point lacework (Borchart de Moreno, 7).

63. For Spain, a key to imperial expansion was work, and the crown aimed to have every sector of the population incorporated into the work force, including women and members of other marginalized groups (Pérez Samper, 200). The possibility of economic expansion was considered to be the greatest in the Americas.

64. *Tornos* were introduced in Europe in the thirteenth and fourteenth centuries from India. The use of mechanical spinning machinery appeared in England around 1764. For a summary of the history of spinning, see Jorge Antonio Delgado Palomino, "Hilados," www.monografias.com/trabajos38/hilados/hilados.shtml.

65. Martínez Compañón included an illustration in which men were seen consuming *chicha*. Illustration "E60: Yndios merendando en chichería" shows a woman serving the drink to two men, one of them already drunk and almost asleep, while the other keeps consuming the drink. However, the woman is a provider, not a consumer. For an in-depth study of the consumption and production of *chicha* as related to indigenous cultural memory and identity in Peru, see Morales. Also, for a discussion of women as active producers of *chicha* in everyday commerce, see Mangan, 76–105.

66. The illustrations included in the volumes pertaining to natural history also worked as a means to monitor and control natural resources.

67. According to the *Diccionario de la lengua española de la Real Academia Española*, uta comes from the Quechua and refers to "enfermedad de úlceras faciales muy común en las quebradas hondas del Perú" (a disease composed of facial ulcers that is very common in the deep ravines of Peru) (1456).

68. Foucault also argues that "disease" was viewed in the eighteenth century "as a political and economic problem for social collectivities," and as such was perceived as a problem that needed to be under government control (*Power/Knowledge*, 166).

69. David J. Weber states that integration was "widespread throughout the Empire," as it was promoted with the intention of turning the population, especially Indians, into "useful vassals and sociable men" (102, 104).

70. Bennett adds that objects placed in a museum become "on the plain meaning, facsimiles of themselves. They announce a distance between what they are and what they were through their very function, once placed in the museum, of representing their own pastness and, thereby, a set of past social relations" (129). Of course, these facsimile representations of social relationships are characterized by their own limitations, as visual images can never capture the fluidity of those relationships.

71. For Rodríguez Campomanes, economic progress should be a must for all those who love their "glorious nation." The works by Campomanes and Ward were cited in eighteenth-century Spanish American newspapers, such as the *Papel periódico de Santafé de Bogotá*, which attests to the familiarity of American intellectuals with such works.

72. Rodríguez Campomanes clearly argues in *Discurso sobre el fomento de industria popular* that "los verdaderos principios de su engrandecimiento [de la nación] son la ocupación útil de todos sus habitantes de ambos sexos y la riqueza del pueblo" (The

true principles of the progress of the nation consist of the useful occupation of all the inhabitants of both sexes and the richness of its people) (63).

## CHAPTER 3

1. The article was published in three different issues (nos. 84–86) in October 1791. According to the members of the Academic Society, they based their news article on an unpublished written account ("memorias inéditas") found in the monastery. The account gathered the documentation located in the monastery's archives. They did not mention the author of the account or the year in which it was written. I will return to this article later in the chapter.
2. As Kristine Ibsen suggests, "in the Americas, the establishment of monasteries paralleled consolidation and expansion of colonial rule" (3). Josefina Muriel has also noted how monasteries in colonial Spanish America became a social need ("necesidad social") (130). They helped the church impose and spread its ideology through the religious education provided in their institutions, while also facilitating the maintenance of moral purity in cities and towns where they were established. In this regard, Kathleen Ann Myers has commented that as "Christianity took hold, Spanish urban centers developed around a central church or cathedral, and vast sums of money were donated to the founding of nunneries and monasteries" (3).
3. The need for contributions was a major concern of many female institutions because in Spanish America, monasteries were required by the crown to "guarantee their own subsistence through endowments" (McKnight, 78).
4. The monastery still exists today, and is also known as Monasterio de las Trinitarias Descalzas de San Miguel Arcángel de Lima. It is one of the few enclosed nunneries in the Peruvian capital. Despite efforts to access their archives, I was never granted the permit needed.
5. A fifth provincial council was held in 1601 under the direction of bishop and future saint Toribio de Mogrovejo. Mogrovejo had also established the 1582 council that took place in Lima. For a succinct discussion of how the crown imposed numerous decrees to establish its supremacy over the church, see Fisher, *Bourbon Peru*.
6. The discalced orders "followed strict vows of poverty and accepted novices without dowries" (Socolow, 96). They usually walked barefoot as a sign of humiliation and poverty.
7. Lavrin maintains that the king's orders constituted an attempt to subdue the church under the power of the state and to facilitate "the consolidation of royal power" (182).
8. For a discussion of specific cases, see Martín, chaps. 8 and 9.
9. I do not pretend to offer in this chapter a detailed discussion of the economic difficulties endured by the Peruvian monasteries in the eighteenth century. For a more extensive discussion of this issue, see the works of Vargas Ugarte and Burns.
10. For an excellent discussion of the financial difficulties suffered by Peruvian monasteries in Cuzco during the eighteenth century, see Burns, especially chap. 6.
11. On this topic, see Walker, "Desde el terremoto a las bolas de fuego," and his most recent book, *Shaky Colonialism*.
12. Susan Socolow comments that the number of nuns allowed in the monasteries was sometimes "limited by the Crown" (94).
13. Esteban Sánchez-Tagle argues that in the Viceroyalty of New Spain, the new hygienic projects caused the ruin of many monasteries once they were required to cover such expenses (153).

14. Lavrin mentions that "royal aid came in the form of small sums of money for annual contributions over limited periods of time, for the sustenance of the community, or for providing oil for the main altar lamps" ("Female Religious," 179).
15. Walker adds that "the excessive dominance of the Church in financial and real estate markets, its moral decline, and the concomitant need to strengthen the state" were the reasons behind many of these reforms (*Shaky Colonialism*, 129).
16. Not every nun in colonial Spanish America was literate. Most of the texts discovered to date depict the lives of very exceptional women. Biographies, *vidas*, autobiographies, hagiographies, chronicles, and *relaciones* represent some of the writings in which nuns expressed their spiritual paths. Some works, as Myers and Powell indicate, promoted church ideology. Meanwhile, others offered a more problematic view of women's lives in their quest for spiritual perfection (327). Some of these women were forced to write, while others took the initiative themselves. They were all aware, however, that their works had the opportunity to reach a broad audience. Most of them went through intense scrutiny by confessors who closely examined and edited their writings. As a result, some manuscripts were never published, and those that were suffered transformations. Furthermore, the confessors' roles in the elaboration and final result of these texts were so significant that they "influenced the tone and narrative strategies of the accounts, at times problematizing the role of a nun as an author and a subject" (Myers and Powell, 317).
17. For an in-depth look at the characteristics of the different female religious genres, see Myers and Powell; Myers, *Neither Saints nor Sinners*; McKnight; Muriel, *Cultura femenina*; Bravo Arriaga; Lavrin, "La vida femenina"; and Arenal and Schlau.
18. I refer to the *Historia de la fundación* as a chronicle based on the eighteenth-century connotation of the word. In the *Diccionario de autoridades* the word *crónica* is defined as "Historia ò Annáles en que se trata de la vida de los Reyes, ù de otras personas heróicas en virtud, armas, ò letras" (History or Annals that deal with the lives of Kings, or other heroic people in virtue, arms, or letters) (335). Because Sor María Josefa was collecting the history of the lives of many of the founders and members of the monasteries, and also because she referred to them as women "heroicas en virtud," I believe her work can be considered a chronicle. However, one must not forget that Sor María Josefa entitled the work *Historia*. When reading Sor María Josefa's *Historia de la fundación* one realizes that her intention was also to create a continuous narration that paid particular attention to the most renowned actions and events that occurred in the monastery ("historia"). Due to the loss of written documentation that could attest to the events as they actually occurred, the *Historia* suffers at times from a lack of continuity. Nevertheless, the goal to create a truthful written document that recorded facts as well as events of the past was what probably guided Sor María to entitle her work *Historia de la fundación*. In this chapter, I will refer to the text as a chronicle.
19. As mentioned in note 2 of the Introduction, "Nación," as connoted up until the early eighteenth century, referred to "lugar de Nacimiento" (place of birth) or "la coleccion de los habitadores en alguna Provincia, Pais o Reino" (the group of inhabitants of a Province, Country, or Kingdom) (*Diccionario de autoridades*, 644). Its regional connotation also alluded to the racial, linguistic, and cultural affinities that define a group of people from the same region (see Mazzotti, 4).
20. The modern edition of the text refers to this part as "Introducción." Nevertheless, this part of the text coincides in format with the definition of proem at the time. According to the *Diccionario de autoridades*, it was considered "the exordium that precedes and serves as a prologue to a work" (394). As a prologue, its aim consisted

of "informing the reader about the object of the work, or to warn him or her of something" (398–99). I will refer to this part throughout this chapter as a proem or introduction.

21. For an excellent discussion of the definition of the genre of *vida espiritual*, see Myers, *Neither Saints Nor Sinners*, introduction; McKnight, introduction.

22. I refer to Sor María Josefa as a compiler and an editor based on the different tasks involved in each process. A compiler is one "who gathers literary material from different sources for publication in a new form" (*Webster's Universal Dictionary of the English Language*, 341). An editor is someone who "superintends, revises, corrects, and prepares a book . . . for publication" (536). Sor María Josefa is certainly a compiler and to a certain extent an editor because she did engage as well in the process of revising the material she gathered for her *Historia*.

23. One of the reasons listed for why a nun was asked to leave was that the nun in question was not suited for the religious institution (184).

24. I will discuss this issue later in the chapter.

25. Jodi Bilinkoff observes that for Creoles, "saints and their cults proved instrumental in their efforts to prove that their homeland, while only recently Christianized, was just as blessed and beloved by God as was the Old World" (17–18). For saints such as Rosa de Lima, one can see "the convergence of religious faith, pride of place, and an evolving sense of Creole distinctiveness from the European metropole" (xviii). On the conception of Rosa de Lima as redeemer of America, see Myers, " 'Redeemer of America' "; and Myers, *Neither Saints nor Sinners,* chap. 1.

26. As Castro-Klarén points out, following Ignacio Bernal's statements about Mexican patriotism, it is important to stop looking at the phenomenon of nationalism solely as a political matter (180). It is time to study nationalism as a "cultural artifact" or form of expression that goes "beyond the power of alphabetic memory sites such as books, novels, and newspapers" (Castro-Klarén, 164, 177). I would like to add that it is important as well to include within these discussions works that are not usually conceived as political in nature, such as religious texts. This new approach, aside from being more inclusive, forces us to stop looking at the phenomenon of nationalism in Latin America as a manifestation that emerged in the nineteenth century.

27. The *Diccionario de autoridades* describes *pintura* as "an image or an imitation of what is visible" (278). According to the *Diccionario, pintar* was used metaphorically to refer to the act of describing any object through writing or through speech (276). The definition of the act of painting in the *Webster's Universal Dictionary* resembles the Spanish description, as it lists the following connotations: "To represent or to exhibit to the mind; to represent in form or likeness to the intellectual view; to describe clearly; to delineate in speech or in writing" (1170).

28. Frederick A. de Armas reminds us of the connection that has historically existed between writing and vision (7). In his discussion of this connection during the Golden Age, he states that "writing" at the time "had a strongly visual component," to the extent that "poets and other writers of fiction appealed to this sense in particular since it was thought that seeing was a key to memory" (7). A great example of this case in Latin America is Sor Juana Inés de la Cruz.

29. Scarry discusses specifically "the centrality of the body" in the original narratives and the representations of Christ (216). According to her, "Christ is himself embodied in the scriptures, long before any visual descriptions of him" (216). She also adds that the act of embodiment as an act of representation "is itself recognized as an act of description" (223).

30. For a detailed discussion of how a great part of the monastery's documentation was

given over to Dr. Manuel Clerque, who was supposed to write a history of the convent but instead lost all the documents received from the nun, see Meléndez, "¡Si tal era el dedo, cuál sería el cuerpo!"

31. There is no evidence that Sor María Josefa de la Santísima Trinidad's *Historia* was published in 1783. Not even the Biblioteca Nacional in Peru owns a copy that testifies to its publication. The only copy available today was printed in 1957 by Fidel Ma. Tubino, auxiliary bishop and vicar general of Peru at that time. Mother María Rosario de San Antonio, who arrived from Spain at the Monasterio de la Santísima Trinidad in 1916, and who was its abbess at the time, requested its publication. She thought it important to make available what she considered a "precious and hidden treasure" ("tan preciado y escondido tesoro") (7), so it could serve as a model to follow by future generations interested in a spiritual path. To the original text compiled by Sor María Josefa de la Santísima Trinidad, Mother María Rosario de San Antonio added a brief historical review on the origins of the Trinitarian order. She mentions that there was a second volume that accompanied the 1783 manuscript that was given to an honorable person to publish in Spain. However, it never arrived there due to loss in a shipwreck. In 1791 the authors of the newspaper article in the *Mercurio peruano*, cited earlier, did not mention the existence of two volumes. María Josefa specifically declared at the end of her introduction that she had compiled all the materials into one volume (29). María Rosario de San Antonio might have been referring to another volume written after 1783.
32. For a list and discussion of these rules see Myers, *Neither Saints nor Sinners*, 63–65.
33. This explains why her *Historia de la fundación* also followed some of the main rhetorical strategies and language of earlier hagiographical works.
34. The editors did not mention in their article who had been the author of the account they read to gather the information used for their article. However, they did mention that the prodigious life of one of her members, Mother María Antonia de San Joseph, was "published" in 1783 along with the "Oración fúnebre" that was read in 1781 when she died. Sor María Josefa de la Santísima Trinidad's *Historia de la fundación*, written in 1783, includes a very brief summary of the life of María Antonia de San Joseph. Born in 1708, she entered the monastery in 1727, professed her vows in 1728, and died in 1781. This is essentially all the information given. The "Oración fúnebre" was not included in the 1957 publication, although Sor María Josefa de la Santísima Trinidad mentioned at the end of her introduction that her *Historia de la fundación* concluded with the funeral oration mentioned by the editors of the *Mercurio* (29). Based on the close resemblance between Sor María Josefa's account and the *Mercurio peruano* article, it is obvious that the editors of the newspaper used her *Historia* to compose their article.
35. Asunción Lavrin states that "nunneries were part of the urban and regional economy, they partook of the economic cycles of their respective areas, and reflected the general wealth or poverty of certain regions" ("Female Religious," 179).
36. The editors also mentioned all the reforms that had been imposed by the church and the crown since the seventeenth century, aimed to limit the establishment of new monasteries due to their increasing economic burden. They specifically pointed to the royal decree of 1616 sent to Lima, in which all nunneries unable to support eight members were asked to close (3.86 [1791], 157). According to them, the same decree was again sent by Charles IV, making the establishment of new monasteries extremely difficult if not impossible.
37. Mario Cesareo suggests that religious discourse and practice in colonial Latin

America privileged the body as a symbolic space of religious expression and domination (21). He adds that the body represented a "metaphorical machine" that fulfilled a "unifying function" that gave a human dimension to the colonial relationships prevalent at the time (133).
38. Her lack of command when it came to mastering the official discourse was made explicit when she commented: "porque no soy gramática y el latín es para mí tan griego como la virtud, y la virtud es para mí latín y muy griego" (because I am not an expert in grammar and Latin for me is like Greek or impossible to understand, as is virtue, because virtue is for me like Latin, a very Greek Latin) (34).
39. *Beaterios* were considered "congregations of unordained laywomen pursuing private devotions" (Socolow, 106). Unlike convents, the *beaterios* did not require dowry, and "no irrevocable religious vows were made" (Socolow, 106).
40. According to Mother Isabel Francisca de la Presentación, the crown officially approved the founding of the monastery in 1677, but the licenses did not arrive in Lima until 1682. It was not until 1708, one year after Ana de Robles's death, that D. Bernardo Gurmendi, a patron, decided to fully pay the expenses to build a monastery as well as a church that would fulfill the new needs of the nuns. The physical space of the former *beaterio* and later monastery, along with its chapel donated by Ana de Robles, was no longer sufficient to accommodate the number of activities or amount of nuns that were present (Mendiburu, 104). The monastery was in need of a more prestigious locale. It was not until 1722 that the mission was accomplished and the city of Lima celebrated the construction of the new building. According to Mendiburu, these celebrations lasted three days, with members of the high court (*audencia*), town councils (*cabildo*), the army, archbishop, and members of the nobility participating in the activities (105).
41. Sor Isabel states that the amount of money that Ana de Robles donated to the monastery was 100,000 pesos. However, according to Manuel Mendiburu in volume 7 of his *Diccionario histórico-biográfico del Perú*, the founder Ana de Robles donated only 91,000 pesos (104).
42. Mendiburu observes that the dowry demanded for nuns who wanted to enter the monastery consisted of 2,000 pesos (104).
43. It is fascinating that although Ana de Robles was the real founder, the narrator, along with María Josefa de la Santísima Trinidad (in her prologue), both referred to the other eleven nuns who inhabited the monastery at the time as founders as well. I believe this was an attempt on behalf of the authors of the *relaciones* to emphasize the important role of the other eleven nuns, who happened to be natives of Peru, in the establishment and development of the monastery as a prestigious institution in Lima. Of the twelve so-called founders, Ana de Robles was the only nonnative nun.
44. The narrator commented that the first *relación* written about Ana de Robles was lost in the monastery's archives. As a result, she had to depend on oral testimonies given by nuns who knew her.
45. For more information on the functions of the vertebral column, see Thomas, 1721.
46. The *Diccionario de autoridades* defines *refección* as moderate food that people take to regain strength (535).
47. Tobacco was considered a plant native to the Indies to the extent that it was described in the *Diccionario de autoridades* in the eighteenth century as "Planta de Indias" (a plant of the Indies) (201). From the definition given by Covarrubias it always carried a native connotation. According to Covarrubias, who based his description on a passage of Pliny, the plant was discovered by the Devil to give to his priests. In the

eighteenth-century description, it was also perceived as a vice: "ya se ha hecho tan comun, que à pasado a costumbre general, y aun a vicio" (its use is so common that has been become a general custom, and even a vice) (*Diccionario de autoridades*, 201).

48. The Spanish definition says, "falta ligera, que no llega à culpa, ni aun venial; pero la huyen y la deben huir los justos y que aspiran a la perfección" (*Diccionario de autoridades*, 223).

49. The three ways in which tobacco could have been consumed were: (1) as a topical application by warming the green leaves; (2) chewing the leaves, which helped to suppress hunger and thirst; and (3) by smoking, which offset weariness and helped people to relax (Goodman, 45).

50. Jordan Goodman discusses the ecclesiastical controversy surrounding tobacco consumption within the church, as many popes were even addicted to it. In 1725 Pope Benedict XIII allowed the consumption of tobacco in church and the papacy opened its own tobacco factory in 1779 (Goodman, 78).

51. Bynum also explains that it was through illness that many nuns perceived an "active fusing with the death agonies of Christ" in the crucifixion (48).

52. Bynum adds, based on the study of Weinstein and Bell, that between 1000 and 1700 the suffering of illness "was the major element of sanctity" for those women who were "canonized or revered as saints" (188).

53. For more on this disease see Thomas, 1334, 1643.

54. *Suave* was described at the time as something "soft, sweet, delicate and gentle to the senses" ("blando, dulce, delicado, y apacible à los sentidos") (*Diccionario de autoridades*, 166).

55. Dr. D. Melchor de la Nava was a native of Lima who functioned as a priest and subsequent dean of the Cathedral of Lima as well as inspector of the Inquisition. He also occupied the rectorship of the University of San Marcos between 1704 and 1706. In 1711 he became archbishop of Cuzco. Dr. Mesía was Cristóval Messia y Munive, who was the *oidor* of the High Court of Lima. For more information on their lives, see Mendiburu, vol. 6, p. 3, and vol. 5, p. 314, respectively.

56. Dr. Clerque is mentioned as the person who was supposed to write the original history of the monastery.

57. The exact length of the *relaciones* are as follows: Sor Francisca de José: 2 pages; Sor Ventura María de la Encarnación: 6 pages; Madre Josefa de San Pedro: 4 pages; Madre de Jesús María y José: 9 pages; Sor Nicolasa de San José: 3 pages; Sor Micaela de Jesús: 1 page; Sor Inés de la Madre de Dios del Rosario: 35 pages (5 chapters); Sor Petronila de la Santísima Trinidad: 4 pages; Sor Luisa de la Madre de Dios de Belén: 1 ½ pages; Madre Juana de Santa María: 3 pages; Madre Isabel de la Concepción: 1 paragraph.

58. In the context of this chapter I follow Michael Solomon's distinction between *illness* and *disease*. According to Solomon, *disease* is considered as "an objective description of abnormalities (corporeal, behavioral, and social)" that are diagnosed and treated. *Illness* is an experience that "makes itself known in the individual through various forms of pain, dysfunction, deformity, and alienation" (39). In sum, *illness* is what "is experienced individually" while *disease* "is socially constituted" (Solomon, 39–40).

59. In its original use the word *anorexia* comes from the Greek meaning "no appetite." Anorexia nervosa is a diagnosis based on the criterion of "an intense fear of becoming obese" (Thomas, 107).

60. See definition in the *Diccionario de la Real Academia*, 778.

61. According to Bell, holy anorexia differs from fasting in that for anorexia there is no

"stopping point . . . no agreed upon termination," while in fasting "its scope always is limited, its purpose clear" (118).
62. It is interesting to note that Sor Rosa Catalina's accounts ended with a quotation from her confessor stating that there were other miraculous acts that Sor María de la Encarnación performed but were not made public by fellow nuns, due to "the silence of their great humility" (102). Sor Rosa Catalina added that the confessors also did not want to comment on these deeds.
63. The *Diccionario de autoridades* did not list "escrúpulos" as a disease but described it as "knowledge of something that represents some type of appearance against what is believed, thought or doubted without judging the contrary ("conocimiento de algo que representa alguna apariencia, contra lo que se cree, opina ò duda, sin hacer juzgar lo contrario") (575). It also referred to it as "Doubt that one has about something" (575).
64. This is the first time that the figure of the confessor appeared in the *Historia* as someone who seemed to be asking the nun to gather biographical information. The rest of the accounts did not include any comment stating that they were being written as a result of a confessor's request. In another *relación*, that of Mother Juana de Jesús María y José, the narrator quoted from two confessors' accounts but did not acknowledge writing at their request.
65. These are the words quoted by the narrator, Sor María Teresa de la Santísima Trinidad, from Fray Juan de Venavente, a confessor of Mother Juana de Jesús when she was forty-two years old. The friar described her as "someone with virginal purity, profound humility, and of submissive and blind obedience . . . of rigorous penitence and mortification in fasting and disciplines, and of extreme and religious poverty" ("de virginal pureza, de profunda humildad y de muy rendida y ciega obediencia . . . de rigurosa penitencia y mortificación, en ayunos y disciplinas y de extremada y religiosa pobreza") (108–9).
66. These are the comments of Don Felipe Acevedo, Mother Juana's second confessor, who took spiritual care of her during the last years of her life.
67. Osteoporosis can be the result of the body failing to form enough new bone due to the lack of nutrients such as calcium and phosphate. As the bone tissue weakens, it causes fractures that can produce profound pain. A broken rib can be extremely painful, especially when trying to breathe or cough, which could have explained her terrible pain.
68. This *relación* was about one page long and was written by Mother Sor Cipriana María de las Llagas in 1744. The narrator did emphasize that Sor Micaela suffered many illnesses, but she always endured them with great patience.
69. As Jouve Martín argues, in the case of saints in colonial Spanish America, the proclamation of sanctity was a collective endeavor, in which institutions as well as individuals in different realms of society participated many times with very specific objectives (182).
70. The *Diccionario de autoridades* defines *tabardillo* as "a dangerous disease that consists of a malignant fever that provokes exterior spots like flea bites, and sometimes pimples in different colors like purple, yellow, etc." ("Enfermedad peligrosa, que consiste en una fiebre maligna, que arroja al exterior unas manchas pequeñas como de picaduras de pulga, y à veces granillos de diferentes colores: como morados, cetrinos") (202). Later it was named typhoid fever. It could be caused by the consumption of water, milk, and food, especially seafood contaminated by a "mobile bacillus" or "causative organism" known as "Salmonella typhi" (Thomas, 1927–28). As we know

it today, "typhoid fever" is "an acute infectious disease" that if not treated can result in death (Thomas, 1927).
71. The quotation appears in bold in the original text.
72. According to the *Diccionario de autoridades*, in the eighteenth century cancer was considered to be a malignant tumor, sometimes black or yellow, caused by black cholera (108).
73. One must remember, as mentioned earlier, that this "hidropesía" could have been caused by sodium retention, malnutrition, or starvation.
74. There are two other founders for whom there was very little information about their lives because, according to the narrators, their memoirs were lost in the accident mentioned by Sor María Josefa de la Santísima Trinidad in her introduction. For Mother Isabel de la Concepción, we have just one paragraph stating that she was a native of Lima who entered the monastery when she was twenty-one years old, and died when she was thirty-two. For the last nun in the account, Sor María de la Santísima Trinidad, we find just two paragraphs commenting that she was also a native of Lima, and that she was considered the co-founder of the monastery along with Ana de Robles. She joined the Discalced Trinitarians when she was twenty-two years old, in 1682, when the institution was still a *beaterio*. She died in 1745 at the age of one hundred five. Unfortunately, all her written memoirs were lost.
75. Witnesses said that she was always bleeding from her mouth, fainting, and unable to talk or eat for days. Doctors found no physical explanation for these sufferings.
76. It is not a coincidence that the decrease in Spanish American canonization and the tighter control of the publication of *vidas* coincided with a point in time when construction of national identities began to have a profound political and social impact on colonial society. Myers and Powell suggest that this decline had to do not only with "the stricter procedures of canonization" but also "an attempt to dampen *criollo* pride in their role in the Catholic Church" (335). Also, we must remember that in the eighteenth century, viceroys such as D. José Antonio Manso de Velasco (1688–1767) and Don Manuel Amat y Junient (1707–1782) often commented in their *memorias* on the precarious economic situation that many monasteries were experiencing, with lack of sufficient funds to pay for their basic needs. See Manso de Velasco and Amat y Junient.
77. In general, women's religious writings in colonial Spanish America followed many of the themes and rhetorical devices used by peninsular nuns. They were heavily affected by the ideologies of the Counter-Reformation and as such, we find the rhetoric of obedience, humility, and fear, as well as extreme cases of penitence, mortification, suffering, fasting, and self-denigration. Writing also appeared in these texts as an "act of defiance" and as an ambiguous act of freedom and coercion (Arenal and Schlau, 16). As Kathryn McKnight observes, although the models and genres followed by Spanish American colonial nuns were inherited from Spain, "they inject peninsular discourse with colloquialism, they engage with the politics and economics particular to the colonial situations, and they frequently paint their devils with the racial stereotyping specific to the colonial world" (69).
78. These comments were part of a presentation at the Third International Interdisciplinary Symposium on Colonial Studies in the Americas organized by the Colonial Americas Studies Organization (CASO) in Universidad San Francisco de Quito, Ecuador, June 4–10, 2007. His presentation focused on the Viceroyalty of Nueva Granada, arguing that the idea of sanctity in the colonial context became a social phenomenon in the sense that in the promotion of these religious figures, the people saw an opportunity to promote regional ideas.

79. Francisco Echave in his *Estrella de Lima convertida en sol* (1687), in which he writes about the greatness of Lima when it came to religious perfection, devotes a section to the Monastery of Discalced Trinitarians. According to Echave, in a "Cielo, donde luzen las flores, y florecen las Estrellas," the Discalced Trinitarians represented a type of "Heaven in earth" ("Este Cielo mas en la tierra") or a "celestial enclosure" ("Celestial clausura") (175, 233). It constituted one of the many religious stars that made Lima such an extraordinary place of divine perfection.

## CHAPTER 4

1. Cases of cesarean section go back to ancient times, including Hindu, Egyptian, Grecian, Roman, and European folklore. According to Jane Eliot Sewell, "at that time the procedure was performed only when the mother was dead or dying, as an attempt to save the child for a state wishing to increase its population" (2). It was in the sixteenth and seventeenth centuries the procedure came to be known as a cesarean operation. However, only in the nineteenth century did the procedure became safe and more professional, due to advances in medical technology, including the discovery of anesthesia. For a brief history of cesarean section, see Jane Eliot Sewell, "Cesarean Section: A Brief History," Brochure to Accompany an Exhibition on the History of Cesarean Section at the National Library of Medicine, April 30, 1993–August 31, 1993, 1–15. Available at *www.nlm.nih.gov/hmd/pdf/cesarean.pdf*.
2. All quotations from the *Mercurio peruano* come from the facsimile edition published by the Biblioteca Nacional del Peru in 1964, hereafter cited in the text by volume, number, year, and page number.
3. In the eighteenth century *cirugía* referred to the art and science of curing wounds and sores, opening tumors, and cauterizing and cutting parts of the body for which that was the only viable cure. See *Diccionario de autoridades,* 360.
4. The *Mercurio peruano* was the first newspaper founded by Peruvian natives. The three other newspapers that appeared before or during the times of the *Mercurio* were all founded by Spaniards. *La Gazeta de Lima* (1715) was published by the Spanish government. *Diario de Lima* (1790–1792) was founded by the Spanish pedagogue Jayme Bausate y Mesa, and the conservative newspaper *El Semanario crítico* (1791) was established by the Spanish friar José Antonio Olavarrieta. The founding members of *Mercurio peruano* were Hermágoras (José L. Egaña and president of the Academic Society), Aristio (José Hipólito Unanue, the secretary), Hesperióphilo (José Rossi y Rubí) and Homótimo (Demetrio Guasque). Cefalio (José Baquíjano), Théaganes (Tomás Mendes), and Archidamo (Diego Cisneros) were also important members of the Academic Society. According to Manuel de Mendiburu, of the thirty academicians who belonged to the Academic Society, twenty-one were from Lima (vol. 8, 158). All members of the Academic Society became active contributors of the newspaper. For biographical information on some of these contributors, see Mendiburu (vol. 8, 1890). See also Miró Quesada (52–55), for a list of the pseudonyms used by some of the contributors. See also the introduction to vol. 7.210 (1793) where the editor also lists some of the names. For more information on the archival project of the *Mercurio peruano* see Mariselle Meléndez, "Patria, Criollos, and Blacks"; and Clément.
5. The concept of the nation utilized by the editors of the newspaper was endowed with political connotations that aimed to set Peru, and especially Lima, apart from the rest of the world. The nation was no longer perceived as only a place of origin or

an ethnic entity as it had been before the Enlightenment. For the members of the Academic Society, the nation had now become the "patria," the country for which citizens needed to express their sacrifice and love. In this regard we can talk about that sense of "community" that, according to Benedict Anderson, is characteristic of the process of imagining the nation as a "horizontal comradeship" rooted in a sense of provinciality (16). On the limitations of Anderson's argument that the nation in the modern sense of the word emerged in Spanish America in the eighteenth century, see the collection of essays edited by Sara Castro-Klarén and John Charles Chasteen. For a detailed discussion of the concept of the nation as elaborated in the *Mercurio peruano*, see Meléndez, "Patria, Criollos, and Blacks."

6. *Bicípete* is the same as *bicéfalo*, meaning someone or something with two heads. This article has been attributed to Hipólito Unanue, member and secretary of the Academic Society of the Lovers of the Country, who wrote under the pseudonym of Aristio. However, no author's name accompanied the article.

7. This type of monster was considered by Ambroise Paré in his famous work, *Monsters and Marvels (Des monstres et prodiges*, 1573), as an example of "the mixture or mingling of seed" (67). Among the visual illustrations he included are figures of a child being part dog, a monster with the face of a man and the body of a goat, and a pig with the head, hands, and feet of a man (68–71).

8. Covarrubias commented that when the parents witnessed the birth of their own monstrous son, they decided to bury him alive, fearing it to be a bad omen. Eventually the authorities accused the parents of parricide.

9. The definition in Spanish reads, "a parto ú produccion contra el orden de la naturaleza," "lo que es sumamente feo," "desorden grave en la proporcion que deben tener las cosas, segun lo natural ó regular," and "desproporcion, en lo physico ú en lo moral" (598–99).

10. Geoffroy Saint-Hilaire (1772–1844) is considered the founder and father of teratology. He demonstrated "through comparative anatomical studies that a cause of monstrosity was an interruption in the development of the fetus." Nevertheless, it was not until the first half of the nineteenth century that scientists began to focus on the nature of birth defects and eliminated the allusions to imaginary monsters from their studies. For more information on the science of teratology, see "The Eighteenth Century: Monsters as Battleground for Scientific and Philosophical Debates," October 2002, available at *www.nyam.org/initiatives/im-histe_ter9.shtml*.

11. One example given by the author of "*Monstruos* por exceso" was that of a child born in 1694 in Lima having one body and two heads. He referred to the case as described in the work *Desvíos de la naturaleza*, written, according to him, by Pedro Peralta y Barnuevo (1664–1743). This work as well as the controversy about its authorship will be discussed later.

12. *Germ* in the context of these theories referred to "the first rudiment" or part "of an organism" (Thomas, 731).

13. According to Stafford, Malebranche's *Recherche de la verité* and its five editions, published between 1721 and 1722, "brought the entire imaginationist theory of correspondences to the threshold of the eighteenth century" (313). Malebranche believed that "the mother alone . . . was responsive to, and responsible for, the impact of frightful ulcers or beautiful works of art . . . she conferred on the child growing in the womb emotional reactions to what she saw or felt" (313).

14. John Friedman makes interesting suggestions with regard to the reasons behind the belief in the existence of monsters that grew so popular in the Middle Ages. According to him, they could have been the result of "fantasy, escapism, delight in

the exercise of the imagination, and—very important—fear of the unknown" (24). Monsters could also have been a consequence of "errors of perception" (24). During their travels to the East or unknown places, European men could have mistakenly perceived the customs of matriarchal societies (Amazons) as a sign of monstrosity. Tribes that suffered lobster-claw syndrome could have been perceived as a "people who had horses' hooves instead of feet" (16), and baboons or anthropoid apes "may be behind the tales of barking, dog-headed peoples" (24). Finally, the absence of a neck could have been a result of ornamented shield armors used by some tribes. For a more detailed discussion of these errors of conception, see Friedman, 24–26.

15. The *Mercurio peruano* is not the only newspaper that published news pertaining to the birth of monsters in colonial Spanish America. For example, *Gazeta de Mexico* (1784) published many articles related to monstrous births. Other contemporaneous historians, such as Juan de Velasco in his *Historia del Reino de Quito*, also devoted a section to the nature of monsters. However, before the eighteenth century some chroniclers had made interesting observations with regard to the manner in which children born with physical malformations or, as they were termed, "monstrosities," were treated in indigenous cultures. For example, in the sixteenth century Cristóbal de Albornoz mentioned how children who were born with monstrosities were sacrificed to the *huacas*. With regard to Mexico, Hernán Cortés in his *Cartas de relación* also commented that monstrous children or any individuals born with any physical disability in the Aztec society were kept in a special house alienated from the rest of society. However, he noted that Montezuma designated certain individuals whose only job was to care for these "hombres y mujeres monstruos" (female and male monsters) (67). Other mentions of monsters by colonial chroniclers are Cristóbal Colón, Francisco López de Gómara, Pedro Mártir de Anglería, and Gonzalo Fernández de Oviedo, to name a few.

16. According to Martha Few, human dissections were performed in Spanish America as early as hospitals were founded in the early sixteenth century (155). Medical and colonial authorities conducted autopsies to represent and emphasize "the strangeness and extreme effects of the disease on the bodies of native peoples" and "to promote and standardize human biology" (Few, 154).

17. There has been some controversy with regard to the real author of this manuscript. Critics such as Ruth Hill and Jerry Williams argue that the author was Pedro de Peralta y Barnuevo. Their conclusion is based on the fact that contemporaries such as Francisco Ramírez Pacheco and Pablo Petit claimed Peralta as the author (Hill, *Sceptres and Sciences in the Spains*, 155, 180). However, Uriel García Cáceres argues that Rivilla Bonet y Pueyo was the real author of the manuscript. He argues that Rivilla was the surgeon in charge of conducting the autopsy of the bicephalous monster born in Lima in 1694. It was the president of the Protomedicato Tribunal, Francisco Bermejo y Roldán, who selected him for the job. García Cáceres explains that the confusion occurred when Hipólito Unanue, in his article about a bicephalous calf, attributed the authorship to Peralta y Barnuevo based on note 94 of Canto VI of *Lima fundada*, where Peralta made a cryptic reference in the first person singular when describing the monster. García Cáceres explains that the descriptions of the autopsy as well as the surgical interventions recorded during the process were signed by Rivilla y Pueyo (72). For more information on the prolific career of Rivilla y Pueyo as a surgeon in Lima, see García Cáceres, 70–89. Libraries in the United States have catalogued this work under Rivilla Bonet y Pueyo juxtaposed with the name of Terralla y Landa, followed by a question mark.

18. The congenital malformation present in the twins is known today as "xiphopagus,"

which is the case of "symmetrical twins joined at the xiphoid process" (Thomas, 2029).
19. The author describes a monster as "any living component whose spontaneous production lacks the ordinary course of nature" ("todo aquel compuesto animado, en cuya producción espontanea, falta mas o menos enormemente à su acostumbrado orden de la Naturaleza"). As Ruth Hill observes, the author departed from the Renaissance and Counter-Reformation conception of "monster," which was explained as a divine punishment (*Sceptres and Sciences in the Spains*, 162).
20. This specific birth was mentioned also by the author of the article "Descripción de un ternero bicípite seguida de algunas reflexiones sobre los Monstruos," discussed earlier in this section. The author of the article took the opportunity to disagree with Louis Feuillé in his *Journal des observations physiques, mathematiques et botaniques, faites par ordre du roi sur les côtes orientales de l'Amerique méridionale, aux Indes Occidentales. Et dans un autre voïage faite par le même ordre á la Nouvelle Espagne, aux illes de l'Amerique* (1714), who also mentioned the 1694 episode of the bicephalous child. The contributor of the *Mercurio peruano* corrected Feuillé in his statement that the twins were baptized individually; according to the author of the news article, that was not the case. See note 11 of the *Mercurio peruano* article (4.126 [1792], 188).
21. Rivilla also mentioned cases of monstrous children born in England, Italy, Germany, France, Africa, and Spain.
22. Nevertheless, Rivilla emphasized that there was no need for alarm with this kind of monster due to its symbolic nature. He then offered a symbolic interpretation of the creature. That the twins appeared to be embracing was a sign of "union, peace, and love" ("union, paz y amor"), all attributes of the government of the viceroy of Peru, Conde de la Monclova, who had successfully integrated state ("jurisdicciones") and church ("afecto sagrado"). Allegorically, the twins' single head came to represent the union of state and church in one body, as "it is better to have two perfect heads than a deformed one" ("mejores son dos cabezas perfectas que una diforme"). According to Rivilla, two perfect heads were preferred over one that was malformed, a situation in which ideas would tend to confuse one another. The illustration of the monstrous twins inserted in the center of an "escudo" emphasized such a union (see Figure 37). Ironically, when one considers the politics of the time, in which church and state were in constant disagreement in regard to government, economics, and social issues, this metaphorical "union" is a very monstrous ("abnormal") one. But for the political imagery, this "union" was necessary for restitution of order in a society where Creoles, *mestizos*, indigenous groups, and other *castas* were constantly threatening the colonial order. On the influence of Descartes and Bacon on the main premises of this work, see Ruth Hill, *Sceptres and Sciences in the Spains*, 154–64.
23. When the editors refer to Peru as a kingdom they emphasize the idea that Peru was a territory subject to the Spanish king.
24. A *negra* or *negro bozal* was an African slave who had recently arrived to the Americas.
25. Several articles included in the newspaper criticized and mocked the black population of the city, particularly *negros bozales*. For more on the depiction of blacks in the *Mercurio peruano*, see Meléndez, "Patria, Criollos, and Blacks."
26. Haidt mentions that in the eighteenth century surgeons "operated on affected parts of [the body) and performed bleedings," while doctors "consulted, diagnosed 'internal' and 'external' problems and prescribed remedies" (24).

27. The author clarifies that this is a "truthful account" ("caso veridico") relayed to him by reliable sources.
28. Canonistas were judicial advisers of the Church and experts in the laws and regulations that governed it.
29. Since the early arrival of the Spaniards in the Americas, "pecado nefando" was frequently ascribed to the male indigenous population.
30. The author of this newspaper article seemed to follow a more analytical approach, which had become more prevalent in the second half of the eighteenth century. For some medical authorities, "physical enigmas were indicative of hidden causes legible only to specialized interpreters. Whether analyzing a body, a text, or an image, the pattern of reasoning moved from effect to cause, from evident to non-evident, made accessible with the 'right' detector" (Stafford, 84).
31. Dennis Todd refers to the case of Mary Toft, who with the help of her mother-in-law hid rabbit body parts within her vagina, causing the appearance of giving birth to rabbits. She gained the enthusiastic admiration of a surgeon (John Howard), who paid her in return for the use of her body as an object of study. The popularity he gained from having assisted in such births was of great benefit as well. Her case attracted the interest of intellectuals who published in prestigious newspapers in London and devoted part of their discussion to her case. See Todd, 1–37.
32. Cotabamba was a province of Peru that belonged to the district of Apurimac.
33. According to modern medicine, former notions that venereal diseases, such as syphilis, caused malformations were unfounded. However as T. W. Sadler suggests, syphilis "may lead to congenital deafness and mental retardation in the offspring" (118).
34. Rebollar comments that "this custom was very common in barbarous people" (9.311 [1793], 281).
35. For this article, Rebollar follows many of Buffon's remarks on the relationship of monstrous births to the mother's behavior in his work *Historia natural del hombre*, a translation of his *Histoire naturelle, générale et particulière*, published in French in 1749 and in Spanish in 1773. Georges-Louis Leclerc, Comte de Buffon, was a French naturalist and mathematician.
36. As Palencia-Roth explains, cannibalism, bestiality, and civil disorder all became "indices of the monstrous" and an integral part of the "theology of the Conquest" (27).
37. The eighteenth-century debates about monstrous births had a great impact on contemporary medical issues with regard to congenital malformations. Medical texts on embryology today define teratology as "the study of birth defects and their causes" including "investigations pertaining to both structural and behavioral abnormalities" (Sadler, 115). The word *teratogen* is used to refer to the "factors that cause such abnormalities" (Sadler, 115). For example, in current medical terminology a set of conjoined twins is referred to as "double monsters" (Sadler, 112). Congenital malformations were and are considered signs of the abnormal, that which lies outside the norm. With vast advances in knowledge of fetal development and chromosomes, and concomitant development of medical terminology, logical explanations have been found as to the causes of many of the cases that were considered signs of monstrosity in the eighteenth century.
38. *Papeleta* was a type of flyer through which some news items circulated in the public domain.
39. Torpas de Ganarrila summarizes some of the cases discussed by these as well as other contemporary authors.
40. To a certain extent this case is reminiscent of that of Catalina de Erauso, also known

as the Monja Alférez, who in 1620, after living as a male soldier, confessed to the bishop while in Guamanga that she was indeed a woman. An examination was performed, which discovered the truth and revealed that she was also a virgin. This case, as she recounted in her *relación*, became famous in the Indies as well as in Europe.

41. The perineum with regard to women referred to the external area between the vulva and the anus. For men it refers to the area between the scrotum and the anus. This part of the body is composed of skin, muscle, and fasciae (Thomas, 1362).
42. Galen saw no distinction in the external anatomy of female and male bodies. For him, female reproductive organs were in the wrong place and located interiorly (Laqueur 27).
43. As Laqueur explains, it was in the eighteenth century that anatomists "produced detailed illustrations of an explicitly female skeleton to document the fact that sexual difference was more than skin deep" (157).
44. One must remember that anatomy in the eighteenth century was considered a science that dealt with "the organization, shape, form, and location of all the organs of the human body," as well as "the examination of all the parts of the human body, an animal or a bird, which entailed dissection and partitioning in order to learn more about them" (*Diccionario de autoridades*, 281).
45. In the eighteenth century "incontinence" referred to lewdness or lack of control of the sexual appetites.
46. Laqueur explains that before the eighteenth century anatomists believed that the body had one structure, for which the male body was the standard, and that the female body was a variation of the male (62). In the eighteenth century, the first detailed drawing of the female skeleton was produced, heralding a new means to observe and name the female organs (157). However, previous anatomical beliefs about the female body continued to coexist with the new ones.
47. See *Diccionaro de la Real Academia Española*, 780–81.
48. Judovitz adds that "the material process of folding and unfolding that involves inscription, transcription, and interpretation" characterizes the process of embodiment (7).
49. As King states, the word *hysteria* comes from the Greek adjective meaning "from the womb" (213). In ancient Greece and influenced by Hippocrates, it was believed that the womb constituted "the origin of all disease" (King, 213). As King adds, in the eighteenth century "hysteria was increasingly described as 'neurosis'" while "excess blood naturally present in the female body led to increased nervous irritability, especially under the influence of too much meat, coffee or tea, or insufficient exercise" (214). I will return shortly to the influence of Hippocrates on Suadel's dissertation on pregnant women.
50. Richard Manningham was a famous physician who acquired a great reputation in the field of midwifery. His *Artis obstetricariae compendium* included an abstract addressed to the midwives with explanations of anatomical preparations for safely delivering a child. In this compendium he includes a chapter on the nature of monstrous births. He also published, among other medical works, *An exact diary of what was observed during a close attendance upon Mary Toft: the pretended rabbit-breeder of Godalming in Surrey, from Monday Nov. 28, to Wednesday Dec. 7 following: together with an account of her confession of the fraud* (1726); *The symptoms, nature, causes, and cure of the febricula, or little fever: commonly called the nervous or hysteric fever . . .* (1746); and *A discourse concerning the plague and pestilential fevers: plainly proving, that the general productive causes of all plagues of pestilence, are from some*

*fault in the air . . .* (1758). He was one of the physicians who discovered the fraud of Mary Toft, mentioned earlier in this chapter.

51. For a complete definition of the word *economy*, see *Webster's Universal Dictionary*, 534; and also the *Diccionario de autoridades*, 367.

52. For his comments on the negative repercussions of consuming chile peppers, the author relied on the work *Advertencias para beber frío*, which he mentions was published at the beginning of the sixteenth century by a doctor named Matías Porres. I was unable to locate this work after an extensive search in many library catalogs in and outside the United States.

53. King observes that the authority of Hippocrates in the field of medicine grew in the sixteenth century and remained significant until the nineteenth century, heavily influencing the field of gynecology (13). Regarding pregnancy, Hippocrates believed that if a woman's womb was "excessively dense, hot, cold, dry or wet," this could represent an obstacle to pregnancy (King, 31). He also believed that in order to procreate, the womb needed to be "healthy, dry and soft" (King, 141).

54. The *protomedicato* was an institution created by the Spanish government to achieve greater centralization and control of the field of medicine. In the case of Spain as well as Peru, a way in which the Spanish government sought to control the role of midwives in society was by regulations, such as the one established in 1750 by the royal protomedicato to examine and license midwives (Lanning, 299). The government began to request marriage licenses or proofs, certificates of consent by the husbands to practice midwifery, or proofs indicating that the women were "honorably widows" in order for them to be allowed to practice midwifery (Lanning, 298). As Lanning also indicates, "a proof of blood purity, a birth certificate, testimony of 'good conduct and customs' and inevitably, a deposit of 128 pesos to cover fees and other expenses" constituted additional requirements imposed by the government (Lanning, 298).

55. Other venues with posted ads for people interested in buying wet nurses were barbershops, baker's shops, and cafes. Since antiquity, the hiring of wet nurses had made use of special domestic spaces where these women could sell their services. In Rome, for example, wet nurses were requested to attend the forum, where they could be hired by those who were in need (Fildes, 18). It is also known that since medieval times, women had announced their services through songs appearing in town carnivals. The advertisement of wet nurse services in newspapers was very popular in the eighteenth century. Carmen Sarasúa comments that newspapers in Spain, such as *Diario de avisos de Madrid*, printed hundreds of advertisements each year advertising the sale of wet nurses (145–46). Want ads for wet nurses were also published in abundance in North American newspapers.

56. As Bianca Premos observes, "wet nursing fetched an income of 15 to 18 pesos a month," which meant that "any woman who recently had been pregnant could pay the trade to support herself" (*Children of the Father King*, 54). As Premo adds, the women themselves considered wet nursing a "valuable commodity" (*Children of the Father King*, 54).

57. Ann Twinam has indicated that since 1255 the *Fuero Real* "marked the age of three as the first critical transition point, for law obligated mothers to nurture infants before that age" (160).

58. Rousseau argued in his novel *Émile* (1762) that "on the good constitution of mothers depends primarily that of the children; on the care of women depends the early education of men; and on women, again, depend their morals, their passions, their tastes, their pleasures, and even their happiness. Thus the whole education of women ought to be relative to men" (49).

59. Bonells's book was published in 1786 and was entitled *Perjuicios que acarrean al Género Humano y al Estado las Madres que rehúsan criar a sus hijos y medios para contener el abuso de ponerlos en Ama*. Another important book published before that of Bonells was written by another physician, Juan Gutiérrez Godoy, and entitled *Tres discursos para probar que estan obligadas a criar a sus pechos todas las mujeres, quando tienen buena salud, fuerzxas, buen temperamento, buena leche y suficiente para alimentarles* (1629). For more information about these two authors see Sarasúa.
60. According to a census pertaining to Lima in the eighteenth century, the indigenous population fluctuated between 7 and 11 percent, while the white population was diminishing in proportion when compared to the number of inhabitants of mixed races. See Premo, "Misunderstood Love," 237–38.
61. The editors of the newspaper published the letter on January 16, 1791.
62. Premo has demonstrated the important impact that the formative education of children had upon the social measures established by the Bourbon regime. According to Premo, the Spanish authorities "set about producing highly paternalistic reform legislation that could transform the greatest possible number of colonial children into productive workers for a new, revenue-driven, centralized state" ("Misunderstood Love," 236). Three years later, in 1794, the Bourbon regime passed legislation that banned the practice of sending children from urban areas to wet nurses in rural areas. It aimed to prevent the high infant mortality rate at the time, which was consequently leading to population decline. The Bourbons also condemned the practice of nursing several children at once, claiming this act to be detrimental and unhealthy (Premo, "Misunderstood Love," 240). These rulings demonstrate that the Spanish regime was preoccupied with the negative repercussions that wet nursing could have on the future of the children of the empire.
63. For a discussion of the debate between Olavarrieta and the contributors of *Mercurio peruano*, see Premo, *Children of the Father King*, 170–71; also Claudia Rosas Lauro's excellent article, "La visión ilustrada." Olavarrieta claimed that close contact with wet nurses contributed to negative linguistic habits, biological contamination, and insidious cultural habits. According to him, women ought to understand "the abuse of feeding them with foreign, gross or nutritious milk contributing in this manner to disorder and abuse" (Olavarrieta, 5).
64. On this issue see Genevieve Lloyd, who calls attention to the importance of understanding the maleness that characterized the traditional conception of reason and its impact on constructing gender difference. As she suggests, "from the beginnings of philosophical thought, femaleness was symbolically associated with what Reason supposedly left behind—the dark powers of the earth goddesses, immersion in unknown forces associated with mysterious female powers" (2).
65. There is a discrepancy with respect to the manner in which his name was spelled in the second letter: Filomates versus Eustachio Phylomathes.
66. At the time, a *negra criolla* was defined as a black woman born in the Americas who had descended from African parents. For some reason, within the Spanish American context, the word *criollo* has overwhelmingly been used to refer to white citizens born in the Americas but of Spanish descent.
67. Similar characteristics were assigned to servants in general. According to Manuel Fernández Alvárez, the servant was supposed to be submissive, obedient, and isolated from the rest of society (201).
68. Between 1591 and 1605 Reginaldo de Lizárraga stated a similar complaint in his *Descripción del Perú, Tucumán, Río de la Plata y Chile*. According to Lizárraga, the

reason why there were so many ill-mannered children in Peru was that children were being raised by wet nurses (253). For Lizárraga, wet nursing was detrimental to the well-being of society. Wet nurses were considered a dangerous influence for white children, and it was paramount to avoid any contact with them. Lizárraga's solution was for the government to force the husbands to stop hiring wet nurses altogether. Ironically, a century later this perceived problem was still present in Peru, particularly in Lima, as Phylomathes pointed out in his letters. However, the issue was immersed within the politics of the Enlightenment that appealed to the need of progress through the production of healthy citizens.

69. For a detailed discussion of the concept of race as understood before the nineteenth century, see Hill, *Hierarchy, Commerce, and Fraud*, chap. 5. Hill perceives race along with the terms of "*condición, calidad* and *estado*" as "intersecting principles of hierarchy in colonial Spanish America" (*Hierarchy, Commerce, and Fraud*, 215).

70. Premo also contends that both letters "were based on one of the most critical European literary works about Lima published during this period" (*Children of the Father King*, 171). According to her, the poem written by Esteban Terralla y Landa, "Lima por dentro y por fuera," prompted these letters. Following Ricardo Palma's *Tradiciones peruanas*, she cites 1790 as the year in which the poem was published. However, based on existing editions, Terralla y Landa's poem was not published until 1797 in Lima. The Biblioteca Nacional de Peru holds a copy of this edition, which does not list any particular printing house. There is also a more popular edition published in 1798 in Madrid, Spain, by the Imprenta Villalpando. There are twenty-three known copies of this particular edition.

71. As Clément suggests, in the *Mercurio peruano* blacks are viewed as total inferiors (vol. 1, p. 161).

72. According to Premo, the 1794 edicts were modeled after the recent rulings by the absolutist government in France around 1786 that aimed "to promote improvement in care through programs to lower infant mortality and the licensing of wet nurses" ("Misunderstood Love," 242). Phylomathes's letter falls within both rulings, a sign that attests to the awareness of contributors of the Peruvian newspaper with regard to debates on social issues pertaining to the children's well-being.

73. Lefebvre adds, "In the best of circumstances, the outside space of the community is dominated, while the indoor space of family is appropriated" (166).

74. In this sense, the body of the wet nurse was similar to the hesitant body of the monster that Antoine de Bacque describes: "a body endlessly vacillating between fear and laughter, a body led toward its ambiguity by a writing that is itself amphibolous" (179).

75. E. Ann Kaplan is referring to the manner in which women have historically been perceived in society. Based on Julia Kristeva's position on women, Kaplan adds that "women are sometimes reviled as too close to chaos, as outside of culture; but may then be idealized and elevated as supreme defenders against the wilderness that would envelop man" (43).

76. Nussbaum argues that the eighteenth century was when an intense "cult of domesticity" emerged, focusing on the belief that "female of every culture and species should be imagined as loving and nurturant mothers heavily invested in the care of their children" (48). Nussbaum adds, "The metaphors of mother country and the associations of maternity with nationhood elevate women to mystic heights" (48).

77. It is interesting to note that the *Mercurio peruano* mostly pays attention to the bodies of the elite upper-class women and those of black women. These represent

extreme ends of the colonial social spectrum. The indigenous woman is seldom mentioned in the news articles included in the newspaper. The large black population in Lima at the time is an important factor in the decision to discuss cases pertaining to women of African descent.

## EPILOGUE

1. *Polilla* or "a moth" refers literally to any insect or larvae "destructive to fabrics" (*Webster's Universal Dictionary*, 1068). In a figurative sense it implies "one who or that which gradually and systematically eats, consumes, or wastes anything" (*Webster's Universal Dictionary*, 1068).
2. See definition of citizen in the Introduction to this book.

# Works Cited

Adorno, Rolena. "Retórica y resistencia pictóricas: El grabado y la polémica en los escritos sobre el Perú en los siglos XVI y XVII." *Las imágenes de resistencia indígena y esclava.* Ed. Roger Zapata. Lima: Editorial Wari, 1990. 33–77.

Aguirre, Carlos, and Ricardo D. Salvatore. "Writing the History of Law, Crime, and Punishment in Latin America." *Crime and Punishment in Latin America.* Ed. Ricardo D. Salvatore et al. Durham, NC: Duke University Press, 2001. 2–32.

Albornoz, Cristóbal. *La instrucción para descubrir todas las guacas del Pirú y sus camayos y haziendas.* Paris: Musée de l'Homme, 1967.

Alfonso X. *Las Siete partidas del sabio Rey don Alfonso el nono, nuevamente Glosadas por el Licenciado Gregorio Lopez del Consejo Real de Indias de su Majestad.* Salamanca: Andrea de Portonaris, 1555 [1974].

Amat y Junient, Manuel. *Memoria de los virreyes que han gobernado el Perú durante el tiempo del coloniaje español.* Vol. 4. Lima: Librería Central de Felipe Baillo, 1859.

Anderson, Benedict. *Imagined Communities: Reflections on the Origin and Spread of Nationalism.* London: Verso, 1983.

Andrien, Kenneth J. *Andean Worlds: Indigenous History, Culture, and Consciousness under Spanish Rule, 1532–1825.* Albuquerque: University of New Mexico Press, 2001.

Arenal, Electa, and Stacey Schlau. *Untold Sisters: Hispanic Nuns in Their Own Works.* Albuquerque: University of New Mexico Press, 1989.

Arias, Santa, and Mariselle Meléndez. "Space and the Rhetorics of Power in Colonial Spanish America: An Introduction." *Mapping Colonial Spanish America: Places and Commonplaces of Identity, Culture, and Experience.* Lewisburg, PA: Bucknell University Press, 2002. 13–23.

Arze, Silvia, Magdalena Cajías, and Ximena Medinaceli. *Mujeres en la rebelión: La presencia femenina en las rebeliones de Charcas del siglo XVIII.* La Paz: Ministerio del Desarrollo Humano, 1997.

Bacque, Antoine de. *The Body Politic: Corporeal Metaphor in Revolutionary France, 1770–1800.* Trans. Charlotte Mandell. Stanford, CA: Stanford University Press, 1997.

Ballesteros Gaibrois, Manuel. "Un manuscrito colonial del siglo XVIII, su interés etnográfico." *Journal de la Société des Américanistes* 27 (1935): 145–73.

Ballesteros Gaibrois, Manuel, ed. *Trujillo del Perú. Apéndice.* Madrid: Ediciones de Cultura Hispánica, 1994.

Barkan, Leonard. *Nature's Work of Art: The Human Body as Image of the World.* New Haven, CT: Yale University Press, 1975.

Barrera, Antonio. "Empire and Knowledge: Reporting from the New World." *Colonial Latin American Review* 15.1 (2006): 39–54.

Barrionuevo, Alfonsina. *Habla Micaela.* Lima: Ediciones Iberia S.A., 1976.

Bauer, Arnold J. *Goods, Power, History: Latin America's Material Culture*. Cambridge: Cambridge University Press, 2001.
Benjamin, Walter. "The Collector." *The Arcades Project*. Trans. Howard Eiland and Kevin McLaughlin. Cambridge, MA: Harvard University Press, 1999. 203–11.
Bennett, Tony. *The Birth of the Museum: History, Theory, Politics*. New York: Routledge, 2005.
———. "Stored Virtue: Memory, the Body and the Evolutionary Museum." *Regimes of Memory*. Ed. Susannah Radstone and Katharine Hodgkin. London: Routledge, 2003. 40–54.
Berger, John. *Ways of Seeing*. New York: Viking Press, 1972.
Bhabha, Homi. "Introduction: Narrating the Nation." *Nation and Narration*. Ed. Homi Bhabha. New York: Routledge, 1990. 1–7.
Bilinkoff, Jodi. "Introduction." *Colonial Saints: Discovering the Holy in the Americas*. Ed. Allan Greer and Jodi Bilinkoff. New York: Routledge, 2003. xiii–xxii.
Bleichmar, Daniela. "A Visible and Useful Empire: Visual Culture and Colonial Natural History in the Eighteenth-Century Spanish World." *Science in the Spanish and Portuguese Empires 1500–1800*. Ed. Bleichmar et al. Stanford, CA: Stanford University Press, 2009. 290–310.
———. "Visible Empire: Scientific Expeditions and Visual Culture in the Hispanic Enlightenment." *Postcolonial Studies* 12.4 (2009): 441–66.
———. "Training the Naturalist's Eye in the Eighteenth Century: Perfect Global Visions and Local Blind Spots." *Visualising the Unseen, Imagining the Unknown, Perfecting the Natural*. Ed. Andrew Graciano. Newcastle, UK: Cambridge Scholars Publishing, 2008. 1–24.
———. "Painting as Exploration: Visualizing Nature in Eighteenth-Century Colonial Science." *Colonial Latin American Review* 15.1 (2006): 81–104.
Bolo Hidalgo, Salomón. *Micaela Bastidas Puiucagua: La mujer más grande de América*. Lima: n.p., 1976.
Borchart de Moreno, Christiana. "Beyond the Obraje: Handicraft Production in Quito toward the End of the Colonial Period." *The Americas* 52.1 (1995): 1–24.
Bordo, Susan. "The Body and the Reproduction of Femininity." *Writing on the Body: Female Embodiment and Feminist Theory*. Ed. Katie Conboy et al. New York: Columbia University Press, 1997. 90–110.
———. *Unbearable Weight: Feminism, Western Culture, and the Body*. Berkeley: University of California Press, 1995.
Borja, Jaime. "Cuerpos coloniales y vidas ejemplares. Retóricas visuales y narradas." Third International Interdisciplinary Symposium on Colonial Studies in the Americas. The Colonial Americas Studies Organization (CASO). Universidad San Francisco de Quito, Ecuador. June 4–10, 2007.
Bourdieu, Pierre. *The Field of Cultural Production: Essays on Art and Literature*. New York: Columbia University Press, 1993.
Braidotti, Rosi. "Mothers, Monsters, and Machines." *Writing on the Body: Female Embodiment and Feminist Theory*. Ed. Conboy et al. New York: Columbia University Press, 1997. 58–79.
Bravo Arriaga, María Dolores. "El costumbrero del monasterio de Jesús María de México o del lenguaje ritual." *Mujer y cultura en la colonia hispanoamericana*. Ed. Mabel Moraña. Pittsburgh: Biblioteca de América, 1996. 161–70.
Bueno, Cosme. "El conocimiento de los tiempos." *Geografía del Perú virreinal* (1766). Ed. Daniel Valcárcel. Lima: n.p, 1951. 49–67.
Buffon, Georges-Louis Leclerc, Comte de. *Natural History: Containing a Theory of the*

*Earth, a General History of Man, of the Brute Creation, and of Vegetables, Minerals.* London: 1797.
Burkholder, Mark A., and Lyman L. Johnson. *Colonial Latin America.* New York: Oxford University Press, 2001.
Burns, Kathryn. *Colonial Habits: Monasteries and the Spiritual Economy of Cuzco, Peru.* Durham, NC: Duke University Press, 1999.
Busto Duthurburo, José Antonio. *José Gabriel Túpac Amaru antes de su rebelión.* Lima: Pontificia Universidad Católica del Perú, 1981.
Butler, Judith. "Performative Acts and Gender Constitution: An Essay in Phenomenology and Feminist Theory." *Theatre Journal* 40.4 (1988): 519–31. Reprinted in *Writing on the Body: Female Embodiment and Feminist Theory.* Ed. Katie Conboy et al. New York: Columbia University Press, 1997. 401–17.
Bynum, Caroline Walker. *Fragmentation and Redemption: Essays on Gender and the Human Body in Medieval Religion.* New York: Zone Books, 1992.
Campbell, Leon G. "Ideology and Factionalism during the Great Rebellion, 1780–82." *Resistance, Rebellion, and Consciousness in the Andean Peasant World, 18th to 20th Centuries.* Ed. Steve Stern. Madison: University of Wisconsin Press, 1987. 110–39.
———. "Women and the Great Rebellion in Peru, 1780–83." *The Americas: A Quarterly Review* 42.2 (1985): 163–96.
Canguilhem, Georges. "Monstrosity and the Monstrous." *The Body: A Reader.* Ed. Mariam Fraser and Monica Greco. New York: Routledge, 2005. 187–93.
Cañizares-Esguerra, Jorge. *How to Write the History of the New World: Historiographies, Epistemologies, and Identities in the Eighteenth-Century Atlantic World.* Stanford, CA: Stanford University Press, 2001.
Carrera, Magali. *Imagining Identity in New Spain: Race, Lineage, and the Colonial Body in Portraiture and Casta Painting.* Austin: University of Texas Press, 2003.
Carrió de la Vandera, Alonso. *El lazarillo de ciegos caminantes.* Madrid: Editora Nacional, 1980.
Castro-Klarén, Sara. "The Nation in Ruins: Archeology and the Rise of the Nation." *Beyond Imagined Communities: Reading and Writing the Nation in Nineteenth-Century Latin America.* Ed. Sara Castro-Klarén and John Charles Chasteen. Washington, DC: Johns Hopkins University Press, 2003. 161–95.
Castro-Klarén, Sara, and John Charles Chasteen, eds. "Introduction." *Beyond Imagined Communities: Reading and Writing the Nation in Nineteenth-Century Latin America.* Washington, DC: Johns Hopkins University Press, 2003.
Cesareo, Mario. *Cruzados, mártires y beatos: Emplazamientos del cuerpo colonial.* West Lafayette, IN: Purdue University Press, 1995.
Childress, Joseph, and Gary Hentzi. *Columbia Dictionary of Modern Literary and Cultural Criticism.* New York: Columbia University Press, 1995.
Cieza de León, Pedro. *Del señorío de los Incas.* Buenos Aires: Ediciones Argentinas Solar, 1943.
Classen, Constance. *Inca Cosmology and the Human Body.* Salt Lake City: University of Utah Press, 1993.
Clément, Jean-Pierre. *El Mercurio peruano, 1790–1795.* 2 vols. Vol. 1: Estudio. Madrid: Iberoamericana, 1997. Vol. 2: Antología. Madrid: Iberoamericana, 1998.
Cobo, Bernabé. *Historia del Nuevo Mundo.* 1653. 4 vols. Vol. 3. Seville: Imp. de E. Rasco, 1892.
———. *History of the Inca Empire: An Account of the Indians' Customs and Their Origin Together with a Treatise on Inca Legends.* Trans. Roland Hamilton. Austin: University of Texas Press, 1979.

Conboy, Katie, et al. "Introduction." *Writing on the Body: Female Embodiment and Feminist Theory*. Ed. Conboy et al. New York: Columbia University Press, 1977. 1–12.

Corbin, Alain. *Historia del cuerpo*. 3 vols. Vol. 2. Trans. Paloma Gómez et al. Buenos Aires: Taurus, 2005.

Cornblit, Oscar. *Power and Violence in the Colonial City: Oruro from the Mining Renaissance to the Rebellion of Túpac Amaru (1740–1782)*. Trans. Elizabeth Ladd Glick. Cambridge: Cambridge University Press, 1995.

Cornejo Bouroncle, Jorge. *Sangre andina: Diez mujeres cuzqueñas*. Cuzco: H. G. Rozas Suvesores, 1949.

Cortés, Hernán. *Cartas de relación*. Mexico City: Porrúa, 1985.

Cotton, Daniel. *Cannibals and Philosophers: Bodies of Enlightenment*. Baltimore: Johns Hopkins University Press, 2001.

Covarrubias Horozco, Sebastián. 1611. *Tesoro de la lengua castellana o española*. Madrid: Biblioteca Áurea Hispánica, 2006.

Croix, Teodoro de. "Memorias." *Memorias de los virreyes que han gobernado el Perú durante el tiempo del coloniaje español*. 6 vols. Vol 5. Lima,1859.

Curran, Patricia. *Grace before Meals: Food Ritual and Body Discipline in Monastery Culture*. Urbana: University of Illinois Press, 1989.

Dean, Carolyn. *Inka Bodies and the Body of Christ: Corpus Christi in Colonial Cuzco, Peru*. Durham, NC: Duke University Press, 1999.

Dean-Smith, Susan. "Creating the Colonial Subject: Casta Paintings, Collectors, and Critics in Eighteenth-Century Mexico and Spain." *Colonial Latin American Review* 14.2 (2005): 169–204.

De Armas, Frederick A. "Introduction." *Writing for the Eyes in the Spanish Golden Age*. Ed. Frederick A. de Armas. Lewisburg, PA: Bucknell Unversity Press, 2004. 7–20.

Delemeau, Jean. "Miedos de ayer y de hoy." In *El miedo: Reflexiones sobre su dimensión social y cultural*. Ed. Jean Delemeau et al. Medellín: Corporación Región, 2002. 9–21.

De Quirós, C. Bernaldo. *La picota: Crímenes y castigos en el país castellano en los tiempos medios*. Madrid: Librería General de Victoriano Suárez, 1907.

De Vos, Paula S. "The Rare, the Singular, and the Extraordinary: Natural History and the Collection of Curiosities in the Spanish Empire." *Science in the Spanish and Portuguese Empires, 1500–1800*. Ed. Bleichmar et al. Stanford, CA: Stanford University Press, 2009. 271–89.

———. "Research Development, and Empire: State Support of Science in the Later Spanish Empire." *Colonial Latin American Review* 15.1 (2006): 55–79.

*Diario de Lima*. Lima, 1791.

*Diccionario de autoridades*. Madrid: Editorial Gredos, 1990.

*Diccionario de la lengua española de la Real Academia Española*. Madrid: Brosmac, 1992.

Diderot, Denis. "Encyclopédie." *The Portable Enlightenment Reader*. Ed. Isaac Kramnick. New York: Penguin Books, 1995. 17–21.

Dixon, Laurinda S. *Perilous Chastity: Women and Illness in Pre-enlightenment Art and Medicine*. Ithaca, NY: Cornell University Press, 1995.

Douglas, Mary. *Purity and Danger*. New York: Routledge, 2008.

Edney, Matthew H. "Reconsidering Enlightenment Geography and Map Making: Reconnaissance, Mapping, Archive." *Geography and Enlightenment*. Ed. David N. Livingstone and Charles W. J. Withers. Chicago: University of Chicago Press, 1999. 165–98.

Erauso, Catalina. *Historia de la monja Alférez escrita por ella misma*. Madrid: Hiperión, 1986.

Feijoo de Sosa, Miguel. *Relacion descriptiva de la Ciudad y Provincia de Truxillo del Peru, con noticias exactas de su Estado Politico, según la Real orden dirigido al Excelentisimo Señor Virrey Conde de Super-Unda. Escrita por Don Miguel Feijoo.* Madrid, 1763.
Ferguson, George. *Signs and Symbols in Christian Art.* New York: Oxford University Press, 1966.
Fernández Alvarez, Manuel. *Casadas, monjas, rameras y brujas: La olvidada historia de la mujer española en el Renacimiento.* Madrid: Espasa Calpe, 2002.
Feuillé, Louis. *Journal des observations physiques, mathematiques et botaniques, faites par ordre du roi sur les côtes orientales de l'Amerique méridionale, aux Indes Occidentales. Et dans un autre voïage faite par le même ordre à la Nouvelle Espagne, aux illes de l'Amerique.* 1714. Paris, 1725.
Few, Martha. "Indian Autopsy and Epidemic Disease in Early Colonial Mexico." *Invasion and Transformation: Interdisciplinary Perspectives and the Conquest of Mexico.* Ed. Rebecca P. Brienen and Margaret A. Jackson. Boulder: University of Colorado Press, 2008. 153–66.
Filders, Valerie. *Wet Nursing: A History from Antiquity to the Present.* Oxford: Basil Blackwell, 1988.
Finch, Christopher. *Nineteenth Century Watercolors.* New York: Abbeville Press, 1991.
Findlen, Paula. *Possessing Nature: Museums, Collecting, and Scientific Culture in Early Modern Italy.* Berkeley: University of California Press, 1996.
Fisher, John R. *Bourbon Peru 1750–1824.* Liverpool: Liverpool University Press, 2003.
Foucault, Michel. *Discipline and Punish: The Birth of the Prison.* New York: Vintage Books, 1995.
———. *Power/Knowledge.* Ed. Colin Gordon. New York: Pantheon Books, 1980.
———. *The Order of Things: An Archeology of Knowledge.* New York: Vintage, 1970.
Fraser, Miriam, and Monica Greco. "Bodies and Social (Dis)order." *The Body: A Reader.* New York: Routledge, 2005. 67–72.
Freedburg, David. *The Eye of the Lynx: Galileo, His Friends, and the Beginning of Modern Natural History.* Chicago: University of Chicago Press, 2004.
Friedman, John Block. *The Monstrous Races in Medieval Art and Thought.* 1981. Syracuse, NY: Syracuse University Press, 2000.
Garcés, Carlos Alberto. *El cuerpo como texto: La problemática del castigo corporal en el siglo XVIII.* Argentina: Universidad Nacional de Jujuy, 1999.
García Cáceres, Uriel. *Juan del Valle Caviedes: Cronista de la Medicina: Historia de la medicina en el Perú en la segunda mitad del siglo XVII.* Lima: Banco Central de la Reserva, 1999.
García Sáiz, María Concepción. "Portraiture in Viceregal America." *Retratos: 2,000 Years of Latin American Portraits.* Ed. Elizabeth P. Benson et al. New Haven, CT: Yale University Press, 2005. 74–85.
Garret, David T. *The Indian Nobility of Cuzco, 1750–1825.* New York: Cambridge University Press, 2005.
*Gazeta de Mexico.* 1784. Edición facsimilar. Mexico City: Rolston-Bain, 1986.
Gilman, Sander. *Picturing Health and Illness: Images of Identity and Difference.* Baltimore: Johns Hopkins University Press, 1995.
Glave, Luis Miguel. *La rebelión de Túpac Amaru.* Cuzco: Centro de Estudios Rurales Andinos Bartolomé de las Casas, 1982.
Goodman, Jordan. *Tobacco in History: The Cultures of Dependence.* New York: Routledge, 1993.
Granjel, Luis. *Anatomía española de la Ilustración.* Salamanca: Universidad de Salamanca, 1963.

Grosz, Elizabeth. "Refiguring Bodies." *The Body: A Reader*. Ed. Mariam Fraser and Monica Greco. London: Routledge, 2005. 47–51.

———. *Space, Time, and Perversion: Essays on the Politics of Bodies*. New York: Routledge, 1995.

———. *Volatile Bodies: Toward a Corporeal Feminism*. Bloomington: Indiana University Press, 1994.

Guaman Poma de Ayala, Felipe. *Nueva corónica y buen gobierno*. Ed. John Murra and Rolena Adorno. Mexico City: Siglo XXI, 1980.

Guardia, Sara Beatriz. *Voces y cantos de las mujeres*. Lima: Centro de Estudios de La Mujer en la Historia de América Latina, 1991.

Haidt, Rebecca. *Embodying the Enlightenment: Knowing the Body in Eighteenth-Century Spanish Literature and Culture*. New York: St. Martin's Press, 1998.

Hall, James. *Dictionary of Subjects and Symbols in Art*. New York: Harper and Row, 1979.

Hammer, Kirsten. "Monjas Coronadas: The Crowned Nuns of Viceregal Mexico." *Retratos: 2,000 Years of Latin American Portraits*. Ed. Elizabeth P. Benson et al. New Haven, CT: Yale University Press, 2005. 86–101.

Hanafi, Zakiya. *Magic, Medicine, and the Marvelous in the Time of Scientific Revolution*. Durham, NC: Duke University Press, 2000.

Herzog, Tamar. *Defining Nations: Immigrants and Citizens in Early Modern Spain and Spanish America*. New Haven, CT: Yale University Press, 2003.

Higgins, Antony. *Constructing the Criollo Archive: Subjects of Knowledge in the Bibliotheca Mexicana and the Rusticatio Mexicana*. West Lafayette, IN: Purdue University Press, 2000.

Hill, Ruth. *Hierarchy, Commerce, and Fraud in Bourbon Spanish America: A Postal Inspector's Exposé*. Nashville: Vanderbilt University Press, 2005.

———. *Sceptres and Sciences in the Spains: Four Humanists and the New Philosophy (ca. 1680–1740)*. Liverpool: Liverpool University Press, 2000.

Hillman, David, and Carla Mazzio. "Introduction: Individual Parts." *The Body in Parts: Fantasies of Corporeality in Early Modern Europe*. Ed. David Hillman and Carla Mazzio. New York: Routledge, 1997. xi–xxix.

Hobbes, Thomas. *Leviathan*. 1651. New York: Penguin Books, 1985.

Huet, Marie-Hélène. *Monstrous Imaginations*. Cambridge, MA: Harvard University Press, 1993.

Hutton, Patrick. *History as an Art of Memory*. Hanover, NH: University of Vermont Press, 1993.

Hyde, Alan. *Bodies of Law*. Princeton, NJ: Princeton University Press, 1997.

Ibsen, Kristine. *Women's Spiritual Autobiography in Colonial Spanish America*. Gainesville: University of Florida Press, 1999.

———. "'The Hiding Places of My Power': Sebastián Josefa de la Santísima Trinidad and the Hagiographic Representation of the Body in Colonial Spanish America." *Colonial Latin American Review* 7.2 (1998): 251–70.

Impelluso, Lucia. *Nature and Its Symbols*. Trans. Stephen Sartarelli. Los Angeles: J. Paul Getty Museum, 2004.

Jackson, Stevi, Jane Prince, and Pauline Young. "Science, Medicine, and Reproductive Technology." *Women's Studies: Essential Readings*. Ed. Stevi Jackson. New York: New York University Press, 1993. 363–68.

Johnson, Julie Greer. *Satire in Colonial Spanish America: Turning the World Upside Down*. Austin: University of Texas Press, 1993.

Jouve Martín, José Ramón. "En olor de santidad: Hagiografía, cultos locales y escritura religiosa en Lima, siglo XVII." *Colonial Latin American Review* 13.2 (2004): 181–98.

Judovitz, Dalia. *The Culture of the Body: Genealogies of Modernity*. Ann Arbor: University of Michigan Press, 2001.
Kagan, Richard L. *Urban Images of the Hispanic World, 1493–1793*. New Haven, CT: Yale University Press, 2000.
Kaplan, E. Ann. *Motherhood and Representation: The Mother in Popular Culture and Melodrama*. London: Falta Editorial, 1992.
Katzew, Ilona. *Casta Painting: Images of Race in Eighteenth-Century Mexico*. New Haven, CT: Yale University Press, 2004.
Kelly, Veronica, and Dorothea Von Mücke. "Introduction: Body and Text." *Body and Text in the Eighteenth Century*. Ed. Kelly and Von Mücke. Stanford, CA: Stanford University Press, 1994. 1–20.
King, Helen. *Hippocrates' Woman: Reading the Female Body in Ancient Greece*. New York: Routledge, 1998.
Kinsbruner, Jay. *The Colonial Spanish-American City: Urban Life in the Age of Atlantic Capitalism*. Austin: University of Texas Press, 2005.
Klaren, Peter Flindell. *Peru: Society and Nationhood in the Andes*. New York: Oxford University Press, 2000.
Laín Entralgo, Pedro. *El cuerpo humano: Oriente y Grecia Antigua*. Madrid: Espasa Calpe, 1987.
Lanning, John Tate. *The Royal Protomedicato: The Regulation of the Medical Profession in the Spanish Empire*. Durham, NC: Duke University Press, 1985.
Laqueur, Thomas. *Making Sex: Body and Gender from the Greeks to Freud*. Cambridge, MA: Harvard University Press, 1990.
Lavrin, Asunción. "De su puño y letra: Epístolas monasteriales." *El monacato femenino en el Imperio español: Monasterios beaterios, recogimientos y colegios*. Ed. Manuel Ramos Medina. Mexico City: Centro de Estudios de Historia de México, 1995. 43–61.
———. "La vida femenina como experiencia religiosa: Biografía y hagiografía en Hispanoamérica colonial." *Colonial Latin American Review* 2.1 (1993): 27–51.
———. "Female Religious." *Cities and Society in Colonial Latin America*. Ed. Louisa Schell Hoberman and Susan Migden Socolow. Albuquerque: University of New Mexico Press, 1986. 165–95.
———. "Ecclesiastical Reform of the Nunneries in New Spain in the Eighteenth Century." *The Americas* 12.2 (1982): 182–203.
Lefebvre, Henri. *The Production of Space*. Trans. Donald Nicholson-Smith. Oxford: Blackwell, 1998.
Lequanda, Joseph Ignacio de. "Descripción geográfica de la ciudad y partido de Truxillo." *Mercurio peruano*. 1793.
Lingis, Alphonso. *Foreign Bodies*. New York: Routledge, 1994.
Lizárraga, Reginaldo de. *Descripción del Perú, Tucumán, Río de la Plata y Chile*. Madrid: Historia, 1987.
Lloyd, Genevieve. *The Man of Reason: "Male" and "Female" in Western Philosophy*. Minneapolis: University of Minnesota Press, 1993.
Loayza, Francisco A., ed. *Mártires y heroínas. Documentos inéditos del año de 1780 a 1782*. Lima: Librería e Imprenta D. Miranda, 1945.
López Serrano, Matilde. *Trujillo del Perú en el siglo XVIII*. Madrid: Editorial Patrimonio Nacional, 1976.
Low, Setha M. *On the Plaza: The Politics of Public Space and Culture*. Austin: University of Texas Press, 2000.
Lupton, Deborah. *Risk*. London: Routledge, 1999.
Macera, Pablo. "El tiempo del Obispo Martínez de Compañón." *Trujillo del Perú. Baltasar*

Martínez de Compañón. Siglo XVIII. Ed. Pablo Macera et al. Lima: Ausonia S.A., 1997. 13–80.
Mangan, Jane. *Trading Roles: Gender, Ethnicity, and the Urban Economy in Colonial Potosi*. Durham, NC: Duke University Press, 2005.
Manningham, Richard. *Artis Obstetricariæ Compendium*. London: Edward Littleton, 1739.
Manso de Velasco, José Antonio. *Memoria de los virreyes que han gobernado el Perú durante el tiempo del coloniaje español*. Vol. 5. Lima: Librería Central de Felipe Baillo, 1859.
Marchena, Juan F. "Su Majestad quiere saber. Información oficial y reformismo borbónico en la América de la Ilustración." *Recepción y difusión de textos ilustrados*. Ed. Diana Soto Arango et al. Madrid: Colección Actas Tavara, S.L., 2003. 151–85.
María Josefa de la Santísima Trinidad. *Historia de la fundación del monasterio de Trinitarias descalzas de Lima. 1783*. Lima: n.p, 1957.
Martín, Luis. *Daughters of the Conquistadores: Women of the Viceroyalty of Peru*. Dallas: Southern Methodist University Press, 1989.
Martínez Compañón, Baltasar. *Trujillo del Perú*. 1789. 9 vols. Madrid: Ediciones de Cultura Hispánica, 1998.
———. "Apéndice III." *Trujillo del Perú*. Ed. Manuel Ballesteros Gaibrois. Madrid: Ediciones de Cultura Hispánica, 1994.
———. "Copia de la dedicatoria con que ofrecio a S.M. un cunplido Mapa de la Intendencia y Obispado de Truxillo su Dignisimo Prelado el Illmo. Señor Don Baltasar Jayme Martínez Compañón." 1786. *Mercurio peruano* 347.11 (1794).
Mazio, Carla. "Sins of the Tongue." *The Body in Parts: Fantasies of Corporeality in Early Modern Europe*. Ed. David Hillman and Mazzio. New York: Routledge, 1997. 53–79.
Mazzeo, Cristina. "El comercio libre de 1778 y sus repercusiones en el mercado limeño." *El Perú en el Siglo XVIII. La era borbónica*. Ed. Scarlett O'Phelan Godoy. Lima: Pontificia Universidad Católica del Perú, 1999. 127–45.
Mazzotti, José Antonio. "Resentimiento criollo y nación étnica: el papel de la épica novo-hispana." *Agencias criollas: La ambigüedad "colonial" en las letras hispanoamericanas*. Ed. José Antonio Mazzotti. Pittsburgh: Biblioteca de América, 2000. 143–60.
McClintock, Anne. *Imperial Leather: Race, Gender, and Sexuality in the Colonial Contest*. New York: Routledge, 1995.
McCormack, Sabine. *Religion in the Andes: Vision and Imagination in Early Colonial Peru*. Princeton, NJ: Princeton University Press, 1991.
McKnight, Kathryn Joy. *The Mystic Nun of Tunja: The Writings of Mother Castillo, 1671–1742*. Amherst: University of Massachusetts Press, 1998.
Meléndez, Mariselle. "An Eighteenth-Century Visual Representation of *Truxillo del Peru*: Picturing Cultural and Social Difference in the Black Population." *Bulletin of Spanish Studies* 86, nos. 7–8 (Fall 2009): 119–42.
———. "Patria, Criollos, and Blacks: Imagining the Nation in the *Mercurio peruano*, 1791–1795." *Colonial Latin American Review* 15.2 (2006): 207–27.
———. "¡Si tal era el dedo, cuál sería el cuerpo! The Archival Project of María Josefa de la Santísima Trinidad (1783)." *Hispanic Review* 74.3 (2006): 251–77.
———. "Visualizing Difference: The Rhetoric of Clothing in Colonial Spanish America." *The Latin American Fashion Reader*. Ed. Regina Root. Series "Dress, Body, Culture." New York: Berg, 2005. 17–30.
———. "La dimensión discursiva del miedo y la economía del poder en las cartas y autos de Micaela Bastidas, 1780–1781." *DIECIOCHO (Hispanic Enlightenment)* 21.2 (1998): 181–93.
Mendiburu, Manuel de. *Diccionario Histórico-Biográfico del Perú*. 8 vols. Vol. 7. Lima, 1887. Vol. 8. Lima, 1890.

Merback, Mitchell B. *The Thief, the Cross, and the Wheel: Pain and the Spectacle of Punishment in Medieval and Renaissance Europe*. Chicago: University of Chicago Press, 1999.
*Mercurio peruano, 1790–1795*. Lima: Biblioteca Nacional del Perú, 1964.
Miró Quesada, Carlos. *Historia del periodismo peruano.*Lima: Librería Internacional del Perú, 1957.
Mitchell, W. J. T. *Picture Theory*. Chicago: University of Chicago Press, 1999.
———. *Iconology: Image, Text, Ideology*. Chicago: University of Chicago Press, 1987.
Morales, Mónica. "Alcohol Drinking as Cultural Construction from Colonial to Early Twentieth-Century South America." Ph.D. diss., Purdue University, 2001.
Mundi, Barbara. *The Mapping of New Spain: Indigenous Cartography and the Maps of Relaciones Geográficas*. Chicago: University of Chicago Press, 1996.
Muriel, Josefina. *Las mujeres de Hispanoamérica. Época colonial*. Madrid: Mapfre, 2002.
———. *Cultura femenina novohispana*. Mexico City: Universidad Nacional Autónoma, 1944.
Mutis, José Celestino. "Oración fúnebre que en las exequias funerales hechas por el Monasterio de la Enseñanza de Santafe de Bogotá; a su insigne benefactor y padre, el Ilmo. Señor Arzobispo de esta Metropolitana D. Baltazar Jayme Martínez Compañón." December 19, 1797.
Myers, Kathleen Ann. *Neither Saints Nor Sinners: Writing the Lives of Women in Spanish America*. Oxford: Oxford University Press, 2003.
———. "'Redeemer of America': Rosa de Lima (1586–1617): The Dynamics of Identity and Canonization." *Colonial Saints: Discovering the Holy in the Americas*. Ed. Allan Greer and Jodi Bilinkoff. New York: Routledge, 2003. 251–75.
Myers, Kathleen, and Amanda Powell. *A Wild Country Out in the Garden: The Spiritual Journals of a Colonial Mexican Nun*. Bloomington: Indiana University Press, 1999.
New York Academy of Medicine. "The 18th Century: Monsters as Battleground for Scientific and Philosophical Debates." October 2002. www.nyam.org/initiatives /im-histe_ter9.shtml.
———. "Teratology." October 2002. www.nyam.org/initiatives/im-histe_ter1.shtml.
Novas, Carlos, and Nikolas Rose. "Genetic Risk and the Birth of the Somatic Individual." *The Body: A Reader*. New York: Routledge, 2005. 237–41.
Nussbaum, Felicity. *Torrid Zones: Maternity, Sexuality, and Empire in Eighteenth-Century English Narratives*. Baltimore: Johns Hopkins University Press, 1995.
Olavarrieta, Juan Antonio de. *Semanario Crítico*. Lima, 1791.
O'Phelan Godoy, Scarlett. "Repensando el movimiento nacional Inca del siglo XVIII." *El Perú en el siglo XVIII: La era borbónica*. Lima: Pontificia Universidad Católica del Perú, 1999. 263–77.
———. *La gran rebelión en los Andes: De Túpac Amaru a Túpac Catari*. Cuzco: Centro de Estudios Regionales Andinos Bartolomé de las Casas, 1995.
Outram, Dorinda. *The Enlightenment*. 1995. New York: Cambridge University Press, 2006.
Palencia-Roth, Michael. "Enemies of God: Monsters and the Theology of the Conquest." *Monsters, Tricksters, and Sacred Cows: Animal Tales and American Identities*. Ed. A. James Arnold. Charlottesville: University Press of Virginia, 1996. 23–49.
Palma, Ricardo. *Tradiciones peruanas completas*. Madrid: Aguilar S.A. Ediciones, 1953.
Paniagua y Pérez, Jesús. "El monacato femenino en la Audencia de Quito." *El monacato femenino en el Imperio español: Monasterios, beaterios, recogimientos y colegios*. Ed. Manuel Ramos Medina. Mexico City: Centro de Estudios de Historia de México, 1995. 273–318.

Peralta Ruiz, Víctor. "Las razones de la Fe. La Iglesia y la Ilustración en el Perú, 1750–1800." *El Perú en el Siglo XVIII: La era borbónica*. Ed. Scarlett O'Phelan Godoy. Lima: Pontificia Universidad Católica del Perú, 1999. 177–204.

Pérez Samper, María Angeles. *La España del Siglo de las Luces*. Barcelona: Ariel Practicum, 2000.

Philo, Chris. "Edinburgh, Enlightenment, and the Geographies of Unreason." *Geography and Enlightenment*. Ed. David N. Livingstone and Charles W. J. Withers. Chicago: University of Chicago Press, 1999. 372–98.

Porras Barrenechea, Raúl. "Carta a Aurelio Miró Quesada a propósito de la obra del Obispo Martínez Compañón sobre Trujillo del Perú en el siglo XVIII." *La obra del Obispo Martínez Compañón sobre Trujillo del Perú en el siglo XVIII*. Madrid: Ediciones Cultura Hispánica, 1978. 18–21.

———. "Informe de Raúl Porras Barrenechea respecto de la obra del Obispo Martínez Compañón sobre Trujillo del Perú en el siglo XVIII." *La obra del Obispo Martínez Compañón sobre Trujillo del Perú en el siglo XVII*. Madrid: Ediciones Cultura Hispánica, 1978. 25–33.

Porter, James I. "Foreword." *The Body and Physical Difference: Discourses on Disability*. Ed. David T. Mitchell and Sharon L. Snyder. Ann Arbor: University of Michigan Press, 1997. xiii–xv.

Premo, Bianca. *Children of the Father King: Youth, Authority, and Legal Minority in Colonial Lima*. Chapel Hill: University of North Carolina Press, 2005.

———. "Misunderstood Love: Children and Wet Nurses, Creoles and Kings in Lima's Enlightenment." *Colonial Latin American Review* 14.2 (2005): 231–61.

Quijano, Aníbal. "Coloniality of Power, Eurocentrism, and Latin America." *Nepantla: Views from the South* 1.3 (2000): 533–80.

Radstone, Susannah, and Katherine Hodgkin. "Regimes of Memory: An Introduction." *Regimes of Memory*. New York: Routledge, 2003. 1–22.

Regalado de Hurtado, Liliana. "Reflexión sobre el cuerpo en el Virreinato del Perú." *Colonial Latin American Review* 11.2 (2002): 305–15.

Renan, Ernest. "What Is a Nation?" *Nation and Narration*. Ed. Homi Bhabha. New York: Routledge, 1990. 8–22.

Restrepo Manrique, Daniel. *La iglesia de Trujillo (Perú) bajo el episcopado de Baltasar Martínez Compañón (1780–1790)*. 2 vols. Bilbao: Servicio Central de Publicaciones del Gobierno Vasco, 1992.

Rich, Adrienne. *Of Woman Born: Motherhood as Experience and Institution*. 1986. New York: W. W. Norton, 1995.

Rico Bovio, Arturo. *Crítica de la corporeidad*. Mexico City: Cuadernos Joaquín Matiz, 1990.

Rivera Ayala, Sergio. *Discurso colonial en textos novohispanos: Espacio, cuerpo y poder*. Woodbridge, UK: Tamesis, 2009.

Rivilla Bonet y Pueyo, José de. *Desvios de la naturaleza O Tratado de el origen de los monstros. A que va anadido un compendio de curaciones chyrurgicas en monstruosos accidentes*. Lima, 1695.

Robin, Corey. *Fear: The History of a Political Idea*. Oxford: Oxford University Press, 2004.

Rodríguez García, Margarita Eva. *Criollismo y patria en la Lima ilustrada (1732–1795)*. Madrid: Miño y Dávila Editores, 2006.

Rosas Lauro, Claudia. "La visión ilustrada de las amas de leche negras y mulatas en el ámbito familiar (Lima, siglo XVIII)." *Passeurs, mediadores culturales y agentes de la primera globalización en el mundo ibérico, siglos XVI–XIX*. Ed. Scarlett O'Phelan

Godoy and Carmen Salazar-Soler. Lima: Pontificia Universidad Católica del Perú, 2005. 311–43.
———. "Madre sólo hay una. Ilustración, maternidad y medicina en el Perú del siglo XVIII." *Anuario de Estudios Americanos* 61.1 (2004): 103–38.
Rosas Moscoso, Fernando. "El miedo en la historia: Lineamientos generales para su estudio." *El miedo en el Perú: Siglos XVI al XX*. Ed. Claudia Rosas Lauro. Lima: Pontificia Universidad Católica del Perú, 2005. 23–32.
Rose, Gillian. *Visual Methodologies*. London: SAGE Publications, 2001.
Rousseau, Jean-Jacques. *Émile* (Selection): *Women, the Family, and Freedom: The Debate in Documents*. Ed. Susan Groag Bell and Karen M. Offen. Stanford, CA: Stanford University Press, 1983. 43–52.
Russo, Mary. "Female Grotesques: Carnival and Theory." *Writing on the Body: Female Embodiment and Feminist Theory*. Ed. Katie Conboy et al. New York: Columbia University Press, 1997. 318–36.
Sadler, T. W. *Medical Embryology*. Baltimore: Williams and Wilkins, 1981.
Saldaña, Juan José. "Ilustración, ciencia y técnica en América." *La Ilustración en la América colonial*. Ed. Diana Soto Arango et al. Madrid: Consejo de Investigaciones Científicas, 1995. 19–53.
Sánchez-Tagle, Esteban. "Las monjas ante la remodelación urbana en el siglo XVIII." *El monacato femenino en el Imperio español: Monasterios, beaterios, recogimientos y colegios*. Ed. Manuel Ramos Medina. Mexico City: Centro de Estudios de Historia de Mexico, 1995. 149–54.
Santa Cruz PachacutiYamqui Salcamaygua, Juan de. 1613. *Relación de antigüedades del Reyno del Perú: Cronistas indios y mestizos*. Comp. Francisco Carrillo. Lima: Editorial Horizonte, 1991. 111–55.
Sarasúa, Carmen. *Criados, nodrizas y amos: El servicio doméstico en la formación del mercado de trabajo madrileño, 1758–1868*. Madrid: Siglo XXI, 1994.
Sawday, Jonathan. *The Body Emblazoned: Dissection and the Human Body in Renaissance Culture*. New York: Routledge, 1995.
Scarry, Elaine. *The Body in Pain: The Making and Unmaking of the World*. New York: Oxford University Press, 1985.
Shklar, Judith N. "The Liberalism of Fear." *Liberalism and the Moral Life*. Ed. Nancy L. Rosenblum. Cambridge, MA: Harvard University Press, 1989. 21–38.
Silverblatt, Irene. *Moon, Sun, and Witches: Gender Ideologies and Class in Inca and Colonial Peru*. Princeton, NJ: Princeton University Press, 1987.
Siracusano, Gabriela. *El poder de los colores: De lo material simbólico en las prácticas culturales andinas. Siglos XVI–XVIII*. Buenos Aires: Fondo de Cultura Económica, 2005.
Socolow, Susan Migden. *The Women of Colonial Latin America*. New York: Cambridge University Press, 2000.
Solomon, Michael. *The Literature of Misogyny in Late Medieval Spain: The Arcipreste de Talavera and the Spill*. New York: Cambridge University Press, 1997.
Sor María Josefa de la Santísima Trinidad. *See* María Josefa de la Santísima Trinidad.
Soto Arango, Diana, and Jorge Tomás Uribe. "Textos ilustrados en la enseñanza y tertulias literarias en Santa Fe de Bogotá en el siglo XVIII." *Recepción y difusión de textos ilustrados*. Ed. Soto Arango et al. Madrid: Colección Actas Tavara, S.L., 2003. 59–75.
Spierenburg, Pieter. *The Spectacle of Suffering: Execution and the Evolution of Repression: From Pre-Industrial Metropolis to the European Experience*. Cambridge: Cambridge University Press, 1984.
Stafford, Barbara Maria. *Body Criticism: Imagining the Unseen in Enlightenment Art and Medicine*. 1991. Boston: MIT Press, 1997.

Stern, Steve. "The Age of Andean Insurrection, 1742–1782." *Resistance, Rebellion, and Consciousness in the Andean Peasant World, 18th to 20th Centuries*. Ed. Steve Stern. Madison: University of Wisconsin Press, 1987. 34–93.
Stoler, Ann Laura. *Race and the Education of Desire: Foucault's History of Sexuality and the Colonial Order of Things*. Durham, NC: Duke University Press, 1995.
Stolley, Karen. "The Eighteenth Century: Narrative Forms, Scholarship, and Learning." *The Cambridge History of Latin American Literature*. Ed. Roberto González Echevarría and Enrique Pupo-Walker. 3 vols. Vol. 1. New York: Cambridge University Press, 1996. 336–74.
Suetonius. *Lives of the Twelve Caesars*. 1506. London: T. Hodgkin for A. and J. Churchill, 1698.
Synnott, Anthony. *The Body Social: Symbolism, Self and Society*. New York: Routledge, 1993.
Szeminski, Jan. "Why Kill the Spaniard? New Perspectives on Andean Insurrectionary Ideology in the 18th Century." *Resistance, Rebellion, and Consciousness in the Andean Peasant World, 18th to 20th Centuries*. Ed. Steve Stern. Madison: University of Wisconsin Press, 1987. 166–92.
Tandeter, Enrique, et al. "Indians in the Late Colonial Markets: Sources and Numbers." *Ethnicity, Markets, and Migration in the Andes: At the Crossroads of History and Anthropology*. Ed. Brooke Larson and Olivia Harris. Durham, NC: Duke University Press, 1995. 196–223.
Thomas, Clayton L., ed. *Taber's Cyclopedic Medical Dictionary*. Philadelphia: F. A. Davis Company, 1989.
Tobin, Beth Fowkes. *Picturing Imperial Power: Colonial Subjects in Eighteenth-Century British Painting*. Durham, NC: Duke University Press, 1999.
Todd, Dennis. *Imagining Monsters: Miscreations of the Self in Eighteenth-Century England*. Chicago: University of Chicago Press, 1995.
Tuana, Nancy. *The Less Noble Sex: Scientific, Religious, and Philosophical Conceptions of Woman's Nature*. Bloomington: Indiana University Press, 1993.
Twinam, Ann. *Public Lives, Private Secrets: Gender, Honor, Sexuality, and Illegitimacy in Colonial Spanish America*. Stanford, CA: Stanford University Press, 1999.
Uribe, María Teresa. "Las incidencias del miedo en la política: Una mirada desde Hobbes." *El miedo: Reflexiones sobre su dimensión social y cultural*. Ed. Jean Delemeau et al. Medellín: Corporación Región, 2002. 25–46.
Uztaris, Geronymo de. *Theórica y práctica de comercio y marina: La España del Siglo de las Luces*. Ed. María Angeles Pérez Samper. Barcelona: Ariel Practicum, 2000.
Varcárcel, Carlos Daniel, ed. *La rebelión de Túpac Amaru*. Mexico City: Fondo de Cultura Económica, 1973.
———. *Colección Documental de la Independencia del Perú*. 4 vols. Vol. 2. Lima: Comisión Nacional del Sesquicentenario de la Independencia del Perú, 1971.
Vargas Ugarte, Rubén. *Historia de la Iglesia en el Perú*. 5 vols. Vol. 4. Burgos: Imprenta de Aldecoa, 1961.
Vega, Inca Garcilaso de la. *Comentarios reales*. Mexico City: Porrúa, 1984.
Vega, Juan José. *José Gabriel Túpac Amaru*. Lima: Ed. Universal S.A., 1969.
Velasco, Juan. *Historia del Reino de Quito en la América Meridional*. 2 vols. Vol. 1. Quito: Impresora El Comercio, 1946.
Vidal, Teodoro. "José Campeche: Portrait Painter of an Epoch." *Retratos: 2,000 Years of Latin American Portraits*. Ed. Elizabeth P. Benson et al. New Haven, CT: Yale University Press, 2005. 102–13.
Viforcos Marinas, María Isabel. "Las reformas disciplinarias de Trento y la realidad de

la vida monástica en el Perú virreinal." *El monacato femenino en el Imperio español: Monasterios, beaterios, recogimientos y colegios.* Ed. Manuel Ramos Medina. Mexico City: Centro de Estudios de Historia de México, 1995. 523–40.

Vlahos, Olivia. *Body: The Ultimate Symbol.* New York: Lippincott, 1979.

Walker, Charles F. *Shaky Colonialism: The 1746 Earthquake-Tsunami in Lima, Peru, and Its Long Aftermath.* Durham, NC: Duke University Press, 2008.

———."Civilize or Control? The Lingering Impact of the Bourbon Urban Reforms." *Political Cultures in the Andes, 1750–1950.* Ed. Nils Jacobsen and Cristóbal Aljovín de Losada. Durham, NC: Duke University Press, 2005. 74–95.

———. "Desde el terremoto a las bolas de fuego: Premoniciones conventuales sobre la destrucción de Lima en el siglo XVIII." *Relaciones* 97.25 (2004): 29–55.

———. "Crime in the Time of the Great Fear: Indians and the State in the Peruvian Southern Andes, 1780–1820." *Crime and Punishment in Latin America.* Ed. Ricardo D. Salvatore et al. Durham, NC: Duke University Press, 2001. 35–55.

———. *Smoldering Ashes: Cuzco and the Creation of Republican Peru, 1780–1840.* Durham, NC: Duke University Press, 1999.

Weber, David J. *Bárbaros: Spaniards and Their Savages in the Age of Enlightenment.* New Haven, CT: Yale University Press, 2005.

*Webster's Universal Dictionary of the English Language.* Cleveland: World Publishing Company, 1940.

# Index

Page numbers in bold refer to illustrations.

Academic Society of Lovers of the Country, 152, 170
accessories, clothing, 56
Acevedo, Felipe, 197n66
achromatism, 145
Acos, 24
Adorno, Rolena, 43, 184n6
Age of Reason, 6
Age of the Andean Insurrection, 14
Aguirre, Carlos, 179n20
Albornoz, Cristóbal de, 201n15
*alcabala*, 14
Alférez, Monja, 204n40
Alfonso X, 24, 162, 179n20, 180n35, 205n57
Almoguera y Ramírez, Juan, 86–87
Álvarez, Manuel Fernández, 206n67
*amas de leche*. *See* wet nurses
"Amas de Leche. Segunda carta de Filomates sobre la educación" (Phylomathes), 164–65
Amat y Junient, Manuel, 187n38
Amerindian bodies, 175n7
Ana de la Santísima Trinidad, 101, 113
Ana de Robles
  illnesses, 104–6
  Monasterio de Trinitarias Descalzas and, 100, 101–2, 109, 195n41, 195n43
  relics of, 108
  tobacco and, 103–4
anal intercourse, 140
anatomy, 141, 147, 149–50, 204n44
Andean criminal law, 177n3
Andean insurrections, 179n19
Anderson, Benedict, 200n5
Andrien, Kenneth J., 14
anemia, 112
anorexia, 113, 196n59. *See also* holy anorexia

anorexia nervosa, 196n59
*antojos*, 155
Archeological Museum of Madrid, 185n15
Archivo de Indias, 187n34
Areche, José Antonio de, 15, 23, 26, 32, 182nn45–46
Arenal, Electa, 84, 92
Arequipa, 30
Aristio (pseud.), 36, 130, 200n6, 202n20
Aristotle, 135, 142
Armendáriz, José de, 61
arms, 31
Arriaga, Antonio de, 12
*arrobamientos*, 111, 121
*Artis obstetricariae compendium* (Manningham), 155, 204–5n50
Arze, Silvia, 179n19
Atahualpa, 33
atlases, geographical, 186n29
Aucapacharuna Indians, 35
*audiencia*, 5, 106
Austin, Alfredo López, 176n7
Auto General de Reforma, 87
autopsies, 136, 201n16

Bacque, Antoine de, 207n74
Ballesteros Gaibrois, Manuel, 185n15, 186n28
Barrenechea, Gabriel de, 114
Barrera, Antonio, 79, 184n11
Bastidas, Antonio, 181n45
Bastidas, Micaela
  biographical details, 15, 178n14
  body of, 2, 27–31, 36, 38, **39**, **40**, 172, 178n10
  death sentence, 13, 23, 24, 25–26, 33, 172, 188n38
  execution, 26–31, 34, 36, 37, 39–40, 172, 181nn44–45

223

Bastidas, Micaela, *continued*
   fear and, 17, 20–22, 172
   letters/edicts by and to, 13, 16–17, 178n8
   memory of, 31, 40, 181n44
   monstrous nature of, 15–23, 39
   respect and obedience toward, 18
   Cecilia Túpac Amaru and, 180n32
   Túpac Amaru and, 15, 21, 178n5
   Túpac Amaru insurrection and, 5, 12–13, 15, 177–78n4, 179n22, 179n25, 183n60
   violence and, 17–18
Batallanos, Maria Josepha, 143–46
Bauer, Arnold J., 54, 68, 188n45, 188n51
Bausate y Mesa, Jayme, 199n4
*beaterios*, 195n39
Bedóa, Diego de, 101
Bell, Rudolph, 112, 196–97n61
Benedict XIII (pope), 196n50
Benjamin, Walter, 78
Bennett, Tony, 80, 187n32, 190n70
Bermejo y Roldán, Francisco, 201n17
Bernal, Ignacio, 193n26
Bhabha, Homi, 123
*bicípete/bicéfalo*, 200n6
Bilinkoff, Jodi, 193n25
birth defects, 136, 137, 200n10. *See also* congenital malformations; monsters/monstrosities; monstrous births
blacks
   black populations, 56, 62, 163, 202n25, 208n77
   black women, 56, **57**, 58, 139–40, 168, 207–8n77
   as inferior, 207n71
   as wet nurses, 160–61, 163
   See also *negra bozal*; *negra criolla*
Bleichmar, Daniela, 43, 185–86n24, 185n17, 189n60
bodies
   abnormal female, 146
   Amerindian bodies, 175n7
   anatomy of female, 141
   architectural bodies, 100, 109
   biological assessments of, 177n17
   burning of, 36, 40
   Christian bodies, 55
   commodification of, 80
   construction of, 7–9
   cosmology and, 176n7
   of criminal or accused, 3
   definition, 7

   dismemberment of, 28, 31, 37–38
   dynamic nature of, 40
   *Historia de la fundación del Monasterio de Trinitarias Descalzas de Lima* and, 99, 102
   idea of, 7–9
   images in *Truxillo del Perú*, 47, 48
   Incas and, 33
   incomplete bodies, 31
   incorruptibility of, 116
   indolent bodies, 171–72
   Judovitz on, 173
   as machines, 152–60
   male bodies, 175–76n7
   male perception of female, 141
   materiality of, 124, 148, 154
   as memory, 48–49, 110
   in *Mercurio peruano*, 128–29
   metaphoric interpretations of, 7, 28, 33, 177n18, 181n41
   monasteries and, 100
   of monsters, 207n74
   naked bodies, 55
   nuns' abuse of, 112
   pain and suffering of, 105
   productive bodies, 6, 63, **64–74**, 66–70, 73–74
   public executions and, 23–31, 181n39
   religious bodies, 1–2, 174
   religious patriotism and, 85
   religious perfection and, 110, 124
   as sacred space, 110
   sick bodies, 74–78, 190nn67–68
   as site of governance, 174
   social bodies, 3
   space and, 29, 63, 100
   state as, 177n18
   symbolic nature of, 124
   as symbolic spaces, 99, 195n37
   as text, 13, 23–31, 37, 117, 181n39
   types, 172
   of wet nurses, 166, 167, 207n74
   *See also* Hanan; Hurin; Tahuantisuyu
Bonells, Jaime, 162–63, 206n59
Bordo, Susan, 13, 147
Bourbon reforms, 4–5, 80, 86, 88, 89, 158–59, 178n12, 206n62
Bourdieu, Pierre, 42, 183n4
Braidotti, Rosi, 146
brain, 102
Bueno, Cosme, 184n8
Buenos Aires, 5, 176n12

Buffon, Comte de, 145, 203n35
burning, of bodies, 36, 40
Burns, Kathryn, 84
Butler, Judith, 148
Bynum, Carolyn, 111, 113, 116, 196n51

Cabinet of Natural Sciences, 44
*cacica*, 24
*caciques*, 176n14
Cajías, Madgalena, 179n19
calf, bicephalous, 130
*calidad*, 52, 188n42
Callanca, 30
Callao, 5, 176n12
Campbell, Leon G., 178n12
cancer, 198n72
Cañizares-Esguerra, Jorge, 49, 91, 187n33, 187n35
cannibalism, 203n36
canonistas, 203n28
canonization, 198n76
Cápac, Huayna, 34
Carabaya, 30
Caranques, 35
*carne*, 180n26
Carrera, Magali, 3, 187n38
"Carta escrita a la Sociedad sobre el abuso de que los hijos tuteen a sus padres" (Phylomathes), 163–64, 206n61
Cartagena de Indias, 186n25
*Cartas de relación* (Cortés), 201n15
"Carta segunda de Erasistrato Suadel relativa a las precauciones que debe observarse en los *Partos* en continuacion de las publicadas en el *Merc.* Num. 45" (Suadel), 158–60
*casta* paintings, 51, 187n38, 188n44
*castas*, 51, 61, 167, 187n37
Castelo, Andrés, 181n45
Castro-Gómez, Santiago, 63
Castro-Klarén, Sara, 36, 91, 93, 181n44, 193n26
*cédulas*, 87
cesarean sections, 127–28, 199n1
Cesareo, Mario, 175–76n7, 194n37
Charles III, 4, 43–44, 46, 86, 87, 150
Charles IV, 4, 46, 194n36
*chicha*, 70, 73, **73**, 190n65
childbirth, 158–60
childrearing, 162–69, 206–7n68
Chimu culture, 45
*cholas/cholos*, 185n21

Chucuyto, Indians of, 183n55
churches, 191n2
Cieza de León, Pedro, 34, 37, 182n48
Cipriana María de las Llagas, 116, 197n68
*cirugia*, 199n3
Cisneros, Francisco, 20
citizens
    becoming, 177n21
    Christian citizens, 95
    concept of, 8, 177n21
    creation of good, 95
    in eighteenth-century Spanish America, 189n59
    productive citizens, 1, 6, 47, 63, 174
    women as productive citizens, 63, 67, 80–81, 190n69
Classen, Constance, 33, 176n7
Clerque, Manuel, 109, 194n30, 196n56
clothing, 53–56, 58–62, 188nn44–45, 188–89n51
cloth trades, 189–90n31
Cobo, Bernabé, 35–36
cocoa, 103, 104
*cofradías*, 185n14
collecting and collections, 42, 78
colonial control, 78
colonial discourse, 168
*Comentarios reales* (Garcilaso), 34
*concilios provinciales*, 86
Condemayta, Tomasa Titu, 24–25, 178n12, 180n34, 181n45
Condorcanqui, José Gabriel. *See* Túpac Amaru
congenital malformations, 147, 203n37. *See also* birth defects; deformities
consumption, 8, 68
*contact zone*, 37, 183n56
convents. *See* monasteries
Cornblit, Oscar, 14
corporal punishment, 34, 36, 78, 179n20
corporeality, 105
*corregidores*, 5, 11, 17, 176n13, 177n1
*corrupto* (term), 119
Cortés, Hernán, 201n15
cosmogony, 176n7
cosmology, 176n7
Cotabamba, 143, 203n32
Council of Indies, 49, 187n35
Council of Trent, 97
Covarrubias, Sebastián de, 131, 195n47, 200n8
creoles, 19–20, 167

*criada*, 46
*criollo*, 206n66
*crónica*, 192n18
*Crónica del Perú* (Cieza), 34, 182n48
*Cruzados, mártires y beatos* (Cesareo), 175–76n7
cuaderno antiguo, 92
*Cuerpo humano e ideología* (Austin), 176n7
cultural practices, 8, 41, 45, 46, 51, 62
Curran, Patricia, 112
Cuzco, 25, 178n5, 183n54

Day of the Dead, 38
Dean, Carolyn, 37
Deans-Smith, Susan, 77, 187n36
De Armas, Frederick A., 193n28
death sentences/penalties, 25, 34, 36, 38
decapitation, 34. *See also* heads
"Dedicatoria" (María Josefa), 90, 91, 92
deformities, 136, 147. *See also* birth defects; congenital malformations; monsters/monstrosities; monstrous births
Delemeau, Jean, 178n9
"Descripción anatómica de un *Monstruo*," 138–39
*Descripción del Perú, Tucumán, Río de la Plata y Chile* (Lizárraga), 206–7n68
"Descripción de un ternero bicípite seguida de algunas reflexiones sobre los Monstruos" (Aristio), 130, 202n20
*Descripciones geográficas de los partidos de Trujillo, Piura, Saña, Lamayeque y Cajamarca* (Lequanda), 186n28
*Desvíos de la naturaleza o Tratado de el origen de los monstros. A que va anadido un compendio de Curaciones Chyrurgicas en Monstruosos accidentes* (Rivilla), **134**, 136–37, 201n17
*Desvíos de la naturaleza* (Peralta y Barnuevo), 200n11
De Vos, Paula S., 184n11, 184n13, 185n16, 188n39
Día de los Muertos, 38
*Diario de Lima* (newspaper), 161, 199n4
Diderot, Denis, 49
diet, 156
disabilities, 139
discalced orders, 87, 191n6
Discalced Trinitarians, 198n74, 199n79
*Discipline and Punish* (Foucault), 175n5

discourses
  colonial discourse, 168
  normative discourses, 7, 146
*discurso colonial en textos novohispanos, El* (Rivera-Ayala), 175–76n7
"Discurso histórico sobre la fundación del exemplar Monasterio de Trinitarias Descalzas de esta Ciudad de Lima," 83, 98, 194n34
"Discurso sobre el destino que debe darse a la gente vaga que tiene Lima" (Lequanda), 171–72
*Discurso sobre el fomento de la industria popular* (Rodríguez Campomanes), 80, 190n72
diseases, 74–78, **74–77**, 111, 196n58. *See also* illnesses; sick bodies; *specific diseases*
"Disertacion de Cirugia sobre un fetus de nueve meses que sacó a una muger por el conducto de la orina el año de 1779 el Autor de ella" (letter), 139
"Disertacion primera en la que se proponen las reglas que deben observar las Mugeres en el tiempo de la preñez" (Suadel), 152–58, 160
dismemberment, 28, 31, 37–38
disorder, 29, 40, 137, 146, 167, 172, 203n36
doctors, 202n26. *See also* surgeons
domestic maternity, 169
domestic space, 167, 168
donadas, 86
Douglas, Mary, 78
dowries, 195n42

earthquakes, 88, 115
Echave, Francisco, 199n79
economics
  of monasteries, 84, 86, 87–89, 99, 191n3, 192n14, 194n36, 198n76
  of Peru, 5
  of Spain, 63, 69, 80–81, 189n60, 190n63
  of Trujillo, 47, 63, 186n26
edema, 111
education
  of colonial citizens, 4
  early, 1, 93, 168, 205n58, 206n62
  during Enlightenment, 93, 94
  religious education, 191n2
  wet nurses and, 160, 165, 168
  of women, 205n58
  women's role in, 95

embodiment, 96, 193n29
*Embodying Enlightenment* (Haidt), 2–3, 175n4
embryology, 147
*Émile* (Rousseau), 162, 205n58
encyclopedias
  definition, 49
  encyclopedic museums, 62
  visual encyclopedias, 49, 62
Enlightenment
  colonial Spanish America and, 6
  education during, 93, 94
  language of, 91
  literature of, 6
  patriotic enlightenment, 129–30
  Philo on, 169
  philosophy and principles of, 129, 148
"En que se trata si una muger se puede convertir en un hombre" (Torpas de Ganarrila), 148
Erauso, Catalina de, 203–4n40
*escribanos*, 20, 179n21
escrúpulos, 115, 197n63
*Espéculo* (Alfonso X), 180n35
*estado*, 167
*Estrella de Lima convertida en sol* (Echave), 199n79
executions, public. *See* public executions
*éxtasis*, 111

*faldellines*, 53, 55
fasting, 111–12, 196–97n61
fear
  Bastidas and, 17, 20–22, 172
  definition, 178n9
  during Great Fear, 21
  Incas and, 36
  memory of, 31
  rhetoric of, 12, 13, 17, 31, 172
  Shklar on, 13
  Túpac Amaru insurrection and, 12–13, 14–15
Feliciana, 141–43
Festival of the Sun, 37, 182n53
Feuillé, Louis, 202n20
Few, Martha, 201n16
Fildes, Valerie, 162
Finantes (painter), 95, 125
Findlen, Paula, 183n3
Fisher, John R., 176n12
flowers, 54, 59–60, 189n53. *See also* roses; tulips

Foucault, Michel, 8, 23, 25, 42, 76, 175n5, 177n17, 190n68
fragmentation, 23, 28
Francisca (black woman), 139–41
Francisca de San José, 110–12
Fraser, Miriam, 22, 31, 180n27
Friedman, John, 200n14
*Fuero Real* (Alfonso X), 180n35, 205n57

Galen, 149, 204n42
Galleguinos, Manuel, 16, 20
gallows, 27
Garcés, Carlos Alberto, 3, 37, 175n5, 179n20
García Cáceres, Uriel, 201n17
Garcilaso de la Vega, 34–35, 37, 182nn49–50
garrote, 23, 27, 180n28
*Gazeta de Lima* (newspaper), 199n4
*Gazeta de Mexico* (newspaper), 201n15
gender
  complementarity, 183n60
  differences, 164, 206n64
Generation of Animals (Aristotle), 135
germ (term), 200n12
Gilman, Sander L., 77
Gil y Lemus, D. Francisco, 48
Goodman, Jordan, 196n50
Great Britain, 176n9
Great Fear, 14, 21
Greco, Monica, 22, 31, 180n27
Grosz, Elizabeth, 39, 167
Gualcayoc Hill, 45
Guaman Poma de Ayala, Felipe, 35, 37, 184n6

haciendas, 88
hagiographies, 91, 95, 97, 123, 192n16
Haidt, Rebecca, 2–3, 8, 141, 151, 175n4, 202n26
hair, 60
Hanafi, Zakiya, 136, 139
Hanan, 33
heads, 29–30, 31, 34, 102. *See also* decapitation
Heliogabalus (Roman emperor), 150–51
herrería, 70, **71**
Herzog, Tamar, 175n2, 177n21
hidropesía, 111, 119, 198n73
hierarchy (term), 175n6
Higgins, Antony, 98
high court, 5, 186n26, 195n40

Hill, Ruth, 175n6, 187n37, 201n17, 202n19, 207n69
Hillman, David, 28
hills, 37–38. *See also specific hills*
Hippocrates, 156, 205n53
*Historia de la fundación del Monasterio de Trinitarias Descalzas de Lima* (María Josefa, ed.)
　aspects of, 90
　bodies and, 99, 102
　"Dedicatoria," 90, 91, 92
　genre of, 91
　introduction, 90, 92–94, 98
　language of, 194n33
　local history in, 95–96
　María Antonia de San Joseph in, 194n34
　María Josefa as compiler and editor, 96–97, 193n22
　as metaphorical body, 96
　as national and religious patrimony, 83–84
　oral testimonies in, 92, 96
　organization of, 91, 192n20
　parts of, 100
　patchwork character of, 92
　physicality in, 99
　productive citizens and, 6
　publication, 97, 120, 194n31
　purpose, 1, 85, 90, 93–94, 98–99, 122, 192n18
　*relaciones*, 109, 118, 120, 196n57, 197n64
　religious patriotism and, 91, 123–26
*Historia del Nuevo Mundo* (Cobo), 35
*Historia del Reino de Quito* (Velasco), 201n15
historiographical production, 49, 187n33
Hobbes, Thomas, 13, 182n50
Hodgkin, Katherine, 110
holy anorexia, 113, 196–97n61. *See also* anorexia
holy people, local, 94–95, 123
homegrown nationalisms, 91
House of Geography and Natural History, 184n13
Howard, John, 203n31
Huamanguinos, 32
Huayna Cápac, 34
Hurin, 33
*huso*, 70
hybris del punto cero, 50

Hyde, Alan, 40, 178n10
hydropesia, 156
hydropsy, 111
hygiene, 152
hysteria, 204n49

Ibsen, Kristine, 109, 177n19, 191n2
Ica, 121
"Idea general del Peru," 137
identity construction, 104
Illescas, Don Juan de, 108
illnesses, 104, 111, 116, 196nn51–52, 196n58. *See also* diseases; *specific illnesses*
images
　Adorno on, 43
　Bleichmar on, 185–86n24
　Deans-Smith on, 187n36
　Mitchell on, 50
　related to disease, 74–78, **74–77**
　of women, 46, 78–81
imitatio Christi, 104, 111
imperfección, 103, 196n48
*Inca Cosmology and the Human Body* (Classen), 176n7
Incas
　bodies and, 33
　culture, 45
　fear and, 36
　legal punishment and, 31–38
　public executions and, 31–38
　punishments imposed by, 182n50
incontinence, 204n45
incorruptibility, 115–16
Indians
　Aucapacharuna Indians, 35
　of Chucuyto, 183n55
　denominations for, 188n47
　Indian men, 67–68, **68**
　Indian women, 54–56, **55**, **57**
　infidel Indians, 74, 76–77, **77**, 188n47
　making national, 188n49
　Martínez Compañón on, 73
Inés del Rosario, 91, 109, 120–22, 198n75
*infidel*, 54, 188n47
infidel Indians, 74, 76–77, **77**, 188n47
Inkarrí myth, 33–34
insurrections, 5, 35, 179n19. *See also* Túpac Amaru insurrection
*intendentes*, 44
intercourse, anal, 140
Inti Raimi (festival), 37, 182n53
Isabel de la Concepción, 198n74

Isabel Francisca de la Presentación, 91, 100, 101–2, 105, 106, 108, 195nn40–41
isolation, spatial and social, 74–78

Jesuits, 4–5
Joaquín de Orellana, 183n55
Josefa de San Pedro, 114–15, 120
Juana de Jesús María y José, 197nn64–65
Juana de Santa María, 117–18
Judovitz, Dalia, 154, 173, 204n48
Jujuy, 175n5
"Jumelles atacheés par les reins," **135**

Kagan, Richard, 186n30
Kaplan, E. Ann, 207n75
Katzew, Ilona, 187n38, 188n42, 188n44
*kaukaypata*, 37
Kelly, Veronica, 39, 183n56
King, Helen, 146, 204n49, 205n53
Kinsbruner, Jay, 182n52
knowledge, 6, 8, 42–43, 45, 49, 78–81, 169, 173
Kristeva, Julia, 207n75
*kurakas*, 176n14

lacking flesh (phrase), 22
*ladina*, 15
Langui, 23
Lanning, John Tate, 205n54
Laqueur, Thomas, 151, 204n43, 204n46
Lauro, Rosas, 167
Lavrin, Asunción, 87, 89, 191n7, 192n14, 194n35
law
   Andean criminal law, 177n3
   codes of Spain, 179n20
   sumptuary laws, 61
Lefebvre, Henri, 100, 207n73
legal punishment, 31–38
legs, 30, 31
Lemery, Nicolas, 133
leprosy, 75, **76**
Lequanda, Joseph Ignacio, 171–72, 186n28, 189nn55–56
*lessa magestad*, 16, 24, 179n20
*Leviathan* (Hobbes), 182n50
*Leyes de Castilla*, 25, 180n35
Lima
   black population, 208n77
   *concilios provinciales* (1772), 86
   earthquake (1746), 88
   indigenous population, 206n60

religious and divine perfection in, 120, 199n79
   trade, 5
   white population, 206n60
Limán, Melchor de, 101, 108
"Lima por dentro y por fuera" (Terralla y Landa), 207n70
*limpieza*, 167
Linan y Cisneros, Melchor de, 115
Livingstone, David, 160
Lizárraga, Reginaldo de, 206n68
Lloyd, Genevieve, 206n64
local history, 95–96
local holy people, 94–95, 123
López Serrano, Matilde, 44, 48
Luisa de Borbón, 46
Luisa de la Madre de Dios de Belén, 118–20
Lupton, Deborah, 176n16

Macera, Pablo, 185n22
Madrid, 44, 148
Malebranche, Nicolas, 200n13
malformations, 132, 146. *See also* congenital malformations; deformities
Manningham, Richard, 155, 204–5n50
Manuel de Moscoso y Peralta, Don Juan, 148
Marchena, Juan F., 44, 184–85n14
María (wet nurse), 165–67
María Antonia de San Joseph, 115, 194n34
María de la Encarnación, 112–13, 197n62
María de la Santísima Trinidad, 198n74
María Josefa, 1–2, 92, 96–97, 173, 174, 193n22. See also *Historia de la fundación del Monasterio de Trinitarias Descalzas de Lima* (María Josefa, ed.)
Mariana (black woman), 149
María Rosario de San Antonio, 194n31
María Teresa de la Santísima Trinidad, 113–14, 115, 197n65
Martín, Jouve, 197n69
Martínez Compañón, Baltasar
   biographical details, 43–44, 48, 186n27
   collections, 44, 185n15
   correspondence, 184n10
   on Indians, 73
   as naturalist, 44, 185n17
   notes and memoirs, 186n28
   on *Truxillo del Perú*, 42–43, 45–46, 47–48
   See also *Truxillo del Perú* (Martínez Compañón)

maternity, 163, 169, 207n76. *See also* mothers
Mazzio, Carla, 28, 29, 181n42
McClintock, Anne, 166
McKnight, Kathryn, 198n77
Medinaceli, Ximena, 179n19
memory, 31, 40, 48–49, 181n44
men, 46, 67–68, **68**
Mendiburu, Manuel de, 195nn41–42
Merback, Mitchell B., 25, 181n37, 181n39
*Mercurio peruano* (newspaper)
    bodies as topic for, 128–29
    founders, 199n4
    goals, 129
    on monasteries, 124, 173
    monstrous birth articles, 136, 137–39, 147, 201n15
    patriotic enlightenment in, 129–30
    wet nursing articles and letters, 160–61, 163–64, 167–68
    women represented in, 207–8n77
*Mercurio peruano* (newspaper): articles
    "Amas de Leche. Segunda carta de Filomates sobre la educación," 164–65
    "Carta escrita a la Sociedad sobre el abuso de que los hijos tuteen a sus padres," 163–64, 206n61
    "Descripción anatómica de un *Monstruo*," 138–39
    "Descripción de un ternero bicípite seguida de algunas reflexiones sobre los Monstruos," 130, 202n20
    "Discurso histórico sobre la fundación del exemplar Monasterio de Trinitarias Descalzas de esta Ciudad de Lima," 83, 98, 194n34
    "Idea general del Peru," 137
    "Operacion Cesarea," 127
Messia y Munive, Cristóval, 108, 196n55
*mestizas*, 59–60, 69–70, **71**, 189n51
*mestizos*, 73, 188–89n51, 189n55
Micaela de Jesús, 116–17, 120
midwives, 158–60, 205n54
*mita* system, 5, 176n13
Mitchell, W. J. T., 50
Moche culture, 45
modernism, religious, 6
modernity (term), 176–77n16
Mogrovejo, Toribio de, 191n5
Molina, Francisco, 19

monasteries
    as architectural bodies, 100, 109
    Bourbon reforms and, 88, 89
    colonial rule and, 191n2
    economics of, 84, 86, 87–89, 99, 191n3, 192n14, 194n36, 198n76
    governing of, 86–87
    hygienic projects and, 191n13
    Lavrin on, 194n35
    María Josefa on, 173
    *Mercurio peruano* on, 124, 173
    new establishments, 194n36
    number of nuns allowed in, 191n12
    nuns on, 191n12
    *paisanas*, 123
    perception of, 89
    religious perfection of, 124
    religious prestige of, 113
    religious reforms and, 86–90
    social and political significance, 84
    social celebrations in, 89
    as social need, 191n2
    spiritual and social value of, 124
Monasterío de las Trinitarias Descalzas de San Miguel Arcángel de Lima, 191n4
Monasterio de Trinitarias Descalzas
    Ana de Robles and, 100, 101–2, 109, 195n41, 195n43
    dowries, 101
    economic difficulties, 99, 101
    exemplarity of, 99
    founders and founding, 101–2, 109–10, 195n40, 198n74
    historical importance, 83
    history of, 98
    map including, **85**
    modern existence, 191n4
    See also *Historia de la fundación del Monasterio de Trinitarias Descalzas de Lima* (María Josefa, ed.)
Monclova, Conde de la, 88
*Monsters and Marvels* (Paré), 200n7
monsters/monstrosities
    belief in, 200–201n14
    bodies and, 207n74
    definition, 16, 130–31, 179n17, 183n59, 200n9
    elements, 132
    malformations and, 138
    origins, 132–33
    Palencia-Roth on, 146–47

Rivilla on, 202n19
study of, 147
as symbol of difference, 141
types, 132, 200n11
"Monstre," **131**
monstrous births
  articles in *Mercurio peruano*, 136, 137–39, 147, 201n15
  aspects, 136
  causes, 132–36, 138–39, 200n10, 201n14, 203n37
  congenital malformations and, 203n37
  fear of, 137
  fraudulent, 143, 203n31
  Rebollar on, 143–46, 203n34
  twins, 136–37, 202n22
Montevideo, 176n12
Moscoso y Peralta, Juan Manuel de, 38–39
mothers, 64–68, **64–69**. *See also* maternity
moths, 171, 208n1
mulattos, 32, 60, 61, **61**, 189n56
Muriel, Josefina, 91, 191n2
museum
  Bennett on, 80, 187n32, 190n70
  Bourdieu on, 42, 183n4
  definition, 42
  in early modern Italy, 183n3
  Foucault on, 42
  recording things in, 183–84n5
Mutis, José Celestino, 186n27
Myers, Kathleen, 95, 97, 123, 191n2, 198n76

*Nación*, 192n19
nation
  concept of, 175n2, 199–200n5
  Peruvian, 2
national identities, 198n76
national interests, 90, 95, 192n19
nationalism, 91, 95, 193n26
natural disasters, 84, 88
natural history, 43
Natural History Cabinet, 184n13
naturalists, 185n17
Nava, Melchor de la, 108, 196n55
*negra bozal*, 138, 139–40, 202nn24–25
*negra criolla*, 165, 167, 206n66
"Négre-pie," **144**
Nicolasa de San José, 116
normative discourses, 7, 146
*Nueva corónica y buen gobierno* (Guaman Poma), 35, 184n6
nunneries, 86–90. *See also* monasteries

nuns
  abuse of bodies, 112
  bodies as discursive tools, 2
  corporeal transformations of, 113, 114, 115–19, 122
  illnesses and, 104, 196nn51–52
  on monasteries, 191n12
  numbers in monasteries, 191n12
  writings of, 90–91, 192n16
Nussbaum, Felicity, 207n76

Oblitas, Antonio, 181n45
*obra gráfica*, 41
obstetrics, 155, 158, 159
Olavarrieta, Juan Antonio, 164, 199n4, 206n63
"Operacion Cesarea," 127
O'Phelan Godoy, Scarlett, 37–38, 176n14
"Oración Fúnebre," 194n34
osteoporosis, 197n67

*Padrón de los domingos* ceremony, 78, **79**
pain, 27–28, 105, 111–12
painting, act of, 96, 193n27
*paisanas*, 123
Palencia-Roth, Michael, 146–47, 203n35
*papeleta*, 203n38
*pardos*, 52
Paré, Ambroise, 200n7
*parótida*, 105, 106
*parteros*, 158
patriotic enlightenment, 129–30
patriotism, 85, 91, 123–26, 128–29, 174
Paul, Saint, 177n18
Paz, Melchor de, 16
*pecado nefando*, 203n29
Peralta y Barnuevo, Pedro, 200n11, 201n17
perineum, 148, 204n41
*Perjuicios que acarrean al Género Humano y al Estado las Madres que rehúsan criar a sus hijos y medios para contener el abuso de ponerlos en Ama* (Bonells), 206n59
Peru
  economics of, 5
  in eighteenth century, 3–7, 8
  insurrections and revolts, 5, 171
  as kingdom, 137, 202n23
  religious modernism in, 6
  religious perfection and sanctity in, 120
  Upper Peru, 5, 14
  *See also* Viceroyalty of Peru
Petronila de la Santísima Trinidad, 113–14

Philo, Chris, 129, 169
Phylomathes, Eustachio, 160–69, 206n61
physicality, 99, 100, 102
Piccho Hill, 30, 38
pigmentation, 145. *See also* skin color
*pintura*, 193n27
place, 63, 189n58
plants, 185n18
*Plaza del Pregón* of the Incas, 25–26, 37
*plaza mayor*, 25, 37
plazas, 25–27, 32, 36–37, 39, 182n52
plethora, 156
pneumonia, 111
*policía*, 26
*polilla*, 171, 208n1
Porras Barrenechea, Raúl, 48, 186n28
ports, 176n12
Powell, Amanda, 198n76
power, 14–15, 175n6
*Pragmática*, 61
Pratt, Mary Louise, 183n56
pregnancy, 153–60, 205n53
Premo, Bianca, 167, 205n56, 206n62, 207n70, 207n72
pride, 90–99, 120
primitiveness, 77
private space, 167, 168
productive citizens, 1, 6, 47, 63, 174
productivity, 8
progress, 8, 80–81, 128, 129, 147, 148, 151, 173
*protomedicato*, 205n54
provincial councils, 191n5
public executions
  of Micaela Bastidas, 34, 36, 37, 39–40, 172, 181nn44–45
  bodies as text and, 23–31, 181n39
  description, 23–24
  dramatization of, 180n29
  Foucault on, 23, 25
  Incas and, 31–38
  length of use, 23
  Merback on, 181n37, 181n39
  in plazas, 25–27
  during Túpac Amaru insurrection, 24–25
public space, 13, 167, 168
public spectacles. *See* public executions
*pueblos*, 95
punishments, 25, 38, 182n50. *See also* corporal punishment; legal punishment
Puquín Hill, 38

*quarterona de mestizo*, 46, 51, **58**, 189n55
Quijano, Aníbal, 176–77n16

race, 207n69
Radstone, Susannah, 110
Ramírez, Susan, 184n9
*Real Provisión* (Charles III), 150
reason, 8, 148, 169, 170
rebellions, 14, 178n12
Rebollar, Francisco de, 143–46, 203nn34–35
*Recherche de la verité* (Malebranche), 200n13
*refección*, 195n46
Regimen de Intendencias, 44
*Relación de antigüedades deste Reyno del Perú* (Santa Cruz Pachacuti), 34
*relaciones geográficas*, 188nn39–40
*Relación suscinta de los principios y progresos del monasterio*, 92, 100, 101–2, 104, 108
relics, 107, 108, 122, 124
religion, 55, 81, 84
religious modernism, 6
religious patriotism, 85, 91, 123–26
religious perfection, 99, 110, 113, 120, 124
religious prestige, 113, 123–25
religious texts, 91
Renan, Ernest, 95
*rengos*, 68, **70**, 190n62
*reparto/repartimiento* system, 5, 176n13
reproductive organs, 204n42. *See also* womb
República (term), 95
"Retrato verdadero de una criatura que nació en 12 de marzo del año corriente," **133**
rhetoric of fear, 12, 13, 17, 31, 172
Riero, Alonso, 101
Rivera-Ayala, Sergio, 175–76n7
Rivilla y Bonet y Pueyo, Joseph de, 136–37, 201n17, 202n19, 202n22
Robin, Corey, 13, 18, 22
Rodríguez Campomanes, Pedro, 80, 190nn71–72
Rodríguez García, Margarita Eva, 157–58
Rosa Catalina de San José, 112, 113, 197n62
Rosa de Lima, Saint, 94, 95, 120, 193n25
Rose, Gillian, 187n31
roses, 54, 60
Rousseau, Jean-Jacques, 162, 205n58
Royal Academy of History, 49
Royal and Public Library, 184n13

sacred space, 110
Sadler, T. W., 203n33
Saint-Hilaire, Geoffroy, 200n10
saints, 113, 116, 193n25, 197n69
Salazar, José, 17
Saldaña, Juan José, 6
Salvatore, Ricardo D., 179n20
*salvoconductos*, 17
Sanca, 17
Sánchez-Tagle, Esteban, 191n13
sanctity, 116, 117, 120, 197n69, 198n78
*sangre de drago*, 185n18
Santa Cruz Pachacuti, Juan de, 34
Sarasúa, Carmen, 205n55
Sawday, Jonathan, 28
Scarry, Elaine, 27–28, 96, 105, 193n29
Schlau, Stacey, 92
scrotum, 148
scruple disease, 115, 197n63
seeing, act of, 43
*Semanario crítico* (newspaper), 164, 199n4
*Señorío de los Incas, Del* (Cieza), 34, 182n48
servants, 86, 206n67
Seven Years War (1754–1763), 176n9
Sewell, Jane Eliot, 199n1
sexual behaviors, 145
Shklar, Judith N., 13
sick bodies, 74–78, 190n68
*Siete partidas* (Alfonso X), 24, 162, 179n20, 180n35
signs, 8, 177n20
Silverblatt, Irene, 183n60
Sirucasano, Gabriela, 185n18
sites of reason, 169, 170
sites of unreason, 129, 169–70
skin color, 60–61, 145. *See also* pigmentation
social control, 14, 24, 78
social disorder, 29, 137, 146, 167
Sociedad Académica de Amantes de Lima, 83, 98
Sociedad Académica de Amantes del País, 129
Sociedad Económica de Amigos del País, 129
Society of Jesus, 4
Socolow, Susan Migden, 189n61, 191n12
sodomy, 34
Solomon, Michael, 196n58
somatization, 22, 180n27
Soto Arango, Diana, 6

space
  bodies and, 29, 63, 100
  definition, 189n58
  domestic space, 167, 168
  private space, 167, 168
  public space, 13, 167, 168
  sacred space, 110
  spatial relations, 39
  symbolic spaces, 99, 195n37
  for women, 167
Spain
  economics, 63, 69, 80–81, 189n60, 190n63
  law codes, 179n20
  territories, 184n11
  Treaty of Paris (1763), 176n9
  *Truxillo del Perú* in, 48
  work force, 190n63
Spaniards, 19–20, 24, 31, 33, 37, 50–51, 56, 189n55. *See also* Spanish women
Spanish America, colonial, 6, 24, 161, 163, 180n31
Spanish women, 52–54, **53**, 59, **59**, 64–68, **64–69**, 69
*spectacle*, 25–26
Spierenburg, Pieter, 27, 28, 180n29
spinning, 70, **71**, **72**, 190n64
Stafford, Barbara, 132, 150, 200n13
Stern, Steve, 14
stigmata, 110
Stoler, Ann Laura, 168
stoning, 35
Suadel, Joseph Erasistrato, 152–60
*suave*, 196n54
sumptuary laws, 61
surgeons, 139, 158, 159, 160, 202n26
symbolic goods, 42, 183n4
symbolic spaces, 99, 195n37
Synnott, Anthony, 80
syphilis, 203n33
Szeminski, Jan, 177n3

*tabardillo*, 111, 118, 197–98n70
Tahuantisuyu, 33
Teodoro de Croix, 186n26
teratology, 132, 147, 200n10, 203n37
Teresa de Avila, Saint, 177n18
Teresa de la Santísima Trinidad, 113
Terralla y Landa, Esteban, 207n70
terror, 23, 25, 27, 28, 36, 38
Tinta, 178n5

tobacco, 103–4, 195n47, 196nn49–50
Tobias, Saint, 104
Tobin, Beth Fowkes, 49
Todd, Dennis, 130, 203n31
Toft, Mary, 203n31, 205n50
tongues, 29, 31, 181n42
*tornos*, 70, **71**, **72**, 190n64
Torpas de Ganarrila, Joseph, 139–40, 148–52
Torres, Don José, 17
torture, 27–28
*trages ordinarios*, 56
treason, 25
Treaty of Paris (1763), 176n9
Trujillo
   Archbishopric of, 184nn8–9
   black population, 56
   economics, 47, 63, 186n26
   location, 184n9
   natural resources, 46
   population, 52
   size, 43
*Truxillo del Perú* (Martínez Compañón)
   artists involved in, 46, 48, 185n22, 186n30
   binding, 48
   colonial body images in, 47, 48
   creation, 8–9, 41
   cultural context of, 49
   description, 41, 45–46, 185n18
   as encyclopedia, 49, 78–81
   as epistemic, 58
   ethnic women's groups in, 50–56, **53**, **55**, **57–59**, 58–63, 61, 64–68, **64–69**
   format, 48
   as governmental, 58
   influences on, 43
   Martínez Compañón on, 42–43, 45–46, 47–48
   men's images in, 46
   mothers in, 64–68, **64–69**
   natural resources in, 46
   organization, 51, 76–77, 188n43
   place in Enlightenment, 45
   productive bodies in, 6, **64–74**, 66–70, 73–74
   in Spain, 48
   statistical chart, 51–52, **52**, 188n39
   Volume 1, 45
   Volume 2, 45, 50–56, 58–63, 74
   Volumes 3–9, 45
   women as productive workers in, 63, **64–74**, 66–70, 73–74
   women's images in, 46, 51, **64–74**, 78–81, 172
Tubino, Fidel Ma., 194n31
Tucumán, 127, 175n5
tulips, 59–60, 189n52, 189n54, 189n57
Tungasuca, 30
Túpac Amaru
   Bastidas and, 15, 21, 178n5
   capture, 23
   Condemayta and, 180n34
   Cuzco attack and, 178n5
   execution, 32–33, 34, 36, 181nn44–45
   military operations of, 38
   Tinta defeat, 178n5
   *See also* Túpac Amaru insurrection
Túpac Amaru, Cecilia, 24, 178n12, 180nn32–33
Túpac Amaru, Francisco, 181n45
Túpac Amaru, Hipólito, 181n45
Túpac Amaru I, 33–34
Túpac Amaru II. *See* Túpac Amaru
Túpac Amaru insurrection
   Bastidas and, 5, 12–13, 15, 177–78n4, 179n22, 179n25, 183n60
   culmination (1781), 12
   fear and, 12–13, 14–15
   initiation (1780), 12
   organization of, 183n60
   power and, 14–15
   public executions during, 24–25
   purpose, 5
   women sentenced during, 24
Turner, Bryan, 180n27
Twinam, Ann, 4, 5, 205n57
twins, 136–37, 202n22, 203n37
typhoid fever, 111, 118, 197–98n70

Unanue, Hipólito, 200n6, 201n17
Upper Peru, 5, 14
uprisings, indigenous, 14. *See also* Túpac Amaru insurrection
urethra, 148
Uribe, Jorge Tomás, 6
*uta*, **74**, 190n67
utilitarianism, 6
utility, 3, 9, 42, 43, 81, 150

Valcárcel, Carlos Daniel, 12
*vecindad*, 177n21

Velasco, Juan de, 201n15
Venavente, Juan de, 197n65
venereal diseases, 144–45, 203n33
Verdejo, José, 181n45
Viceroyalty of La Plata, 5, 14, 175n3
Viceroyalty of Peru, 2, 14, 175n3
*vida espiritual*, 193n21
*vidas*, 109–10, 198n76
violence, 17–18, 27, 38, 78, **79**
violencia selectiva, 38
virginity, 34
Virgin Mary, 118
vision, 96, 193n28
visuality, 48, 187n31
Vlahos, Olivia, 29
Von Mücke, Dorothea, 39, 183n56

Walker, Charles W., 86, 89, 178n5, 180n31, 192n15
watercolor technique, 185n18
Weber, David J., 4, 79–80, 188nn47–48, 190n69
wet nurses
  advertisements for, 161, 205n55
  articles and letters on, 160–61, 163–64, 167–68
  blacks as, 160–61, 163
  bodies and actions of, 166, 167, 207n74
  Bourbon reforms and, 206n62
  characteristics required of, 162
  childrearing and, 162–69, 206–7n68
  in colonial Spanish America, 161, 163
  education and, 160, 165, 168
  ethnicity of, 163
  legislation (1794), 168, 207n72
  Olavarrieta on, 164, 206n63
  Phylomathes on, 160–69
  as profitable market, 161, 205n56
  role of, 161, 165
  social concerns, 162–69
Williams, Jerry, 201n17
womb, 204n49, 205n53
women
  Andean insurrections and, 179n19

  becoming men, 147–52
  black women, 56, **57**, 58, 139–40, 168, 207–8n77
  in cloth trades, 189–90n31
  contributions to society, 183n60
  crimes against, 37, 183n55
  death sentences imposed on, 38
  education of, 205n58
  education role, 95
  ethnic groups in *Truxillo del Perú*, 50–56, **53**, **55**, **57–59**, 58–63, 61, 64–68, **64–69**
  images in *Truxillo del Perú*, 46, 51, **64–74**, 78–81, 172
  images of, 46, 78–81
  Indian women, 54–56, **55**, **57**
  in *Mercurio peruano*, 207–8n77
  mulatto women, 60, **61**
  in peasant rebellions, 178n12
  perception in society, 207n75
  productive, 63, **64–74**, 66–70, 73–74, 80–81, 190n69
  punishments on, 38
  religious writings of, 198n77
  saintly women and corporeality, 105
  sentenced during Túpac Amaru insurrection, 24
  space for, 167
  Spanish women, 52–54, **53**, 59, **59**, 64–68, **64–69**, 69
  spatial relations and, 39
  subordination and, 78, **79**
  violence and, 78, **79**
  writing and, 90
writing, 90, 91, 96, 193n28, 198n77

xiphopagus, 201–2n18

Yahuarcocha, 35
Yépez, Gregorio de, 19
*ynfiel*, 54, 188n47

*Zamba*, 127, 128, 153
*zambo/zamba*, 15